TALES OF OLD CALIFORNIA

Edited by Frank Oppel

CASTLE BOOKS

This edition published in 2005 by

Castle Books ®

a division of Book Sales, Inc.
114 Northfield Avenue
Edison, NJ 08837

ISBN 13: 978-1-55521-538-5
ISBN 10: 1-55521-538-6

Printed in the United States of America

Contents

The City of the Golden Gate
(1875)

SCRIBNER'S MONTHLY.

Vol. X.   JULY, 1875.   No. 3.

THE CITY OF THE GOLDEN GATE.

MARVELOUS has been the growth of San Francisco. Its story reads like a chapter from the "Arabian Nights." Yesterday a dreary waste of sand—to-day a city of a quarter of a million souls, with an aggregate wealth of five hundred millions. The men who laid its foundations—who were present at its birth and christening—are hardly past the prime of life.

Never was there a more unsightly spot for a city. A long ragged peninsula, mottled with mammoth sand dunes, over which swept the sharp winds and chilling fogs of summer, and the pitiless storms of winter; isolated from the main land, barren, verdureless, horrid to the eye, with the broad Pacific dashing its waves against it on one side, and a stormy inland sea beating upon it on the other—no wonder the heart of the pioneer sunk within him as he gazed upon the inhospitable wilds for the first time. It was no less uninviting in its social aspect. An old church, and a cluster of adobe huts at the Mission; a lot of wretched rookeries at the Presidio; a few hide and tallow warehouses on the beach—that was all. The population was made up of Greasers, Digger Indians, a few white traders, deserters from whale ships, and adventurers of no nationality in particular, the whole numbering a few hundred souls. Its very name—"Yerba Buena"—was strange to American ears.

Yet it was manifest to the sharp observer that nature had intended the place for a great city. Nearly twenty years before the first Argonaut had planted his foot upon its site, Captain Bonneville, the famous explorer, predicted that here would rise one of the great marts of commerce and naval stations of the world. The bay of San Francisco is a vast inland sea. It has an extreme length of over seventy miles, a mean width of ten miles, and a circumference—if we include San Pablo and Suisun bays, which are properly its arms—of two hundred and fifty-six miles. Within the circle of its deep water all the navies of the world could safely

7

SAN FRANCISCO IN 1849.

ride at anchor, for the mighty portals of the Golden Gate protect it against the surf of the Pacific. It is as picturesque as it is grand. A noble amphitheater of hills, Grecian in form and contour, exquisitely varied in play of light and shadow, encircles it. It is dotted with islands and margined with sunny slopes; two vast rivers—the Sacramento and the San Joaquin—bring their tribute of water to it, and innumerable minor streams —children of the valley and the mountain— discharge their crystal treasures into its bosom. It is the home of the sea-gull and the pelican, of the porpoise and the sturgeon. Even the shark, the sea-lion and the devil-fish not infrequently visit its deeper recesses.

The stranger who landed in San Francisco in 1849 beheld a unique spectacle. He found men living, for the most part, in tents and shanties. There were few adventurers of the baser sort, and they were speedily exterminated or expelled. The refining influence of woman was almost entirely wanting, yet nowhere was true woman held in profounder respect. Life and property were far more secure than in older communities. Locks and bars were unknown. Men trusted their all to those who were strangers but a few hours before. There were virtually no written laws, but a "higher law" of honor and probity controlled the actions of the people. There was not a school; not a

Protestant church; but men who left Christian homes brought their Bibles with them, and the sweet influences of virtuous home example protected them from vicious courses. Never, perhaps, in a community made up of such heterogeneous elements, attracted by love of adventure and the thirst for gold, were there so few bad men.

But this condition of things did not last long. The fame of the gold discovery attracted a horde of adventurers from all parts of the world. Ruffians and cut-throats, thieves and gamblers, from every land poured in, a foul and fetid stream, tainting the air and polluting the soil. Convicts from Australia; the scum of European cities; "bruisers" from New York and "plug uglies" from Philadelphia; desperadoes from Central and South America; pariahs from India and outcasts from the South Sea Islands, swooped down, a hideous brood, upon the infant city. The effect was soon visible. Crime of almost every conceivable grade ran riot. Gambling dens monopolized the heart of the town. Murderers walked about the streets unchallenged in midday. Leading citizens were murdered in cold blood in their places of business, or on their way home at night. No man's life, no man's property, was safe. Then followed the uprising of the people— the punishment of the principal offenders, sharp, quick, terrible—without the formula of legal proceedings—and the dispersion and flight of more notorious ruffians. A short reign of peace and order—then a repetition in a new and perhaps more danger-

BIRD'S-EYE VIEW OF SAN FRANCISCO—1875.

of municipal corruption. The thieves and cut-throats, intrenching themselves within the precincts of the City Hall, made war upon the life of the community. Again the people rose in righteous anger, and applied the heroic treatment to local abuses. Instead of suspending the Tweeds and Connollys of 1856 from office, they suspended them from second story windows. The remedy was harsh, but it was effective; it was extra-judicial, but it brought order out of anarchy. The Vigilance Committee, having fulfilled its mission, dissolved never to re-appear. The power it had so terribly yet discreetly wielded, passed peacefully into the People's Party, to be exercised through constitutional channels, to be used for the popular good. Henceforward San Francisco became one of the most quiet, law-abiding, well-governed cities in the world. Various efforts to establish corrupt rings have since been made, but, thanks to a vigilant Press and a public opinion with which it is still dangerous to trifle, they have failed. Its rulers have been, with few exceptions, able and upright, identified with its best interests, careful of its good name and proud of the distinction of having proved true to their trusts. The machinery of our local government is simple. The power rests almost absolutely in a single body—the Board of Supervisors. The only direct check upon its actions is the

ous form, of the disorders of 1850 and '51. The era of vulgar ruffianism followed that veto of the Mayor. A corrupt Board could inflict incalculable injury upon the city; yet, so potent is the corrective force of public opinion, so jealous are these people of their rights, so quick to punish unfaithful public servants, that few iniquitous jobs have ever been consummated.

The old landmarks—pride of the pioneer —have nearly all disappeared. The wooden shanty, the dingy adobe hut, the crazy rookery on piles, have given place to palatial structures; and San Francisco is rapidly

THE OLD MISSION CHURCH ("MISSION DÓLORES"), SAN FRANCISCO.

The pioneer loves to dwell on the changes that have taken place in the physical aspect of the city. He will tell you that the greater part of the business portion of the town has been reclaimed from the sea; that where mighty warehouses now stand ships rode at anchor; that where the Babel of commerce roars loudest, the peaceful crab had his home and the festive dolphin disported; that the tide swashed against the sandy shore on the present line of Montgomery street; that where now stands the Cosmopolitan Hotel,

THE OLD MISSION CHURCH (RESTORED).

towered a sand-hill seventy feet high; that the southern limit of the city was Bush street; that all beyond from the junction of Montgomery and Market to the ocean was a howling wilderness.

taking rank architecturally with the great cities of the world. Front and Battery and Sansom are already fine business streets; Kearny, Montgomery, California, and the lower part of Market suggest a town a hundred years old. Some of the public and private buildings are among the most elegant and costly in the country.

The new City Hall, on the site of the ancient burial-ground, will, when completed, cost at least five millions of dollars. The new Mint, on the corner of Fifth and Mission, with its splendid front of Corinthian columns, is one of the finest buildings in America, and has cost the Government about two millions of dollars.

The Palace Hotel, to be opened in September, will be the largest establishment of the kind in the world; it will accommodate twelve hundred guests, and cost between three and four million dollars. All its furniture will be not only of California manufacture, but of California material. It will have three immense inner courts, roofed with glass, a marble-tiled promenade, and a tropical garden with exotic plants; it will have a music pavilion and a band in constant attendance. To run this mammoth caravansary will require over three hundred and fifty people.

Among other noticeable buildings are the new Custom-House, the Nevada Block, the Safe and Deposit Block, the Occidental, Lick and Grand Hotels, and the Railroad Block, corner of Fourth and Townsend.

Many of the private residences are very large, rich and elaborate. The stranger, riding along Bush, Pine, Sutter, Post streets,

NEW CITY HALL, SAN FRANCISCO.

and Van Ness Avenue, will find it difficult to realize that he is in a city only a quarter of a century old. But he will also be struck with the absence of architectural unity.

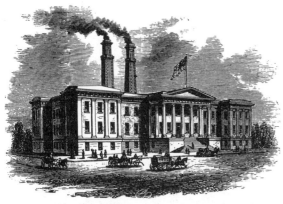

THE NEW UNITED STATES BRANCH MINT, SAN FRANCISCO.

Hardly any two mansions are exactly alike. The "orders" are fearfully and wonderfully mixed. He will find Corinthian, Gothic, Doric, Bysantine huddled together in a chaotic jumble of wood and stone, and brick and iron; yet there is a sort of family likeness running through all—an architectural kinship that is essentially Californian. There is the ubiquitous bay window (the San Franciscan has learned that sunlight makes the doctor's visits rare), and the ambitious Mansard roof, and the elaborate cornices—terror of timid pedestrians in earthquake times—and the somewhat "loud" front entrance. Entering a rich man's house, he will find luxury carried to the utmost limit of the possible; princely halls, and dazzling drawing-rooms; the floors covered with richest carpets; the walls adorned with costly paint-

ings—the splendors of the East and West combined. An invited guest, he will find a royal hospitality dispensed, and sit down to dinners that would tempt an anchorite to forget his vows of abstinence; for these people are generous livers.

A few facts will show the vigor with which this young metropolis has been pushing its way to the front rank of American cities. In 1849 its population was 2,000; in 1850 it was 20,000; in 1860 it was 56,000; in 1870 it was 149,000; in 1874 it was 200,000. Now, it is about 230,000, and, at the present ratio of growth, in 1880 it will be 369,000. Never has the growth been as rapid as now. Over two thousand buildings have been erected within the past twelve months, while Oakland, Alameda, San Rafael, and other suburbs, have been advancing with unexampled rapidity.

The growth of commerce has nearly kept pace with the growth of population. San Francisco is to-day the third city in the Union, measured by the aggregate of its importations and exportations. The early records of the Custom-House were destroyed by fire, and we have no data prior to 1854, when the appraised value of imports was only $5,000,000; in 1864 it was nearly $11,000,-

PALACE HOTEL, SAN FRANCISCO.

ooo; in 1869 it was $16,000,000; in 1874 it was nearly $29,000,000. A comparison of tonnage will perhaps give a better idea of the growth of the business of the port. In 1854 it was only 194,000; in 1874 it was 662,000. A notable feature of the commercial development of the city is the Oriental trade. Until 1869 it was comparatively of little importance—the aggregate tonnage from China and Japan for that year

STARR KING'S CHURCH, GEARY STREET, SAN FRANCISCO.

being 65,752; but with the inauguration of steamship service it received a sudden impetus, swelling up in 1874 to 124,000 tons. And this trade is only in its infancy. The establishment of steam communication with the Australian provinces promises great results. In fact as "all roads lead to Rome," so all the streams of commerce from the vast countries on the western and eastern shores of the Pacific—from the groups of islands lying between here and Australasia—flow by an inevitable law of gravitation to this Western emporium to fertilize and aggrandize it. It could not escape its magnificent destiny if it would. It has greatness literally thrust upon it. How far the men now on the stage will be able to utilize their opportunities is a problem not yet quite solved.

The accumulation of wealth has been very rapid. The aggregate personal and real estate of the city may be safely estimated at $500,000,000. The banking capital amounts to $84,000,000 ; there are more than sixty millionaires. The United States Branch Mint coined during 1874 over $27,000,000. The total coinage from 1854 to the close of 1874 was about $377,329,000, while the aggregate gold product of California, from 1848 to the present time, was about $990,-000,000. This vast volume of the precious

metals has not passed into the general current of the world's circulating medium without leaving its influence on the Golden State. San Francisco is largely—more largely than many of our people are willing to confess—the child of the mines. They gave it its first start; they have generously, though not exclusively, nourished it ever since. They have called into existence a large manufacturing interest, giving employment to tens of thousands of men. They have stimulated every branch of trade and internal commerce, quickened every pulse of industrial life. Nearly all our finest buildings have been erected out of the profits of mining enterprises. Every pound of ore that is taken out of the earth, from Alaska to Arizona, pays tribute here. A man may make his fortune in the desert of Nevada or Idaho, but he is pretty sure to spend it in San Francisco.

California street is the speculator's paradise, or perdition. Here the bulls bellow, and the bears growl their loudest. Here the crowd of stock-jobbers congregate, and the operators put up their "little games." Fortunes are made or lost in a day. A happy turn in stocks makes a millionaire of the man who yesterday could not get trusted for a pair of boots. Nowhere is the temptation to gamble so strong, or the chances of gain or loss so great, as in mines. Nature

BANK OF CALIFORNIA, SAN FRANCISCO.

herself turns gamester and shuffles the cards to suit herself. A single blow of the pick may reveal millions, where before was seen nothing but barren earth; a "horse," a streak of porphyry, a fire, a flood, a cave, may make the richest mine on the Comstock un-

MERCHANTS' EXCHANGE, SAN FRANCISCO.

the speculative debauch is renewed. To all this there is one compensating good: without the speculations of the street and the grinding assessments of the managers, the vast explorations in the mysterious caverns of the earth, resulting in the discovery of great ore bodies in mines, abandoned by less energetic or less wealthy prospectors, would not be prosecuted to the extent they have been.

Wealth is being turned to worthier channels—dedicated to nobler uses. The example of James Lick who, in spite of the revocation of the original Trust, emphasizes his intention to give a fortune of several millions to public objects, will not be barren of results. Already there are rumors in the air of embryo bequests to Education, Art, Science; colossal schemes of benefaction are slowly but surely maturing.

San Francisco is probably the most cosmopolitan city of its size in the world. Nowhere else are witnessed the fusing of so many races, the juxtaposition of so many nationalities, the Babel of so many tongues. Every country on the globe, every state and principality, almost every island of the sea, finds here its representative. Your next

productive for months. Four years ago the Crown Point and Belcher mines were regarded as worthless. The stock of the former went begging in the market at three dollars a share; the stock of the latter was without buyers at any price. But a great "bonanza" stretching across both mines was discovered, and in a few months Belcher and Crown Point rushed up to $1,800 a share. Since then these mines have produced nearly $45,000,000 of bullion and two United States Senators. Two years ago the Consolidated Virginia mine was denounced on the street as a "wild cat;" now its value is modestly estimated at $150,000,000; and the California Mine, which a few months ago was hardly known, is likely to have even a greater future. With such marvelous revelations of the hidden riches of the earth, it is not surprising that these mercurial people occasionally lose their heads, abandon temporarily the more conservative channels of business, and seek their fortune on the street. The sales of the Stock Board for 1873 aggregated over $146,000,000, and for 1874, over $260,000,000; in addition to this, there were sales to the amount of several millions in the "Little Board" and on the street of which no record is kept. A seat in the Board cannot be bought to-day for less than $25,000. But a bonanza with "millions in it" is not struck every week. Stocks may "boom" to-day, but droop to-morrow, and with the crash come remorse and repentance, heartache, and disgust. Then California street curses its fate, puts on sackcloth and ashes, and resolves to sin no more. The good resolution lasts till the next stock-rise, when the old appetite returns, and

"EMPEROR NORTON."

door neighbor may be a native of Central Asia; your vis-à-vis at the restaurant table may have been reared in New Zealand; the man who does your washing may have been born under the shadow of the great wall of China; the man who waits on you at table may be a lascar from the East Indies. If you go to the theater, you may find sitting next you a lady from the Sandwich Islands; if you go to the Opera, you may hear, in the pauses of the music, French, German, Italian, Spanish, Russian, Swedish, Modern Greek,

San Francisco is a generous patron of education. Its public school buildings compare favorably with those of Eastern cities; its teachers are generally able and efficient, and better paid than in any other place in the world. The average yearly salary is $1,033, while in Boston it is $940, and in Chicago and St. Louis, less than $800. Since the

THE GOLDEN GATE.

spoken by people dressed in the most scrupulous evening costume. If you take a ride in the horse-cars, you may find yourself wedged in between a parson from Massachusetts and a parsee from Hindostan; if you go to the bank, you may be jostled by a gentleman from Damascus, or a prince of the Society Islands. In three minutes' walk from your place of business, you enter an Oriental city—are surrounded by the symbols of a civilization older than that of the Pharaohs. If you are tired of French or American cookery, you may feast on the royal delicacies of bird's-nest soup, shark's fin, and fricasseed puppies. If you are fond of the drama, you may vary your amusements by witnessing a play spoken in the language of Confucius, performed with all the appointments of the barbaric stage. You will find thousands listening on Sabbath to the Christian Gospel, and thousands listening to the dogmas of Buddha, and kneeling at the shrine of Joss.

organization of our city government, we have spent over $6,000,000 for school purposes, and between $200,000 and $300,000 will be put into new school buildings during the current year. About 21 per cent. of the municipal revenue is devoted to educational purposes; in Chicago only 16 per cent. goes to the schools, and in Boston only 18 per cent. The average attendance at public schools is over 57 per cent. of all the children between six and seventeen, and in Chicago, only 33 per cent.

The condition of the working classes is exceptionally prosperous. Labor is more remunerative here than in any other city of the Union. Strikes are rare. There are over fifty millions of dollars deposited in our Savings Banks—more than twice as much as in Chicago or St. Louis, which have nearly double the population. There were on the 30th of June, 1874, fifty-six thousand depositors in these institutions, over one-fourth the entire population: a larger percentage than in any city on the globe. From these vast accumulations of the people's savings over two millions of dollars were paid out in dividends last year. A very large proportion of our mechanics own

THE BUMMER.

their homesteads. The curse of tenement-houses is unknown. The cost of fuel is nominal, for fires, even in the coldest days, are rather a luxury than a necessity. The habits of our people are extravagant, and it costs perhaps quite as much to live here as in most Eastern cities; but the mere necessaries of life—bread, fruit, vegetables, are very cheap. Our markets supply almost every conceivable want of hungry humanity. The products of every clime are laid in profusion at our doors. There is not a day in the year when one may not enjoy the luxuries of green peas, fresh tomatoes, celery, and cauliflower. Even strawberries may be a perennial delight.

San Francisco is famed for its restaurants. In no city in America are these establishments so numerous in proportion to the population. They number between two and three hundred, and it is safe to say that at least thirty thousand people take their meals at them. They are of all grades and prices—from the "Poodle Dog," Martin's, and the Maison Dorée, where a meal costs from $1.50 to $20—down to the Miners'

Restaurant, where it costs only forty cents. Between these extremes are a large number of French, German, and Italian restaurants, where one may get a royal breakfast for half a dollar, a lunch for twenty-five cents, and a dinner, including claret, for seventy-five cents, *à la carte*. A tenderloin steak (and there is no better beef in the world than here), potatoes, bread and butter, and a cup of coffee will cost fifty cents; a lamb chop, potatoes, bread and butter, and coffee twenty-five cents; salmon, bread and butter, and coffee twenty-five cents; an omelet or eggs boiled, fried or scrambled, with coffee, and bread and butter, thirty-five cents. A grade lower down, but in places cleanly and entirely respectable, one gets three dishes for twenty-five cents, and may find quite a decent meal for twenty to thirty cents.

San Francisco is the elysium of "bummers." Nowhere else can a worthless fellow, too lazy to work, too cowardly to steal, get on so well. The climate befriends him, for he can sleep out of doors four-fifths of the year, and the free lunch opens to him boundless vistas of carnal delights. He can gorge himself daily for a nominal sum; get a dinner that a king might envy for fifty cents. There are two classes of saloons where these midday repasts are furnished— "two bit" places and "one bit" places. In the first he gets a drink and a meal; in the second a drink and a meal of inferior quality. He pays for the drink (twenty-five or fifteen cents, according to the grade of the place), and gets his meal for nothing. This consists, in the better class of establishments, of soup, boiled salmon, roast beef of the best quality, bread and butter, potatoes, tomatoes, crackers and cheese. Many of these places are fitted up in a style of almost Oriental grandeur. A stranger, entering one of them casually, might labor under the delusion that he had found his way, by mistake, to the *salon* of a San Francisco millionaire. He would find immense mirrors reaching from floor to ceiling; carpets of the finest texture and the most exquisite patterns; luxurious lounges, sofas, and arm-chairs; massive tables covered with papers and periodicals; the walls embellished with expensive paintings. A large picture which had adorned a famous drinking and free-lunch house was sold the other day for $12,500. Some of the keepers are men of education and culture. One is an art critic of high local repute, who has written a book, and a very readable one, of San Francisco reminiscences.

San Francisco has rather more than her share of eccentric characters. Foremost among these is the "Emperor Norton," a harmless creature, who firmly believes that he is the legitimate sovereign of the United States and Mexico; issues frequent pronunciamentos; exacts tribute from such citizens as humor his delusion; spends his days walking about the streets, his evenings at the theater, and his nights at a cheap lodging-house. He has the run of the hotel reading-rooms, appears on public occasions in tattered regalia, visits the different churches to see that heresies dangerous to the peace of the Empire are not promulgated, calls at the newspaper offices to warn the conductor against the consequences of treasonable utterances—in short, is up early and late regulating the affairs of the world in general, and the city and State in particular.

A familiar figure for many years was the "Gutter Snipe." His shoulders were covered all seasons with an old white oil-cloth cape. He went about the streets head down, rummaging among the gutters, picking up bits of vegetables and fruit, wiping the dirt off with his sleeve, and eating them. He never spoke to any one, never looked at any one, would accept no food or money. He slept in a hole in the sand-hills. He was not a sightly object to look at, and one day a fastidious policeman "took him in charge"; a commission of lunacy sat upon him, and he was seen no more. Disappointment in love was his complaint.

Li Po Tai, the Herculean Chinese doctor, deserves a place among our local eccentrics. He is the prince of quacks and high priest of charlatans, who has amassed a large fortune by playing upon the credulity of the public, and has set up a Joss house (heathen temple). His rooms are thronged with visitors of all conditions and nationalities, who come to consult him touching their various ailments. His diagnosis is direct and simple. The seat of all disorder is the liver, and it is to the correction of that rebellious organ that all his energies are directed. His medicines are something dreadful to think of; all the vile drugs of the celestial and Christian pharmacopœia concentrated in potions (measured by the pint) so nauseating, so abhorrent to taste and smell, as to make one pause to consider which of the two evils is the greater, death or Dr. Li Po Tai.

All San Franciscans know "Crisis." He is a sort of American howling dervish with a religious twist in his brain, who holds forth on street corners, warning sinners to flee from the wrath to come, and predicting the speedy collapse of this wicked world of ours. He also peddles tracts written in atrocious English, and filled with most dismal prophecies. He wears a hat that looks as if it might have fallen overboard from the Ark and been drifting about ever since, and his general appearance is that of incorrigible seediness. There are many other odd characters which I have not time to

"HAVE YOUR RAZORS GROUND!"

STREET MARKET SCENE IN SAN FRANCISCO.—FROM A PAINTING BY WM. HAHN.

sketch, among them Krause, the Poet Laureate of the Pave, who, like Homer, wanders about hawking hexameters, and the old fellow whose "Have your razors ground!" is familiar to the ears of all San Franciscans.

The Hoodlum is a distinctive San Francisco product. Certainly no treatise on the resources of California would be complete that did not include him. He may be somewhat vaguely defined as a ruffian in embryo. Young in years, he is venerable in sin. He knows all the vices by heart. He drinks, gambles, steals, runs after lewd women, sets buildings on fire, rifles the pockets of inebriated citizens going home in the small hours, parades the streets at night singing obscene songs, uttering horrid oaths, and striking terror to the heart of the timid generally. Occasionally he varies the programme of his evil doings by perpetrating a highway robbery, blowing open a safe, or braining an incautious critic of his conduct. One of his chief diversions, when he is in a more pleasant mood and at peace with the world at large, is stoning Chinamen. This he has reduced to a science. He has acquired a dexterity in the use of missiles, a delicacy and firmness of handling, an accuracy of aim and precision of movement, that seldom fail to bring the hated heathen down. Ac-

cording to the Hoodlum ethical code, to stone Chinamen is no sin. It is better than pastime—it is a work of righteousness.

The Hoodlum is of no particular nationality. He must simply be young and depraved. He must have broken most of the commandments before he has got far into his teens. He may be the son of a beggar, he may be the son of a millionaire. There is no aristocracy in this republic of crime. The great mass of recruits are, of course, gathered from the lower classes, but "our best society" has bequeathed to the order some of its most brilliant representatives.

This sudden efflorescence, of a sharply defined criminal class among boys—for the Hoodlum first appeared only three or four years ago—is somewhat alarming. It shows that there is a screw loose somewhere in our social mechanism. The selfish "Trades Unions," which virtually exclude apprentices from the mechanical pursuits, have been, I think, the principal cause of Hoodlumism. But there are other causes. Nowhere else are the restraints of parental authority so lax as here. A large portion of the people have no homes. They live, or rather they exist, in hotels, in boarding-houses, in lodging-houses, eat at restaurants, spend their days at their places of business, and their evenings at resorts of amusement. Their children are allowed to run wild, learn slang at their mother's breast, swear in pinafores, and prattle in the jargon of the street. The distracted parents, failing to govern them, give up the fight, allow them to go out nights and have their own way in everything. From this point the road to ruin is so short and direct that it needs no guide-board to point the way. Hoodlumism is a disease so virulent, so rapid in its spread, that moral physicians are at their wit's end how to treat it. All sorts of remedies are proposed, but the most practical was that adopted by Mr. Ralston, the great banker, who, confronted by a combination of workmen who put up a "corner" on lathing for the Palace Hotel, cut the controversy short by setting several hundred boys to work to learn the business. This is the key to the whole case. Give the boys work, and Hoodlumism will disappear like a hateful excrescence.

The popular speech of San Francisco is strongly flavored with localisms. You hear on every side the jargon of the mining camp, the *patois* of the frontier. If a man fails in business he is "gone up a flume;" if he makes a lucky speculation he "has struck it rich;" if he dies he has "passed in his checks." Of a man of sound sense it is said "his head is level;" a good business is said to "pan out well." The genuine Californian never says he has made a fortunate investment, but he has "struck a lead;" never says he has got rich, but he has "made his pile." A good dinner he calls a "square meal;" a cheat is always a "bilk;"getting at the real character of a man is "coming down to the bed rock." "Clean out," "freeze out," are synonyms for rascally operations in business. When stocks are active they are said to be "booming;" a panic in the market is expressed by the term "more mud;" a man who is hurt in a mining transaction is "cinched;" a weak man is said to have "no sand in him;" a lying excuse is denounced as "too thin." In the slang vernacular, an eating-place is a "hash-house," a "pretty waiter girl" is a "beer-slinger," and a newspaper reporter an "ink-slinger."

For a young city, San Francisco is very much wedded to petty traditions. It clings to the "bit" with a death-like tenacity; clings to it against all reason and against its own interests. The bit is a mythical quantity. It is neither twelve and a-half cents, nor half of twenty-five; it is neither fifteen cents nor ten cents. If you buy a "bit's"

worth and throw down twenty-five cents, you get ten cents back; if you offer the same ten cents in lieu of a "bit," you are looked upon as a mild sort of a swindler. And yet the "bit" is the standard of mini-

THE DEAD BEAT.

mum monetary value. Of no fixed value itself, it is the measure of the value of a large share of what the people buy and sell. Until within the past few years five-cent pieces were nearly unknown, and are even yet looked upon with disdain by the more conservative residents. Some time ago the leading Bank tried the dangerous experiment of introducing pennies, and imported several hundred dollars' worth. They were scornfully rejected as unworthy the notice of broad-brained Californians, and speedily disappeared.

San Franciscans are remorseless critics. They pride themselves on their ability to form independent judgments, and their contempt for the opinions of the rest of mankind. This is shown in their treatment of distinguished dramatic and musical artists. They condemned Edwin Forrest after a single hearing, gave Madame Celeste the cold shoulder, and declined to go into raptures over Edwin Booth. But they gave Charles Kean a glorious welcome, took Boucicault to their bosoms, and went wild over "Dundreary." They opened their purses and their hearts to Parepa-Rosa, gave an ovation to Ole Bull, but permitted Wieniawski to discourse his divine harmonies to empty benches. Gough drew, but Josh Billings cracked his awful jokes on unsympathetic ears. Rev. Dr. Lord's historical lectures were crowded, but Charles Kingsley was generally voted a bore. They flocked to hear Hepworth Dixon the first night, declared that he would not do, and left him so severely alone, that he declined to make his appearance after the second attempt, and left in disgust.

The pioneers must not go unnoticed. Death has been cruelly busy among them of late, but they still constitute a large and perhaps dominant element of our population. Taken as a whole, the world has seldom known such brave and hardy spirits. They were the picked men of the age—the flower of the adventurous chivalry of the time. They found the country a wilderness, and made it blossom like the rose. They founded a great city, and added a rich, powerful, and vigorous member to the commonwealth of States.

There is another, and, fortunately, smaller class of pioneer of whom little that is good can be spoken. So far as his influence is felt at all, it is obstructive. He is the Bourbon of California. Intellectually, he has no recognized status; morally, you must date him somewhere down in the Silurian age. He has no visible means of support. He is above the vulgar plane of labor. He lives wholly in the past. He dates the Creation of the world from the discovery of gold at Sutter's Mills, the Deluge from the great flood at Sacramento. He went to sleep immediately after the collapse of the Vigilance Committee, and has been asleep ever since. The world has moved on; the city has increased in population sixfold; a new race of men has come upon the stage, but he knows it not. He sighs for the halcyon days when a man could get a dollar an hour for work; when the dulcet voice of the derringer was heard in the land at all hours; when one could settle his little disputes with his neighbor in Judge Lynch's Court of Last Resort. I asked a friend the other day where one of these incorrigibles could be found, as I wished to deliver a message to him.

"You will find him in the —— Saloon, in the midst of a lot of bummers, drinking out of the same old bottle that he drank from eighteen years ago."

"But how does he live?"

"Sponges on his friends and 'strikes' newcomers."

An amusing illustration of the conservatism of these case-hardened Argonauts occurred the other day. The recently elected officers of the Pioneer Society—men of progressive ideas, who have fully kept abreast of the times—ventured on a dangerous innovation. They removed the bar. This was an outrage on "vested rights" not to be endured. The bibulous fossils rose in their wrath, held an indignation meeting, and threatened to depose the offending officials.

"But," said the acting President, "the Pioneer Hall ought to be something more than a whisky shop. The Society ought to do something for the future."

"You don't understand the thing at all," replied the thirsty veteran; "the Society was organized over a bar, and a bar it must and shall have."

San Franciscans make a hobby of their climate. They roll it as a sweet morsel under their tongue. It is their *pièce de résistance* in the catalogue of blessings. "The derned place seems shaky on her pins," said a citizen just after the great earthquake of 1868; "but there's one consolation, anyhow, we've got the best climate in the world." It is a climate of strong contrasts. It is eccentric; it is tantalizing; it is seductive. We are piqued at its capriciousness, yet it unfits us for living anywhere else. Summer hardens into winter; winter is glorified into summer. Roses and sunny skies in January; verdureless waste, cold winds, and chilling fogs in July.

"Did you ever see such a summer as this?" said one Irishman to another.

"No, be jabers, not since the middle of last winter."

We cry for thick blankets while you are sweltering in the dog-day heats; we throw open our doors and windows while you are cowering beneath the sharp stings of winter. Not that all days in summer are cold, and all days in winter warm; but the general rule is, that June, July, and August are detestable, and the rest of the year unequaled for loveliness of weather. There are not only days, but weeks, when the skies are indescribably glorious. The Nile Valley is not so sweetly balmy, Southern Italy not so rich in mellow splendor. The golden sunshine permeates every pore, quickens every pulse of life. The air has an indefinable softness and sweetness—a tonic quality that braces the nerves to a joyous tension, making the very sense of existence a delight. The contrast of temperature between summer and winter is less apparent than real. The remarkable equability of the climate will appear from the following: In June, 1874, the highest thermometer was 67°, the lowest, 58°; in January of the same year, the highest was 59°, the lowest, 54°. In December, the range was between 60° and 52°; in August it was between 68° and 60°.

cottages, and picnic grounds. The city has been fortunate in its Park Commissioners and Engineer. They are intelligent, unselfish, and public-spirited—the former serving without pay. No taint of jobbery, no suspicion of political management attaches to their administration.

Society has greatly changed for the better within the past few years, but is still somewhat "mixed." The lines of class and caste

HOODLUMS AT THE STREET CORNER, SAN FRANCISCO.

San Francisco begins to talk of its Park. It is a crude affair as yet, but promises great things. It comprises about 1,100 acres, and extends from the western limit of the city to the sea. It commands a series of magnificent views, taking in a vast panorama of ocean, bay, mountain and plain. Like everything in this country, it is a thing of rapid growth. Three years ago it was a howling waste of sand; to-day it has several miles of drives, lovely plateaus covered with grass, flowers, and young trees; sheltered nooks, where the weary citizen may enjoy balmy air, and delicious sunshine; labyrinths of meandering roads and by-paths, rustic

are often vague and shadowy. Your coachman of yesterday may be your landlord to-day. The man who supplied you with vegetables a few years ago may now rank with you socially. The woman who did your washing in the early days may look down with pitying eyes upon you to-morrow. Bridget, who was your maid-of-all-work when you first came to the country, lives in a grand house, rejoices in a coachman in livery, and goes to all the great parties. Don't feel hurt if she cuts you, for she is "in society," and cannot afford to be too promiscuous in her acquaintants. It is natural that in a community so largely made up of fortune-hunters wealth should be a controlling social power; but it would be unjust to say that wealth is the sole standard of social position. Occupation, how one lives, and

JAMES LICK.

wnere one lives have something to do with it. There is a story of a rich man—I will not vouch for its truth—who some years ago gave a famous party. He had a large circle of acquaintances, but he could not invite everybody. "We must draw the line somewhere, you know," he said, and he drew it bravely between wholesale and retail. The man who sold soap and candles by the box was decreed to be within the "sacred pale" of society's most elect. The man who sold soap and candles by the pound was voted a social Philistine. A rich lady was about to give a large party, and called in a friend to talk over the question of invitations. After reading the list the latter said:

"But I don't see the Bierstadts! Surely you will invite the Bierstadts?"

"Bierstadt! who's Bierstadt?"

"Why, the great painter!"

"Is he one of them ar' California painters? because, if he is, I won't have him."

Living at a first-class hotel is a strong presumption of social availability, but living in a boarding-house, excepting two or three which society has indorsed as fashionable, is to incur grave suspicions that you are a mere nobody. But even in a boarding-house the lines may be drawn between those who have a single room and those who have a suite. Said a lady to a little woman recently arrived:

"I see, my dear, you have but one room. This will not do; you will never get into society until you have a suite."

"But, my husband can't afford it."

"He must afford it."

But all rich people are not shoddies, and all poor people are not socially outcast. There are many—and the number is rapidly multiplying—whom wealth has not spoiled —has not made proud and insolent; to whose houses good men and women with clean antecedents, and small bank accounts, are welcome and honored guests; to whose homes successful rascals and purse-proud boobies are never admitted; who make riches ministers of beneficence, and in conferring pleasures upon their less prosperous fellows, confer happiness upon themselves. I see many signs of healthful social growth.

Our rich men are beginning to learn that there are nobler investments than stocks and bonds; that life has something grander and sweeter than the pursuit of sordid gain; that he who would leave an honored name behind him must do something for the future as well as for the past, for the public as well as for self.

What manner of person the "Coming Man" of San Francisco is to be is not so clear; but some things may be pretty safely predicted of him.

He will be a fine man physically, clearbrained, if not broad-brained; bold, speculative, dashing—a man of great projects, if not great fulfillments. He will be iconoclastic, unconventional, a hater of shams.

He will have little reverence for the past, little respect, for traditions little pa-

CHINESE THIEF.

tience with precedents, little regard for the opinions of his elder brothers. He will strike out into new paths of progress, dash forward with striding step, rudely jostle more slow-going travelers, as if he were monarch of the road, and born for conquest. He will have boundless faith in himself, will be fertile in resources, quick to see his advantage, prompt to act, possibly careless in the use of means by which to attain ends. In a word, he will typify in his character the dry, clear, intensely electric air of this land of the Setting Sun.

A sketch of San Francisco would be very incomplete that omitted the Chinaman. He is ubiquitous and all-pervading. For good or for evil, he is firmly rooted to our soil. You can no more expel him than you can the rats. He came here early and evidently means to stay late. He does not mind persecution; I am not sure that it does not agree with him. His skull is reasonably thick, and can stand a vast amount of stoning. It does not seem to make him feel very bad to be called hard names. Even taxing does not vitally hurt him, or he would have been driven off long ago. He is patient, docile, slow to anger, seldom strikes back, and is never vindictive. He is free from most of the grosser Christian vices. He does not drink; he does not blaspheme; he does not engage in broils; he does not go howling about the streets at night, insulting peaceable citizens, garroting unwary pedestrians or pistoling policemen. He is the most industrious creature in the world. You find him at work when you get up in the morning, and when you retire at night. And this tireless industry, this apparent love of work for work's sake, this irrepressible desire to be doing something and earning something, is what fills the souls of his enemies with despair. If he would only be shiftless and lazy—squander his substance in riotous living—he might be endured. But

this heathenish thrift of his is something inexpressibly hard to bear. It cannot be fought against; it cannot be put down by bludgeons, legislative statutes, or resolutions of Labor Leagues.

But John has his little vices too. He will gamble; he will drug himself with opium; he will lie to get himself out of a scrape; he will steal on the sly. His morals are of the negative order, and his religion anything but Christ-like. His conscience— I sometimes doubt if he have one—is elastic,

ALLEY IN CHINESE QUARTER, SAN FRANCISCO.

and permits him to do pretty much as he pleases. He will unblushingly tamper with the virtue of a guileless revenue inspector or license collector. He will even bribe his god Joss, in order to obtain celestial favors. John is not a humorist, but is occasionally given to sharp sayings and biting repartees. One day he was twitted about his heathen practices and proclivities by a Jew. John retorted: "You worse than Chinaman, you kill Melican man's Joss."

As a domestic servant, John is occasionally trying to the housewife. He is capri-

CHINESE OPIUM DEN, SAN FRANCISCO.

cious, sometimes moody, and if things go wrong, will indulge in a mild sort of impudence that is very exasperating. He takes curious freaks; will stop in the midst of his work, pack up his duds, demand his pay and walk off. If you ask for an explanation, he will tersely reply: "Me no likee; too muchee work." Persuasion, appeals to his moral sense, even an offer of better pay, have no effect. Then he may take a sudden notion that he wants to go back to China. You say to him· "John, I am very sorry you are going; who can we get to take your place?" He replies: "My cousin (he always has a cousin—indefinite· relays of cousins for all emergencies), him belly good Chinaman, all same as me." The "cousin," three times out of four, proves a snare and a delusion—not infrequently a blockhead or a thief.

The Chinese quarter is a system of alleys and passages, labyrinthian in their sinuosities, into which the sunlight never enters; where it is dark and dismal, even at noonday. A stranger attempting to explore them, would be speedily and hopelessly lost. Many of them seem mere slits in the flanks of the streets—dirty rivulets flowing into the great stream of life. Often they have no exit—terminating in a foul court, a dead wall, a gambling or opium den. They literally swarm with life; for this human hive is never at rest. Every dent and angle—every nook and cranny in the wall—every foot of surface on the ground is animate. The ultimate problem of Mongolian existence seems to be, how to get the greatest number of human beings into the least possible space. They herd together like cattle in their workshops, eating-houses, and places of social resort. A lodging-house represents an almost solid mass of human anatomy. The authorities, some time since, found it necessary, for sanitary reasons, to pass an ordinance, prescribing five hundred cubic feet of air (equal to a space eight feet square) to each person in Chinese tenements; but such contempt have these creatures for oxygen, that they constantly evade or ignore it. You might suppose these slums would be breeding-places of pestilence, but such does not seem to be the fact. No epidemic has violently raged in the Chinese quarter. When, some years ago, the small-pox was carrying off the Caucasian at the rate of nearly one hundred a week, the Mongolian passed unharmed. This remarkable exemption is due partly to the fact that all Chinamen are inoculated in childhood, and that they pay more strict regard to certain essential sanitary laws. The bath is a part of their religion; so is the tooth-brush, both of which are daily used under all circumstances.

Not altogether uninteresting is an opium den. Under the escort of a police officer, we grope our way through a dismal court, pass throngs of Chinese of both sexes—the men mostly gamblers, the women all prostitutes; stumble over heaps of rubbish, cooking utensils, etc.; squeeze through a narrow entry, open a door, and are in the den. The reek of the place is horrible. The air is thick with the fumes of the deadly drug. At first, all is nebulous and indistinct,

and offers us his pipe with, "You smokee? Him belly fine." We decline and pass on. Another stares at us with glazed eyes, looking the picture of hopeless imbecility. Our guide says, "John, you smokee too much opium; by'm bye you go to Mission" (you die). "Me no care," responded the wretch; "me likee he," pointing to his little opium box, "me smokee all same." Many of these creatures live in these dens. They have their bunks, for which they pay so much rent, and in which they keep their worldly possessions. They do their cooking in a little court outside, pass the few waking hours of their existence in listless misery, seldom go out on the street, and long for

CHINESE GAMBLING DEN, SAN FRANCISCO.

but in a few moments the eye takes in the outlines of the room. It is filled with men, all lying down on mats, on benches, on the floor; some on their sides; some on their backs. They are in every stage of narcotism from the dreamy languor induced by the first few whiffs of the opium pipe to soggy insensibility. Some are hilarious; some are sullen and scowl viciously at us; some are given to the most seductive reveries; some are murmuring incoherent words in their dreams; one or two are sleeping the heavy death-like sleep of souls utterly subjugated by the insidious poison. One old fellow raises himself up on his haunches, extends a withered hand in token of friendly greeting,

the night, when they may repeat the Lethean debauch. Others work a part of the day and repair to the opium den at night, where they spend all their earnings. The amount consumed varies from a few grains to an ounce a night. The opium is not furnished by the keeper, but is brought in by the consumer.

The opium pipe consists of a straight, or slightly curved stem, about eighteen inches long, with a bowl three inches round, in the center of which is a small circular hole. This leads to a smaller reservoir in the center of the bowl, and a channel runs from this to the end of the pipe, which the smoker places in his mouth. He takes a bit of wire and dips the end into prepared opium, which is about the consistency of mucilage. The drop of the drug that adheres to the wire is held in the flame of a lamp, and, under the influence of the heat, it bubbles and changes blers will stand a siege, and the only way to capture them is to batter down the door with sledge hammers, or cut a passage through the roof. The principal game of chance is very simple, and is called " Tan."

CHINESE THEATER, SAN FRANCISCO.

color like boiling molasses. It is now smoking hot, and upon being placed in the hole of the bowl, will yield the smoker several whiffs. He easily draws the smoke from the stem, sends it into his lungs, and finally discharges it through his nostrils.

The gambling dens are a characteristic feature of the Chinese quarter. There are, or were until recently—for the police have been remorselessly swooping down upon them—no less than three hundred of these establishments. Many of them are petty fortresses, approached by a series of narrow passages, with doors of thick Oregon pine, securely barred and bolted. Sentinels are on the look-out, who, on the approach of danger, give warning ; the lights are instantly extinguished ; the door shut, and the inmates scamper off like rats through secret rear exits, or over the roofs of the adjoining houses. The retreat being cut off, the gam-

A square, or oblong table, covered with matting, stands in the middle of the room. The dealer takes a handful of beans, or small coin, and throws them on the board. He then divides the pile into four parts with a hooked stick. The gamblers stake their wagers on what the remainder will be after the pile has been divided by four, whether one, two, three, or nought. Those who have money on the lucky chance receive double the amount of their wager, and the remainder of the coin goes to the bank. The game is very exciting, the players frequently staking their all on a single venture. There are various other games with dice and dominoes, and cards, while the lottery is a favorite form of gambling.

The theater is one of the show places of Chinatown. It will seat nearly a thousand people, and has a pit, gallery, and boxes. The men sit on one side of the house, the women on the other—the former with their hats on. All are smoking; the men, cigars and pipes; the women, cigarettes. The performance usually begins at seven in the evening, and closes at two in the morning; but on festive occasions it begins at two in the afternoon, and closes at four in the morning. An historical play is usually about six months long, being continued from night to night until the end. If one dies before it is finished, I suppose his heirs get the benefit of what is left. The stage is a cold and barren affair, with no scenery or appointments to speak of. There is no curtain even. When the hero dramatically dies, and the heroine faints, after lying still a reasonable time they get up and walk off. The orchestra sit in the back part of the stage with their hats on, puffing away at villainous cigars. There are no female performers, feminine parts being assumed by men or lads. The text of the piece is spoken in a drawling, sing-song tone; the gestures apparently absurd and meaningless. The music is inexpressibly ear-splitting and nerve-shattering—all the discords blended into one.

There are eight heathen temples, or Joss houses, in San Francisco. Some of them are fitted up with considerable splendor. The divine Joss sits on a throne, with an assisting deity on each side. He is a hideous-looking fellow, fierce and brutal of countenance, dressed in showy costume, and decked with a profusion of ornaments. In one corner is a sort of furnace in which is burnt every morning the effigies of those who slew the god. The women have a special female Joss in a separate apartment, whom they worship, and to whom they present offerings. A visit to one of these temples does not give us an exalted idea of Mongolian devotion.

There is apparently very little sentiment of reverence. To all appearances, John is sadly wanting in respect for his divinity. He walks into the Joss house in a shambling, indifferent sort of way, makes his offering, and walks out. He has even been seen to laugh and crack jokes in the sacred presence.

The Farallon Islands
(1874)

HARPER'S
NEW MONTHLY MAGAZINE.

No. CCLXXXVII.—APRIL, 1874.—Vol. XLVIII.

THE FARALLON ISLANDS.
By CHARLES NORDHOFF.

RUNNING THE ROOKERIES—GATHERING MURRE EGGS.

IF you approach the harbor of San Francisco from the west, your first sight of land will be a collection of picturesque rocks known as the Farallones, or, more fully, the Farallones de los Frayles. They are six rugged islets, whose peaks lift up their heads in picturesque masses out of the ocean, twenty-three and a half miles from the Golden Gate, the famous entrance of San Francisco Bay. Farallon is a Spanish word, meaning a small pointed islet in the sea.

These rocks, probably of volcanic origin, and bare and desolate, lie in a line from southeast to northwest—curiously enough the same line in which the islands of the Hawaiian or Sandwich Island group have been thrown up. Geologists say they are the outcrop of an immense granite dike.

The southernmost island, which is the

LIGHT-HOUSE.

largest—just as Hawaii, the southernmost of the Sandwich Island group, is also the biggest—extends for nearly a mile east and west, and is 340 feet high. It is composed of broken and water-worn rocks, forming numerous angular peaks, and having several caves; and the rock, mostly barren and bare, has here and there a few weeds and a little grass. At one point there is a small beach, and at another a depression; but the fury of the waves makes landing at all times difficult, and for the most part impóssible.

The Farallones are seldom visited by travelers or pleasure-seekers. The wind blows fiercely here most of the time; the ocean is rough; and to persons subject to seasickness the short voyage is filled with the misery of that disease. Yet they contain a great deal that is strange and curious. On the highest point of the South Farallon the government has placed a light-house, a brick tower seventeen feet high, surmounted by a lantern and illuminating apparatus. It is a revolving white light, showing a prolonged flash of ten seconds duration once in a minute. The light is about 360 feet above the sea, and with a clear atmosphere is visible, from a position ten feet high, twenty-five and a half miles distant; from an elevation of sixty feet it can be seen nearly thirty-one miles away; and it is plainly visible from Sulphur Peak on the main-land, 3471 feet high and sixty-four and a half miles distant. The light-house is in latitude 37° 41′ 8″ north, and longitude 122° 59′ 05″ west.

On our foggy Western coast it has been necessary to place the light-houses low, because if they stood too high their light would be hidden in fog-banks and low clouds. The tower on the South Farallon is therefore low; and this, no doubt, is an advantage also to the light-keepers, who are less exposed to the buffetings of the storm than if their labor and care lay at a higher elevation.

As the Farallones lie in the track of vessels coming from the westward to San Francisco, the light is one of the most important, as it is also one of the most powerful on our Western coast; and it is supplemented by a fog-whistle which is one of the most curious contrivances of this kind in the world. It is a huge trumpet, six inches in diameter at its smaller end, and blown by the rush of air through a cave or passage connecting with the ocean.

One of the numerous caves worn into the rocks by the surf had a hole at the top, through which the incoming breakers violently expelled the air they carried before them. Such spout-holes are not uncommon on rugged, rocky coasts. There are several on the Mendocino coast, and a number on the shores of the Sandwich Islands. This one, however, has been utilized by the ingenuity of man. The mouth-piece of the trumpet or fog-whistle is fixed against the aperture in the rock, and the breaker, dashing in with venomous spite, or the huge bulging wave which would dash a ship to pieces and drown her crew in a single effort, now blows the fog-whistle and warns the mariner off. The sound thus produced has been heard at a distance of seven or eight miles. It has a peculiar effect, because it has no regular period; depending upon the irregular coming in of the waves, and upon their similarly irregular force, it is blown somewhat as an idle boy would blow his penny trumpet. It ceases entirely for an

ARCH AT WEST END, FARALLON ISLANDS.

hour and a half at low water, when the mouth of the cave or passage is exposed.

The life of the keepers of the Farallon light is singularly lonely and monotonous. Their house is built somewhat under the shelter of the rocks, but they live in what to a landsman would seem a perpetual storm; the ocean roars in their ears day and night; the boom of the surf is their constant and only music; the wild scream of the sea-birds, the howl of the sea-lions, the whistle and shriek of the gale, the dull threatening thunder of the vast breakers, are the dreary and desolate sounds which lull them to sleep at night, and assail their ears when they awake. In the winter months even their supply vessel, which for the most part is their only connection with the world, is sometimes unable to make a landing for weeks at a time. Chance visitors they see only occasionally, and at that distance at which a steamer is safe from the surf, and at which a girl could not even recognize her lover. The commerce of San Francisco passes before their eyes, but so far away that they can not tell the ships and steamers which sail, by them voiceless and without greeting; and of the events passing on the planet with which they have so frail a social tie they learn only at long and irregular intervals. The change from sunshine to fog is the chief variety in their lives; the hasty landing of supplies the great event in their months. They can not even watch the growth of trees and plants; and to a child born and reared in such a place, a sunny lea under the shelter of rocks is probably the ideal of human felicity.

Except the rock of Tristan d'Acunha in the Southern Atlantic Ocean, I have never seen an inhabited spot which seemed so utterly desolate, so entirely separated from the world, whose people appeared to me to have such a slender hold on mankind. Yet for their solace they know that a powerful government watches over their welfare, and— if that is any comfort—that, thirty miles away, there are lights and music and laughter and singing, as well as crowds, and all the anxieties and annoyances incidental to what we are pleased to call civilization.

But though these lonely rocks contain but a small society of human beings—the keepers and their families—they are filled with animal life; for they are the home of a multitude of sea-lions, and of vast numbers of birds and rabbits.

The rabbits, which live on the scanty herbage growing among the rocks, are descended from a few pair brought here many years ago, when some speculative genius thought to make a huge rabbit-warren of these rocks for the supply of the San Francisco market. These little animals are not very wild. In the dry season they feed on the bulbous roots of the grass, and sometimes they suffer from famine. In the winter and spring they are fat, and then their meat is white and sweet. During summer and fall they are not fit to eat.

They increase very rapidly, and at not infrequent intervals they overpopulate the island, and then perish by hundreds of starvation and the diseases which follow a too meagre diet. They are of all colors, and though descended from some pairs of tame white rabbits, seem to have reverted in color to the wild race from which they originated

The Farallones have no snakes. The sea-lions, which congregate by thousands upon the cliffs, and bark and howl and shriek and roar in the caves and upon the steep sunny slopes, are but little disturbed, and one can usually approach them within twenty or thirty yards. It is an extraordinarily interesting sight to see these marine monsters, many of them bigger than an ox, at play in the surf, and to watch the superb skill with which they know how to control their own motions when a huge wave seizes them, and seems likely to dash them to pieces against the rocks. They love to lie in the sun upon the bare and warm rocks; and here they sleep, crowded together, and lying upon each other in inextricable confusion. The bigger the animal, the greater his ambition appears to be to climb to the highest summit; and when a huge, slimy beast has with infinite squirming attained a solitary peak, he does not tire of raising his sharp-pointed, maggot-like head, and complacently looking about him. They are a rough set of brutes—rank bullies, I should say; for I have watched them repeatedly, as a big fellow shouldered his way among his fellows, reared his huge front to intimidate some lesser seal which had secured a favorite spot, and first with howls, and if this did not suffice, with teeth and main force, expelled the weaker from his lodgment. The smaller sea-lions, at least those which have left their mothers, appear to have no rights which any one is bound to respect. They get out of the way with an abject promptness which proves that they live in terror of the stronger members of the community; but they do not give up their places without harsh complaints and piteous groans.

Plastered against the rocks, and with their lithe and apparently boneless shapes conformed to the rude and sharp angles, they are a wonderful, but not a graceful or pleasing sight. At a little distance they look like huge maggots, and their slow, ungainly motions upon the land do not lessen this resemblance. Swimming in the ocean, at a distance from the land they are inconspicuous objects, as nothing but the head shows above water, and that only at intervals. But when the vast surf which breaks in mountain waves against the weather side of the Farallones with a force which would in a single sweep dash to pieces the biggest

SEA-LIONS.

Indiaman—when such a surf, vehemently and with apparently irresistible might, lifts its tall white head, and with a deadly roar lashes the rocks half-way to their summit— then it is a magnificent sight to see a dozen or half a hundred great sea-lions at play in the very midst and fiercest part of the boiling surge, so completely masters of the situation that they allow themselves to be carried within a foot or two of the rocks, and at the last and imminent moment, with an adroit twist of their bodies, avoid the shock, and, diving, re-appear beyond the breaker.

As I sat, fascinated with this weird spectacle of the sea-lions, which seemed to me like an unhallowed prying into some hidden and monstrous secret of nature, I could better realize the fantastic and brutal wildness of life in the earlier geological ages, when monsters and chimeras dire wallowed about our unripe planet, and brute force of muscles and lungs ruled among the populous hordes of beasts which, fortunately for us, have perished, leaving us only this great wild sea-beast as a faint reminiscence of their existence. I wondered what Dante would have thought—and what new horrors his gloomy imagination would have con-

THE GULL'S NEST.

jured, could he have watched this thousand or two of sea-lions at their sports.

The small, sloping, pointed head of the creature gives it, to me, a peculiarly horrible appearance. It seems to have no brain, and presents an image of life with the least intelligence. It is in reality not without wits, for one needs only to watch the two or three specimens in the great tank at Woodward's Gardens, when they are getting fed, to see that they instantly recognize their keeper, and understand his voice and motions. But all their wit is applied to the basest uses. Greed for food is their ruling passion, and the monstrous lightning-like lunges through the water, the inarticulate shrieks of pleasure or of fury as he dashes after his food or comes up without it, the wild, fierce eyes, the eager and brutal vigor with which he snatches a morsel from a smaller fellow-creature, the reliance on strength alone, and the abject and panic-struck submission of the weaker to the stronger—all this shows him a brute of the lowest character.

Yet there is a wonderful snake-like grace in the lithe, swift motions of the animal when he is in the surf. You forget the savage blood-shot eyes, the receding forehead, the clumsy figure and awkward motion as he wriggles up the steep rocks, the moment you see him at his superb sport in the breakers. It seemed to me that he was another creature. The eye looks less baleful, and even joyous; every movement discloses conscious power; the excitement of the sport sheds from him somewhat of the brutality which re-appears the moment he lands or seeks his food.

So far as I could learn, the Farallon sea-lions are seldom disturbed by men seeking profit from them. In the egging season one or two are shot to supply oil to the lamps of the eggers; and occasionally one is caught for exhibition on the main-land. How do they catch a sea-lion? Well, they lasso him; and, odd as it sounds, it is the best and probably the only way to capture this beast. An adroit Spaniard, to whom the lasso or reata is like a fifth hand, or like the trunk to the elephant, steals up to a sleeping congregation, fastens his eye on the biggest one of the lot, and, biding his time, at the first motion of the animal, with unerring skill flings his loose rawhide noose, and then holds on for dear life. It is the weight of an ox and the vigor of half a dozen that he has tugging at the other end of his rope, and if a score of men did not stand ready to help, and if it were not possible to take a turn of the reata around a solid rock, the seal would surely get away.

Moreover, they must handle the beast tenderly, for it is easily injured. Its skin, softened by its life in the water, is quickly cut by the rope; its bones are easily broken; and its huge frame, too rudely treated, may be so hurt that the life dies out of it. As quickly as possible the captured sea-lion is stuffed into a strong box or cage, and here, in a cell too narrow to permit movement, it roars and yelps in helpless fury, until it is transported to its tank. Wild and fierce as it is, it seems to reconcile itself to the tank life very rapidly. If the narrow space of its big bath-tub frets it, you do not perceive this, for hunger is its chief passion, and with a moderately full stomach the animal does well in captivity, of course with sufficient water.

The South Farallon is the only inhabited one of the group. The remainder are smaller; mere rocky points sticking up out of the Pacific. The Middle Farallon is a single rock, from fifty to sixty yards in diameter, and twenty or thirty feet above the water. It lies two and a half miles northwest by west from the light-house. The North Farallon consists in fact of four pyramidal rocks, whose highest peak, in the centre of the group, is one hundred and sixty feet high; the southern rock of the four is twenty feet high. The four have a diameter of 160, 185, 125, and 35 yards respectively, and the most northern of the islets bears north 64° west from the Farallon light, six and three-fifths miles distant.

All the islands are frequented by birds; but the largest, the South Farallon, on which the light-house stands, is the favorite resort of these creatures, who come here in astonishing numbers every summer to breed; and it is to this island that the eggers resort at this season to obtain supplies of sea-bird's eggs for the San Francisco market, where they have a regular and large sale.

The birds which breed upon the Farallones are gulls, murres, shags, and sea-parrots, the last a kind of penguin. The eggs of the shags and parrots are not used, but the eggers destroy them to make more room for the other birds. The gull begins to lay about the middle of May, and usually ten days before the murre. The gull makes a rude nest of brush and sea-weed upon the rocks; the murre does not take even this much trouble, but lays its eggs in any convenient place on the bare rocks.

The gull soon gets done, but the murre continues to lay for about two months. The egging season lasts, therefore, from the 10th or 20th of May until the last of July. In this period the egg company which has for eighteen years worked this field gathered in 1872 17,952 dozen eggs, and in 1873 15,203 dozen. These brought last year in the market an average of twenty-six cents per dozen. There has been, I was assured by the manager, no sensible decrease in the number of the birds or the eggs for twenty years.

From fifteen to twenty men are employed during the egging season in collecting and shipping the eggs. They live on the island during that time in rude shanties near the usual landing-place. The work is not amusing, for the birds seek out the least accessible places, and the men must follow, climbing often where a goat would almost hesitate. But this is not the worst. The gull sits on her nest, and resists the robber who comes for her eggs, and he must take care not to get bitten. The murre remains until her enemy is close upon her; then she rises with a scream which often startles a thousand or two of birds, who whirl up into the air in a dense mass, scattering filth and guano over the eggers.

Nor is this all. The gulls, whose season of breeding is soon past, are extravagantly fond of murre eggs; and these rapacious birds follow the egg-gatherers, hover over their heads, and no sooner is a murre's nest uncovered than the bird swoops down, and the egger must be extremely quick, or the gull will snatch the prize from under his nose. So greedy and eager are the gulls that they sometimes even wound the eggers, striking them with their beaks. But if the gull gets an egg, he flies up with it, and, tossing it up, swallows what he can

catch, letting the shell and half its contents fall in a shower upon the luckless and disappointed egger below.

Finally, so difficult is the ground that it is impossible to carry baskets. The egger therefore stuffs the eggs into his shirt bosom until he has as many as he can safely carry, then clambers over rocks and down precipices until he comes to a place of deposit, where he puts them into baskets, to be carried down to the shore, where there are houses for receiving them. But so skillful and careful are the gatherers that but few eggs are broken.

The gathering proceeds daily, when it has once begun, and the whole ground is carefully cleared off, so that no stale eggs shall remain. Thus if a portion of the ground has been neglected for a day or two, all the eggs must be flung into the sea, so as to begin afresh. As the season advances, the operations are somewhat contracted, leaving a part of the island undisturbed for breeding; and the gathering of eggs is stopped entirely about a month before the birds usually leave the island, so as to give them all an opportunity to hatch out a brood.

The murre is not good to eat. If undisturbed it lays two eggs only; when robbed, it will keep on laying until it has produced six or even eight eggs; and the manager of the islands told me that he had found as many as eight eggs forming in a bird's ovaries when he killed and opened it in the beginning of the season. The male bird regularly relieves

SHAGS, MURRES, AND SEA-GULLS.

THE GREAT ROOKERY.

the female on the nest, and also watches to resist the attacks of the gull, which not only destroys the eggs, but also eats the young. The murre feeds on sea-grass and jelly-fish, and I was assured that though some hundreds had been examined at different times, no fish had ever been found in a murre's stomach.

The bird is small, about the size of a half-grown duck, but its egg is as large as a goose egg. The egg is brown or greenish, and speckled. When quite fresh, it has no fishy taste, but when two or three days old, the fishy taste becomes perceptible. They are largely used in San Francisco by the restaurants and bakers, and for omelets, cakes, and custards.

During the height of the egging season the gulls hover in clouds over the rocks, and when a rookery is started, and the poor birds leave their nests by hundreds, the air is presently alive with gulls flying off with the eggs, and the eggers are sometimes literally drenched.

There is thus inevitably a considerable waste of eggs. I asked some of the eggers how many murres nested on the South Farallon, and they thought at least one hundred thousand. I do not suppose this an extravagant estimate, for, taking the season of 1872, when 17,952 dozen eggs were actually sold in San Francisco, and allowing half a dozen to each murre, this would give nearly 36,000 birds; and adding the proper number for eggs broken, destroyed by gulls, and not gathered, the number of murres and gulls is probably over one hundred thousand. This on an island less than a mile in its greatest diameter, and partly occupied by the light-house and fog-whistle and their keepers, and by other birds and a large number of sea-lions!

When they are done laying, and when the young can fly, the birds leave the island, usually going off together. During the summer and fall they return in clouds at intervals, but stay only a few days at a time, though there are generally a few to be found at all times; and I am told that eggs in small quantities can be found in the fall.

CONTEST FOR THE EGGS.

The murre does not fly high, nor is it a very active bird, or apparently of long flight. But the eggers say that when it leaves the island they do not know whither it goes, and they assert that it is not abundant on the neighboring coast. The young begin to fly when they are two weeks old, and the parents usually take them immediately into the water.

The sea-parrot has a crest, and somewhat resembles a cockatoo. Its numbers on the South Farallon are not great. It makes a nest in a hole in the rocks, and bites if it is disturbed.

The island was first used as a sealing station; but this was not remunerative, there being but very few fur seal, and no sea-otters. This animal, which abounds in Alaska, and is found occasionally on the southern coast of California, frequents the masses of kelp which line the shore; but there is no kelp about the Farallones.

In the early times of California, when provisions were high-priced, the egg-gatherers sometimes got great gains. Once, in 1853, a boat absent but three days brought in one thousand dozen, and sold the whole cargo at a dollar a dozen; and in one season thirty thousand dozen were gathered, and brought an average of but little less than this price.

Of course there was an egg war. The prize was too great not to be struggled for; and the rage of the conflicting claimants grew to such a pitch that guns were used and lives were threatened, and at last the government of the United States had to interfere to keep the peace. But with lower prices the strife ceased; the present company bought out, I believe, all adverse claims, and for the last fifteen or sixteen years peace has reigned in this part of the county of San Francisco—for these lonely islets are a part of the same county with the metropolis of the Pacific.

Pioneer Spanish Families in California

The Missions of Alta California (1891)

PIONEER SPANISH FAMILIES IN CALIFORNIA.

WITH SPECIAL REFERENCE TO THE VALLEJOS.

DON ARTURO BANDINI IN THE OLD SPANISH RIDING DRESS OF HIS FATHER.

THE most attractive literary material left in California is to be found in the recollections and traditions of descendants of the pioneer Spanish families. But these men and women must be met with sympathy for their misfortunes, and with an unfeigned interest in the old ranch and Mission days. As soon as their confidence is fairly won they tell all they know, with almost childlike eagerness to help in the restoration of the past. One immediately observes the great stress laid upon family connections, the pleasure taken in stories of former times, and the especial reverence for the founders of the province, the governors and other officials, and the heads of the Missions. Politics, though of course on an extremely small scale, occupies a large part of the recollections of the older men, and the animosities of the petty revolutions of half a century ago, of the years just before the American conquest, and of the conquest itself, still divide families from each other. A glance at the subjoined list of the governors of California will show the reader how closely united were the social and political features of the life of the province. At first the governors had much power; the great families were hardly established in their almost feudal relations to the soil; and the long terms of office,— fourteen years in one case,— and the peaceful progress of events, show that it was the age of settlement. As the Mexican revolution of 1835 approached the Californians grew restive and gave their governors more and more trouble; at last every noted ranchero family had a different candidate for the governorship, and that "year of revolutions," 1836, saw four successive occupants of the office. Picos, Castros, Alvarados, and a dozen other families, with

THE CAMULOS RANCH,—THE SCENE OF H. H.'S "RAMONA,"—ABOUT TWENTY-FIVE MILES FROM SAN BUENAVENTURA.

DON JUAN B. CASTRO.

tions. The Estradas, for instance, were relatives of the Alvarados, and Don José Abrego, of Monterey, treasurer of the province from 1839 to 1846, married an Estrada. This made the Abregos allies of the Alvarados. Don José's son married a daughter of Jacob P. Leese, the American, son-in-law of General Vallejo; his daughter married Judge Webb of Salinas: the Alvarado-Vallejo connection had drawn the Abregos towards the Americans. The founder of the Alvarado family was Juan B., a settler of 1769, whose son José was sergeant at Monterey, and whose grandson was the governor. The mother of the governor was Maria Josefa Vallejo; his wife was Martina Castro. The founder of the Arguello family was Don José Dario, who arrived in 1781; his wife was a daughter of the Moragas, and their children intermarried with the best families of the province. One daughter was the famous Maria de la Concepcion Marcela, born in 1790, and remembered because of her romance, of which Bret Harte has told the story. There is little to add to the outlines of the poem, except that the tale of the lady Concepcion Arguello is familiar to all the Spanish families, and one often hears it used to illustrate the " simple faith of the ancient days." One of the ladies of the Vallejo family retired to a convent. The lady Apolinaria Lorenzana, of Santa Barbara and San Diego, whose lover died, devoted her

their adherents and relatives, were struggling for social and political supremacy.[1]

The great families of the Spanish pioneer period have mostly representatives at the present day; some of them have retained wealth and influence, especially in the southern counties. Don Romualdo Pacheco, whose mother was Ramona Carrillo, became State senator, lieutenant-governor, and one of the leaders of the Republican party. The grandson of Captain Antonio del Valle, who came from Mexico to California in 1819, is now one of the most prominent politicians in the State. Don Juan B. Castro has held many offices of trust and profit in Monterey County. Don Ignacio Sepulveda, a thoroughly educated lawyer, married an American wife, and was long a superior judge in Los Angeles. A number of similar cases might be mentioned in which individuals of the conquered race have found their opportunity in the material development of the Pacific coast. Still, these were but exceptions; most of the old families sank into obscurity, and it is now difficult to trace their connections. Only about thirty Spanish families of California have retained any wealth or influence.

Among the families of the first rank as regards wealth, influence, dignity, and pride of birth were the Castros, Picos, Arguellos, Bandinis, Carrillos, Alvarados, Vallejos, Avilas, Ortegas, Noriegas, Peraltas, Sepulvedas, Pachecos, Yorbas, and their numerous connec-

DON MANUEL CASTRO.

life to teaching and to charity, and was known for half a century as "*La Beata*," to whom all doors were open and all sorrows brought. She

---

[1] The Spanish and Mexican governors of California and the dates of their accession were as follows : Gaspar de Portola, 1767; Felipe de Barri, 1771; Felipe de Neve, 1774; Pedro Fages, 1782; José Antonio Romen, 1790; José J. de Arrillaga, 1792; Diego de Borica, 1794; José J. de Arrillaga, 1800; José Dario Arguello, 1814; Pablo Vicente de Sola, 1815; Luis Antonio Arguello, 1823; José Maria de Echeandia, 1825; Manuel Victoria, 1831; Pio Pico, 1832; José Figueroa, 1833; José Castro, 1835; Nicolas Gutierrez, 1836; Mariano Chico, 1836; Nicolas Gutierrez, 1836; Juan B. Alvarado, 1836; Manuel Micheltorena, 1842; Pio Pico, 1845.

planted the famous grapevine of Montecito, long known as the largest in the world, and bearing six thousand clusters in a single season.

PIO PICO, GOVERNOR OF CALIFORNIA IN 1845.
(FROM A PHOTOGRAPH BY BUTTERFIELD & SUMMERS.)

There were other women as worthy of saintship, of whom the elders still speak.

The well-known family of Pico was founded in 1782, by Don José Maria, the father of the governor. The northern branch of this family sprang from Don José Dolores, who arrived in 1790. The first of the Sotos was Don Ignacio, a pioneer of 1776; and the Moraga family date from the same year, their founder being Comandante José Joaquin, of San Francisco Presidio and San José Pueblo. A large and prominent Los Angeles family, that of the Avilas, was founded by Cornelio Avila in 1783. Alcalde Avila was killed in the revolution of 1836. Several daughters married Americans. The Lugos are often spoken of in histories. They descend from a Mexican soldier, Francisco Lugo, who arrived in 1769, the date which ranks among Spanish Californians as 1849 does among American pioneers. His four daughters married into the four prominent families of Ruiz, Cota, Vallejo, and Carrillo. The town of Martinez, near Monte Diablo, takes its name from the Martinez family, whose founder was an early alcalde of San Francisco, and three of whose daughters married Americans. A far later arrival was the Jimeno family, one of whom was Governor

Alvarado's Secretary of State, whose widow became the wife of Dr. Ord, and whose two sons were taken to the Atlantic States by Lieutenant Sherman in 1850 to be educated. An intimate friend of this famous secretary was Don José M. Romero, the most widely known teacher and author of the province, who wrote and printed the "Catecismo de Ortologia" at Monterey in 1836, and established an advanced school, the best in California until the days of Enrique Cambuston and José Maria Campina, whom Governor Alvarado brought from Mexico.

The Bandinis descended from an Andalusian family of high rank, and were in California by 1771. Old Captain José Bandini was the first to raise the Mexican flag, which he did on the ship *Reina*, at San Blas, in 1821. His son Juan married Dolores Estudillo, and, after her death, Refugio Arguello, and was very prominent in the province from 1825 to 1845. The extensive Carrillo family and also the great Ortega family date their Californian record from 1769. The Ortegas founded Santa Barbara. The Carrillos in the second generation married into the Vallejos, Castros, Pachecos, and many other proud families. At the time of the conquest they had connections in every part of the province. The late Judge Covarrubias, of Santa Barbara, one of the most prominent jurists of Southern California, was connected by marriage with the Carrillos. Captain Noriega, of Santa Barbara, also married a Carrillo, and when he died, in 1858, he left more than a hundred descendants. There were large families in those days of simple,

GENERAL ANDRES PICO.
(FROM A PHOTOGRAPH IN POSSESSION OF PIO PICO.)

healthy outdoor life; one often reads in the old documents of from twelve to twenty sons and daughters of the same parents. Don Cristobal Dominguez, who owned the Las Virgenes ranch, left fourteen living children, and one hundred and ten living descendants.

The founders of the early families came from

MARIA DE JESUS VALLEJO (SISTER MARIA TERESA).

thing which "astonished all his friends," for it was not seemly; no other Californian did so. The officer who founded Branciforte, Colonel Pedro Albertia, was a Catalan. The first of the Alvisos, the Valencias, and the Peraltas were from Sonora. José Mariano Bonilla, from the city of Mexico, was one of the first lawyers in the province. The Vacas, descendants of the famous *conquistadore* Captain Vaca, who was under Cortez, came from New Mexico. Don Manuel Requena of Los Angeles came to California from Yucatan. The Suñols, who owned one of the most beautiful of valleys, were from Spain, and the sons were sent to Paris to be educated. Lieutenant Valdez, who was in the Malaspina expedition of 1791, returned to Europe and was killed at Trafalgar. This noted expedition, under Alejandro Malaspina, consisted of two royal corvettes of Spain, which left Cadiz in 1789, reached California in 1791, and went around the world. In ways like these, and from a thousand channels of commerce and adventure, every province of Spain and Mexico became represented among the pioneer families of California.

THE Vallejo family traces its descent from soldiers and nobles of the heroic days of Spain, and is as well known in the mother country as in California. A copy of the genealogical record of the family, which has been kept with great precision, was filed in 1806 in the Spanish archives of Alta California. It states that Don Alonzo Vallejo commanded the Spanish troops on board the vessel which brought the

all parts of the Spanish dominions. The Castros were from Sinaloa, and so were the Lugos. Old Don Aguirre, a wealthy ship-owner and merchant, who first came in his vessel the *Guipuscuana*, was a Basque, and his family is still represented in San Diego and Santa Barbara. Another Basque pioneer was Don José Amesti, a rough, honest fellow, alcalde of Monterey, and afterwards the governor's secretary, who married Prudencia Vallejo. General Castro once told me that Don José "would even say 'carajo' before his children," a

royal commissioner Bobadilla to America with orders to carry Columbus a prisoner to Spain. Another famous Vallejo was a captain under Cortez, followed that illustrious cutthroat to the complete conquest of Mexico, and became governor of the province of Panuco, lord of great silver mines, and master of peons innumerable.

Bilbao, the ancient capital of Burgos, Spain, was the place from which the branch of the Vallejos that is known in California started for the New World. Of this branch came Don

THE MOTHER OF GENERAL VALLEJO, BORN
MARIA ANTONIA LUGO.

gation works of the Missions and pueblos, and becoming the owner of extensive and valuable estates.

Don Ignacio's engagement and marriage are noted in most of the chronicles of the period. The great Missions were being founded, and, outside of priests and Indians, few people were in the country; California, as late as in the "golden prime of '49," was a masculine community, and women of the better sort were hard to find. When, therefore, the young soldier of fortune saw, at San Luis Obispo, in 1776, on the day of her birth, an infant daughter of the Lugo family, then as now prominent among the Spanish families of Southern California, he did not delay his wooing. Using all the dignity and formality that the aristocratic *gentils de razon* of the period considered essential in such matters, he obtained an interview with the parents, and negotiated a solemn contract of engagement with the day-old Señorita Maria Antonia Lugo, subject to the girl's future consent. She grew up to be an exceedingly attractive and intelligent young woman, and in due season they were married. It proved an extremely happy and fortunate union, and the success of the founder of the Vallejo family in California in speaking for an infant in arms became almost a family proverb from San Diego to Sonoma. Don Ignacio's home was notable, even in that pioneer age, for its patriarchal simplicity, and he maintained to the day of his death, in 1831, a noble and dignified leadership of the family. Señora Vallejo survived her husband until 1851, and a painting made a short time before her death shows the almost puritanical severity and strength of character of this old Spanish lady of the Arcadian period of California.

Ignacio Vicente Vallejo, born in 1748, in the city of Guadalaxara, Mexico, and designed, as were many of the family before him, for holy orders and the service of the Church. The young man rebelled, volunteered under Captain Rivera y Moncada in Padre Junipero Serra's famous expedition, landing at San Diego in 1769, and thus became a pioneer among the Spanish pioneers themselves. He soon became prominent in the colony, and was not only made military commander of various towns, but was long the only civil engineer in the province, laying out most of the greater irri-

None of the Spanish pioneer families have more carefully preserved the traditions and

DE LA GUERRA MANSION.

relics of the past than have the Vallejos. With them, as with others, the time of greatest prosperity was between 1820 and 1846. Among the great families with which they were closely connected by marriage or friendship were the De la Guerras, whose founder, Don José de la Guerra y Noriega, was born in Santander, Spain, of a family which dates back to the Moorish wars. Early in the century the family owned no fewer than eight large ranches, and as late as 1850 Don José sold nearly $100,-000 worth of cattle annually, and was one of the great men of the pastoral period, with hundreds of herdsmen scattered over leagues of territory. His wife, Maria Antonia Carrillo, the daughter of Don Raymundo, one of the first commanders at San Diego and Santa of every visitor. The freedom from care, the outdoor life and constant exercise, and the perfect climate of California had re-created the Andalusian type of loveliness. In the Ortega family, for instance, the women, who all had brown hair and eyes and were of pure Castilian stock, were so renowned for their beauty that their fame extended to the city of Mexico, and General Ramirez came from there with letters of introduction to win a daughter of the Ortegas. Another of the famous beauties of her day was the Señora Maria Isabel Cota de Pico, who was born in 1783 and died in 1869, leaving over three hundred living descendants. Señorita Guadalupe Ortega married young Joseph Chapman, a New Englander who landed on the coast in 1818 from

ADOBE HOUSE, SONOMA, ERECTED BY GENERAL VALLEJO, 1834.

Barbara, was called in common speech "that most benevolent lady." The seventh of their eleven children was several times mayor of Santa Barbara. The eldest daughter married W. P. Hartnell, of London. The youngest daughter, Antonia, afterwards Mrs. Oreña, was called in her day the greatest beauty on the Pacific coast.

It is remarkable how many of the daughters of the best families of the old Californian towns married Americans and Englishmen of standing. In the Carrillo family four daughters married foreigners; the Ortegas, Noriegas, and many others showed a similar record. The grace, beauty, and modesty of the women of the time were the admiration the Buenos Ayrean privateer which Bouchard commanded, and who was captured by Corporal Lugo, whose sister married Don Ignacio Vallejo. With true Spanish hospitality Lugo made him a guest of the family, and in a year or two secured his social recognition among the leading families. Chapman became prominent at the Mission San Gabriel, and at Los Angeles and Santa Barbara, where he died in 1849.

A multitude of stories of the social life of the Spanish period might be told here, but it is sufficient to give the outline as told by the descendants of those old families. Each town on the coast was the center of the hide and tallow trade for a hundred miles or more. The low adobe stores there held piles of costly and beautiful goods in the days of which Farnham and Dana wrote — the days when the great cattle princes came from their ranches to hold festival. The young cavaliers rode in on fiery but well-trained and gaily caparisoned horses, and all the wonderful feats of horsemanship of as fine a race of riders as the world has ever seen were performed daily on mesa and sea-beach and plaza. But the home life of these great families was simplicity itself. In many a Spanish house there was no fireplace, window, or chimney. The fire for cooking was built on a clay floor, partly roofed, outside of the main building. The household utensils were few — a copper or iron kettle, a slab of rock on which to pound corn or wheat, a soapstone griddle for the tortillas. Dishes, tableware, and furniture came slowly, and were of the most simple description. For years a raw hide stretched on the floor with a blanket spread over it formed the usual bed in early California. Everything was kept exquisitely clean, and though the Spanish families learned to spend more on their houses and belongings, they seemed to look upon such things as only affording opportunities for a more generous hospitality.

DOÑA VALLEJO, WIDOW OF GENERAL VALLEJO,
BORN FRANCISCA BENICIA CARRILLO.

In the old days there was not a hotel in California, and it was considered a grievous offense even for a stranger, much more for a friend, to pass by a ranch without stopping. Fresh horses were always furnished, and in many cases on record when strangers appeared to need financial help a pile of uncounted silver was left in the sleeping apartment, and they were given to understand that they were to take all they needed. This money was covered with a cloth, and it was a point of honor not to count it beforehand nor afterwards. It was "guest silver," and the custom continued until its abuse by travelers compelled the native Californians to abandon it. Among themselves no one was ever allowed to suffer or struggle for lack of help. The late Dr. Nicholas Den, of Santa Barbara, who married into the Ortega family, once needed money to carry through a speculation, and thought of going to Los Angeles to borrow it. Old Father Narciso, hearing of the matter, sent his Indian boy to him with a "cora," or four-gallon tule basket, full of gold, and the message that he ought to come to his priest whenever he needed help.

The collections of "Documents relating to the History of California" made by General Vallejo and his brother Don J. J. Vallejo, and now in the Bancroft library, and the very graphic and careful series of manuscript notes and memoranda by General Vallejo, entitled "Historia de California," all cast light upon the social and economic conditions in these Arcadian days. A very large number of the old families, such as the Castros, Picos, Arces, and Peraltas, and many of the Americans who had married native Californians, furnished manuscripts, letters, and various documents of permanent value. In fact it may be doubted if the pioneer period of any other American State has had a more complete mass of original authoritative data made ready for the historian's use. Much still remains to be collected from first hands, and many minor historical questions will probably be solved by documents still held by the native Californian families, who treasure every scrap of written paper.

The link between the old and the new, between the quiet and happy pastoral age of the beginning of the century and the age of American growth and change that followed fast on

the capital of the province, and died January 18, 1890, in Sonoma, once the northern fortress of the province and guarded by the young general's soldiers. At the age of sixteen he was an officer in the army and the private secretary of the governor of California. In 1829, when only twenty-one, he became lieutenant-commander of the northern department, which included all the country north of Santa Cruz, and made his headquarters at the presidio. Here he organized the first town government of Yerba

WASHING-DAY ON A RANCH.

Buena, and for five years exercised both civil and military functions there. The Solis rebellion against Governor Echeandia, who had removed the seat of government from Monterey to San Diego, began in the fall of 1829, and Vallejo aided in the defeat of the insurgents at

the conquest, was that remarkable man, General Mariano Guadalupe Vallejo,[1] whose children, as he once told me, "were born under three administrations—Spanish, Mexican, and American." One of his daughters said, "Two of us, when we were small, were called by our brothers and sisters 'the little Yankees.'" General Vallejo, the eighth of the thirteen children of Don Ignacio, was born in 1808, in the old seaport town of Monterey, long

Santa Barbara. He was a member of the territorial deputation in 1831, and brought articles of impeachment against Governor Victoria, who was defeated and driven from California in the revolution which followed. The next year General Vallejo married Señorita Francisca Benicia Carrillo, by whom he had seventeen children, nine of whom are now living.[2]

By 1840 the young lieutenant had reached

[1] See portrait in THE CENTURY for December, 1890.
[2] The eldest became the wife of General John B. Frisbie; the others are the wife of Dr. Frisbie, Mrs. Attila Haraszthy, Mrs. E. Emperan, Mrs. J. Henry Cutter, Dr. Platon Vallejo, Andronica Vallejo, Ulla Vallejo, and Napoleon Vallejo.

THE FANDANGO.

the rank of lieutenant-general, and was the one man in California to whom the entire province turned with perfect confidence in every emergency. When Gutierrez was deposed Vallejo took control of affairs, and he made his nephew Alvarado civil governor, retaining military control himself. Micheltorena, who succeeded him as governor, confirmed all his acts, and appointed him military commander of the whole territory north of Monterey. Vallejo then founded the town of Sonoma, making it his military headquarters, and spent more than a quarter of a million dollars there. He sent to Mexico for a printing press and type, set up with his own hands his orders and proclamations, and printed and bound several pamphlets. This was in 1839. The famous Zamorano press of Monterey, which began work in November, 1834, with carnival ball invitations, had printed the " Catecismo " and many public documents, which are much prized by collectors. Paper was so scarce that the proof-sheets and defective prints were saved and used for fly-leaves of the curious little *arisméticas* and other text-books that were issued a few years later for the schools of the province.

One has to go back to the days of the famous Spanish "marches," or frontier towns built and defended in Spain's heroic age by her proudest knights, to find a fit parallel in history to the position held by General Vallejo during the closing years of the Mexican rule in California. He had absolute sway for a hundred miles or more, and he "kept the border." His men rode on horseback to Monterey and to Captain Sutter's fort on the Sacramento, bringing him news and carrying his letters. Spanish families colonized the fertile valleys under his protection, and Indians came and built in the shadows of the Sonoma Mission. He owned, as he believed by unassailable title, the largest and finest ranch in the province, and he dispensed a hospitality so generous and universal that it was admired and extolled even among the old Spanish families. J. Quinn Thornton, who visited the coast in 1848 and published his experiences, says: " Governor-General Vallejo owns 1000 horses that are broken to the saddle and bridle, and 9000 that are not broken. Broken horses readily bring one hundred dollars apiece, but the unbroken ones can be purchased for a trivial sum." More and more in the closing years of the epoch and the days of the conquest General Vallejo became the representative man of his people, and so he has received, among many of the old families, the reproachful name of a traitor to California and to his nation. The quiet intensity of this bitterness, even to-day, is a startling thing. I have seen men of pure blood, famous in provincial history, leave the room at the name of Vallejo.

In 1844–45 the native Californians drove out Governor Micheltorena, and began to discuss the feasibility of establishing a separate government. In 1846 the famous Santa Barbara convention of leading ranchers occurred, and, according to General Vallejo's memo-

OLD SWISS HOUSE OF GENERAL VALLEJO AT SONOMA, IMPORTED IN PARTS FROM SWITZERLAND.

randa, English influences were very strong. He exerted all his personal influence, and secured an adjournment of the convention to Monterey, where that fine old American, Consul Thomas O. Larkin, helped him in his struggle. Here Vallejo made a bold speech against an English protectorate, against a separate republic, and in favor of annexation to the United States and ultimate statehood. He was thoroughly equipped for the task, the best educated man among the native Californians, and inspired by the American ideal. The convention closed with its leaders, such as his nephews Castro and Alvarado, ready to adopt the views of Vallejo, and the way seemed prepared for a hearty welcome to the Americans. But the Bear Flag episode followed, Vallejo was carried a prisoner to Sutter's Fort, and the opportunity of peaceful conquest was lost. Nevertheless, as soon as he was released he threw himself heart and soul into the work of organizing a government. He aided in framing a temporary code of laws, and in securing its support by the Spanish population. He laid out the town sites of Benicia and Vallejo on the strait of Carquinez, and he was a leading member of the constitutional convention. General Vallejo's whole career showed that he was actuated by a large and noble ambition to be recognized as the foremost citizen of the State. Nothing marked this element in his nature more clearly than the magnificent plans for his proposed capital

at Vallejo. He offered to construct public buildings and give large areas of land. The long-forgotten scheme, which was laid before the legislature of 1850, who accepted, and was ratified by the people, was in every respect worthy of his magnificent liberality. He began to build his new city, but, contrary to the pledges of the State, the capital was removed to Sacramento at the next session of the legislature. Squatters began to settle upon his great Suscol and Petaluma ranches, and ultimately the Supreme Court of the United States rejected the title to the larger part of his estates. He spent the rest of his life on a comparatively small homestead, " Lachryma Montis," near the old town of Sonoma.

Lachryma Montis is one of the few historical mansions of the Pacific coast. The dwelling house, built in 1850–51, cost nearly $60,000 and came from all parts of the world — the mantelpieces from Honolulu, the iron from China, the bricks from South America. Carpenters' wages were then seventeen dollars a day, and the great redwoods that were hewn in the Sonoma forests were " whip-sawed " by hand for the plank required. The spring on the mountain side that gave the mansion its name was walled in, and a lake which supplied the town with water and fed fountains in the orange, lemon, and olive groves was thus formed. More nopal hedges were planted, and the old ones extended. A chalet imported in parts from Switzerland was erected near the mansion. Farther away were the old adobes. A pavilion of iron, glass, and bamboo, imported from China, cost, as members of the family tell me, more than a hundred thousand dollars. When the estates were lost the beautiful grounds began to fall into ruins, through lack of means to keep them up, and in 1890 General Vallejo died a comparatively poor man.

Sonoma Valley is full of stories of his generosity. Father Lorenzo Waugh, an early Methodist circuit-rider of the region, saw the squatters taking up land in the valley while waiting for a decision respecting Vallejo's title. He went to the general, and was told to go ahead and settle on a quarter-section, and he would do all in his power to secure him a title. Father Waugh did so, and nine years later, while Vallejo was away, the lines of this particular district were settled, and his lawyer, against orders, sold the tract on which Waugh lived. As soon as Vallejo learned this he gave him a title to three hundred acres of better land, a part of the home estate. No one will ever know how many hundreds of American pioneers owed their start in the world to General Vallejo, even while he was struggling against immense financial difficulties and losing his lands, not by acres, but by square leagues.

in 1849, in Alameda County. "You can keep it; I cannot."

After General Vallejo found his estate slipping away he devoted himself more and more to horticulture and to the education of his children. He occasionally appeared in public, and the greatness of his services to the commonwealth was recognized by every thoughtful citizen. The general's name is mentioned in nearly every book of travels or magazine article relating to early California. In his later years he gathered up and put on record a surprising wealth of material relating to the old Spanish days of California. From him the historians have drawn most of their important details. His manuscript, now in the Bancroft collection, is written with such exquisite care and fidelity to truth that, like General Bidwell's recollections of early days in the Sacramento Valley, it has become the primary authority upon all within its range.

General Vallejo's readiness of apt anecdote was always remarkable. Patti once dined with him, and asked the old soldier if he enjoyed the first opera he ever heard.

"Why, no," said Vallejo; "and yet I confess I shall never forget it."

This reply aroused Patti's curiosity, and she

AN ADOBE IN SONOMA.

Many others of the old Californians made a distinction between the "Gringo thieves" and the pleasant, manly pioneers who were good neighbors. A volume could be written about the unsolicited gifts of land — fifty acres here, a hundred there — made to young Americans to whom the great rancheros had taken a fancy, or who had rendered them a service. "Take the land," said Don Alviso to a Connecticut man

demanded when and where the event took place.

"In 1828, on the site of the Palace Hotel, San Francisco."

"Indeed! And who was the prima donna so long ago as that?"

"Well, I can't say," was the smiling answer; "but there were at least five hundred coyotes in the chorus."

THE VALLEJO CHARIOT FOR POSTILION AND
FOOTMAN, BROUGHT FROM MEXICO EARLY IN THIS CENTURY.

foothills. November 23, 1774, Captain Rivera, with sixteen soldiers and Father Palou, made another expedition to the bay. They entered the Santa Clara Valley and skirted the western shore of the bay of San Francisco, following the level plains past the sites of Palo Alto, Belmont, and many other towns of to-day, and crossing to the ocean beach at Laguna de la Merced, they reached Point Lobos, and climbed the cliff to look down on the Golden Gate. December 4 they planted the cross. The general says in his commemoration address, "That cross I saw myself in the year 1829." The expedition returned to Monterey "by way of San Pedro, Spanishtown, Half Moon Bay, Point New Year, Santa Cruz, Watsonville, Castroville, and Salinas." In 1775 Captain Ayala sailed the *San Carlos* into the bay of San Francisco, and "remained forty days, exploring it in all directions." In the spring of 1776 Colonel Anza and Lieutenant Moraga led another land expedition to the region and returned to Monterey.

A volume of description could not give a more complete picture of the loneliness of the peninsula at that time.

In his younger days General Vallejo not only knew almost every one of the five thousand Spanish Californians in the province, the greater part of the Mission Indians, and the chiefs of the wild tribes, but he gathered up, even in his youth, the traditions of the pioneers, and tested their accuracy by every possible documentary and other evidence. His journals are full of variety, and form a complete picture of the entire Spanish period. One of his memoranda speaks of the galleon *San Augustin*, which was wrecked in Tomales Bay in 1595, and of which portions drifted into the Golden Gate in 1830, where they were found by Don José Antonio Sanches and identified by General Vallejo! He has traced the track of every exploring expedition from the earliest settlement, and determined most of their camps. His story of the discovery of San Francisco Bay illustrates the slowness of the progress of settlement. It was late in 1769 that the Portala party and Captain Rivera, with whom was Don Ignacio Vallejo, worked northward from San Diego, past Monterey, and down the San Mateo peninsula, till, on November 2, two hunters of the expedition first looked upon the bay of San Francisco, and November 4 the whole party saw the great bay. In March, 1772, Captain Fages and Father Crespi made that notable exploration which extended from Monterey across the Salinas Valley, through the hills to the Santa Clara Valley, up the east side of the bay past San José and Oakland, and along the shores of San Pablo and Suisun to where Antioch now stands. The San Joaquin River was crossed at this point, and recrossed by the expedition, which returned to Monterey through the Monte Diablo

Then came the foundation of the Mission and the Presidio. The military force, under Lieutenant Moraga, consisted, says General Vallejo, of one sergeant, two corporals, and ten soldiers, with their wives and children. These conveyed Fathers Palou and Cambon, with two Indian servants and three neophyte Indians, who cared for eighty-six head of Mission cattle, partly their own, partly belonging to the king. June 27, 1776, they camped at the lagoon or lake of Dolores, near where the Mission was soon afterwards built. The soldiers erected barracks of tule, soon replaced by wood. The day of the foundation of the Mission was fixed at October 4, the day of St. Francis, and October 8 the actual building was begun. Among those present were Don Ignacio Vallejo, Lieutenant Moraga, and members of the families of Briones, Galindo, Castro, Pacheco, Bojorques, Bernal, Peralta, Higuera, and others of prominence in Spanish California.

The historians of Spanish Californian days must draw on such traditions as these, obtained from General Vallejo's conversations, or written in his memoranda. A single magazine article can contain only a small part of the wealth of tradition that has gathered about the old Sonoma homestead of the Vallejos — that homestead which is in the highest degree typical of all Spanish homesteads of the first rank on the Pacific coast. Everywhere, in the most picturesque portions of California, are the old adobes that once were social centers of the stately life of nearly a century ago. Most of them are merely ruins, but many are still the homes of the descendants of the first families of the province. The years that brought such change and wreck to the old days have now carried them so far back into the mists of tradition that they seem centuries away. Vallejo's fortress on the frontier is now a town, as dull and unromantic as Yonkers. About the ancient pueblo of Los Angeles has sprung up an intensely modern city. A railroad extends through the very graveyard of San Miguel Mission. Much needs to be done by Cali-fornians to preserve the memorials of the past that was so fair and so fruitful a beginning of the story of the commonwealth. The agency through which this is to be accomplished is likely to be the association known as the Native Sons of the Golden West, under whose public-spirited direction was conducted the recent successful celebration of the admission of California.

Charles Howard Shinn.

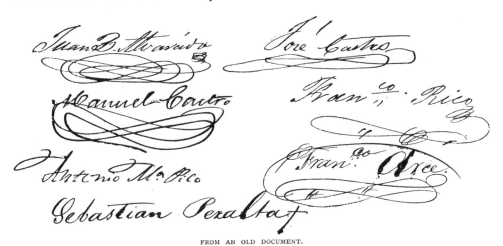

FROM AN OLD DOCUMENT.

THE MISSIONS OF ALTA CALIFORNIA.[1]

CROSS AT MONTEREY MARKING THE LANDING PLACE OF JUNIPERO SERRA.

ALTHOUGH the peninsula of Lower California was discovered as early as 1534, and many attempts were made to colonize it, it remained wholly unoccupied by Spain down to 1697. In February of that year two Jesuit fathers, Juan Maria Salvatierra and Francisco Eusebio Kino, asked permission to attempt the spiritual conquest of the country, which was granted on condition that the king should not be called on for any part of the expense involved, and that possession should be taken distinctly in the name of the Spanish crown. Armed with this authority and the sanction of their superiors in the order, the two missionaries set about collecting funds for their undertaking, and in a short time succeeded in obtaining sufficient means to commence it. These funds, subscribed by charitable individuals, whose names and contributions the gratitude of the fathers has preserved for us to this day, increased, in progress of time, to an aggregate of sufficient importance to find frequent mention in Mexican legislation and history, under the name of the "Pious Fund of the Californias." It constituted afterwards the endowment and support of the Missions on all the west coast of the continent as far north as claimed by Spain, the whole of which was called by the general name of the Californias.

The thirteen Missions founded by the Jesuits

[1] See also "Father Junipero and his Work: A Sketch of the Foundation, Prosperity, and Ruin of the Franciscan Missions in California," by "H. H.," in this magazine for May and June, 1883.—EDITOR.

in Lower California extended from Cape San Lucas, at the extremity of the peninsula, northwards. Details regarding them are deemed out of place here: they were in a flourishing condition at the time of the expulsion of the order in 1768, and the establishments remain to the present day; ruined indeed and deserted by the population that once clustered round them, but attesting still the pious zeal of their founders.

In 1767 the Spanish monarch, by a "pragmatic sanction," directed that the Society of abroad. A few moments only were allowed to them to snatch their breviaries, beads, prayer-books, and necessary clothing, and within an hour after the first knock at the door of the establishment the whole body of inmates was in motion towards the coast, where they were with equal suddenness and despatch shipped off to Rome. During their journey to the point of embarkation no intercourse was allowed either with friends or with persons casually met on the road. They vanished

THE FIRST MISSION IN CALIFORNIA (SAN DIEGO).

Jesus should be expelled from his dominions. With a refinement of cruelty this decree was directed to be put into force in every part of the kingdom at the same instant. At a given hour of the night, long after the inmates were in profound sleep, a train of vehicles was drawn up at the door of every Jesuit college, novitiate, or other establishment of any kind, and the porter was roused from sleep and directed, in the name of the king, to summon all the members of the community to instant assembly in the chapel or refectory. Hastily putting on their garments, the members obeyed the summons, bewildered to conjecture its cause. The roll was called, the laggards, if there were any, were brought in, and the assembled members were then informed that his Majesty had been pleased to banish them forever from his dominions. Carriages were awaiting them below, and relays of animals were provided for their transportation to the nearest seaport, where vessels were prepared to convey them from Spain, and from all the European possessions of Spain, as silently and as rapidly as a morning mist.

It was not possible to enforce this barbarous decree with the same cruel precision in California. The place was too remote, and its resources inadequate. It was necessary to supply the Missions with other missionaries, else the Indians, who had been with so much trouble and effort reduced to habits of civilization, would infallibly have relapsed again into savagery and paganism, and the whole work of conquest would have to be recommenced. Thus the necessities of the situation somewhat modified the cruelty of the proceedings in California. The missionaries were assembled in La Paz in February, 1768, and amid the tears and lamentations of their Indian flocks, who, from every Mission in the peninsula, sent delegations to accompany their spiritual fathers, they finally embarked, and, after a toilsome pilgrimage across Mexico, finally took ship at Vera

MISSION OF SAN JOSÉ. (DRAWN AFTER A DAGUERREOTYPE
TAKEN IN 1853, NOW OWNED BY J. L. BEARD.)

BELLS AND FONT AT SAN JOSÉ.

Cruz on the 13th of April. From the magnitude of the Pious Fund the hungry politicians, who hoped to profit by their expulsion, looked for large amounts of money from the plunder of the California Missions. The total of all sums found at them proved less than a hundred dollars.

Arrangements had been made by the viceroy by which Franciscan friars, drawn from the convent of San Fernando de Zacatecas, took the place of the expelled Jesuits in the several Missions; and adopting the rules and practices of their predecessors they gradually slid into the confidence of the simple-hearted natives, and carried on the work as it had been commenced.

At this time the Marquis de Croix was Viceroy of New Spain, and José de Galvez was sent over from the mother country as Visitador General, armed with extraordinary powers. Apprehensions of an attempt by the English to enlarge their possessions in America and to obtain a foothold on the Pacific made it appear unsafe to permit the northwest coast to remain longer unoccupied, and Galvez determined to colonize it on a large scale. He was a man of immense zeal and untiring industry, well chosen for an occasion requiring energetic action. Fortunately he met with an ecclesiastic to second his movements who possessed the same qualities in as high a degree, perhaps in a higher, and who joined to them a humble piety, a zealous devotion to duty, and a self-abnegation even more remarkable. This was Father Junipero Serra, president of the Missions.

Father Michael Joseph Serra was born in the island of Majorca, in the year 1713. After pursuing his studies in the Lullian University there he evinced a preference for a religious life, and was admitted to the order of St. Francis, taking instead of his baptismal names that of Junipero, by which only he is known in history. The Franciscans and Dominicans were, about that period, extending their Missions among the Indians of America in rivalry with the Jesuits, and Father Serra with three of his fellow-members became inflamed with the desire to take part in these pious enterprises. The other associates were Fathers Rafael Verger, Francisco Palou, and Juan Crespi. They obtained permission to join a body of missionaries which in 1749 was assembled at Cadiz to embark for the New World, and after a ninety-nine days' voyage they landed in Vera Cruz. Palou has left us a quaint history of their journey, which in these days of rapid transit is rather amusing. The voyage from Majorca to Malaga was made in a small English coaster,

the captain of which [says he] was a stubborn, cross-grained heretic, of a disposition so aggravating that, during the fifteen days our passage to Malaga lasted, he gave us not a minute's peace. We scarce had time to read our office, from his everlasting and

missionaries overboard, and on one occasion clapped a dagger at Father Serra's throat, threatening his life. It is not surprising that the missionaries rejoiced at again reaching *terra firma* after fifteen days of tossing in a Mediterranean vessel and enjoying from the officers these social amenities.

After many years' successful missionary efforts in the Sierra Gorda, Father Serra was selected to take principal charge of the Missions of California, now confided to the Franciscans, and he arrived at the port of Loreto with fifteen associates on the 2d of April, 1768. After having made the necessary dispositions for occupying the various establishments of the peninsula — a task which occupied many months, as they extended over a territory seven hundred

MISSION OF SAN ANTONIO OF PADUA, ABOUT TWENTY MILES FROM MONTEREY.

persistent craving to dispute about religion and wrangle over doctrinal points. He understood no language save English and a mere smattering of Portuguese, and in the latter he conducted his disputations. With the English version of the Bible in his hand he would read a text of the Holy Scripture and proceed to interpret it according to his own ideas. But our Father Junipero was so well versed in dogmatic theology and so familiar with the Holy Scriptures that he would at once point out the error and misinterpretation, and frequently refer to another text in confirmation. The captain would thereupon rummage his greasy old Bible, and when he could find no other escape would declare that the leaf was torn and he could n't find the verse he wanted.

The captain, as Father Palou states, remained " doggedly perverse " till the last, and in fact the disputes waxed so hot at times that he more than once threatened to throw the

miles in length — he was ready to coöperate with Galvez in the subjection of Upper California to the practical dominion of the crown of Spain and the Christian religion. Two expeditions were organized for the purpose, one by sea and the other by land. The latter was formed into two detachments, which, after a toilsome march from San Fernando de Vellicata, on the Indian frontier of Lower California, were, on the 1st of July, 1769, reunited at the bay of San Diego, where the schooners *San Carlos* and *San Antonio*, which had come up the coast to meet them, were also safely anchored. San Diego was a place of which at that time nothing more was known than that there was an excellent harbor, which had been visited by Sebastian Vizcayno in his voyage of 1601–2. This journey to San Diego occupied ninety-three days, during which Father Serra suffered

MISSION OF SAN BUENAVENTURA.

excruciatingly from an injury to one of his legs, so that at times he could neither walk nor ride.

The first Mission of Upper California was founded at San Diego, and before the lapse of a fortnight a second expedition was organized, under Don Gaspar de Portola, which was directed to proceed up the coast as far as Monterey and to found a Mission there. Monterey was also a place made known to Spanish geographers by Vizcayno's voyage of 1602, in his report of which he had described it in glowing terms as a magnificent harbor, fit to shelter the navies of the world. Fathers Juan Crespi and Francisco Gomez were the chaplains of this expedition, which was also to have the coöperation of the two schooners, which were directed to the same destination.

How this land expedition toiled up the coast from San Diego, of its "moving accidents by flood and field, of hairbreadth 'scapes, ... of antres vast and deserts idle, rough quarries, rocks and hills," of how in its search for Monterey it stumbled on the bay of San Francisco and first made known to civilized man the garden of the present State of California, I have related elsewhere and will not here repeat. Suffice it to say, that having penetrated as far up the coast and over the Coast Range as to look down from the crest over what is now Searsville on the broad expanse of the Santa Clara Valley, and on the great estuary which its historian described as a "Mediterranean sea," the expedition, compelled by the approach of winter, the scarcity of food, and the increasing hostility of the aborigines, turned on the 11th of November to retrace its steps to San Diego.

On again reaching Point Pinos and the supposed place of the bay of Monterey, nearly a

PULPIT AND CONFESSIONAL OF SAN BUENAVENTURA.

fortnight was devoted to a vigorous exploration of the rugged coast in search of the magnificent port described by Vizcayno, but in vain. The locality did not correspond in any degree to the traveler's glowing description of it. Failing to discover the harbor they were looking for, the leaders concluded it had been either destroyed by some convulsion of nature, or filled with silt, and so obliterated. They erected a large wooden cross at the north and another at the south side of Point Pinos as a memorial of their visit, and for the purpose of attracting the attention of the expedition by sea, which had been despatched to coöperate with them. On the cross erected at the south side was cut the legend: " Dig at the foot of this and you will find a writing "; and at its foot accordingly

cisco on the 11th of November, passed Point Año Nuevo on the 19th, and reached this point and harbor of Pinos on the 27th of the same month. From that date until the present, 9th of December, we have used every effort to find the bay of Monterey, searching the coast thoroughly notwithstanding its ruggedness, but in vain. At last undeceived, and despairing of finding it after so many efforts, sufferings, and labors, and having left of all our provisions but fourteen small sacks of flour, we leave this place to-day for San Diego. I beg of Almighty God to guide it, and for you, traveler, who may read this, that he may guide you to the harbor of eternal salvation.

Done in this harbor of Pinos, the 9th of December, 1769.

NOTE.—That Don Michael Constanzo, the engineer, observed the latitude of various places on the coast, and the same are as follows.

MISSION OF SAN MIGUEL, SAN LUIS OBISPO COUNTY.

they buried a brief account of their journey. Its text is set forth in the diary of Father Crespi as follows :

The overland expedition which left San Diego on the 14th of July, 1769, under the command of Don Gaspar de Portola, Governor of California, reached the channel of Santa Barbara on the 9th of August and passed Point Concepcion on the 27th of the same month. It arrived at the Sierra de Santa Lucia on the 13th of September, entered that range of mountains on the 17th of the same month, and emerged from it on the 1st of October. On the same day caught sight of Point Pinos and the harbors on its north and south sides without discovering any indications or landmarks of the bay of Monterey. Determined to push on farther in search of it, and on the 30th of October got sight of Point Reyes and the Farallones at the bay of San Francisco,[1] which are seven in number. The expedition strove to reach Point Reyes, but was hindered by an immense arm of the sea, which, extending to a great distance inland, compelled it to make an enormous circuit for that purpose. In consequence of this and other difficulties, the greatest of all being the absolute want of food, the expedition was compelled to turn back, believing that it must have passed the harbor of Monterey without discovering it.

Started on return from the estuary of San Fran-

[1] The bay of San Francisco of the old Spanish geographers and navigators was what we now call " Sir Francis Drake's Bay."

Here follow the latitudes of various points, after which the letter continues :

If the commanders of the schooners, either the *San José* or the *Principe,* should reach this place within a few days after this date, on learning the contents of this writing, and the distressed condition of this expedition, we beseech them to follow the coast closely towards San Diego, so that, if we should be happy enough to catch sight of them, we may be able by signals of flags or firearms to apprise them where succor and provisions may reach us.

" Glory be to God," says the pious chronicler, " the cross was erected on a little hillock, close to the beach of the small harbor on the south side of Point Pinos, and at its foot we buried the letter."

The cross erected at the north side of the Point bore the simple inscription, cut on its transverse arm with a razor: " The overland expedition from San Diego returned from this place on the 9th of December, 1769, starving."

Their prayer for succor was in vain; it never reached those to whom it was addressed. The schooners, after beating up the coast as far as the latitude of Monterey, were driven back by adverse winds, and, after months of fruitless effort to make port there, returned to San Diego, arriving just in time to relieve the infant colony from starvation. The land party plodded its weary way down the coast, encountering sickness, suffering, privation, and occasionally death, until on the 21st of January, 1770, its surviving members reached tion in California. There were interred the remains of Fathers Junipero Serra, Juan Crespi, and Rafael Verger.

San Diego and Monterey served to mark the extremes of the first Spanish occupancy;

San Diego, whence it had set out six months and twelve days before.

The effort at missionary colonization was not, however, abandoned. In 1770 another expedition moved up the coast, following the track of the first explorers, whose diary was their guide, and founded the Mission of San Carlos on the bay of Monterey, close to which was established the presidio of the same name. The place first selected proved unsuitable for the site of a Mission, and before the close of 1771 the establishment was removed a few miles to the southward and planted on the banks of the Carmel River, overlooking the charming little bay of the same name. This new foundation was called "El Carmelo." The presidio retained its site and subsequently became the capital city of the department.

Monterey has become in our day a famous watering-place frequented by visitors from the ends of the earth, and the ancient Mission, El Carmelo, now little better than a ruin, continues to attract the attention of travelers from its picturesque site and from the fact that it contains the remains of the venerable men whose pious efforts created the Missions and laid the foundations of civiliza-

MISSION OF SANTA BARBARA.

the interval was filled up and the area of missionary conquest gradually extended by other similar establishments. The names of these institutions, founded in rapid succession, are as follows:

1771.—San Gabriel, San Fernando, San Antonio.
1772.—San Luis Obispo.
1776.—San Juan Capistrano, San Francisco de Assisi.
1777.—Santa Clara.
1782.—San Buenaventura.
1786.—Santa Barbara.
1787.—La Purissima.
1791.—La Soledad, and Santa Cruz.
1797.—San Juan Bautista, San José, San Miguel.
1798.—San Luis Rey.
1802.—Santa Ynez.

After this missionary efforts seem to have relaxed, but a revival at a later date led to the foundation of San Rafael in 1817, and

The Mission building is in the form of a hollow square of about one hundred and fifty yards front, along which a gallery extends. The church forms one of the wings. The edifice, a single story in height, is elevated a few feet above the ground. In the interior is a court adorned with a fountain and planted with trees, on the corridor extending around which open the apartments of the friars and the major-domo as well as those used for workshops, schoolrooms, and storehouses, and the chambers set apart for the accommodation of travelers and guests.

The male and female infirmaries, as well as the schoolrooms, are placed in the most quiet portions of the premises. The young Indian girls occupy a

San Francisco Solano in 1823. Sonoma, at which this last was located, was as far north as the missionaries penetrated.

These Missions were, of course, designed for the instruction of the rude aborigines in the truths of Christianity and in the arts of civilized life. The scheme of life and discipline was devised by the Jesuits, who in the sixteenth and seventeenth centuries organized and carried on the most extensive system of missions in every quarter of the heathen and pagan world. India, China, Japan, both coasts of Africa, a large part of Central Asia, and both North and South America were the scenes of their indefatigable labors.

MISSION AND BELLS OF SAN GABRIEL, NEAR LOS ANGELES.

The Franciscans, who succeeded the Jesuits in California, followed their system. In order to induce the Indians to abandon their nomadic tribal life, and to exchange their reliance for food on the fruits of the chase and the spontaneous products of the forest for the ways of civilized men, they were at first supplied by the missionaries with food and clothing and afterwards taught to cultivate the earth and support themselves. Timber was felled wherever accessible and transported to a suitable site, where, with unburned brick and tiles, the Mission church and buildings were erected. The following description of San Luis Rey, condensed from the account of an intelligent traveler who saw it in its palmy days, will convey a fair idea of the establishments of which it was a type.

set of apartments secluded from the rest and commonly called the "nunnery," and they themselves are familiarly styled the "nuns." They are thus entirely protected from intrusion, and, being placed under the guardianship of staid and trustworthy matrons of their own race, are taught to spin and weave wool, flax, and cotton, and do not leave the nunnery until marriageable.

The Indian children attend the same schools with those of the white colonists, and are educated with them. Those who exhibit the most talent are taught some music, as the plain chant of the church, as well as the violin, flute, horn, violoncello, and other instruments. Such as attain superior proficiency, either as carpenters, smiths, or even agricultural laborers, are made foremen, by the name of alcaldes, and placed in charge of the other workmen.

Two ecclesiastics are stationed at each Mission; the elder is charged with the internal administration and the duty of religious instruction, the

MISSION OF SAN FERNANDO, LOS ANGELES.

younger, with the direction of the agricultural and mechanical labor. The Franciscans assiduously cultivate the study of the Indian dialects, of which they have compiled dictionaries and grammars, some of which are still extant.

Industry is inculcated and encouraged by the constant example of the Fathers, who are always the first to put their hands to the work; and considering the meagerness of their resources, and the absence of European labor, the works they have executed with the aid of unskilled savages, of low intelligence, are marvels of architecture and mechanical skill. These comprise mills, machinery, bridges, roads, and canals for irrigation, besides extensive agricultural labors. For the erection of nearly all the Mission buildings large beams had to be transported from the mountains eight and ten leagues off, and the Indians taught to burn lime, cut stone, make bricks, tiles, etc.

Opposite the Mission building is usually a guard-house for lodging the escort of the priests, consisting of four cavalry soldiers, under command of a sergeant, who act as couriers, carrying correspondence and orders from one Mission to another, besides protecting the Mission from the incursions of hostile Indians.

CLOISTERS AND BELL OF SAN FERNANDO.

The following is a summary of the ordinary day's work at a Mission. At sunrise the bell sounded for the Angelus and the Indians assembled in the chapel, where they attended morning prayers and mass and received a short religious instruction. Then came breakfast, after which, distributed in squads as occasion required, they repaired to their work. At 11 A. M. they ate dinner, and after that rested until 2 P. M. Work was then resumed, and continued until an hour before sunset, when the bell again tolled for the Angelus. After prayers and the rosary the Indians supped, and then were free to take part in a dance or some such innocent amusement. Their diet consisted of fresh beef or mutton in abundance, with vegetables and tortillas made of flour or corn-meal. They made drinks of the same ingredients, which were called *atole* and *pinole* respectively. Their dress consisted of a shirt of linen, a pair of pantaloons, and a woolen smock. The alcaldes and head workmen had also cloth clothes like those of the Spaniards; the women received every year two changes of underclothing, a smock, and a new gown.

The Indians of California were not the sturdy warlike race of the eastern side of the continent, nor did they possess the intelligence or partial civilization of the natives of the tableland of Mexico. They were originally of low intelligence and brutish habits. Besides what they obtained from fishing and hunting — in which they do not appear to have been specially dexterous — their food consisted largely of acorns, pine nuts, and the like, and their clothing was practically *nil*. Though neither as subtle nor as fierce as the Iroquois, Algonquins, and Hurons of Canada, with whom Parkman's brilliant pages have made us familiar, they were not wanting in cunning, treachery, or ferocity, and on more than one occasion the missionaries sealed their faith with their blood — a sacrifice from which, to their honor be it said, the Franciscans never flinched, any more than the followers of Ignatius.

As conversions made progress among the natives, and the young people, instructed from their childhood, came to maturity, they were taught various industries, besides farming. Ordinary smith's and carpenter's work they learned to do fairly well; their saddlery was of a superior sort, and is still sought for. As weavers, tailors, and shoemakers they would

PRESENT CHAPEL OF SAN JUAN CAPISTRANO.

not perhaps have obtained recognition in Paris, London, or New York, but they made serviceable blankets, serapes, cloth, and shoes, and I have seen creditable specimens of their work in silver. Domestic animals were introduced and they increased with astonishing rapidity, and in the care and management of them the Indians became very dexterous and serviceable — in fact, some of the most skillful horsemen in the world.

Hides, tallow, grain, wine, and oil were sold to ships visiting the coast. From the proceeds the friars distributed to the Indians handkerchiefs, clothing, tobacco, rosaries, trinkets, etc., and employed the surplus profits in the embellishment of the churches, the purchase of musical instruments, pictures, ornaments for the altar, etc. Where lands were found suitable for the purpose the fathers established outlying farms as appurtenances of the particular Mission on which they were made to depend. At these were gathered considerable colonies of civilized Indians selected from the most reliable.

Besides instructing the natives and incidentally fulfilling the duties of parochial clergy, the Missions extended a bountiful hospitality to all travelers and wayfarers. Planted at intervals of about a day's journey, on the natural route of travel along the coast, they became the usual resting-place for all travelers in either direction. Horses were the only means of locomotion, and at the end of his hard day's ride the weary traveler stopped at the door of the Mission building as naturally, and with as little thought of intrusion, as one might now at a public hotel. Throwing his rein to an Indian *arriero*, he was received by the missionary priest, or in his absence by the sacristan, with the patriarchal hospitality that Abraham extended to Lot. A bath was provided, followed by a plentiful meal and a comfortable bed. He was at liberty to stay as long as his convenience required, and on leaving was provided with a fresh horse and directions, or, if needed, a guide, for his further journey. Perhaps it is a tradition from these early days, but travelers still speak kindly of the hospitality of California.

Serus in cœlum redeat !

The Missions in this State were in all twenty-one. They may be said to have attained their maximum of prosperity during the first quarter of the present century. The Indian tribes of the coast, as far north as Sonoma, had by that time been reduced to pupilage at the various establishments described, and those of the younger generations had been sufficiently instructed in the simple arts of domestic life not only to carry on the various industries mentioned, but to make useful servants to the rancheros and white settlers, whose numbers, recruited from discharged and superannuated soldiers, a few voluntary—and some involun-

and sale. The cattle were valued mainly for their hides and tallow, which with soap and other exportable products were sold to vessels trading along the coast, and paid for in dry-goods, cutlery, tools, clothing, etc. The archives contain a good deal of statistical information as

MISSION OF SAN JUAN CAPISTRANO.

tary—immigrants from Mexico, occasional trappers, runaway sailors, or other adventurous foreigners, *quos ratio dederat aut fors objecerat*, had by this time become sufficiently considerable to create a demand for such services. There were still wild tribes in the mountains, to the north and east, but they gave little trouble, and the friars seem to have lost the spirit of missionary enterprise which characterized the companions and immediate successors of Father Junipero, and settled down to a quiet life among their neophytes and white neighbors, producing from the soil all the necessaries and many of the simple luxuries of life, and accumulating, for the Indian communities they governed, pastoral wealth, in the shape of countless herds of cattle, horses, sheep, goats, and swine.

The grain raised on the Mission ranches was threshed out, just as in Egypt and Mesopotamia twenty-five hundred or three thousand years ago, by spreading it on the ground and turning in a band of horses to trample it. A rude mill, generally turned by hand or by horse-power, furnished flour, though at two or three of the Missions water-power was utilized for this purpose. At each Mission gardens and orchards were inclosed, wherein, besides ordinary vegetables, fruits of various sorts were cultivated, including the fig, the orange, the olive, and the vine. The last two gave the missionaries oil and wine in abundance, for use

to Mission products, but I am not aware that it has ever been tabulated. An idea of them may be formed from the statement that in the year 1820 the Mission cattle are quoted at 140,000 head; the horses at 18,000, the sheep at 190,000, etc. The average annual product of grain, from 1811 to 1820, is given at over 113,000 bushels.

But the increase of white settlers, bringing with them the wants, ambitions, and freedom of modern life, was incompatible with the continued success of institutions based, as the Missions were, on paternal authority. The Indians were infants in all respects except age and capacity for evil; and the settlers were subject to no restraints except those of the civil authority, which was of the weakest kind.

Contact and intercourse with them corrupted the Indians and relaxed the bonds of discipline among them. Moreover the broad acres and the vast herds of the Missions excited the cupidity of the settlers, who did not regard the property of the friars and Indians in the same light as that of white people. Under these influences the Mexican congress, in 1833, passed a law for secularizing the Missions, converting them into parishes, replacing the missionary priests by curates, and emancipating the Indians from their pupilage to the Church. Administrators were to be ap-

malign, that the Government became alarmed and suspended the operation of the law. But it was too late; the mischief had been accomplished and the establishments thenceforth visibly decayed. A traveler of 1840–41 says that at the Mission of San José as late as 1837 Father Gonzales turned over to the administrators 17,000 head of cattle, of which as many as 8000 remained unappropriated in 1840, as well as 200 horses and 9000 sheep, while four hundred Indians remained even at that late day gathered about the Mission. He was also much interested by a school, still in existence,

INTERIOR OF SAN LUIS REY.

pointed for the temporalities of the Missions, the proceeds of which, after a small allowance for the maintenance of the priest and the charges of public worship, were to be applied to public purposes.

Under this law the greedy politicians of the day were enabled to plunder the Missions pretty nearly to their heart's content. Administrators were appointed, who administered away the tangible property in favor of themselves and their friends with marvelous industry and celerity. People whose names were held in esteem among the colonists, members of the "first families," leaders in public opinion and public affairs, are recorded as having despoiled the Missions of their lands and cattle by wholesale. The desolation wrought was so rapid and complete, and its effects on the Indian population so

where sixty Indian children surprised him by their progress in elementary studies, especially arithmetic. In 1834 (after the secularization) San Luis Rey had an Indian population of 3500 and possessed over 24,000 cattle, 10,000 horses, and 100,000 sheep. It harvested 14,000 fanegas of grain and 200 barrels of wine. In the same year San José had 2300 neophytes, 20,000 cattle, 11,000 horses, and 19,000 sheep, and harvested 10,000 fanegas of grain and 60 barrels of wine.

The ruin of the Missions was completed by the American conquest. The few remaining Indians were speedily driven or enticed away, for the rough frontiersmen who came over the plains knew nothing of missionary friars or civilized Indians; they came here to squat on public land and respected no possession beyond 160

THE MISSION OF SAN LUIS REY, SAN DIEGO COUNTY.

acres, and that only in the hands of one familiar with the English language and modern weapons. None of the establishments retains its original character. Where population has grown up around the site, as at Santa Clara, San Francisco, and San Rafael, they became parish churches. At other places squatters took possession of them, extruding priest and mayor-domo impartially, and in more than one case even the churches were sacrilegiously degraded to the use of stables and the like. In others many parts of the buildings were demolished for the sake of the timber, tiles, and other building material they afforded.

The most extensive of the old establishments was that of San Luis Rey. I visited it with a companion in the summer of 1862. We left San Juan Capistrano at an early hour, and reached San Luis at about 2 P. M., without meantime meeting a human being or seeing a house or a fence. Our way had taken us along a faintly marked wagon trail in the rugged foothills of the Sierra, through tangled chemisal and underbrush, crossed by many steep barrancas, which out of California would scarce be deemed practicable for wheels. After many hours of this monotonous travel we suddenly emerged from the chain of hills to the prospect of a charming valley, through which meandered a little stream of crystal water,

which after many windings found its way to the sea, which then opened on our sight, bounding the western horizon. In the middle of the valley, on a slight elevation, rose the towers of the old church, the red-tiled roof of which, and of the adjoining buildings of the ancient Mission, shone bright and ruddy in the glare of an almost tropical sun.

The landscape was magnificent, and we paused a short time to enjoy it before hastening on to examine the spot. The walls of the quadrangle remained in fair condition, and the graveled approach to the main entrance appeared so neat that I was persuaded it had lately been swept, and that I should find some inhabitants within. I effected an entrance without much difficulty, and wandered through the interior rooms and corridors searching for the aged sacristan my imagination had suggested; but I searched in vain. No shadow was cast there except my own; I heard no sound but the echo of my own footsteps. The inte-

INTERIOR OF SAN LUIS OBISPO.

SANTA YNEZ, SANTA BARBARA COUNTY.

rior court, once a garden, bright with flowers and the lustrous leaves of the orange and lemon tree, was rank with weeds and spontaneous vegetation; the fountain was dried up, and the walls which confined its basin split by the swelling roots of neglected and overgrown trees. Great spider webs hung from the columns of the corridor, and the stillness was broken only by the drowsy hum of dragonflies and humming-birds. I entered the venerable old church, and while endeavoring to accustom my eyes to the dim, uncertain light which shrouded its interior I was disturbed by the startled cry and hasty flight of an enormous owl, which left its perch over where the high altar had stood and rustled over to a window at the opposite end. I ascended one of the towers to the belfry, where I provoked another flight of unclean birds. The old chime of bells still hung there inscribed with the maker's name and "Boston, 1820," telling plainly of the intercourse of the old missionaries with the whaling fleets and the hide drogers which half a century ago wintered on the coast. Probably the order for these bells had been given in 1818, and they had been received, in pursuance of it, in 1821 or 1822. There was no express in those days between Boston and California; the journey was made *via* Cape Horn, and a couple of years elapsed between the departure and the return of a vessel. The Mission gardens, particularly that in front of the main building, retained many traces of former beauty. But the hedgerows, once carefully trimmed, now grown rank and wild; the old rustic seats crumbling to decay; the vines and fruit trees, which for want of pruning had ceased to produce; and the garden flowers growing neglectedly — all told of decay and ruin. From the remains of the fountain two clear streams of water still issued, and from the little rivulet they formed, bordered with cress as green as an emerald, a lazy fish looked deliberately up at me without moving — so unaccustomed to man as not to fear him. Just before the American conquest this Mission had harbored an industrious Indian population of several thousand. It had been occupied by our troops as a military post during the Mexican war and for some time after its close. When it ceased to be so used the Government, as I have heard General Beale say, caused an estimate to be made of the expense of repairing and restoring it to its former condition. The figures were two millions of dollars, and the project of repairing was, of course, given over.

It stands there to-day, magnificent, even in its ruins, a monument of the piety, devotion, industry, and disinterestedness of the venerable monks who wear the habit and cord of St. Francis, and who were the first colonists of Alta California.

John T. Doyle.

A FAMILY CHAPEL (CAMULOS).

Life in California Before the Gold Discovery

Ranch and Mission Days in Alta California (1890)

THE CENTURY MAGAZINE.

VOL. XLI.   DECEMBER, 1890.   NO. 2.

LIFE IN CALIFORNIA BEFORE THE GOLD DISCOVERY.

BY JOHN BIDWELL (PIONEER OF '41).

SUTTER'S BOOT. (IN THE
PIONEER SOCIETY'S ROOMS, SACRAMENTO.)

THE party whose fortunes I have followed across the plains[1] was not only the first that went direct to California from the East; we were probably the first white people, except Bonneville's party of 1833, that ever crossed the Sierra Nevada. Dr. Marsh's ranch, the first settlement reached by us in California, was located in the eastern foothills of the Coast Range Mountains, near the northwestern extremity of the great San Joaquin Valley and about six miles east of Monte Diablo, which may be called about the geographical center of Contra Costa County. There were no other settlements in the valley; it was, apparently, still just as new as when Columbus discovered America, and roaming over it were countless thousands of wild horses, of elk, and of antelope. It had been one of the driest years ever known in California. The country was brown and parched; throughout the State wheat, beans, everything had failed. Cattle were almost starving for grass, and the people, except perhaps a few of the best families, were without bread, and were eating chiefly meat, and that often of a very poor quality.

Dr. Marsh had come into California four or five years before by way of New Mexico. He was in some respects a remarkable man. In command of the English language I have scarcely ever seen his equal. He had never studied medicine, I believe, but was a great reader: sometimes he would lie in bed all day reading, and he had a memory that stereotyped all he read, and in those days in California such a man could easily assume the rôle of doctor and practise medicine. In fact, with the exception of Dr. Marsh there was then no physician of any kind anywhere in California. We were overjoyed to find an American, and yet when we became acquainted with him we found him one of the most selfish of mortals. The night of our arrival he killed two pigs for us.[2] We felt very grateful, for we had by no means recovered from starving on poor mule meat, and when he set his Indian cook to making tortillas (little cakes) for us, giving one to each,— there were thirty-two in our party,— we felt even more grateful; and especially when we learned that he had had to use some of his seed wheat, for he had no other. Hearing that there was no such thing as money in the country, and that butcher-knives, guns, ammunition, and everything of that kind were better than money, we expressed our gratitude the first night to the doctor by presents — one giving a can of powder, another a bar of lead or a butcher-knife, and another a cheap but serviceable set of surgical instruments. The next morning I rose early, among the first, in order to learn from our host something about California,— what we could do, and where we could go,— and, strange as it may seem, he would scarcely answer a question. He seemed to be in an ill humor, and among other things he said, "The company has already been over a hundred dollars' expense to me, and God knows whether I will ever get a *real* of it or not." I was at a loss to account for this, and went out and told some of

---

[1] See "The First Emigrant Train to California," in THE CENTURY for November, 1890.

[2] Men reduced to living on poor meat, and almost starving, have an intense longing for anything fat.

the party, and found that others had been snubbed in a similar manner. We held a consultation and resolved to leave as soon as convenient. Half our party concluded to go back to the San Joaquin River, where there was much game, and spend the winter hunting, chiefly for otter, the skins being worth three dollars apiece. The rest — about fourteen — succeeded in gaining information from Dr. Marsh by which they

exposed than any other to the ravages of the Horse-thief Indians of the Sierra Nevada (before mentioned). That valley was full of wild cattle,—thousands of them,—and they were more dangerous to one on foot, as I was, than grizzly bears. By dodging into the gulches and behind trees I made my way to a Mexican ranch at the extreme west end of the valley, where I staid all night. This was one

SACRAMENTO VALLEY.

started to find the town of San José, about forty miles to the south, then known by the name of Pueblo de San José, now the city of San José. More or less of our effects had to be left at Marsh's, and I decided to remain and look out for them, and meantime to make short excursions about the country on my own account. After the others had left I started off traveling south, and came to what is now called Livermore Valley, then known as Livermore's Ranch, belonging to Robert Livermore, a native of England. He had left a vessel when a mere boy, and had married and lived like the native Californians, and, like them, was very expert with the lasso. Livermore's was the frontier ranch, and more

of the noted ranches, and belonged to a Californian called Don José Maria Amador — more recently, to a man named Dougherty.[1] Next day, seeing nothing to encourage me, I started to return to Marsh's ranch.

On the way, as I came to where two roads, or rather paths, converged, I fell in with one of the fourteen men, M. C. Nye, who had started for San José. He seemed considerably agitated, and reported that at the Mission of San José, some fifteen miles this side of the town of San José, all the men had been arrested and put in prison by General Vallejo, Mexican commander-in-chief of the military under Governor Alvarado, he alone having been sent back to tell Marsh and to have him come forth-

---

[1] The rancheros marked and branded their stock differently so as to distinguish them. But it was not possible to keep them separate. One would often steal cattle from the other. Livermore in this way lost cattle by his neighbor Amador. In fact it was almost a daily occurrence — a race to see which could get and

kill the most of the other's cattle. Cattle in those days were often killed for the hides alone. One day a man saw Amador kill a fine steer belonging to Livermore. When he reached Livermore's — ten or fifteen miles away — and told him what Amador had done, he found Livermore skinning a steer of Amador's !

with to explain why this armed force had invaded the country. We reached Marsh's after dark. The next day the doctor started down to the Mission of San José, nearly thirty miles distant, with a list of the company, which I gave him. He was gone about three days. Meanwhile we sent word to the men on the San Joaquin River to let them know what had taken place, and they at once returned to the ranch to await results. When Marsh came back he said ominously, " Now, men, I want you all to come into the house and I will tell you your fate." We all went in, and he announced, " You men that have five dollars can have passports and remain in the country and go where you please." The fact was he had simply obtained passports for the asking; they had cost him nothing. The men who had been arrested at the Mission had been liberated as soon as their passports were issued to them, and they had at once proceeded on their way to San José. But five dollars! I don't suppose any one had five dollars; nine-tenths of them probably had not a cent of money. The names were called and each man settled, giving the amount in something, and if unable to make it up in money or effects he would give his note for the rest. All the names were called except my own. There was no passport for me. Marsh had certainly not forgotten me, for I had furnished him with the list of our names myself. Possibly his idea was—as others surmised and afterwards told me—that, lacking a passport, I would stay at his ranch and make a useful hand to work.

The next morning before day found me starting for the Mission of San José to get a passport for myself. Mike Nye, the man who had brought the news of the arrest, went with me. A friend had lent me a poor old horse, fit only to carry my blankets. I arrived in a heavy rain-storm, and was marched into the calaboose and kept there three days with nothing to eat, and the fleas were so numerous as to cover and darken anything of a light color. There were four or five Indians in the prison. They were ironed, and they kept tolling a bell, as a punishment, I suppose, for they were said to have stolen horses; possibly they belonged to the Horse-thief tribes east of the San Joaquin Valley. Sentries were stationed at the door. Through a grated window I made a

GENERAL M. G. VALLEJO.
(FROM A PHOTOGRAPH BY BRADLEY & RULOFSON, LENT BY LOYALL FARRAGUT.)

motion to an Indian boy outside and he brought me a handful of beans and a handful of *manteca*, which is used by Mexicans instead of lard. It seemed as if they were going to starve me to death. After having been there three days I saw through the door a man whom, from his light hair, I took to be an American, although he was clad in the wild picturesque garb of a native Californian, including serape and the huge spurs used by the vaquero. I had the sentry at the door hail him. He proved to be an American, a resident of the Pueblo of San José, named Thomas Bowen, and he kindly went to Vallejo, who was right across the way in the big Mission building, and procured for me the passport. I think I have that passport now, signed by Vallejo and written in Spanish by Victor Prudon, secretary of Vallejo. Every one at the Mission pronounced Marsh's action an outrage; such a thing was never known before.

We had already heard that a man by the name of Sutter was starting a colony a hundred miles away to the north in the Sacramento Valley. No other civilized settlements had been attempted anywhere east of the Coast Range; before Sutter came the Indians had reigned supreme. As the best thing to be done I now determined to go to Sutter's, afterward called "Sutter's Fort," or New Helvetia. Dr. Marsh said we could make the journey in two days, but it took us eight. Winter had come in earnest, and winter in California then, as now, meant rain. I had three companions. It was wet when we started, and much of the time we traveled through a pouring rain. Streams were out of their banks; gulches were swimming; plains were inundated; indeed, most of the country was overflowed. There were no roads, merely paths, trodden only by Indians and wild game. We were compelled to follow the paths, even when they were under

Moreover, our coming was not unexpected to him. It will be remembered that in the Sierra Nevada one of our men named Jimmy John became separated from the main party. It seems that he came on into California, and, diverging into the north, found his way down to Sutter's settlement perhaps a little before we reached Dr. Marsh's. Through this man Sutter heard that our company of thirty men were already somewhere in California. He immediately loaded two mules with provisions taken out of his private stores, and sent two men with them in search of us. But they did not find us, and returned, with the pro-

OLD RUSSIAN BUILDING.   FORT ROSS.

water, for the moment our animals stepped to one side down they went into the mire. Most of the way was through the region now lying between Lathrop and Sacramento. We got out of provisions and were about three days without food. Game was plentiful, but hard to shoot in the rain. Besides, it was impossible to keep our old flint-lock guns dry, and especially the powder dry in the pans. On the eighth day we came to Sutter's settlement; the fort had not then been begun. Sutter received us with open arms and in a princely fashion, for he was a man of the most polite address and the most courteous manners, a man who could shine in any society.

visions, to Sutter's. Later, after a long search, the same two men, having been sent out again by Sutter, struck our trail and followed it to Marsh's.

John A. Sutter was born in Baden in 1803 of Swiss parents, and was proud of his connection with the only republic of consequence in Europe. He was a warm admirer of the United States, and some of his friends had persuaded him to come across the Atlantic. He first went to a friend in Indiana with whom he staid awhile, helping to clear land, but it was business that he was not accustomed to. So he made his way to St. Louis and invested what means he had in merchandise, and went out as a New Mexi-

GENERAL JOHN A. SUTTER.
(FROM A PHOTOGRAPH BY BRADLEY & RULOFSON.)

can trader to Santa Fé. Having been unsuccessful at Santa Fé, he returned to St. Louis, joined a party of trappers, went to the Rocky Mountains, and found his way down the Columbia River to Fort Vancouver. There he formed plans for trying to get down to the coast of California to establish a colony. He took a vessel that went to the Sandwich Islands, and there communicated his plans to people who assisted him. But as there was no vessel going direct from the Sandwich Islands to California, he had to take a Russian vessel by way of Sitka. He got such credit and help as he could in the Sandwich Islands and induced five or six natives to accompany him

to start the contemplated colony. He expected to send to Europe and the United States for his colonists. When he came to the coast of California, in 1840, he had an interview with the governor, Alvarado, and obtained permission to explore the country and find a place for his colony. He came to the bay of San Francisco, procured a small boat and explored the largest river he could find, and selected the site where the city of Sacramento now stands.

A short time before we arrived Sutter had bought out the Russian-American Fur Company at Fort Ross and Bodega on the Pacific. That company had a charter from Spain to take furs, but had no right to the land. The

SUTTER'S FORT. (REDRAWN FROM A PHOTOGRAPH OF AN OLD PRINT.)

charter had about expired. Against the protest of the California authorities they had extended their settlement southward some twenty miles farther than they had any right to, and had occupied the country to, and even beyond, the bay of Bodega. The time came when the taking of furs was no longer profitable; the Russians were ordered to vacate and return to Sitka. They wished to sell out all their personal property and whatever remaining right they had to the land. So Sutter bought them out — cattle and horses; a little vessel of about twenty-five tons burden, called a launch; and other property, including forty odd pieces of old rusty cannon and one or two small brass pieces, with a quantity of old French flint-lock muskets pronounced by Sutter to be of those lost by Bonaparte in 1812 in his disastrous retreat from Moscow. This ordnance Sutter conveyed up the Sacramento River on the launch to his colony. As soon as the native Californians heard that he had bought out the Russians and was beginning to fortify himself by taking up the cannon they began to fear him. They were doubtless jealous because Americans and other foreigners had already commenced to make the place their headquarters, and they foresaw that Sutter's fort would be for them, especially for Americans, what it naturally did become in fact, a place of protection and general rendezvous; and so they threatened to break it up. Sutter had not as yet actually received his grant; he had simply taken prelim-

inary steps and had obtained permission to settle and proceed to colonize. These threats were made before he had begun the fort, much less built it, and Sutter felt insecure. He had a good many Indians whom he had collected about him, and a few white men (perhaps fifteen or twenty) and some Sandwich Islanders. When he heard of the coming of our thirty men he inferred at once that we would soon reach him and be an additional protection. With this feeling of security, even before the arrival of our party Sutter was so indiscreet as to write a letter to the governor or to some one in authority, saying that he wanted to hear no more threats of dispossession, for he was now able not only to defend himself but to go and chastise them. That letter having been despatched to the city of Mexico, the authorities there sent a new governor in 1842 with about six hundred troops to subdue Sutter. But the new governor, Manuel Micheltorena, was an intelligent man. He knew the history of California and was aware that nearly all of his predecessors had been expelled by insurrections of the native Californians. Sutter sent a courier to meet the governor before his arrival at Los Angeles, with a letter in French, conveying his greetings to the governor, expressing a most cordial welcome, and submitting cheerfully and entirely to his authority. In this way the governor and Sutter became fast friends, and through Sutter the Americans had a friend in Governor Micheltorena.

The first employment I had in California was in Sutter's service, about two months after our arrival at Marsh's. He engaged me to go to Bodega and Fort Ross and to stay there until he could finish removing the property which he had bought from the Russians. I remained there fourteen months, until everything was removed; then I came up into Sacramento Valley and took charge for Sutter of his Hock farm (so named from a large Indian village on the place), remaining there a little more than a year—in 1843 and part of 1844.

Nearly everybody who came to California made it a point to reach Sutter's Fort.[1] Sutter was one of the most liberal and hospitable of men. Everybody was welcome—one man or a hundred, it was all the same. He had peculiar traits: his necessities compelled him to take all he could buy, and he paid all he could pay; but he failed to keep up with his payments. And so he soon found himself immensely — almost hopelessly — involved in debt. His debt to the Russians amounted at first to something near one hundred thousand dollars. Interest increased apace. He had agreed to pay in wheat, but his crops failed. He struggled in every way, sowing large areas to wheat, increasing his cattle and horses, and trying to build a flouring mill. He kept his launch running to and from the bay, carrying down hides, tallow, furs, wheat, etc., returning with lumber sawed by hand in the redwood groves nearest the bay and other supplies. On an average it took a month to make a trip. The fare for each person was five dollars, including board. Sutter started many other new enterprises in order to find relief from his embarrassments; but, in spite of all he could do, these increased. Every year found him worse and worse off; but it was partly his own fault. He employed men — not because he always needed and could profitably employ them, but because in the kindness of his heart it simply became a habit to employ everybody who wanted employment. As long as he had anything he trusted any one with everything he wanted — responsible or otherwise, acquaintances and strangers alike. Most of the labor was done by Indians, chiefly wild ones, except a few from the Missions who spoke Spanish. The wild ones learned Spanish so far as they learned

SUTTER'S FORT AS IT IS NOW.
(REDRAWN FROM A PHOTOGRAPH BY H. S. BEALS.)

anything, that being the language of the country, and everybody had to learn some-

---

[1] Every year after the arrival of our party, in 1841, immigrant parties came across the plains to California; except in 1842, when they went to Oregon, most of them coming thence to California in 1843. Ours of 1841 being the first, let me add that a later party arrived in California in 1841. It was composed of about twenty-five persons who arrived at Westport, Mo., too late to come with us, and so went with the annual caravan of St. Louis traders to Santa Fé, and thence *via* the Gila River into Southern California.

Among the more noted arrivals on this coast I may mention :

1841.— Commodore Wilkes's Exploring Expedition, a party of which came overland from Oregon to California, under Captain Ringgold, I think.

1842.— Commodore Thomas ap Catesby Jones, who raised the American flag in Monterey.

1843.— *First.* L. W. Hastings, *via* Oregon. He was ambitious to make California a republic and to be its first president, and wrote an iridescent book to induce immigration,— which came in 1846,— but found the American flag flying when he returned with the immigration he had gone to meet. Also among the noted arrivals in 1843 was Pierson B. Redding, an accomplished gentleman, the proprietor of Redding's ranch in Shasta County, and from whom Fort Redding took its name. Samuel J. Hensley was also one of the same party. *Second.* Dr. Sandels, a very intelligent man.

1844.— *First.* Frémont's first arrival (in March); Mr. Charles Preuss, a scientific man, and Kit Carson with him. *Second.* The Stevens-Townsend-Murphy party, who brought the first wagons into California across the plains.

1845.— *First.* James W. Marshall, who, in 1848, discovered the gold. *Second.* Frémont's second arrival, also Hastings's second arrival.

1846.— Largest immigration party, the one Hastings went to meet. The Donner party was among the last of these immigrants.

thing of it. The number of men employed by Sutter may be stated at from 100 to 500 — the latter number at harvest time. Among them were blacksmiths, carpenters, tanners, gunsmiths, vaqueros, farmers, gardeners, weavers (to weave coarse woolen blankets), hunters,

corral; then three or four hundred wild horses were turned in to thresh it, the Indians whooping to make them run faster. Suddenly they would dash in before the band at full speed, when the motion became reversed, with the effect of plowing up the trampled straw to the

A CALIFORNIA CART.

sawyers (to saw lumber by hand, a custom known in England), sheep-herders, trappers, and, later, millwrights and a distiller. In a word, Sutter started every business and enterprise possible. He tried to maintain a sort of military discipline. Cannon were mounted, and pointed in every direction through embrasures in the walls and bastions. The soldiers were Indians, and every evening after coming from work they were drilled under a white officer, generally a German, marching to the music of fife and drum. A sentry was always at the gate, and regular bells called men to and from work.

Harvesting, with the rude implements, was a scene. Imagine three or four hundred wild Indians in a grain field, armed, some with sickles, some with butcher-knives, some with pieces of hoop iron roughly fashioned into shapes like sickles, but many having only their hands with which to gather by small handfuls the dry and brittle grain; and as their hands would soon become sore, they resorted to dry willow sticks, which were split to afford a sharper edge with which to sever the straw. But the wildest part was the threshing. The harvest of weeks, sometimes of a month, was piled up in the straw in the form of a huge mound in the middle of a high, strong, round

very bottom. In an hour the grain would be thoroughly threshed and the dry straw broken almost into chaff. In this manner I have seen two thousand bushels of wheat threshed in a single hour. Next came the winnowing, which would often take another month. It could only be done when the wind was blowing, by throwing high into the air shovelfuls of grain, straw, and chaff, the lighter materials being wafted to one side, while the grain, comparatively clean, would descend and form a heap by itself. In this manner all the grain in California was cleaned. At that day no such thing as a fanning mill had ever been brought to this coast.

The kindness and hospitality of the native Californians have not been overstated. Up to the time the Mexican régime ceased in California they had a custom of never charging for anything; that is to say, for entertainment — food, use of horses, etc. You were supposed, even if invited to visit a friend, to bring your blankets with you, and one would be very thoughtless if he traveled and did not take a knife with him to cut his meat. When you had eaten, the invariable custom was to rise, deliver to the woman or hostess the plate on which you had eaten the meat and beans — for that was about all they had — and say,

CAÑON OF THE AMERICAN RIVER.

ON THE SUMMIT OF THE SIERRA.

Baptiste Ruelle had been in Sutter's employ several months, when one day he came to Sutter, showed him a few small particles of gold, and said he had found them on the American River, and he wanted to go far into the mountains on that stream to prospect for gold. For this purpose he desired two mules loaded with provisions, and he selected two notedly stupid Indian boys whom he wanted to go into the mountains with him, saying he would have no others. Of course he did not get the outfit. Sutter and I talked about it and queried, What does he want with so much provision — the American River being only a mile and the mountains only twenty miles distant? And why does he want those two stupid boys, since he might be attacked by the Indians? Our conclusion was that he really wanted the outfit so that he could join the party and go to Oregon and remain. Such I believe was Ruelle's intention; though in 1848, after James W. Marshall had discovered the gold at Coloma, Ruelle, who was one of the first to go there and mine, still protested that he had discovered gold on the American River in 1843. The only thing that I can recall to lend the least plausibility to Ruelle's pretensions would be that, so far as I know, he never, after that one time, manifested any desire to go to Oregon, and remained in California till he died. But I should add, neither did he ever show any longing again to go into the mountains to look for gold during the subsequent years he remained with Sutter, even to the time of Marshall's discovery.

Early in the spring of 1844, a Mexican working under me at the Hock Farm for

Sutter came to me and told me there was gold in the Sierra Nevada. His name was Pablo Gutierrez. The discovery by Marshall, it will be remembered, was in January, 1848. Pablo told me this at a time when I was calling him to account because he had absented himself the day before without permission. I was giving him a lecture in Spanish, which I could speak quite well in those days. Like many Mexicans, he had an Indian wife; some time before, he had been in the mountains and had bought a squaw. She had run away from him, and he had gone to find and bring her back. And it was while he was on this trip, he said, that he had seen signs of gold. After my lecture he said, "Señor, I have made an important discovery; there surely is gold on Bear River in the mountains." This was in March, 1844. A few days afterward I arranged to go with him up on Bear River. We went five or six miles into the mountains, when he showed me the signs and the place where he thought the gold was. "Well," I said, "can you not find some?" No, he said, because he must have a *batea*.

faithfully kept his promise. It would have taken us a year or two to get money enough to go. In those days there were every year four or five arrivals, sometimes six, of vessels laden with goods from Boston to trade for hides in California. These vessels brought around all classes of goods needed by the Mexican people. It would have required about six months each way, five months being a quick passage. But, as will be seen, our plans were interrupted. In the autumn of that year, 1844, a revolt took place. The native chiefs of Cali-

THE ANCHORAGE OF MONTEREY FROM THE OLD BURIAL-GROUND.

He talked so much about the "batea" that I concluded it must be a complicated machine. "Can't Mr. Keiser, our saddle-tree maker, make the batea?" I asked. "Oh, no." I did not then know that a batea is nothing more nor less than a wooden bowl which the Mexicans use for washing gold. I said, "Pablo, where can you get it?" He said, "Down in Mexico." I said, "I will help pay your expenses if you will go down and get one," which he promised to do. I said, "Pablo, say nothing to anybody else about this gold discovery, and we will get the batea and find the gold." As time passed I was afraid to let him go to Mexico, lest when he got among his relatives he might be induced to stay and not come back, so I made a suggestion to him. I said, "Pablo, let us save our earnings and get on a vessel and go around to Boston, and there get the batea; I can interpret for you, and the Yankees are very ingenious and can make anything." The idea pleased him, and he promised to go as soon as we could save enough to pay our expenses. He was to keep it a secret, and I believe he

fornia, José Castro and ex-Governor Alvarado, succeeded in raising an insurrection against the Mexican governor, Micheltorena, to expel him from the country. They accused him of being friendly to Americans and of giving them too much land. The truth was, he had simply shown impartiality. When Americans had been here long enough, had conducted themselves properly, and had complied with the colonization laws of Mexico, he had given them lands as readily as to native-born citizens. He was a fair-minded man and an intelligent and good governor, and wished to develop the country. His friendship for Americans was a mere pretext; for his predecessor, Alvarado, and his successor, Pio Pico, also granted lands freely to foreigners, and among them to Americans. The real cause of the insurrection against Micheltorena, however, was that the native chiefs had become hungry to get hold again of the revenues. The feeling against Americans was easily aroused and became their main excuse. The English and French influence, so far as felt, evidently leaned towards the side of the Californians. It was not open but it was felt, and not a few expressed the hope that England or France would some day seize and hold California. I believe the Gachupines — natives of Spain, of whom there were a few — did not participate in the feeling against the Americans, though few did much, if anything, to allay it. In October Sutter went from Sacramento to Monterey, the capital, to see the governor. I went with him. On our way thither, at San José, we heard the first mutterings of the insurrection. We hastened to Monterey, and were the first to communicate the fact to the governor. Sutter, alarmed, took the first opportunity to get away by water. There were in those days no mail routes, no public conveyances of any kind, no regular line of travel, no public highways. But a vessel happened to touch at Monterey, and Sutter took passage to the bay of San Francisco, and thence by his own launch reached home. In a few days the first blow was struck, the insurgents taking all the horses belonging to the government at Monterey, setting the governor and all his troops on foot. He raised a few horse as best he could and pursued them, but could not overtake them on foot. However, I understood that a sort of parley took place at or near San José, but no battle, surrender, or settlement. Meanwhile, having started to return by land to Sutter's Fort, two hundred miles distant, I met the governor returning to Monterey. He stopped his forces and talked with me half an hour and confided to me his plans. He desired me to beg the Americans to be loyal to Mexico; to assure them that he was their friend, and in due time would give them all the lands to which they were entitled. He sent particularly friendly word to Sutter. Then I went on to the Mission of San José and there fell in with the insurgents, who had made that place their headquarters; I staid all night, and the leaders, Castro and Alvarado, treated me like a prince. The two insurgents protested their friendship for the Americans, and sent a request to Sutter to support them. On my arrival at the fort the situation was fully considered, and all, with a single exception, concluded to support Micheltorena. He had been our friend; he had granted us land; he had promised, and we felt that we could rely upon, his continued friendship; and we felt, indeed we knew, we could not repose the same confidence in the native Californians. This man Pablo Gutierrez, who had told me about the gold in the Sierra Nevada, was a native of

Sinaloa in Mexico, and sympathized with the Mexican governor and with us. Sutter sent him with despatches to the governor, stating that we were organizing and preparing to join him. Pablo returned, and was sent again to tell the governor that we were on the march to join him at Monterey. This time he was taken prisoner with our despatches and was hanged to a tree, somewhere near the present town of Gilroy. That of course put an end to our gold discovery; otherwise Pablo Gutierrez might have been the discoverer instead of Marshall.[1]

But I still had it in my mind to try to find gold; so early in the spring of 1845 I made it a point to visit the mines in the south discovered by Ruelle in 1841. They were in the mountains about twenty miles north or northeast of the Mission of San Fernando, or say fifty miles from Los Angeles. I wanted to see the Mexicans working there, and to gain what knowledge I could of gold digging. Dr. John Townsend went with me. Pablo's confidence that there was gold on Bear River was fresh in my mind; and I hoped the same year to find time to return there and explore, and if possible find gold in the Sierra Nevada. But I had no time that busy year to carry out my purpose. The Mexicans' slow and inefficient manner of working the mine was most discouraging. When I returned to Sutter's Fort the same spring Sutter desired me to engage with him for a year as bookkeeper, which meant his general business man as well. His financial matters being in a bad way, I consented. I had a great deal to do besides keeping the books. Among other undertakings we sent men southeast in the Sierra Nevada about forty miles from the fort to saw lumber with a whipsaw. Two men would saw of good timber about one hundred or one hundred and twenty-five feet a day. Early in July I framed an excuse to go into the mountains to give the men some special directions about lumber needed at the fort. The day was one of the hottest I had ever experienced. No place looked favorable for a gold discovery. I even attempted to descend into a deep gorge through which meandered a small stream, but gave it up on account of the brush and the heat. My search was fruitless. The place where Marshall discovered gold in 1848 was about forty miles to the north of the saw-pits at this place. The next spring, 1849, I joined a party to go to the mines on and south of the Cosumne and

1 The insurrection ended in the capitulation — I might call it expulsion — of Micheltorena. The causes which led to this result were various, some of them infamous. Pio Pico, being the oldest member of the Departmental Assembly, became governor, and Castro commander-in-chief of the military. They reigned but one year, and then came the Mexican war. Castro was made governor of Lower California, and died there. Pio Pico was not a vindictive man; he was a mild governor, and still lives at Los Angeles.

THE OLD CUARTEL AT MONTEREY.

Mokelumne rivers. The first day we reached a trading post — Digg's, I think, was the name. Several traders had there pitched their tents to sell goods. One of them was Tom Fallon, whom I knew. This post was within a few miles of where Sutter's men sawed the lumber in 1845. I asked Fallon if he had ever seen the old saw-pits where Sicard and Dupas had worked in 1845. He said he had, and knew the place well. Then I told him how I had attempted that year to descend into the deep gorge to the south of it to look for gold.

"My stars!" he said. "Why, that gulch down there was one of the richest placers that have ever been found in this country"; and he told me of men who had taken out a pint cupful of nuggets before breakfast.

Frémont's first visit to California was in the month of March, 1844. He came *via* eastern Oregon, traveling south and passing east of the Sierra Nevada, and crossed the chain about opposite the bay of San Francisco, at the head of the American River, and descended into the Sacramento Valley to Sutter's Fort. It was there I first met him. He staid but a short time, three or four weeks perhaps, to refit with fresh mules and horses and such provisions as he could obtain, and then set out on his return to the United States. Coloma, where Marshall afterward discovered gold, was on one of the branches of the American River. Frémont probably came down that very stream. How strange that he and his scientific corps did not discover signs of gold, as Commodore Wilkes's party had done when coming overland from Oregon in 1841! One morning at the breakfast table at Sutter's, Frémont was urged to remain a while and go to the coast, and among other things which it

would be of interest for him to see was mentioned a very large redwood tree (*Sequoia sempervirens*) near Santa Cruz, or rather a cluster of trees, forming apparently a single trunk, which was said to be seventy-two feet in circumference. I then told Frémont of the big tree I had seen in the Sierra Nevada in October, 1841, which I afterwards verified to be one of the fallen big trees of the Calaveras Grove. I therefore believe myself to have been the first white man to see the mammoth trees of California. The Sequoias are found nowhere except in California. The redwood that I speak of is the *Sequoia sempervirens*, and is confined to the sea-coast and the west side of the Coast Range Mountains. The *Sequoia gigantea*, or mammoth tree, is found only on the western slope of the Sierra Nevada — nowhere farther north than latitude 38° 30'.

Sutter's Fort was an important point from the very beginning of the colony. The building of the fort and all subsequent immigrations added to its importance, for that was the first point of destination to those who came by way of Oregon or direct across the plains. The fort was begun in 1842 and finished in 1844. There was no town till after the gold discovery in 1848, when it became the bustling, buzzing center for merchants, traders, miners, etc., and every available room was in demand. In 1849 Sacramento City was laid off on the river two miles west of the fort, and the town grew up there at once into a city. The first town was laid off by Hastings and myself in the month of January, 1846, about three or four miles below the mouth of the American River, and called Sutterville. But first the Mexican war, then the lull which always follows excitement, and then the rush and roar of the gold discovery, prevented its building up till it was too late. Attempts were several times made to revive Sutterville, but Sacramento City had become too strong to be removed. Sutter always called his colony and fort "New Helvetia," in spite of which the name mostly used by others, before the Mexican war, was Sutter's Fort, or Sacramento, and later Sacramento altogether.

Sutter's many enterprises continued to create a growing demand for lumber. Every year, and sometimes more than once, he sent parties into the mountains to explore for an available site to build a sawmill on the Sacramento River or some of its tributaries, by which the lumber could be rafted down to the fort. There was no want of timber or of water power in the mountains, but the cañon features of the streams rendered rafting impracticable. The year after the war (1847) Sutter's needs for lumber were even greater than ever, although his embarrassments had increased and his ability to undertake new enterprises became less and less. Yet, never discouraged, nothing daunted, another hunt must be made for a sawmill site. This time Marshall happened to be the man chosen by Sutter to search the mountains. He was gone about a month, and returned with a most favorable report.

James W. Marshall went across the plains to Oregon in 1844, and thence came to California the next year. He was a wheelwright by trade, but, being very ingenious, he could turn his hand to almost anything. So he acted as carpenter for Sutter, and did many other things, among which I may mention making wheels for spinning wool, and looms, reeds, and shuttles for weaving yarn into coarse blankets for the Indians, who did the carding, spinning, weaving, and all other labor. In 1846 Marshall went through the war to its close as a private. Besides his ingenuity as a mechanic, he had most singular traits. Almost every one pronounced him half crazy or harebrained. He was certainly eccentric, and perhaps somewhat flighty. His insanity, however, if he had any, was of a harmless kind; he was neither vicious nor quarrel-

some. He had great, almost overweening, confidence in his ability to do anything as a mechanic. I wrote the contract between Sutter and him to build the mill. Sutter was to furnish the means; Marshall was to build and run the mill, and have a share of the lumber for his compensation. His idea was to haul lumber part way and raft it down the American River to Sacramento, and thence, his part of it, down the Sacramento River, and through Suisun and San Pablo bays to San Francisco for a market. Marshall's mind, in some respects at least, must have been unbalanced. It is hard to conceive how any sane man could have been so wide of the mark, or how any one could have selected such a site for a sawmill under the circumstances. Surely no other man than Marshall ever entertained so wild a scheme as that of rafting sawed lumber down the cañons of the American River, and no other man than Sutter would have been so confiding and credulous as to patronize him. It is proper to say that, under great difficulties, enhanced by winter rains, Marshall succeeded in building the mill — a very good one, too, of the kind. It had improvements which I had never seen in sawmills, and I had had considerable experience in Ohio. But the

A SPANISH-CALIFORNIAN TYPE.

mill would not run because the wheel was placed too low. It was an old-fashioned flutter wheel that propelled an upright saw. The gravelly bar below the mill backed the water up, and submerged and stopped the wheel. The remedy was to dig a channel or tail-race through the bar below to conduct away the water. The wild Indians of the mountains were employed to do the digging. Once through the bar there would be plenty of fall. The digging was hard and took some weeks. As soon as the water began to run through the tail-race the wheel was blocked, the gate raised, and the water permitted to gush through all night. It was Marshall's custom to examine the race while the water was running through in the morning, so as to direct the Indians where to deepen it, and then shut off the water for them to work during the day. The water was clear as crystal, and the current was swift enough to sweep away the sand and lighter materials. Marshall made these examinations early in the morning while the Indians were getting their breakfast. It was on one of these occasions, in the clear shallow water, that he saw something bright and yellow. He picked it up— it was a piece of gold! The world has seen and felt the result. The mill sawed little or no lum-

BULL AND BEAR FIGHT.

ber; as a lumber enterprise the project was a failure, but as a gold discovery it was a grand success.

There was no excitement at first, nor for three or four months — because the mine was not known to be rich, or to exist anywhere except at the sawmill, or to be available to any one except Sutter, to whom every one conceded that it belonged. Time does not permit me to relate how I carried the news of the dis-

covery to San Francisco; how the same year I discovered gold on Feather River and worked it; how I made the first weights and scales to weigh the first gold for Sam Brannan; how the richness of the mines became known by the Mormons who were employed by Sutter to work at the sawmill, working about on Sundays and finding it in the crevices along the stream and taking it to Brannan's store at the fort, and how Brannan kept the gold a secret as long as he could till the excitement burst out all at once like wildfire.

Among the notable arrivals at Sutter's Fort should be mentioned that of Castro and Castillero, in the fall of 1845. The latter had been before in California, sent, as he had been this time, as a peace commissioner from Mexico. Castro was so jealous that it was almost impossible for Sutter to have anything like a private interview with him. Sutter, however, was given to understand that, as he had stood friendly to Governor Micheltorena on the side of Mexico in the late troubles, he might rely on the friendship of Mexico, to which he was enjoined to continue faithful in all emergencies. Within a week Castillero was shown at San José a singular heavy reddish rock, which had long been known to the Indians, who rubbed it on their hands and faces to paint them. The Californians had often tried to smelt this rock in a blacksmith's fire, thinking it to be silver or some other precious metal. But Castillero, who was an intelligent man and a native of Spain, at once recognized it as quicksilver, and noted its resemblance to the cinnabar in the mines of Almaden. A company was immediately formed to work it, of which Castillero, Castro, Alexander Forbes, and others were members. The discovery of quicksilver at this time seems providential in view of its absolute necessity to supplement the imminent discovery of gold, which stirred and waked into new life the industries of the world.

It is a question whether the United States could have stood the shock of the great rebellion of 1861 had the California gold discovery not been made. Bankers and business men of New York in 1864 did not hesitate to admit that but for the gold of California, which monthly poured its five or six millions into that financial center, the bottom would have dropped out of everything. These timely arrivals so strengthened the nerves of trade and stimulated business as to enable the Government to sell its bonds at a time when its credit was its life-blood and the main reliance by which to feed, clothe, and maintain its armies. Once our bonds went down to thirty-eight cents on the dollar. California gold averted a total collapse, and enabled a preserved Union to come forth from the great conflict with only four billions of debt instead of a hundred billions. The hand of Providence so plainly seen in the discovery of gold is no less manifest in the time chosen for its accomplishment.

I must reserve for itself in a concluding paper my personal recollections of Frémont's second visit to California in 1845-46, which I have purposely wholly omitted here. It was most important, resulting as it did in the acquisition of that territory by the United States.

John Bidwell.

RANCH AND MISSION DAYS IN ALTA CALIFORNIA.

IT seems to me that there never was a more peaceful or happy people on the face of the earth than the Spanish, Mexican, and Indian population of Alta California before the American conquest. We were the pioneers of the Pacific coast, building towns and Missions while General Washington was carrying on the war of the Revolution, and we often talk together of the days when a few hundred large Spanish ranches and Mission tracts occupied the whole country from the Pacific to the San Joaquin. No class of American citizens is more loyal than the Spanish Californians, but we shall always be especially proud of the traditions and memories of the long pastoral age before 1840. Indeed, our social life still tends to keep alive a spirit of love for the simple, homely, outdoor life of our Spanish ancestors on this coast, and we try, as best we may, to honor the founders of our ancient families, and the saints and heroes of our history since the days when Father Junipero planted the cross at Monterey.

The leading features of old Spanish life at the Missions, and on the large ranches of the last century, have been described in many books of travel, and with many contradictions. I shall confine myself to those details and illustrations of the past that no modern writer can possibly obtain except vaguely, from hearsay, since they exist in no manuscript, but only in the memories of a generation that is fast passing away. My mother has told me much, and I am still more indebted to my illustrious uncle, General Vallejo, of Sonoma, many of whose recollections are incorporated in this article.

When I was a child there were fewer than fifty Spanish families in the region about the bay of San Francisco, and these were closely connected by ties of blood or intermarriage. My father and his brother, the late General Vallejo, saw, and were a part of, the most important events in the history of Spanish California, the revolution and the conquest. My grandfather, Don Ygnacio Vallejo, was equally prominent in his day, in the exploration and settlement of the province. The traditions and records of the family thus cover the entire period of the annals of early California, from San Diego to Sonoma.

What I wish to do is to tell, as plainly and carefully as possible, how the Spanish settlers lived, and what they did in the old days. The story will be partly about the Missions, and partly about the great ranches.

The Jesuit Missions established in Lower California, at Loreto and other places, were followed by Franciscan Missions in Alta California, with presidios for the soldiers, adjacent pueblos, or towns, and the granting of large tracts of land to settlers. By 1782 there were nine flourishing Missions in Alta California — San Francisco, Santa Clara, San Carlos, San Antonio, San Luis Obispo, San Buenaventura, San Gabriel, San Juan, and San Diego. Governor Fajés added Santa Barbara and Purissima, and by 1790 there were more than 7000 Indian converts in the various Missions. By 1800 about forty Franciscan fathers were at work in Alta California, six of whom had been among the pioneers of twenty and twenty-five years before, and they had established seven new Missions — San José, San Miguel, Soledad, San Fernando, Santa Cruz, San Juan Bautista, and San Luis Rey. The statistics of all the Missions, so far as they have been preserved, have been printed in various histories, and the account of their growth, prosperity, and decadence has often been told. All that I wish to point out is that at the beginning of the century the whole system was completely established in Alta California. In 1773 Father Palou had reported that all the Missions, taken together, owned two hundred and four head of cattle and a few sheep, goats, and mules. In 1776 the regular five years' supplies sent from Mexico to the Missions were as follows: 107 blankets, 480 yards striped sackcloth, 389 yards blue baize, 10 pounds blue maguey cloth,

A SPANISH WINDOW.

etables. Poultry was raised by the Indians, and sold very cheaply; a fat capon cost only twelve and a half cents. Beet and mutton were to be had for the killing, and wild game was very abundant. At many of the missions there were large flocks of tame pigeons. At the Mission San José the fathers' doves consumed a cental of wheat daily, besides what they gathered in the village. The doves were of many colors, and they made a beautiful appearance on the red tiles of the church and the tops of the dark garden walls.

The houses of the Spanish people were built of adobe, and were roofed with red tiles. They were very comfortable, cool in summer and warm in winter. The clay used to make the bricks was dark brown, not white or yellow as the adobes in the Rio Grande region and in parts of Mexico. Cut straw was mixed with the clay, and trodden together by the Indians. When the bricks were laid, they were set in clay as in mortar, and sometimes small pebbles from the brooks were mixed with the mortar to make bands across the house. All the timber of the floors, the rafters and crossbeams, the doorways, and the window lintels were "built in" as the house was carried up. After the house was roofed it was usually plastered inside and out to protect it against the weather and make it more comfortable. A great deal of trouble was often taken to obtain stone for the doorsteps, and curious rocks were sometimes brought many miles for this purpose, or for gate-posts in front of the dwelling.

The Indian houses were never more than one story high, also of adobe, but much smaller and with thinner walls. The inmates covered the earthen floors in part with coarse mats woven of tules, on which they slept. The missions, as fast as possible, provided them with blankets, which were woven under the fathers' personal supervision, for home use and for sale. They were also taught to weave a coarse serge for clothing.

It was between 1792 and 1795, as I have heard, that the governor brought a number of artisans from Mexico, and every mission wanted them, but there were not enough to go around. There were masons, millwrights, tanners, shoemakers, saddlers, potters, a ribbonmaker, and several weavers. The blankets and the coarse cloth I have spoken of were first woven in the southern missions, San Gabriel, San Juan Capistrano, and others. About 1797 cotton cloth was also made in a few cases, and the cotton plant was found to grow very well. Hemp was woven at Monterey. Pottery was

4 reams paper, 5 bales red pepper, 10 arrobas of tasajo (dried beef), beads, chocolate, lard, lentils, rice, flour, and four barrels of Castilian wine. By 1800 all this was changed: the flocks and herds of cattle of California contained 187,000 animals, of which 153,000 were in the mission pastures, and large areas of land had been brought under cultivation, so that the missions supplied the presidios and foreign ships.

No one need suppose that the Spanish pioneers of California suffered many hardships or privations, although it was a new country. They came slowly, and were well prepared to become settlers. All that was necessary for the maintenance and enjoyment of life according to the simple and healthful standards of those days was brought with them. They had seeds, trees, vines, cattle, household goods, and servants, and in a few years their orchards yielded abundantly and their gardens were full of veg-

made at Mission Dolores, San Francisco. Soap was made in 1798, and afterwards at all the Missions and on many large ranches. The settlers themselves were obliged to learn trades and teach them to their servants, so that an educated young gentleman was well skilled in many arts and handicrafts. He could ride, of course, as well as the best cow-boy of the Southwest, and with more grace; and he could throw the lasso so expertly that I never heard of any American who was able to equal it. He could also make soap, pottery, and bricks, burn lime, tan hides, cut out and put together a pair of shoes, make candles, roll cigars, and do a great number of things that belong to different trades.

The California Indians were full of rude superstitions of every sort when the Franciscan fathers first began to teach them. It is hard to collect old Indian stories in these days, because they have become mixed up with what the fathers taught them. But the wild Indians a hundred years ago told the priests what they believed, and it was difficult to persuade them to give it up. In fact, there was more or less of what the fathers told them was "devil-worship" going on all the time. Rude stone altars were secretly built by the Mission Indians to "Cooksuy," their dreaded god. They chose a lonely place in the hills, and made piles of flat stones, five or six feet high. After that each Indian passing would throw something there, and this act of homage, called "pooish," continued until the mound was covered with a curious collection of beads, feathers, shells from the coast, and even garments and food, which no Indian dared to touch. The fathers destroyed all such altars that they could discover, and punished the Indians who worshiped there. Sometimes the more ardent followers of Cooksuy had meetings at night, slipping away from the Indian village after the retiring-bell had rung and the alcalde's rounds had been made. They prepared for the ceremony by fasting for several days; then they went to the chosen place, built a large fire, went through many dances, and called the god by a series of very strange and wild whistles, which always frightened any person who heard them. The old Indians, after being converted, told the priests that before they had seen the Spaniards come Cooksuy made his appearance from the midst of the fire in the form of a large white serpent; afterward the story was changed, and they reported that he sometimes took the form of a bull with fiery eyes.

Indian alcaldes were appointed in the Mission towns to maintain order. Their duty was that of police officers; they were dressed better than the others, and wore shoes and stock-

ings, which newly appointed officers dispensed with as often as possible, choosing to go barefoot, or with stockings only. When a vacancy in the office occurred the Indians themselves were asked which one they preferred of several suggested by the priest. The Mission San José had about five thousand Indian converts at the time of its greatest prosperity, and a number of Indian alcaldes were needed there. The alcaldes of the Spanish people in the pueblos were more like local judges, and were appointed by the governor.

The Indians who were personal attendants of the fathers were chosen with much care, for their obedience and quickness of perception. Some of them seemed to have reached the very perfection of silent, careful, unselfish service. They could be trusted with the most important matters, and they were strictly honest. Each father had his own private barber, who enjoyed the honor of a seat at the table with him, and generally accompanied him in journeys to other Missions. When the Missions were secularized, this custom, like many others, was abolished, and one Indian barber, named Telequis, felt the change in his position so much that when he was ordered out to the field with the others he committed suicide by eating the root of a poisonous wild plant, a species of celery.

The Indian vaqueros, who lived much of the time on the more distant cattle ranges, were a wild set of men. I remember one of them, named Martin, who was stationed in Amador Valley and became a leader of the hill vaqueros, who were very different from the vaqueros of the large valley near the Missions. He and his friends killed and ate three or four hundred young heifers belonging to the Mission, but when Easter approached he felt that he must confess his sins, so he went to Father Narciso and told all about it. The father forgave him, but ordered him to come in from the hills to the Mission and attend school until he could read. The rules were very strict; whoever failed twice in a lesson was always whipped. Martin was utterly unable to learn his letters, and he was whipped every day for a month; but he never complained. He was then dismissed, and went back to the hills. I used to question Martin about the affair, and he would tell me with perfect gravity of manner, which was very delightful, how many calves he had consumed and how wisely the good father had punished him. He knew now, he used to say, how very hard it was to live in the town, and he would never steal again lest he might have to go to school 'til he had learned his letters.

It was the custom at all the Missions, during the rule of the Franciscan missionaries, to keep the young unmarried Indians separate. The young girls and the young widows at the Mission San José occupied a large adobe building, with a yard behind it, inclosed by high adobe walls. In this yard some trees were planted, and a *zanja*, or water-ditch, supplied a large bathing-pond. The women were kept busy at various occupations, in the building, under the trees, or on the wide porch; they were taught spinning, knitting, the weaving of Indian baskets from grasses, willow rods and roots, and more especially plain sewing. The treatment and occupation of the unmarried women was similar at the other Missions. When heathen Indian women came in, or were brought by their friends, or by the soldiers, they were put in these houses, and under the charge of older women, who taught them what to do.

The women, thus separated from the men, could only be courted from without through the upper windows facing on the narrow village street. These windows were about two feet square, crossed by iron bars, and perhaps three feet deep, as the adobe walls were very thick. The rules were not more strict, however, than still prevail in some of the Spanish-American countries in much higher classes, socially, than these uneducated Indians belonged to; in fact, the rules were adopted by the fathers from Mexican models. After an Indian, in his hours of freedom from toil, had declared his affection by a sufficiently long attendance upon a certain window, it was the duty of the woman to tell the father missionary and to declare her decision. If this was favorable, the young man was asked if he was willing to contract marriage with the young woman who had confessed her preference. Sometimes there were several rival suitors, but it was never known that any trouble occurred. After marriage the couple were conducted to their home, a hut built for them among the other Indian houses in the village near the Mission.

The Indian mothers were frequently told about the proper care of children, and cleanliness of the person was strongly inculcated. In fact, the Mission Indians, large and small, were wonderfully clean, their faces and hair fairly shining with soap and water. In several cases where an Indian woman was so slovenly and neglectful of her infant that it died she was punished by being compelled to carry in her arms in church, and at all meals and public assemblies, a log of wood about the size of a nine-months'-old child. This was a very effectual punishment, for the Indian women are naturally most affectionate creatures, and in every case they soon began to suffer greatly, and others with them, so that once a whole

Indian village begged the father in charge to forgive the poor woman.

The padres always had a school for the Indian boys. My mother has a *novena*, or "nine-days' devotion book," copied for her by one of the Indian pupils of the school at the Mission San José, early in the century. The handwriting is very neat and plain, and would be a credit to any one. Many young Indians had good voices, and these were selected with great care to be trained in singing for the church choir. It was thought such an honor to sing in church that the Indian families were all very anxious to be represented. Some were taught to play on the violin and other stringed instruments. When Father Narciso Duran, who was the president of the Franciscans in California, was at the Mission San José, he had a church choir of about thirty well-trained boys to sing the mass. He was himself a cultivated musician, having studied under some of the best masters in Spain, and so sensitive was his ear that if one string was out of tune he could not continue his service, but would at once turn to the choir, call the name of the player, and the string that was out of order, and wait until the matter was corrected. As there were often more than a dozen players on instruments, this showed high musical ability. Every prominent Mission had fathers who paid great attention to training the Indians in music.

A Spanish lady of high social standing tells the following story, which will illustrate the honor in which the Mission fathers were held:

Father Majin Catala, one of the missionaries early in the century, was held to possess prophetic gifts, and many of the Spanish settlers, the Castros, Peraltas, Estudillos, and others, have reason to remember his gift. When any priest issued from the sacristy to celebrate mass all hearts were stirred, but with this holy father the feeling became one of absolute awe. On more than one occasion before his sermon he asked the congregation to join him in prayers for the soul of one about to die, naming the hour. In every case this was fulfilled to the very letter, and that in cases where the one who died could not have known of the father's words. This saint spent his days in labor among the people, and he was loved as well as feared. But on one occasion, in later life, when the Mission rule was broken, he offended an Indian chief, and shortly after several Indians called at his home in the night to ask him to go and see a dying woman. The father rose and dressed, but his chamber door remained fast, so that he could not open it, and he was on the point of ordering them to break it open from without, when he felt a warning, to the effect that they were going to murder him. Then he said, " To-morrow I will visit your sick : you are forgiven; go in peace." Then they fled in dismay, knowing that his person was protected by an especial providence, and soon after confessed their plans to the father.

Father Real was one of the most genial and kindly men of the missionaries, and he surprised all those who had thought that every one of the fathers was severe. He saw no harm in walking out among the young people, and saying friendly things to them all. He was often known to go with young men on moonlight rides, lassoing grizzly bears, or chasing deer on the plain. His own horse, one of the best ever seen in the valley, was richly caparisoned, and the father wore a scarlet silk sash around his waist under the Franciscan habit. When older and graver priests reproached him, he used to say with a smile that he was only a Mexican Franciscan, and that he was brought up in a saddle. He was certainly a superb rider.

It is said of Father Amoros of San Rafael that his noon meal consisted of an ear of dry corn, roasted over the coals. This he carried in his sleeve and partook of at his leisure while overseeing the Indian laborers. Some persons who were in the habit of reaching a priest's house at noontime, so as to be asked to dinner, once called on the father, and were told that he had gone to the field with his corn in his *manguilla*, but they rode away without seeing him, which was considered a breach of good manners, and much fun was made over their haste.

The principal sources of revenue which the Missions enjoyed were the sales of hides and tallow, fresh beef, fruits, wheat, and other things to ships, and in occasional sales of horses to trappers or traders. The Russians at Fort Ross, north of San Francisco, on Bodega Bay, bought a good deal from the Missions. Then too the Indians were sent out to trade with other Indians, and so the Missions often secured many valuable furs, such as otter and beaver, together with skins of bears and deer killed by their own hunters.

The *embarcadero*, or " landing," for the Mission San José was at the mouth of a salt-water creek four or five miles away. When a ship sailed into San Francisco Bay, and the captain sent a large boat up this creek and arranged to buy hides, they were usually hauled there on an ox-cart with solid wooden wheels, called a *carreta*. But often in winter, there being no roads across the valley, each separate hide was doubled across the middle and placed on the head of an Indian. Long files of Indians, each carrying a hide in this manner, could be seen trotting over the unfenced level land through the wild mustard to the *embarcadero*, and in

a few weeks the whole cargo would thus be delivered. For such work the Indians always received additional gifts for themselves and families.

A very important feature was the wheat harvest. Wheat was grown more or less at all the Missions. If those Americans who came to California in 1849 and said that wheat would not grow here had only visited the Missions they would have seen beautiful large wheatfields. Of course at first many mistakes were made by the fathers in their experiments, not only in wheat and corn, but also in winemaking, in crushing olives for oil, in grafting trees, and in creating fine flower and vegetable gardens. At most of the Missions it took them several years to find out how to grow good grain. At first they planted it on too wet land. At the Mission San José a tract about a mile square came to be used for wheat. It was fenced in with a ditch, dug by the Indians with sharp sticks and with their hands in the rainy season, and it was so deep and wide that cattle and horses never crossed it. In other places stone or adobe walls, or hedges of the prickly pear cactus, were used about the wheatfields. Timber was never considered available for fences, because there were no sawmills and no roads to the forests, so that it was only at great expense and with extreme difficulty that we procured the logs that were necessary in building, and chopped them slowly, with poor tools, to the size we wanted. Sometimes low adobe walls were made high and safe by a row of the skulls of Spanish cattle, with the long curving horns attached. These came from the *matanzas*, or slaughter-corrals, where there were thousands of them lying in piles, and they could be so used to make one of the strongest and most effective of barriers against man or beast. Set close and deep, at various angles, about the gateways and corral walls, these cattle horns helped to protect the inclosure from horse-thieves.

When wheat was sown it was merely " scratched in " with a wooden plow, but the ground was so new and rich that the yield was great. The old Mission field is now occupied by some of the best farms of the valley, showing how excellent was the fathers' judgment of good land. The old ditches which fenced it have been plowed in for more than forty years by American farmers, but their course can still be distinctly traced.

A special ceremony was connected with the close of the wheat harvest. The last four sheaves taken from this large field were tied to poles in the form of a cross, and were then brought by the reapers in the " harvest procession " to the church, while the bells were rung, and the father, dressed in his robes, carrying the cross and accompanied by boys with tapers and censers, chanting the Te Deum as they marched, went forth to meet the sheaves. This was a season of Indian festival also, and one-fifth of the whole number of the Indians were sometimes allowed to leave the Mission for a certain number of days, to gather acorns, dig roots, hunt, fish, and enjoy a change of occupation. It was a privilege that they seldom, or never, abused by failing to return, and the fact shows how well they were treated in the Missions.

Governor Neve proposed sowing wheat, I have heard, in 1776, and none had been sown in California before that time. At the pueblo of San José, which was established in 1777, they planted wheat for the use of the presidios, and the first sowing was at the wrong season and failed, but the other half of their seed did better. The fathers at San Diego Mission sowed grain on the bottom lands in the willows the first year, and it was washed away; then they put it on the mesa above the Mission, and it died; the third year they found a good piece of land, and it yielded one hundred and ninety-five fold.

As soon as the Missions had wheatfields they wanted flour, and mortars were made. Some of them were holes cut in the rock, with a heavy pestle, lifted by a long pole. When La Pérouse, the French navigator, visited Monterey in 1786, he gave the fathers in San Carlos an iron hand-mill, so that the neophyte women could more easily grind their wheat. He also gave the fathers seed-potatoes from Chili, the first that were known in California. La Pérouse and his officers were received with much hospitality at San Carlos. The Indians were told that the Frenchmen were true Catholics, and Father Palou had them all assembled at the reception. Mrs. Ord, a daughter of the De la Guerra family, had a ·drawing of this occasion, made by an officer, but it was stolen about the time of the American conquest, like so many of the precious relics of Spanish California. La Pérouse wrote: " It is with the sweetest satisfaction that I shall make known the pious and wise conduct of these friars, who fulfil so perfectly the object of their institution. The greatest anchorites have never led a more edifying life."

Early in the century flour-mills by water were built at Santa Cruz, San Luis Obispo, San José, and San Gabriel. The ruins of some of these now remain; the one at Santa Cruz is very picturesque. Horse-power mills were in use at many places. About the time that the Americans began to arrive in numbers the Spanish people were just commencing to project larger mill enterprises and irrigation ditches for their own needs. The difficulties with land titles put an end to most of these plans, and some of them were afterward carried out by Americans when the ranches were broken up.

One of the greatest of the early irrigation projects was that of my grandfather, Don Ygnacio Vallejo, who spent much labor and money in supplying San Luis Obispo Mission with water. This was begun in 1776, and completed the following year. He also planned to carry the water of the Carmel River to Monterey; this has since been done by the Southern Pacific Railway Company. My father, Don J. J. Vallejo, about fifty years ago made a stone aqueduct and several irrigation and mill ditches from the Alameda Creek, on which stream he built an adobe flour-mill, whose millstones were brought from Spain.

I have often been asked about the old Mission and ranch gardens. They were, I think, more extensive, and contained a greater variety of trees and plants, than most persons imagine. The Jesuits had gardens in Baja California as early as 1699, and vineyards and orchards a few years later. The Franciscans in Alta California began to cultivate the soil as soon as they landed. The first grapevines were brought from Lower California in 1769, and were soon planted at all the Missions except Dolores, where the climate was not suitable. Before the year 1800 the orchards at the Missions contained apples, pears, peaches, apricots, plums, cherries, figs, olives, oranges, pomegranates. At San Diego and San Buenaventura Missions there were also sugar canes, date palms, plantains, bananas, and citrons. There were orchards and vineyards in California sufficient to supply all the wants of the people. I remember that at the Mission San José we had many varieties of seedling fruits which have now been lost to cultivation. Of pears we had four sorts, one ripening in early summer, one in late summer, and two in autumn and winter. The Spanish names of these pears were the *Presidenta*, the *Bergamota*, the *Pana*, and the *Lechera*. One of them was as large as a Bartlett, but there are no trees of it left now. The apples, grown from seed, ripened at different seasons, and there were seedling peaches, both early and late. An interesting and popular fruit was that of the *Nopal*, or prickly pear. This fruit, called *tuna*, grew on the great hedges which protected part of the Mission orchards and were twenty feet high and ten or twelve feet thick. Those who know how to eat a *tuna*, peeling it so as to escape the tiny thorns on the skin, find it delicious. The Missions had avenues of fig, olive, and other trees about the buildings, besides the orchards. In later times American squatters and campers often cut down these trees for firewood, or built fires against the trunks, which killed them. Several hundred large and valuable olive trees at the San Diego Mission were killed in this way. The old orchards were pruned and cultivated with much care, and the paths were swept by the Indians, but after the sequestration of the Mission property they were neglected and ran wild. The olive-mills and wine-presses were destroyed, and cattle were pastured in the once fruitful groves.

The flower gardens were gay with roses, chiefly a pink and very fragrant sort from Mexico, called by us the Castilian rose, and still seen in a few old gardens. Besides roses, we had pinks, sweet-peas, hollyhocks, nasturtiums which had been brought from Mexico, and white lilies. The vegetable gardens contained pease, beans, beets, lentils, onions, carrots, red peppers, corn, potatoes, squashes, cucumbers, and melons. A fine quality of tobacco was cultivated and cured by the Indians. Hemp and flax were grown to some extent. A fine large cane, a native of Mexico, was planted, and the joints found useful as spools in the blanket factory, and for many domestic purposes. The young shoots of this cane were sometimes cooked for food. Other kinds of plants were grown in the old gardens, but these are all that I can remember.

In the old days every one seemed to live out-doors. There was much gaiety and social life, even though people were widely scattered. We traveled as much as possible on horseback. Only old people or invalids cared to use the slow cart, or *carreta*. Young men would ride from one ranch to another for parties, and whoever found his horse tired would let him go and catch another. In 1806 there were so many horses in the valleys about San José that seven or eight thousand were killed. Nearly as many were driven into the sea at Santa Barbara in 1807, and the same thing was done at Monterey in 1810. Horses were given to the runaway sailors, and to trappers and hunters who came over the mountains, for common horses were very plenty, but fast and beautiful horses were never more prized in any country than in California, and each young man had his favorites. A kind of mustang, that is now seldom or never seen on the Pacific coast, was a peculiar light cream-colored horse, with silver-white mane and tail. Such an animal, of speed and bottom, often sold for more than a horse of any other color. Other much admired colors were dapple-gray and chestnut. The fathers of the Mission sometimes rode on horseback, but they generally had a somewhat modern carriage called a *volante*. It was always drawn by mules, of which there were hundreds in the Mission pastures, and white was the color often preferred.

Nothing was more attractive than the wedding cavalcade on its way from the bride's house to the Mission church. The horses were more richly caparisoned than for any other ceremony, and the bride's nearest relative or family representative carried her before him, she sitting on the saddle with her white satin shoe in a loop of golden or silver braid, while he sat on the bear-skin covered *anquera* behind. The groom and his friends mingled with the bride's party, all on the best horses that could be obtained, and they rode gaily from the ranch house to the Mission, sometimes fifteen or twenty miles away. In April and May, when the land was covered with wild-flowers, the light-hearted troop rode along the edge of the uplands, between hill and valley, crossing the streams, and some of the young horsemen, anxious to show their skill, would perform all the feats for which the Spanish-Californians were famous. After the wedding, when they returned to lead in the feasting, the bride was carried on the horse of the groomsman. One of the customs which was always observed at the wedding was to wind a silken tasseled string or a silken sash, fringed with gold, about the necks of the bride and groom, binding them together as they knelt before the altar for the blessing of the priest. A charming custom among the middle and lower classes was the making of the satin shoes by the groom for the bride. A few weeks before the wedding he asked his betrothed for the measurement of her foot, and made the shoes with his own hands; the groomsman brought them to her on the wedding-day.

But few foreigners ever visited any of the Missions, and they naturally caused quite a stir. At the Mission San José, about 1820, late one night in the vintage season a man came to the village for food and shelter, which were gladly given. But the next day it was whispered that he was a Jew, and the poor Indians, who had been told that the Jews had crucified Christ, ran to their huts and hid. Even the Spanish children, and many of the grown people, were frightened. Only the missionary father had ever before seen a Jew, and when he found that it was impossible to check the excitement he sent two soldiers to ride with the man a portion of the way to Santa Clara.

A number of trappers and hunters came into Southern California and settled down in various towns. There was a party of Kentuckians, beaver-trappers, who went along the Gila and Colorado rivers about 1827, and then south into Baja California to the Mission of Santa Catalina. Then they came to San Diego, where the whole country was much excited over their hunter clothes, their rifles, their traps, and the strange stories they told of the deserts, and fierce Indians, and things that no one in California had ever seen. Captain Paty was the oldest man of the party, and he was ill and worn out. All the San Diego people were very kind to the Americans. It is said that the other Missions, such as San Gabriel, sent and desired the privilege of caring for some of them. Captain Paty grew worse, so he sent for one of the fathers and said he wished to become a Catholic, because, he added, it must be a good religion, for it made everybody so good to him. Don Pio Pico and Doña Victoria Dominguez de Estudillo were his sponsors. After Captain Paty's death the Americans went to Los Angeles, where they all married Spanish ladies, were given lands, built houses, planted vineyards, and became important people. Pryor repaired the church silver, and was called " Miguel el Platero." Laughlin was always so merry that he was named " Ricardo el Buen Mozo." They all had Spanish names given them besides their own. One of them was a blacksmith, and as iron was very scarce he made pruning shears for the vineyards out of the old beaver traps.

On Christmas night, 1828, a ship was wrecked near Los Angeles, and twenty-eight men escaped. Everybody wanted to care for them, and they were given a great Christmas dinner, and offered money and lands. Some of them staid, and some went to other Missions and towns. One of them who staid was a German, John Gronigen, and he was named " Juan Domingo," or, because he was lame, " Juan Cojo." Another, named Prentice, came from Connecticut, and he was a famous fisherman and otter hunter. After 1828 a good many other Americans came in and settled down quietly to cultivate the soil, and some of them became very rich. They had grants from the governor, just the same as the Spanish people.

It is necessary, for the truth of the account, to mention the evil behavior of many Americans before, as well as after, the conquest. At the Mission San José there is a small creek, and two very large sycamores once grew at the Spanish ford, so that it was called *la aliso.* A squatter named Fallon, who lived near the crossing, cut down these for firewood, though there were many trees in the cañon. The Spanish people begged him to leave them, for the shade and beauty, but he did not care for that. This was a little thing, but much that happened was after such pattern, or far worse.

In those times one of the leading American squatters came to my father, Don J. J. Vallejo, and said : " There is a large piece of your land where the cattle run loose, and your vaqueros have gone to the gold mines. I will fence the field for you at my expense if you will give me half." He liked the idea, and assented, but when the tract was inclosed the

American had it entered as government land in his own name, and kept all of it. In many similar cases American settlers in their dealings with the rancheros took advantage of laws which they understood, but which were new to the Spaniards, and so robbed the latter of their lands. Notes and bonds were considered unnecessary by a Spanish gentleman in a business transaction, as his word was always sufficient security.

Perhaps the most exasperating feature of the coming-in of the Americans was owing to the mines, which drew away most of the servants, so that our cattle were stolen by thousands. Men who are now prosperous farmers and merchants were guilty of shooting and selling Spanish beef " without looking at the brand," as the phrase went. My father had about ten thousand head of cattle, and some he was able to send back into the hills until there were better laws and officers, but he lost the larger part. On one occasion I remember some vigilantes caught two cattle-thieves and sent for my father to appear against them, but he said that although he wanted them punished he did not wish to have them hanged, and so he would not testify, and they were set free. One of them afterward sent conscience money to us from New York, where he is living in good circumstances. The Vallejos have on several occasions received conscience money from different parts of the country. The latest case occurred last year (1889), when a woman wrote that her husband, since dead, had taken a steer worth twenty-five dollars, and she sent the money.

Every Mission and ranch in old times had its *calaveras,* its " place of skulls," its slaughter-corral, where cattle and sheep were killed by the Indian butchers. Every Saturday morning the fattest animals were chosen and driven there, and by night the hides were all stretched on the hillside to dry. At one time a hundred cattle and two hundred sheep were killed weekly at the Mission San José, and the meat was distributed to all, " without money and without price." The grizzly bears, which were very abundant in the country,— for no one ever poisoned them, as the American stock raisers did after 1849,— used to come by night to the ravines near the slaughter-corral where the refuse was thrown by the butchers. The young Spanish gentlemen often rode out on moonlight nights to lasso these bears, and then they would drag them through the village street, and past the houses of their friends. Two men with their strong rawhide reatas could hold any bear, and when they were tired of this sport they could kill him. But sometimes the bears would walk through the village on their way to or from the corral of the butchers, and so scatter the people. Several times a serenade party, singing and playing by moonlight, was suddenly broken up by two or three grizzlies trotting down the hill into the street, and the gay *caballeros* with their guitars would spring over the adobe walls and run for their horses, which always stood saddled, with a reata coiled, ready for use, at the saddle bow. It was the custom in every family to keep saddled horses in easy reach, day and night.

Innumerable stories about grizzlies are traditional in the old Spanish families, not only in the Santa Clara Valley, but also through the Coast Range from San Diego to Sonoma and Santa Rosa. Some of the bravest of the young men would go out alone to kill grizzlies. When they had lassoed one they would drag him to a tree, and the well-trained horse would hold the bear against it while the hunter slipped out of the saddle, ran up, and killed the grizzly with one stroke of his broad-bladed *machete*, or Mexican hunting knife. One Spanish gentlemen riding after a large grizzly lassoed it and was dragged into a deep *barranca*. Horse and man fell on the bear, and astonished him so much that he scrambled up the bank, and the hunter cut the reata and gladly enough let him go. There were many cases of herdsmen and hunters being killed by grizzlies, and one could fill a volume with stories of feats of courage and of mastery of the reata. The governor of California appointed expert bear hunters in different parts of the country, who spent their time in destroying them, by pits, or shooting, or with the reata. Don Rafael Soto, one of the most famous of these men, used to conceal himself in a pit, covered with heavy logs and leaves, with a quarter of freshly killed beef above. When the grizzly bear walked on the logs he was shot from beneath. Before the feast-days the hunters sometimes went to the foothills and brought several bears to turn into the bull-fighting corral.

The principal bull-fights were held at Easter and on the day of the patron saint of the Mission, which at the Mission San José was March 19. Young gentlemen who had trained for the contest entered the ring on foot and on horseback, after the Mexican manner. In the bull and bear fights a hindfoot of the bear was often tied to the forefoot of the bull, to equalize the struggle, for a large grizzly was more than a match for the fiercest bull in California, or indeed of any other country. Bull and bear fights continued as late as 1855. The Indians were the most ardent supporters of this cruel sport.

The days of the *rodeos*, when cattle were driven in from the surrounding pastures, and the herds of the different ranches were separated, were notable episodes. The ranch owners elected three or five *juezes del campo* to govern the proceedings and decide disputes. After the rodeo there was a feast. The great feast-days, however, were December 12 (the day of our Lady Guadalupe), Christmas, Easter, and St. Joseph's Day, or the day of the patron saint of the Mission.

Family life among the old Spanish pioneers was an affair of dignity and ceremony, but it did not lack in affection. Children were brought up with great respect for their elders. It was the privilege of any elderly person to correct young people by words, or even by whipping them, and it was never told that any one thus chastised made a complaint. Each one of the old families taught their children the history of the family, and reverence towards religion. A few books, some in manuscript, were treasured in the household, but children were not allowed to read novels until they were grown. They saw little of other children, except their near relatives, but they had many enjoyments unknown to children now, and they grew up with remarkable strength and healthfulness.

In these days of trade, bustle, and confusion, when many thousands of people live in the Californian valleys, which formerly were occupied by only a few Spanish families, the quiet and happy domestic life of the past seems like a dream. We, who loved it, often speak of those days, and especially of the duties of the large Spanish households, where so many dependents were to be cared for, and everything was done in a simple and primitive way.

There was a group of warm springs a few miles distant from the old adobe house in which we lived. It made us children happy to be waked before sunrise to prepare for the "wash-day expedition" to the *Agua Caliente*. The night before the Indians had soaped the clumsy carreta's great wheels. Lunch was placed in baskets, and the gentle oxen were yoked to the pole. We climbed in, under the green cloth of an old Mexican flag which was used as an awning, and the white-haired Indian *ganan*, who had driven the carreta since his boyhood, plodded beside with his long *garrocha*, or ox-goad. The great piles of soiled linen were fastened on the backs of horses, led by other servants, while the girls and women who were to do the washing trooped along by the side of the carreta. All in all, it made an imposing cavalcade, though our progress was slow, and it was generally sunrise before we had fairly reached the spring. The oxen pulled us up the slope of the ravine, where it was so steep that we often cried, "Mother, let us dismount and walk, so as to make it easier." The steps of the carreta were so low that we could climb in or out without stopping the oxen. The watchful mother guided the whole party, seeing that none strayed too far after flowers, or loitered too long talking with the others. Sometimes we heard the howl of coyotes, and the noise of other wild animals in the dim dawn, and then none of the children were allowed to leave the carreta.

A great dark mountain rose behind the hot spring, and the broad, beautiful valley, unfenced, and dotted with browsing herds, sloped down to the bay as we climbed the cañon to where columns of white steam rose among the oaks, and the precious waters, which were strong with sulphur, were seen flowing over the crusted basin, and falling down a worn rock channel to the brook. Now on these mountain slopes for miles are the vineyards of Josiah Stanford, the brother of Senator Leland Stanford, and the valley below is filled with towns and orchards.

We watched the women unload the linen and carry it to the upper spring of the group, where the water was best. Then they loosened the horses, and let them pasture on the wild oats, while the women put home-made soap on the clothes, dipped them in the spring, and rubbed them on the smooth rocks until they were white as snow. Then they were spread out to dry on the tops of the low bushes growing on the warm, windless, southern slopes of the mountain. There was sometimes a great deal of linen to be washed, for it was the pride of every Spanish family to own much linen, and the mother and daughters almost always wore white. I have heard strangers speak of the wonderful way in which Spanish ladies of the upper classes in California always appeared in snow-white dresses, and certainly to do so was one of the chief anxieties of every household. Where there were no warm springs the servants of the family repaired to. the nearest *arroyo*, or creek, and stood knee-deep in it, dipping and rubbing the linen, and enjoying the sport. In the rainy season the soiled linen sometimes accumulated for several weeks before the weather permitted the house mistress to have a wash-day. Then, when at last it came, it seemed as if half the village, with dozens of babies and youngsters, wanted to go along too and make a spring picnic.

The group of hot sulphur-springs, so useful on wash-days, was a famed resort for sick people, who drank the water, and also buried themselves up to the neck in the soft mud of the slope below the spring, where the waste waters ran. Their friends brought them in litters and scooped out a hole for them, then put boughs overhead to shelter them from the hot sun, and placed food and fresh water within reach, leaving them sometimes thus from sunrise to sunset. The Paso Robles and Gilroy Springs were among the most famous on the coast in those days, and after the annual *rodeos* people often went there to camp and to use the waters. But many writers have told about the medicinal virtues of the various California springs, and I need not enlarge upon the subject. To me, at least, one of the dearest of my childish memories is the family expedition from the great thick-walled adobe, under the olive and fig trees of the Mission, to the *Agua Caliente* in early dawn, and the late return at twilight, when the younger children were all asleep in the slow carreta, and the Indians were singing hymns as they drove the linen-laden horses down the dusky ravines.

Guadalupe Vallejo.

CALIFORNIANA.

Trading with the Americans.

IN the autumn of 1840 my father lived near what is now called Pinole Point, in Contra Costa County, California. I was then about twelve years old, and I remember the time because it was then that we saw the first American vessel that traded along the shores of San Pablo Bay. One afternoon a horseman from the Peraltas, where Oakland now stands, came to our ranch, and told my father that a great ship, a ship " with two sticks in the center," was about to sail from Yerba Buena into San Pablo and Suisun, to buy hides and tallow.

The next morning my father gave orders, and my brothers, with the peons, went on horseback into the mountains and smaller valleys to round up all the best cattle. They drove them to the beach, killed them there, and salted the hides. They tried out the tallow in some iron kettles that my father had bought from one of the Vallejos, but as we did not have any barrels, we followed the common plan in those days. We cast the tallow in round pits about the size of a cheese, dug in the black adobe and plastered smooth with clay. Before the melted tallow was poured into the pit an oaken staff was thrust down in the center, so that by the two ends of it the heavy cake could be carried more easily. By working very hard we had a large number of hides and many pounds of tallow ready on the beach when the ship appeared far out in the bay and cast anchor near another point two or three miles away. The captain soon came to our landing with a small boat and two sailors, one of whom was a Frenchman who knew Spanish very well, and who acted as interpreter. The captain looked over the hides, and then asked my father to get into the boat and go to the vessel. Mother was much afraid to let him go, as we all thought the Americans were not to be trusted unless we knew them well. We feared they would carry my father off and keep him a prisoner. Father said, however, that it was all right: he went and put on his best clothes, gay with silver braid, and we all cried, and kissed him good-by, while mother clung about his neck and said we might never see him again. Then the captain told her : "If you are afraid, I will have the sailors take him to the vessel, while I stay here until he comes back. He ought to see all the goods I have, or he will not know what to buy." After a little my mother let him go with the captain, and we stood on the beach to see them off. Mother then came back, and had us all kneel down and pray for father's safe return. Then we felt safe.

He came back the next day, bringing four boat-loads of cloth, axes, shoes, fish-lines, and many new things. There were two grindstones and some cheap jewelry. My brother had traded some deerskins for a gun and four tooth-brushes, the first ones I had ever seen. I remember that we children rubbed them on our teeth till the blood came, and then concluded that after all we liked best the bits of pounded willow root that we had used for brushes before. After the captain had carried all the hides and tallow to his ship he came back, very much pleased with his bargain, and gave my father, as a present, a little keg of what he called Boston rum. We put it away for sick people.

After the ship sailed my mother and sisters began to cut out new dresses, which the Indian women sewed. On one of mine mother put some big brass buttons about an inch across, with eagles on them. How proud I was! I used to rub them hard every day to make them shine, using the tooth-brush and some of the pounded egg-shell that my sisters and all the Spanish ladies kept in a box to put on their faces on great occasions. Then our neighbors, who were ten or fifteen miles away, came to see all the things we had bought. One of the Moragas heard that we had the grindstones, and sent and bought them with two fine horses.

Soon after this I went to school, in an adobe, near where the town of San Pablo now stands. A Spanish gentleman was the teacher, and he told us many new things, for which we remember him with great respect. But when he said the earth was round we all laughed out loud, and were much ashamed. That was the first day, and when he wrote down my name he told me that I was certainly "La Cantinera, the daughter of the regiment." Afterward I found out it was because of my brass buttons. One girl offered me a beautiful black colt she owned for six of the buttons, but I continued for a long time to think more of those buttons than of anything else I possessed.

Martinez.   *Prudencia Higuera.*

"The Date of the Discovery of the Yosemite."

Your correspondent, Mr. Bunnell, in the September Century, writes an interesting account of his discovery of the Yosemite, March 5, 1851. I am sorry to despoil him of the honor of being the *first*

discoverer, but a truthful regard for history makes it my duty to fix an earlier date.

During the month of January, 1851, I was making a tour of observation along the western slope of the Sierra of California in company with Professor Forrest Shepard of New Haven, Conn., and Professor Nooney, formerly of Western Reserve College, Ohio. Between the 12th and 15th of January we halted at the trading post established by Coulter, who was then and there doing a prosperous business in selling supplies to the gold miners in the vicinity. The locality, I believe, is now known as Coulterville, and is about twenty-five miles west of the Yosemite Cañon. We stopped there overnight, and during our stay heard from some of the men assembled in Coulter's store the following incidents, of which they said they had been witnesses or participants.

There had been some friction and disturbance in the relations of Indians and whites, but the open and general hostility which gave occasion for the subsequent movements of the "Mariposa Battalion" had not commenced at the time of our visit. The first serious quarrel occurred a few days before, when six Indians came to a trading tent in the Coulter camp and a drunken ruffian from Texas, without any reasonable cause, stabbed to the heart the chief of their party. The other five Indians with their bows and arrows at once shot the Texan, and having killed him retreated to the forest. Two nights later a pack of sixteen mules were stolen from Coulter's corral and driven off into the mountains by Indians.

Great excitement prevailed, and a company of about one hundred men from the camp and vicinity armed themselves and started on the trail. They followed the tracks into the great cañon and surprised the Indians, who had already converted the mules into jerked meat and had hung it up to dry. They had the satisfaction of slaughtering a large number of the Indians, with their squaws and papooses. They noticed especially the grandeur that surrounded the battlefield. They had returned from the expedition just before our arrival. In narrating their story they gave no name to the cañon, but gave us a description such as could apply to no place on earth other than the Yosemite. I made no record of the names of these discoverers, for what with the big trees, big lumps of gold, and other wonders that were seen and heard of daily, a big rift in the mountains would not be thought exceptional or extraordinary.

If Mr. Coulter or any of his associates are still living they can probably give the names, besides adding other valuable information.

I fix the date of the fight at the Yosemite, and thus of the discovery by the company of men who went from Coulter's January 10, 1851, as proximate, if not exact, both from memory and from corroborative records.

Montclair, N. J.   *Julius H. Pratt.*

The Extraordinary Story of the Utica Mine (1901)

EVERYBODY'S MAGAZINE

VOL. V.   NOVEMBER, 1901.

PANORAMA OF ANGEL'S, CALIFORNIA.

In the distance, toward the right, may be seen the main hoist of the Utica and Chlorination Gold Mines.

THE EXTRAORDINARY STORY OF THE UTICA MINE.

How John Selkirk sold the Richest Mine in California for Fifty Dollars— Abandoned by the Purchasers—Taken up by James G. Fair and abandoned again—Seven Million Dollars taken from it by Lane and Hayward —Dramatic Incidents of the Mine's History.

BY BAILEY MILLARD.

SICK from overwork on a worthless quartz claim in the foothills of the Sierras, and with a nostalgic ache in his heart, John Selkirk rode his tired mule into Angel's Camp. It was that same Angel's of which Bret Harte has romanced and sung, but it knew not of any romancer or singer in those days of delving and eager seeking after gold. The story was yet to be written, the song was yet to be sung.

John Selkirk came in the dry summer of 1854, when men who had made their way to California to dig for gold were scratching all over Calaveras County, eagerly prospecting for the yellow metal. They were burrowing in the red earth like gophers ; they were changing the courses of streams and washing out their old beds ; they were shoveling gravel like mad, and rocking and sluicing and overhauling the face of nature generally.

Some worked to much purpose and were getting rich, and others were merely making a good living ; but for John Selkirk there had been nothing but the buffets of fortune and none of her rewards. Indeed, his lust for gold had nearly burned itself out. He was weary of soul and would have been glad that day if his mule had borne him to his old Massachusetts home instead of setting him down at Angel's.

Silently John Selkirk rode through the slovenly little camp without a word to anybody and with barely a look to right or left. Coming to a bushy place on a hillside a little way beyond the last shanty, he stopped and tied his mule to a scrub oak. He unpacked his blankets, his pick, shovel, and pan from the back of his saddle, and carelessly threw them down on the earth. Then he built a fire, put his coffee upon it to boil, and pre-

THE CROSS HOISTING WORKS.

paused suddenly in his search and picked up a small gray stone. He was raising it to fling at the jay, when of a sudden his eye caught in the grain of the stone the glint of yellow gold. He broke the little piece of quartz into fragments with the back of his hand-axe. The pieces were heavy with gold. Then he began eagerly to search about for more outcroppings. At the base of a small mass of rocks he made a good-sized prospect hole and found rich and still richer specimens. It "looked right," he said, and he was satisfied with the prospect. So he cut some sticks from

pared a scrappy dinner of which he ate only a small part. He lay idly about on the ground for a while after dinner, smoking his pipe and thinking of home.

"I've had enough of this California country," he said to himself. "I'll light out of here in a few hours and go back to the folks."

A noisy jay interrupted his meditations, yelling at him scoldingly from the brush. The harsh sound disturbed him and, without getting up, he irritably looked about for something to throw at the bird. With his eyes upon the ground and his beard sweeping over it, he

THE CHLORINATION WORKS.

the oak tree, and driving them into the earth at four corners of a rectangular piece of hillside containing fifteen or twenty acres, he staked the great Utica Mine, the richest known gold deposit in California.

John Selkirk worked hard for the next few months. The ceaseless toil, day after day, with pick and drill took all the spring out of the man. He found little gold near the surface, but on going deeper he came upon a rich ledge, some of the rock containing two hundred dollars in gold to the ton. But Selkirk, with his crude arrastra, worked by mule power, and his other primitive methods for crushing the hard rock and extracting

THE STICKLE HOIST.

The logs are ready to use for supporting the "stopes" or excavations.

the gold from it, stored up very few yellow bars, and in time these all went for high-priced necessities. He knew there was gold enough in the ground he had staked to buy him a ship to sail home in and to freight it with treasure, but how to wrest the riches from the hard, unyielding rock? That was the problem.

He went to Sacramento and to Benicia and laid his case before men of wealth.

"You can make a heap of money by going mines and thousands of specimens. To Mammon the prospect was not alluring. It wished him well of his mine, but would none of it.

Back again to Angel's, and back again to another month of wearying, wearing work. Then John Selkirk became more homesick and more heartsick than ever. A prospecting party came along, looked down into the hole and saw the dirty, sweat-stained miner wearily pecking away at the hard rock.

THE SIXTY-STAMP UTICA HOIST AND MILL.

in with me," he said to them, "and I can make money, too, but I must have help. It is a good mine, wonderfully rich. Look at these specimens."

But wise Mammon smiled incredulously. As if John Selkirk were the only man with a hole in the ground into which good money could be sunk! As if John Selkirk's piece of glittering quartz selected from the richest pocket in the mine, or, perhaps, from another hole a hundred miles from it, bore any significance! There had been others with mines and specimens of ore—hundreds of

"What have you got down there?" asked one of the new-comers.

"Biggest thing in the world," said Selkirk, coming up the ladder and sitting down to rest and talk in the bright sunshine.

"Want to sell?" asked one of the party.

"Yes, I *would* sell, if I could get my price."

"What is your price?"

John Selkirk's eye ran up the slope to a far-away smoke-hazed butte. He looked that way for a minute, and then said:

"I'll tell you, I'm sick and worn out, and

CARS OF ORE FROM THE GOLD CLIFF MINE.

marts of California as that of Mackay or of Huntington or of Stanford.

But the men who bought the mine did not know what they were buying. They never had the discerning power of John Selkirk, who knew when he gave it up that he was giving away millions. They opened the vein more freely and set up a twenty-stamp mill. But they were not thrifty men and did not know all there was to know about quartz mining. Then, too, they were almost as poor as John Selkirk.

When they received their bullion from the smelter, there were many ways for it to go, and what they divided among them after the monthly debts were paid was not much. One by one the mine workers of the Selkirk claim became disgusted and left the camp to look for better properties. The last man took a contemptuous look into the shaft one day, found that it was half full of water, and in a fit of disgust packed up his little kit and left the place.

if you'll give me two hundred dollars to get home on I'll let you have it."

The men went down in the mine and looked about by the light of Selkirk's candle. They broke some of the ore, but did not like the look of it.

"We'll give you fifty dollars," said the spokesman. "It don't look like much, does it, Jim?"

"No," said Jim. "Fifty's a big price."

"All right," said Selkirk, very wearily, "I'll take it."

"And throw in the mule?"

"No, siree; I need him to get down to the river on."

The price was paid, and so for a mean little fifty dollars the great Utica Mine was sold by its original discoverer, who, had he stuck to it, might have made the name of Selkirk as mighty in the money

So again the great mine, with all its wonderful store of wealth, was abandoned. Weeds grew up in the track of the old ore-cars, the twenty-stamp mill was dismantled,

AN ORE TRAIN IN THE MINE.

A STATION IN THE UTICA MINE.

being carried off piecemeal by the miners of the neighborhood, some of whom were taking much yellow gold from the ground. In fact, Angel's had come to be regarded as one of the best camps in California. From the time that Henry Angel and James H. Carson found gold there in 1848 it had been esteemed a "good camp." The Winter brothers in 1852 had washed out nine thousand dollars from a piece of ground only two hundred feet square, and in sinking had discovered a ledge yielding two hundred dollars to the ton. But for a few years nothing wonderful had been heard from Angel's. Now, however, stories were being told of rich quartz strikes and marvellous pay ore. The stories reached Sacramento, and a young man full of plans for money-getting, and full of that certain shrewdness which begets money, heard them. This man was James G. Fair, who at that time had a few thousand dollars, all he possessed, in one little sack of dirty "town dust," which did not represent in value more than three-fourths the same amount in good, clean, honest dust from the mines,

being adulterated with black sand as it passed from trader to trader.

Young Fair took the stage for Angel's. With a trusted guide he looked all over the camp, and at last he came to Selkirk's hole-in-the-ground.

"What's down in there?" he asked, peering into the old shaft.

"Nothing but water," said the trusted guide. "There's a good property back on the hill there that I want to show you."

"But I'm going to see this first," said Fair. Pulling off his coat and taking a candle in his hand, he prepared to descend the ladder.

"Look out, Fair! It's old and rotten," said the trusted guide, referring to the ladder.

But Fair was half-way down the shaft and into a drift to which the water had not reached. He held his candle on this side and on that, and sniffed about for the dangerous drift damp which is known to lurk in old mines. He picked up several pieces of straggling quartz that had been chipped off by the last workers in the mine,

DESCENDING THE SHAFT.

and came out with these to the shaft and up the rickety ladder into the sunlight. A few curious idlers had gathered about the mouth of the shaft. What could anybody want down in Selkirk's old hole? Fair looked sharply at the quartz bits. Some he threw away; others he cracked between hard rocks, while the idlers looked on and shrugged their shoulders and smiled. Fair liked the looks of the quartz, but he said nothing. Trust James Fair for keeping his shrewd money-mouth shut when he was examining a mine in which he had suddenly become interested. Yet it was noted that while he gazed intently at one of the richest specimens, his eye, squinting half-shut in the sharp sunlight, glittered like a crumb of broken glass.

Soon afterward an expert miner went carefully through the drifts of the old Selkirk mine, and a few weeks later a skip was at work bailing out the stagnant liquid from the hole.

"Somebody's working the old Selkirk mine," they said in a camp gathering.

"Well, he can work all right enough," was the response, "but he'll be good salt pork before he ever makes it pay."

But they did not know James G. Fair. He was satisfied with the assays of the quartz, and he was prepared to spend the last grain of the dirty "town dust" in his sack in a vigorous prosecution of the work of developing the mine, which he called the Utica. He set up a mill, put men at work underground to delve and drift along the vein, and put men at work above ground, cutting and hauling timber to hold up the walls of shaft and stope; and by working on a scale of which poor John Selkirk had dreamed, but could never realize for himself, Fair saw a goodly stream of gold beginning to pour out of the mine—gold enough, indeed, to pay and feed all hands, keep the machinery in repair, and see a neat surplus coming in every month.

But though the gold flowed into Fair's coffers from the Utica, there were seasons of much discouragement. Fair found that the gold-bearing quartz vein was nearly vertical, with a slight variation toward the east. In places the ground was loose, shifty, and dangerous to dig in. Then, again, quartz would be found of an adamantine nature. The deposit, being thus complicated, often presented difficult problems, particularly when on penetrating the earth it was found to vary from the solid rock to that of a schistose character. The ground was not easy to timber, and the walls of the stopes had to be well and carefully supported. It was also necessary that the ground should be thoroughly prospected as the work proceeded.

MINERS COMING OFF THE SHIFT OF THE UTICA MINE.

THE MAN AT THE HOIST.

Fair knew that the Utica was a mine of magnificent prospects, but he also knew that it was baffling, rebellious, and expensive. His few thousands had brought him in many thousands, but he was not satisfied. This process of gaining great wealth was too slow. He heard of the riches of the Comstock ledge, which were reported to be greater than "all Bokhara's vaunted gold," and he went to visit the place which had begun to attract men of money. There were those who scoffed incredulously, but he did not listen to them. He liked the lay of the land on the Comstock, and the prospect seemed to him a very inviting one. If men wanted to dig and delve in the too-hard and too-soft earth at Angel's Camp, let them do it. He would pin his faith to the Comstock.

So, with the gold he had taken from the Utica, Fair bought mines in the richest centres of the great Comstock ledge. He prospered with dazzling quickness. Soon he joined with Flood, Mackay, and O'Brien, and in the Hale and Norcross mine these four men made their first million. Within a short time this was doubled and trebled. Fair bought more mines, and more riches became his. He left the slow old Utica to take care of itself, and went on amassing wealth until he had gained an enormous es-

LEDGE OVERHEAD IN "UPRAISE" OF THE UTICA MINE. DISCOVERING THE VEINS OF GOLD.

tate—an estate famous in his own day, and more famous since his death and the desperate fight made over it by his heirs in court.

When James G. Fair abandoned the Utica, the mill he built was dismantled, and the timbering in the shaft and stopes, as well as the buildings and the plant generally, were left to the mercy of marauders and the unkindly elements. Here it was, ready to make any man's fortune, but nobody wanted it. Everybody knew it was a hard nut to crack. Above ground and below, the Utica presented the appearance of a picturesque ruin when, in 1880, Charles D. Lane bought it for $10,000. Lane was warned against making the purchase.

"Nobody can make anything out of a mine that Jim Fair has abandoned," they said to him.

"Fair is a shrewd man," replied Lane, "and he rarely lets go of a thing that has any money in it; but I'm going to begin where he left off, and see what I can do."

Lane's friends solemnly assured each other that he was going crazy.

"It's a fool's scheme," they said. "The mine is nothing but a prospect, with three or four hundred feet of development work. Any man must be a lunatic who would try to work that rock."

Lane had very little money, but he had some ideas. Whether he derived these from a real knowledge of mining affairs or whether he got them from the spirit-world it is hard to say. There is a Mrs. Robinson, a spirit medium in San Francisco, who stoutly avers that it was she who told Lane of the real worth of the Utica. This esoteric adept declares that she can take a piece of quartz in her hand, and that, without removing the paper or cloth in which it is wrapped, she can tell all there is worth knowing about it. She says that Lane was boarding at her house at the time he was examining the Utica prospect.

"A man named Hunt had a bond on the Utica," says Mrs. Robinson, "but he failed to make the mine pay.

MEASURING A LEDGE IN FACE OF DRIFT.

and, despite his wife's declaration that no good would come of it, Lane became the owner of the mine.

He worked hard year after year in the big burrow, and his wife had plenty of opportunity for "I-told-you-so's." Still he persevered. He took out some gold, but the rich ore was not yet in sight. Lane had a sort of bulldog pertinacity which stood him in good stead in his attempt to develop the Utica, which he persisted in, though he exhausted every dollar of his own resources and was about fifteen thousand dollars in debt. His credit was entirely exhausted, and he was considered a mild sort of mining crank. Those who knew him were not surprised at the way he stuck to what seemed a hopeless enterprise.

Mr. Lane, who had been looking into it, brought a piece of rock from the prospect and put it into my hands. 'That is your fortune,' I said, holding up the rock. 'There isn't any doubt about it. Stick to that mine, and you'll be a millionaire.'"

Lane was not convinced, but secretly sent quartz specimens to the medium by different persons. In every case the spirits declared the mine to be rich, and so finally Lane set to work to raise money to buy the Utica. The money was gathered together at last, He was a hardy specimen of vigorous manhood, and remains so to-day, in his sixty-fifth year—tall, raw-boned, and fit to fight his way anywhere. He could "stay with his work" until other men had dropped from exhaustion. In those fighting days there was not an ounce of superfluous flesh on him. He could then, and he can now, undergo much privation and hardship, and issue forth from each succeeding ordeal none the worse for wear. He can remain in wet clothes and

STARTING A RAISE.
"The miners working straight up through the roof to the surface, many hundreds of feet."

The figure was conspicuous because it was one of the few ever seen there topped by a stiff silk hat. From under the brim of the hat peered the sharp eyes of Alvinza Hayward, one of the shrewdest of the old-time mining men of the Coast. Hayward had a little money, and Lane, hearing he was in town, determined to interest him in the Utica. The newcomer examined the prospect. He did not like the look of it, and would not accept Lane's assurance that the spirits had promised him much gold would be found there. Hayward was also a confirmed believer in the power of spirit mediums; they had already told him of the location of other good mining properties; but he could not accept the story of a layman, no matter how great that layman's faith.

"Well, go and have the rock read yourself," said Lane. "You'll find that it's all right."

"I'll see about it," said the non-committal Hayward. He took a few rubber boots all day. He can tramp across the roughest Alaskan country and smile at fatigue.

But while he was such a giant for endurance, he was easy with the men of the mine, and was to them, as he is to all who know him now, a congenial companion and all-round "good fellow."

"You had better give it up, Charley," said Mrs. Lane to her husband, when, deep in debt and all his credit gone, the plucky miner looked desperately about for assistance.

"Not yet," was the quiet reply. "There's gold there, and I'm going to have it." And the resolute man kept pegging away, determined to win the vast deposits of rich metal which the spirits had promised he should get out of the mine.

It was at this low tide of the Lane fortune that a gaunt, shambling figure appeared in Angel's.

AT WORK IN "STOPES."

samples of the quartz to San Francisco, and it was a good while before Lane heard from him again. Even then he did not know, of course, what Hayward's medium had reported. Lane and Hayward dickered over an arrangement for joining forces in the Utica. Lane wanted Hayward to advance him money enough to pay his debts and enable him to prosecute the work. Thirty thousand dollars would do it. But Hayward could not raise so much capital. He induced a man named W. S. Hobart, who had some money, to join him, and an arrangement was finally made by which Lane surrendered to the two other men two-thirds of the Utica property, and retained one-third himself, the mine remaining under his superintendence.

"My medium told me just what yours did about that rock," said Hayward to Lane.

"I knew she did," said Lane. "You wouldn't have come in if she hadn't. It's a big thing. Now we'll go to work in earnest."

Lane paid his debts, increased the working force, and within a few months the report went ringing through Angel's and all over the Coast that a large body of rich ore had been struck in the Utica Mine. The report was true. The spirits had "read the rock" aright. Here were millions of gold right at hand for the mere digging.

"What did I tell you?" asked Lane of his wife. "Didn't I say you'd be wearing diamonds? Those spirits never lie."

He and his partners grimly exulted over their new fortunes. But they were quiet men. There was no wild hurrah, no violent conviviality. They kept at their work.

And now there was a great stir at Angel's. Hundreds of men were set to work at the Utica. Stamp mills of the most improved design were erected, as well as reduction works and metal-saving machinery for working the tailings and getting the last response from Mother Earth that she could be made to give in gold.

It was determined to follow the almost vertical vein by probing straight down into the ground to any depth that might be nec-

"SPITTING" THE FUSE.

essary to reach and bring up the richest quartz. A shaft four by eight feet with two compartments was sunk. The cost of this was considerable, being at the rate of seventeen dollars a foot, and only two feet a day could be excavated. The same harsh and baffling conditions were encountered as those which had resisted Selkirk and Fair, but no efforts were spared in preparing to wrest the gold from the bowels of the earth.

It was Homeric labor. Far in the forest an army of men were cutting down yellow pines, and more men were loading them upon wagons hauled by long teams to the mine. Other men were sawing and hewing the great timbers, and were lowering them by cables down deep into the earth, and still others were setting them up and bolting them fast to keep the treacherous walls from breaking down and destroying the miners who were plying their drills and moving mountains of rock to be hoisted aloft by great engines, and to be crushed by other engines, and washed and sifted and strained in the gathering of the golden specks for which men give their best blood.

But thick and strong as were the timbers bracing the walls of the shaft and stopes, there were times when they were not strong enough. There would come a warning rumble, when the men would flee, and a mighty crash would resound through the deeps, and the stout timbers would be splintered and broken into bits.

A tremendous cave occurred in the summer of 1888, when a great section of the timbering was destroyed. The cave reached to the surface, and shows to-day in a great depression in the ground near the hoisting works.

It was found necessary to use heavier and still heavier timbers, and in the end, as simple timbering was found ineffective, a system known as timbering and storming was

A MINER. CHARACTER SKETCH.

adopted, and is now used throughout the mine.

Four shafts have been sunk in the ledge, the deepest being nearly two thousand feet. One of these has been almost entirely retimbered twice with pine and oak, involving much expense and much loss of time in mining. In order to construct speedily a new shaft, not only was the work begun at the top, but a level was run over from the first Utica shaft at its bottom, and a "raise" started, the miners working straight up through the roof to the surface, many hundreds of feet, while the rocks they blasted and the earth they shovelled fell down through the man-way of their platform into what they called the "bull-pen," and were hauled to the Utica shaft and there hoisted and dumped. This was exceedingly hazardous work—first, because of the constant danger of caving; and, secondly, because the gas caused by the blasts would nearly smother the men. Sometimes it would be three hours before the air would clear so that the miners could return to their drilling. This work, as well as nearly all that done in the mine, and particularly the timbering, has been very expensive.

So that while the present owners have tamed the rebellious Utica, and made it the great gold-bearing power that it is, it has

AIR-DRILLING FACE OF DRIFT.

cost them millions to do it. But the returns have been colossal.

And now Bret Harte's Angel's was in a fair way to forget itself and its old traditions. The opening of the rich quartz deposit was a great thing for the quiet, sleepy little town. It changed its rough aspect completely.

To-day only a trace of the frontier mining town remains in its precincts. It is a pretty town—typical of a hundred places in California—and no more. The bones of Abner Dean perhaps lie mouldering somewhere on the hillside, but his spirit doubtless regrets the old, wild days as it hovers above the rugged cañons. There is one main street in Angel's now, and the people are very proper indeed. The town wears an appearance of prosperity. The residence portion radiates from the one business street out into a rolling country, with the typical characteristics of the central part of California in the foothills of the Sierras. It is now the supply centre of a large mining section.

MINERS AT WORK CROSS-CUTTING FROM A STATION.

As the three partners proceeded with their labors, their company absorbed other mining properties adjacent to the Utica, chief of these being the Stickles, which had been fairly developed.

Through seasons of non-productiveness, when new shafts were being made, or when, because of accident, the works of the mine have been shut down, the owners have had their faith in the Utica severely tested, but they have believed in it from the first of their labors there, and their faith has been greatly rewarded. They are said to have taken from the shafts of their great mine over seven million dollars in gold. As much as nine

hundred thousand dollars' worth of bullion has been secured in a single month.

The Utica is the greatest gold mine on the Pacific Coast, one of the wonders of wonderful California. It is a place of potent fascination to the traveller, and it well repays a student of mining to make careful observation of the methods pursued in taking out and treating the quartz. Indeed, so perfect are the appliances, and so educational the study of them, that the philanthropic owners have founded and fostered at the Utica what is known as the "Gold-Mining Kindergarten," composed chiefly of students of the State University at

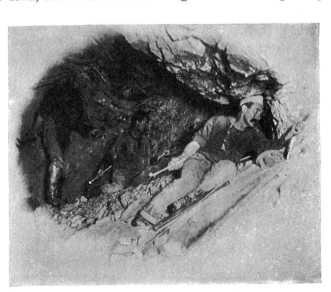

IN THE "STOPES."

Berkeley. In this school practical mining is learned by a class of young men who advance far more rapidly than those who take a merely theoretical course. This is conceded to be of great benefit to the State, where mining development, no doubt, will be going on for centuries to come.

"The Utica runs Angel's," is the saying there, and, in turn, Angel's runs the Utica, for there is where the real masters of the mine, the men of brawn who delve in its deeps and darks, reside. They have braved its terrors of caving earth, its foul damps, its roaring blasts, and the subterranean sea of flames that has run through the drifts and shafts, demons of the underland, seeking out men to destroy them.

It was these dauntless men who, under their brave leader, Superintendent Tom Lane, fought the big fire of July, 1895. Each year they had been putting twelve thousand great forest trees into the mine, and the element which destroys dead wood had always been ready to consume the miles of dry timbering. Nobody knows how the fire began.

"Put up a bulkhead—here!" shouted Lane.

The men, half-blinded by the smoke and choking with the fumes, set to work. They piled high a breastwork of timbers and stones to keep the flames within bounds,

DUMPING THE WASTE.

and smother them, if possible. But hardly had the bulkhead been built before there was a tremendous explosion, and the whole mass of which it was composed was blown back, the fragments scattering far. Luckily, none of the brave workers were killed, though many were nearly suffocated, and required medical assistance at once. Other bulkheads were built, but the gas formed behind each of them, and they were blown away as it ignited from the flames. Explosion after explosion could be heard inside the mine, and there was a rattling of stones and a crashing of earth as the timbers gave way.

"Well," said Lane, "there's only one thing to be done now—fill her up with water. Start the engines there! Get your monitors to work!"

This flooding of the great mine meant the loss of hundreds of thousands of dollars and a long delay. Ninety hours there were from the time the big monitors began to discharge their great streams into the mine to the time when the last blazing stick of pine was submerged.

Then began the work of hoisting the water out of the mine. Night and day for eight weeks the great skips and pumps, regular and extra—all that could be set to work—were kept constantly employed. When the water was lowered sufficiently, the miners went back to their damp stations, and soon the drills were clanking again.

And what has been done with the gold taken from the great mine?

Hayward has used his money to make money, and certainly the influence of his share of the Utica gold has been widely felt. Under the advice of the spirits he has invested in various other mines, nearly all of which have been productive. He has bought large areas of land in California, and buildings and lots. He owns one of the tallest skyscrapers in San Francisco, a great store and office building, erected at the behest of his spiritual guides. He has a large villa tract in San Mateo. Here in a fine mansion, surrounded by beautiful, well-kept grounds, a deer park, and ample conservatories, he lives and enjoys life in a quiet way. He is a man of power and hard to combat in a financial fight, as the men who fought him in an Alameda County water-supply contest found to their sorrow. He was bound to dictate in the matter of the control and distribution of water for the city of Oakland and the neighboring towns

CLEAN-UP OF MILL.

Some of the stamps of the Utica Mine may be seen beneath the letters " A," " B."

on the east side of the Bay of San Francisco. Here Utica gold played a potent part, and Utica gold and native shrewdness, backed by the advice of who shall say how many spirits, won the day, and bred more gold for the hardy Hayward.

The good people of San Mateo have had a taste of his fighting power. They wanted to incorporate their town, and fixed limits to include Hayward's home acres; but incorporation would mean more taxes, and Hayward refused to be incorporated. The good people laughed at him. They said one man could do little against a whole town, but one man did a good deal—enough, in fact, to make the map of San Mateo town look like a congressional district in Ohio, all one-sided, elongated, crescented, with the Hayward acres left out.

Alvinza Hayward is a man of medium height. His hair is almost white, and he wears a close-cropped Vandyke beard. He is never seen without a high silk hat. This is the only head-gear that he ever wears.

This hat has a peculiar sort of flat brim. He wears a dark suit, generally with a frock coat. He has very few friends whom he admits to any degree of intimacy, for he is very self-contained, and does not wear his heart upon his sleeve. He is, however, in a quiet way an exceedingly charitable man, and those who think he loves money for its own sake make a great mistake.

It is difficult to differentiate between Lane and Hayward when it comes to their belief in spirits. Undoubtedly it is the truth to say that they are both devout believers. To them the occult as a governing force is as important as the rise and fall of the markets, and as real. It enters into all their daily calculations. They are both reverent believers in spiritualism, and the arguments for their faith, which they will sometimes advance to their friends, are many and often convincing.

Hobart, the man whom Hayward induced to join him in the Utica enterprise, did not live to enjoy his share of the gold. He died in 1893, leaving an enormous estate. His interest in the Utica is now owned by his son, Walter S. Hobart.

As for Lane, who struggled so long to develop the Utica, and who has had his share of the gold, his investments at home and far afield have prospered exceedingly. He has not gone in for town lots or country lands. With him it has been mines, mines, mines. Utica gold, under spiritual guidance, was directed to La Fortuna Mine, in Arizona. This is one of the great bonanzas of the Pacific Coast, and from its veins were taken the largest pockets of high-grade ore ever dug from the depths of any American mine. A large number of stamps are pounding there at present, and the prospect for future wealth is said to be very great.

In 1896 Lane subscribed one hundred thousand dollars for the purpose of the Bryan campaign. This at once brought him to the front as a national figure in politics, and if the Bryan movement had been successful, he would have been assigned a post very near to the person of the great Democratic leader. But Lane is in no sense a local politician. He is, however, always prepared to support any broad national movement in which he takes an interest.

Utica gold has gone north to breed more gold in the Arctic. Mr. Lane has put more money into Alaskan mining enterprises than any other man in the world. He has sailed ships to Nome freighted with all manner of mining-camp supplies. He has built stores and warehouses and piled up mountains of coal on the Arctic beach, where fuel was not, and carried much lumber there. He built and equipped the northernmost railroad in the world, that from Nome to Anvil City, on which I travelled last summer in a journey over the tundra to the wonderful placers which Mr. Lane was developing along the bleak Anvil Creek. To see Lane seated on a rough bench on a flat car, swaying and rocking over the great marsh, one would not recognize in him the millionaire. But there I saw the man who had the grit to take up the Utica when shrewd James G. Fair had abandoned it, and spend his money like water before a penny was returned. His Nome enterprise was not less hazardous than the Utica, but he will double his money in Alaska this year.

And so, first and last, the Utica has been a great power. The influence of its wonderful store of gold has been felt in many quarters near to and far away from Angel's. Directly and indirectly many a man has prospered because of the unearthing of its great wealth.

The spirits did it all? Who shall say? Happy spirits if they can so control the fortunes of mortals! And happy mortals if they can get for guides such benign, far-seeing spirits!

A STATION IN THE UTICA MINE.

A Miner's Sunday in Coloma

California (1891)

A MINER'S SUNDAY IN COLOMA.

(FROM THE WRITER'S CALIFORNIA JOURNAL, 1849–50.)

THE principal street of Coloma was alive with crowds of moving men, passing and repassing, laughing, talking, and all appearing in the best of humor: Negroes from the Southern States swaggering in the expansive feeling of runaway freedom; mulattoes from Jamaica trudging arm-in-arm with Kanakas from Hawaii; Peruvians and Chilians claiming affinity with the swarthier Mexicans; Frenchmen, Germans, and Italians fraternizing with one another and with the cockney fresh from the purlieus of St. Giles; an Irishman, with the dewdrop still in his eye, tracing relationship with the ragged Australian; Yankees from the Penobscot chatting and bargaining with the genial Oregonians; a few Celestials scattered here and there, their pigtails and conical hats recalling the strange pictures that took my boyish fancy while studying the geography of the East; last of all, a few Indians, the only indigenous creatures among all these exotics, lost, swallowed up — out of place like

"rari nantes in gurgite vasto."

It was a scene that no other country could ever imitate. Antipodes of color, race, religion, language, government, condition, size, capability, strength and morals were there, within that small village in the mountains of California, all impressed with but one purpose,— impelled with but one desire.

A group of half a dozen Indians especially attracted my attention. They were strutting about in all the glory of newly acquired habiliments; but with this distinction — that one suit of clothes was sufficient to dress the whole crowd. The largest and best-looking Indian had appropriated the hat and boots, and without other apparel walked about as proudly as any city clerk. Another was lost in an immense pair of pantaloons. A third sported nothing but a white shirt with ruffled bosom. A fourth flaunted a blue swallow-tailed coat, bespangled with immense brass buttons. A fifth was decked with a flashy vest; while the sixth had nothing but a red bandana, which was carefully wrapped around his neck. Thus what would scarcely serve one white man just as effectually accommodated six Indians.

The street was one continuous din. Thimble-riggers, French monte dealers, or string-game tricksters were shouting aloud at every corner: "Six ounces, gentlemen, no one can tell where the little joker is!" or "Bet on the jack, the jack's the winning card! Three ounces no man can turn up the jack!" or "Here's the place to git your money back! The veritable string game! Here it goes! Three, six, twelve ounces no one can put his finger in the loop!" But rising above all this ceaseless clamor was the shrill voice of a down-east auctioneer, who, perched on a large box in front of a very small canvas booth, was disposing of the various articles in the shebang behind him, "all at a bargain." What a ragged, dirty, unshaven, good-natured assemblage! — swallowing the stale jests of the "crier" with the greatest guffaws, and bidding with all the recklessness of half-tipsy brains and with all the confidence of capacious, well-stuffed bags. Behind a smaller box, to the left of the Yankee, was a Jew in a red cap and scarlet flannel shirt, busy with his scales and leaden weights, to weigh out the "dust" from the various purchasers. There was no fear of the weights being heavier than the law allows, or that the tricky Jew by chance should place the half-ounce on the scales when there was but a quarter due. That there should be a few pennyweights too many made no difference; it is only the hungry purse that higgles about weights or prices. A little bad brandy and a big purse made a miner wonderfully important and magnanimous; and he regarded everything below an ounce as unworthy of attention.

This German Jew was also barkeeper. Beside him were a few tin cups, and a whole army of long and short necked, gaily labeled bottles, from which he dealt out horrible compounds for fifty cents a drink. His eye brightened as he perceived coming up the street a crowd of rollicking, thirsty, sunburned fellows, fresh from their "diggins" among the hills. But the quick eye of the auctioneer also singled them out and read their wants.

"Here's a splendid pair of brand-new boots! cowhide, double-soled, triple-pegged, waterproof boots! The very thing for you, sir, fit your road-smashers exactly; just intended, cut out, made for your mud-splashers alone; going for only four ounces and a half — four and a half! and gone — for four and a half ounces; walk up here and weigh out your dust."

"Wet your boots, old boy!" sang out the companions of the purchaser.

The barkeeper, with his weights already on the scales, exclaimed, "Shtand back, poys, and let de shentlemens to de bar."

The newcomers approached, crowding tumultuously around their companion of the boots, who, drawing out a long and well-filled buckskin bag, tossed it to the expectant Jew with as much carelessness as if it were only dust.

"Thar's the bag, old feller! weigh out the boots and eight lickers. Come, boys, call for what you like; it's my treat — go it big, fellers! all one price."

"Vat ye takes?" asks the barkeeper, after weighing out the amount due and handing the purse back to its owner.

"Brandy straight," "brandy punch," "brandy sling," "gin cocktail," and thus they went on, each one calling for a different drink.

Then the bargaining began. Butcher-knives for crevicing, tin pans, shovels, picks, clothing of all colors, shapes, and sizes; hats and caps of every style; coffee, tea, sugar, bacon, flour, liquors of all grades in stiff-necked bottles — in a word, almost everything that could be enumerated — were disposed of at a furious rate; so that in an hour's time the contents of the little grocery were distributed among the jolly crowd.

Suddenly there was a great noise of shouting and hurrahing away up the street, and, the crowd heaving and separating upon either side, on came a dozen half-wild, bearded miners, fine, wiry, strapping fellows, on foaming horses, lashing them to the utmost, and giving the piercing scalp-halloo of the Comanches! They suddenly halted in front of Winter's hotel, and while the greater number dismounted and tumultuously entered the bar-room for refreshment a few of the remainder made themselves conspicuous by acts of daring horsemanship — picking up knives from the ground while at full gallop, Indian-like whirling on the sides of their steeds, then up and off like the wind and, while apparently dashing into the surrounding crowd, suddenly reining in their horses upon their haunches, and whirling them upon their hind legs, then without a stop dashing off as furiously in the opposite direction. These few proved to be Doniphan's wild riders, who even excelled the Mexican caballeros in their feats of horsemanship. At last, all together once more they came sweeping down the street, apparently reckless of life and limb. As they passed, the scurrying footmen cheered them on with great good nature. The crowd closed again and in a brief time everything was as restless as ever.

Passing up the street, I came to a large unfinished frame-house, the sashless windows and doorway crowded with a motley crew, apparently intent upon something solemn happening within. After a little crowding and pushing I looked over the numberless heads in front, and saw — could I believe my eyes? — a preacher, as ragged and as hairy as myself, holding forth to an attentive audience. Though the careless and noisy crowd was surging immediately without, all was quiet within. He spoke well and to the purpose and warmed every one with his fine and impassioned delivery. He closed with a benediction but prefaced it by saying: "There will be divine service in this house next Sabbath — if, in the meantime, I hear of no new diggin's!"

The audience silently streamed out, the greater part directing their steps to a large, two-story frame-house across the street. This was

AN AUCTION IN COLOMA.

the hotel *par excellence* of the town; one could easily perceive that by its long white colonnade in front, and its too numerous windows in the upper story.

A large saloon occupied the whole front of the building. Filling up the far side of the room was the gaudy and well-stocked bar, where four spruce young fellows in shirt-sleeves and flowing collars were busily engaged dealing out horrible compounds to thirsty customers strung along the whole length of the counter. The other three sides of the saloon were crowded with monte tables, each one of which was surrounded with a crowd of old and young so that it was almost impossible to obtain a glimpse of the dealers or their glittering banks. There was a perfect babel of noises! English, French, Spaniards, Portuguese, Italians, Kanakas, Chilians, all were talking in their respective languages. Glasses were jingling, money was rattling, and, crowning all, two fiddlers in a distant corner were scraping furiously on their instruments, seemingly the presiding divinities of this variegated pandemonium!

Crowding, inch by inch, into one of these motley groups, I found myself at last in front of a large table, neatly covered with blue cloth, upon which was a mass of Mexican silver dollars piled up in ounce or sixteen-dollar stacks. Immediately facing me was the banker; a well-dressed, middle-aged, quiet little man, with one of the most demure countenances imaginable. Beside him was the croupier, a very boy, whose duty it was to rake in the winnings and pay out the losses, which he did with wonderful dexterity.

Fronting the dealer, and dividing the silver into two equal portions, was a large Chinese box of exquisite construction. Upon it were ranged half a dozen packs of French and Spanish cards, several large masses of native gold, and a dozen or more buckskin bags of all sizes and conditions containing dust. Dollars and half-dollars were piled upon these purses — some with a few, others with a greater number thereon. One unacquainted with the game might guess for a day and not be able to hit upon the object of this arrangement, but a close observer might read elation or depression in the anxious eyes of the players, as the weight upon these bags was either diminished or increased. These purses were in pawn; the dollars and half-dollars were the counters wherewith the banker numbered the ounces or half-ounces that might be owing to the bank.

"There's another millstone on the pile," groaned a thin-faced, watery-eyed little fellow in a hickory shirt and walnut pantaloons, as he saw another dollar added to his dust-bag.

"Take off two o' them air buttons," laughed a fat-faced man in red shirt and Chinese cap.

"I won two ounces on the deuce; another bet like that, and my bag's not for your mill, old feller!"

The cards were all out, and the "old feller" was shuffling them for a new deal; during which operation he cast a furtive glance about the table to see if there were any new customers to bite at his game, or, perhaps, to note if any of those who had bitten seemed to be cooling off — a weakness which he hastened to counteract by singing out: "Barkeeper!" and inquiring "What will the gentlemen take to drink?" This invitation was given in such a quiet and insinuating manner that one hesitated to decline for fear of wounding the delicate sensibilities of the banker. Each called for what he wished, and all concluded to "fight the tiger" a little while longer. The sprightly barkeeper was back in a twinkling, with a large waiter covered with glasses. These he distributed with wonderful dexterity, remembering perfectly what each one had ordered; so that, much to the player's surprise, he found his own glass chosen from among twenty and placed before him. That barkeeper had a niche in his brain for every man at the table.

The drinking over, the glasses were whisked away, and all hands were again ready 'for the game.

"It's your cut," said the banker, reaching the cards towards our watery-eyed acquaintance.

"Jack and deuce! Make your bets, gentlemen."

The jack appeared to be the favorite; ounce after ounce was staked upon it; two more cards were thrown out.

"Seven and ace. Come down, gents; come down!" The seven was the favorite by odds.

"All down, gents?" inquired the dealer, as he rapped his knuckles on the table.

"Hold on!" exclaimed a shrill, puerile voice, as if coming from under the table. Every one looked down; and there was apparently a curly-headed boy, whose mouth was little above the level of the bank. He cautiously, coolly and methodically thrust forth a small hand, and laid down two dimes upon the ace. Every one laughed — all but the dealer, who with the same placidity thrust back the dimes and dampened the little fellow's ardor by observing:

"We don't take dimes at this bank."

But no, the little fellow had spunk; he was not so easily dashed. Picking up his dimes, his hand suddenly reappeared, this time holding a very weighty buckskin bag apparently filled with the yellow dust. This he tossed upon the ace, exclaiming:

"There! I guess you'll take that. Six ounces on the ace!"

Every one was astonished. All looked around

THE FARO PLAYERS.

to see if he had any relatives or friends in the crowd. He appeared to be entirely alone and a stranger to every one; but the play began—and, strange to say, the ace won!

"Good!" "Bully!" "Lucky boy!" were the exclamations on every side. The fortunate little gambler pocketed his bag and placed upon the deuce the six ounces he had just won.

"Bar the porte!" shouted the boy as the dealer was about to turn the cards. It was well for him that he cried out in time, for the jack was in the door. It was a narrow escape, but the little fellow was safe for this time. The cards were brushed aside and others took their places. The betting went bravely on. The boy laid his money on the deuce and, wonderful to say, it won! He was now the gainer by twelve ounces. He was the hero of the table; all eyes were upon him; and it was seen that he was not as young as he seemed—an old head upon a child's shoulders! For the remainder of the deal old players regulated their bets by his, and he carried them along upon the wave. The bank looked a little sickly from this bleeding.

The deal being out, the banker, the same cool imperturbable figure, chose another pack of cards, and shuffled and cut and reshuffled them until the patience of the crowd was almost exhausted. It was the boy's cut, and a lay-out was made.

"Jack and queen. Come down with your dust. Gentlemen, make your bets."

The little fellow was very much puzzled; it was a hard matter to choose between the jack and the queen. Another lay-out was made: the deuce against the seven.

"Twenty-five ounces on the deuce," said the little man, piling all his winnings around the card. But few other bets were made; the older hands were afraid this sudden luck would change, and they all held back. The plucky lad was pitted against the man of fifty—youth, enthusiasm and a dare-all luck arrayed against the craft and cunning of an experienced gambler! How our sympathies were warmed by the fearlessness of the boy! The play began; the deck was faced; and, as I live, the deuce was in the door! The boy won the full amount of his bet.

The successful urchin was the least excited person in the room. He hauled in his winnings as carelessly as if those stacks of dollars were only chips. Another shuffle, and another lay-out was made. The field was now given up entirely to the two antagonists. The ace and the five were the cards; against all our hints the boy staked his fifty ounces on the five. We were breathless with fear; the dealer himself paused a little before drawing the cards,—but at length the deck was faced, and slowly and

cautiously the cards were drawn, one by one—deuce, tray, king, queen, and seven appear in succession—and then—the five! The boy was again victorious: his fifty ounces were now one hundred. The last round made a huge chasm in the appearance of the bank, and the table immediately in front of the little hero was absolutely covered with money.

The banker was as cool and methodical as ever; taking a fresh pack he shuffled it carefully and made another lay-out. The boy bet his hundred ounces and was again victorious! Two hundred ounces were now piled up before him. We advised him to desist, not to tempt his luck too far; but he coolly replied: "I'll break that bank or it'll break me!"

Did any one ever hear of such determination, even in a man? He increased in our estimation, and we liked him all the better for his grit. More than half the bank was his already, a fortune in itself! but the little, round, gray eyes of the boy were not upon his winnings, but were feeding eagerly upon the moiety that was not yet his.

"Queen and tray. Come down," said the dealer.

"How much have you in the bank?" asked the boy.

"A hundred and fifty ounces."

"I tap the bank upon the queen."

This would decide the game. A stillness as of death was upon the crowd; our breath was hushed; our very hearts almost ceased to beat; the suspense became painful; even the banker paused, and wiped the cold drops from his brow.

The deck was faced at last, and calmly, steadily, and without hurry the cards were drawn, one by one. One—two—three—four—five—he had lost! The queen had thrown him; and his entire winnings were ruthlessly swept away by the sharp croupier beyond.

Dizzy and sick with the result, we turned our eyes upon the loser; he bore himself bravely, and did not seem to feel the loss half as sensibly as ourselves. He looked about with a stern, defying air, as if to chide us for our sympathy. As yet he had lost nothing; his large buckskin bag was still intact. Laying it upon the table, with the air of a Cæsar, he put his all upon the throw, defying fate to do her worst! Our pity was suddenly changed to admiration. We felt that he was lost; but we were sure he would die game.

The cards were again shuffled and cut. The seven and the king were laid out; the boy chose the king. The cards were drawn, slowly and steadily; at last the seven appeared; and the game was ended. He saw his well-filled purse stowed away along with many others within that Chinese box and, whistling "O Californy," turned his back upon the scene. The crowd parted sympathetically to let him through; and he strutted out with all the importance of a noted hero, the eyes of the astonished and admiring assemblage following him to the door.

I passed out silently after him and joined him in the street. I could scarcely find words to express my sympathy for his loss. He looked

At the next corner I stopped for a few minutes to watch the manœuvers of a tall, slim man, who was explaining the mysteries of thimble-rigging to a crowd of lately arrived gold hunters. He was young, and had a long, high-bridged nose, blue eyes, a florid complexion, and thin flaxen hair, without even the slightest appearance of a beard upon his chin. From

COLOMA IN 1857. (PHOTOGRAPHED BY E. SIMAS, FROM AN EARLY PICTURE.)

[The site of the Marshall Monument is on the hill back of the town on a line vertical with the bridge. The site of Sutter's mill, which was torn down in 1856, is at the extreme right of the picture where the race is shown.]

at me furtively with one eye, without ceasing to whistle. I took his arm and, leading him around the corner of the house, begged to know the amount of his loss, and if he had any money on which to come and go. He did not cease his whistling, but planted himself firmly before me and looked up. I took out my purse, and offered him a part; the whistling instantly ceased; his face swelled out into a broad and homely grin. Looking cautiously around for fear of being overheard, he whispered:

"Mum's the word; I believe you're a good egg! You want to know how much was in that bag? Well, I'll tell you; just four pounds of duck-shot mixed,—and—nothing more; what a swa'rin' and a cussin' when they open it!" and the little imp laughed till the tears were in his eyes. I, too, tried to laugh, but my sympathies were shocked; and I turned away from that premature scamp and strode off with a heavy weight upon my spirits. But I had not gone far until the trick was even too much for my feelings; and I laughed long and heartily at its audacity.

his language I saw that he was English—"a Sydney chap," no doubt, fresh from the galleys; there were thousands like him in the country. He was standing with his left foot upon a low box, so as to make a table of his thigh, on which were three small wooden thimbles, and a little pellet of paper, with the movements of which he completely mystified his audience. With what dexterity he moved the little joker from cup to cup! and yet so slowly that every one could see it in its passage. Now you would be willing to swear it was safely ensconced under the farthest thimble, for you saw it distinctly when the cup was raised; but you might as well give up your money at once as to stake it on the movements of the little joker, who was the very genius of the thimble; even, like him of Aladdin's lamp, becoming visible or invisible as its owner willed. In vain did he invite a bet; no one was bold enough to risk six ounces. Then the thimble-rigger changed his tactics; he saw there were many willing and anxious to bet, were they but half assured there was no hidden trickery in this manual dexterity. His movements, therefore, became slow and careless, as though he supposed there was no one there disposed to risk his money on the game. He was so absent-minded as to turn his head away, as though looking for some one beyond the crowd, but still moving his thimbles and the joker so carelessly that the little pellet was at last left outside of one of the cups, when it should have been totally concealed within. The gambler's mind was evidently not on his game, or he never would have made this mistake, which might be taken advantage of by some of his sharp-sighted auditors. A black-eyed little fellow had been intently watching him for some time past. He had the dress and appearance of a miner, but his hands were soft and delicate — a fact you noted as, taking advantage of the thimble-rigger's carelessness, he cautiously reached forward, and very dexterously swept the joker from the gambler's thigh, without the latter being aware of his conduct. This trick created a marked sensation among the bystanders; so much so, that the Englishman's attention was recalled to his game.

There was now an evident willingness to bet on the part of three or four of the lookers-on, but a swarthy miner, with his face covered with an immense black beard, got the start of all the rest and, trembling with excitement, exclaimed:

" I 'll bet you ten ounces the 's no ball under thar at all."

" Put down your dust," replied the gambler. The miner drew a well-filled buckskin bag from his pocket, but, before he staked his money, had the foresight to declare that the gambler must not touch the thimbles, that he himself must have the privilege of lifting the cups. The Englishman assented to this. Without the least hesitation the miner put down his dust. We all circled closer, laughing within ourselves at the evident discomfiture of the careless gambler. The miner raised the nearest thimble, the ball was not there; he lifted the second, it was not there; he laid his fingers on the third and last and, with a triumphant laugh at his evident good luck, lifted it likewise. But his laugh was suddenly changed to a short, quick, smothered cry of astonishment. We all looked down; and there, lying as cozy as an egg in its nest, was the wonderful little joker!

The miner had been completely fooled. There had been two little paper pellets, and the dark-eyed man was a confederate.

Leaving the thimble-rigger, I passed along under the colonnade of the hotel, my ears almost deafened by the rattling of money and the hubbub of various dialects; and, piercing all, like the shrieking of termagants, came the noise of the tortured fiddles. The saloon was filled with a mass of men, laughing, talking, gambling, drinking, and all apparently in the best of humor. It was no use trying for admittance, so I stepped down to the next house, where there was another large assemblage filling up half the street and intently watching something that was happening in the midst of them.

Edging my way with a good deal of difficulty, I at last saw a long, slab-sided, sleepy-looking Yankee, who was expatiating on the wonders of a small brass padlock, which he held up to the admiration of the crowd, declaring it to be " the wonder of the world," " the very essence of mechanical ingenuity," and " a thing that puzzles the scientific, considerable." And, as a voucher for the truth of his statement, he was willing and ready to wager any amount from ten ounces to a hundred that no man in the crowd could open it within the space of two minutes.

The crowd was agape with wonder; the lock was passed from hand to hand; it was twisted, turned, and tried in a hundred different ways, but all to no purpose,—it withstood the most rigid scrutiny. Some were willing to give it up in despair; but there were others whom the very difficulty of the undertaking impelled to still greater exertions. At last it fell into the hands of a rough, hairy, raw-boned fellow with the mouth and jaw of a bulldog, every feature of whose countenance showed an inflexibility of purpose to overcome every obstacle, whether for evil or for good. He twisted and turned the miniature lock into every conceivable position, searching for the hidden spring. At last he found it. He was astounded at his own success. He gave a furtive look at the owner, to see if he had been observed; but the Yankee was absorbed in conversation with a neighbor, to whom he was narrating the history of the wonderful lock, and did not even appear to know that this bulldog fellow had it in his possession. The latter, now satisfied with his success, gave his neighbor, a thick-headed German, a nudge with his elbow. The two withdrew somewhat from the crowd, and there, in a measure secure from observation, he showed his companion the hidden spring, and advised him to bet twenty ounces on the result, and agreed to " go his halves." The German eagerly accepted the proposition; and the two reëntered the ring with the triumph of discovery in their faces. The German laid down his bag, and on the top of it the Yankee piled his twenty Spanish doubloons. The gambler drew out his watch to note the time; and handing the wizard lock to his opponent, told him to begin.

The German took the lock, and with a smile

A SUNDAY AFTERNOON SPORT.

of derision put his finger on the spring; and lo! the lock was still a lock. Perhaps he mistook the knob whereon to press; but no! that was the boss that but a moment since unhasped the lock. He pressed it again with a firmer hand; but it was of no use, the clasp was still unclasped. The German felt dimly that he had been victimized; the two minutes were rapidly passing away; large drops of perspiration oozed from his forehead,—his hands trembled with excitement,—every knob on the brazen puzzle was convulsively pressed,—but all in vain. The time was up — and his money lost! With a pitiable countenance he turned to his partner in misfortune, but he had gone! His spirit sank within him. He must bear the loss himself! His missing partner was of course a confederate of the Yankee's, and before the money was staked had quietly neutralized the spring upon which the German had so confidently relied.

By this time my appetite began to warn me of the near approach of noon. There were any number of eating-houses and booths, but which to choose I could not tell. However, suffering myself to be guided in a measure by the crowd which was now streaming to the other side of the river, I soon found myself in front of " Little's Hotel," the largest frame building on the right bank of the river, serving in the treble capacity of post-office, store, and tavern. Here I found all my acquaintances, who, like me, were on the search for a good dinner; and who

had been induced to go there by the encomiums of " older hands," who every Sunday had made a custom of visiting Coloma for the express purpose of having one good dinner in the week. The first sounding of the gong had already brought a hungry crowd, apparently large enough to carry away the whole building. They were assembled in front of the closed door of the long dining-room, anxiously awaiting the second signal, when they were to be admitted.

While awaiting the opening of the door, my attention was directed to a diminutive, middle-aged Irishman, who was busily engaged narrating to a companion the various wonders and mysteries that " complately bothered him in this wondther of a place." After many famous adventures he had found himself on the bank of the river, hunting for a " quicksilver masheen," when the gong sounded for dinner; and he thus continued his narrative:

" An' do ye see, Dinnis, I jist went down be the wather to indivor to git a sight of a quicksilver masheen; for I niver seen the loike in this counthry yit; an' I had a great inclination to luck at one, ef it was oney to see the shape ov it, but I did n't see ony thing like the quicksilver masheen at all, at all; but a man that was there prospectin' tould me for to come up to the tavern, an' there wos wun there sittin' out ov doors jist forninst the house. Jist thin I heerd a clatherin' as ov that big mounthin wos tumblen down on us. I did n't know the manen' ov it far a long time; whin it sthruck me right strate — it wos nothin' but the quicksilver masheen. So I hurried up the bank, an' thin I saw evry wan runnin' up this way, as ef it wos a rale Irish foight they were goin' to see, an' not the quicksilver masheen at all. Whin I sees thim all runnin' like pigs afther pratee skins—stir your stumps, Condy, says I, or you 'll niver git near the baste. An' thin, I run loike the rist ov thim; an' whin I got to where the noise come from,— what do you think I seen, Dinnis? Why, nothin' but a big nagur batin' the tamboreen!"

We had scarcely time enough to laugh at Condy's disappointment in search of the

ners. At home, one would associate such a crowd with the deck of a Mississippi steamboat, or the platform of an Alleghany River raft, with iron forks and spoons, and tin plates spread on a rough pine board for a table; but here they lorded it over every luxury that money could procure. There was not a single coat in the whole crowd, and certainly not over half a dozen vests, and neither neckties nor collars. But then, to make amends for these deficiencies, there were any number and variety of fancy shirts, from the walnut-stained homespun of the Missourian to the embroidered blouse of the sallow Frenchman. Never before was I so fully impressed with the truth

"ROUGHS IN TOWN." (ADAPTED FROM A SKETCH BY HUBERT BURGESS OF AN INCIDENT IN THE MINES.)

"quicksilver masheen" when the "tamborine" again sounded; the door flew open, and in a few minutes the long, narrow, dining-room was crowded with at least three hundred miners, seated at a well-furnished table and enjoying the unusual luxury of a chair to sit on, with silver-plated forks and spoons, and other little knickknacks of civilized society. The dinner was really excellent, and every one appeared heartily to enjoy it.

When the edge of my appetite had in a measure been ground away, I took occasion to look up and down the table, and I could but wonder how I happened among such a collection of uncouth men. The contrast was certainly startling between the snow-white tablecloth, china dishes, silver forks and spoons, and the unwashed, half-famished, sunburnt crowd of hungry and bearded mi-

of the old adage that "dress makes the man," for I doubt if the whole world could present to a stranger's eye a crowd of rougher or apparently lower characters than were then seated around that hospitable table. And yet many of these men were lawyers and physicians, and the rest principally farmers and mechanics from the "States"; who now with their long beards and fierce mustaches looked anything else than the quiet citizens they were at home. Men who formerly were effeminacy itself in dress and manners were here changed into rough and swaggering braves, with a carelessness of appearance and language that a semi-civilized condition of society alone could permit.

Men pocketed their pride in California in those days. I met in the mines lawyers and physicians, of good standing at home, who were acting as barkeepers, waiters, hostlers, and teamsters. An ex-judge of oyer and terminer was driving an ox-team from Coloma to Sacramento. One man who had been a State senator and secretary of state in one of our western commonwealths was doing a profitable business at manufacturing " cradles," while an ex-governor of one of our southwestern States played the fiddle in a gambling saloon. These things were hardly remarked. Every one went to the Slope with the determination to make money; and if the mines did not afford it, the next inquiry was what pursuit or business would the sooner accomplish the desired end. Thousands who had not the necessary stamina for the vicissitudes of a miner's life, nor yet the means of going into any of the various channels of trade, were for a time compelled to serve in capacities far beneath their deserts, until time and means should justify them in choosing for themselves.

Charles B. Gillespie.

"BROKE."

CALIFORNIANA.

ANECDOTES OF THE MINES.

BY HUBERT BURGESS.

One Way of Salting a Claim.

To " salt a claim " is to sprinkle gold dust about it in certain places in order to deceive those who may be seeking investment. In this way in the early days of California worthless claims were made to appear rich, and were often sold for large sums of money. In the course of time this practice became so common that purchasers were always on their guard, and it was necessary to exercise much ingenuity in order to deceive them. I know of one instance where solid earth was removed to the depth of six feet and, after coarse gold had been mixed with it, was replaced and covered with rubbish in such a way as to look firm and natural. Soon after, a party came along who wished to buy, and judging from appearances they selected the very place for prospecting which had been salted for them, deeming it less likely to have been tampered with than the rest of the claim. Of course they thought they had " struck it rich," but they realized only the salt. Sometimes claims were pronounced worthless before sufficient work had been done on them. When these were salted and sold to persevering miners they frequently netted large fortunes to those who had unwittingly purchased them.

In 1851 a party of American miners had been working a claim near Columbia, Tuolumne County, California, and not having even found the " color " they became discouraged; the more so as a company of Chinamen a short distance above them were doing very well. The Americans having expressed a willingness to sell, one day three Chinamen went to look at the claim. They talked it over among themselves and finally asked the owners at what price they would sell. Of course the Americans made it out rich and put a high figure on it, though in fact they were resolved to sell out at any price, being sure that the ground was worthless. It was decided that the Chinamen should bring their picks and pans next day to prospect, and if they were satisfied they would buy at the figure agreed upon.

The miners, thinking it would probably be their last chance to sell, determined to salt the claim. It was a large piece of ground and the trouble was where to put the " salt." One of the men soon hit upon a very ingenious plan. He took his gun and went, as he said, to get a quail or two, but in reality to kill a snake. As there were a great many about the place, he soon killed a large gopher-snake, which resembles the rattlesnake in appearance but is perfectly harmless to man. Putting his game into a bag, he returned to camp.

On being asked by his companions what he had brought back for supper, he shook out the snake and explained his idea thus :

" Now, boys, when the Chinamen come to-morrow, they won't allow any of us to be too near, because they 're afraid of ' salt.' Well, Jim, you walk along on top of the bank and have that dead snake in your pocket. Bill and me will stay talking to the Johns, I 'll have my gun over my shoulder as if I was going for a rabbit, only you see I 'll put ' salt' into the gun instead of shot. We 'll find out where they 're going to pan out next, and you be looking on, innocent like, with the snake ready to drop where I tell you. When them fellers start to walk there, just slide him down the bank, and when we all get there, I 'll holler ' Hold on, boys ! ' and before they know what 's up, I 'll fire the ' salt' all around there and make believe I killed the snake. How 'll that do ? "

Next morning four Chinamen came prepared for work. They tried a few places, but of course did not get the "color." The Americans kept at a distance so that there could be no complaint.

"Well, John," said the schemer, "where you try next, over in that corner?"

The Chinamen were suspicious in a moment. They were familiar with salted claims and were well on their guard. "No likee dis corn'. Tlie him nudder corn'," pointing to the opposite one.

Jim, with his hands in his pockets, was above on the bank, many feet away, watching; when he saw them point in that direction, his partner gave a nod and he pitched the snake on the ground near the place. The leader exclaimed, "Hold on boys!" and fired before they could tell which way to look. Going up to the snake, he pushed the gun under it and carried it away hanging over the barrel. Jim walked off and Bill sat on a wheelbarrow on the opposite side from where they were at work. The Chinamen had no suspicion. They carried away several pans of dirt to wash in a stream near by, and when they returned Bill felt pretty sure they had struck some of the "salt," but the Chinamen said nothing except, "Claim no good. Melikin man talkee too muchee."

The Americans, knowing the game, refused to take less than the specified price, which the Chinamen finally paid and in two days the sellers were off to new diggings.

The strangest part of the story is that the claim turned out to be one of the richest in the district. The Chinamen made a great deal of money, sold out and went home.

"Hold on boys, till I make this shot."

IN 1851 Mokelumne Hill was one of the worst camps in California. "Who was shot last week?" was the first question asked by the miners when they came in from the river or surrounding diggings on Saturday nights or Sundays to gamble or get supplies. It was very seldom that the answer was "No one."

Men made desperate by drink or losses at the gambling table, would race up and down the thoroughfares, in single file, as boys play the game of "follow my leader," each imitating the actions of the foremost. Selecting some particular letter in a sign they would fire in turn, regardless of everything but the accuracy of the aim. Then they would quarrel over it as though they were boys, playing a game of marbles, while every shot was likely to kill or wound some unfortunate person.

The gambling tents were large and contained not only gaming tables but billiard tables. At one of these I was once playing billiards with a man named H——. A few feet from us, raised upon a platform made for the purpose, were seated three Mexican musicians, playing guitars; for these places were always well supplied with instrumental music. The evening seldom passed without disputes, and pistols were quickly drawn to settle quarrels. Upon any outbreak men would rush from all parts of the room, struggling to get as near as possible to the scene of action, and often they paid the penalty for their curiosity by being accidentally shot. While H—— and I were engaged in our game, we could hear the monotonous appeal of the dealers, "Make your game, gentlemen, make your game. Red wins and black loses." Suddenly *bang, bang, bang* went the pistols in a distant part of the tent. The usual rush followed. *Bang, bang,* again, and this time the guitar dropped from the hands of one of the unoffending musicians, who fell forward to the ground with a bullet through his neck. His friends promptly undertook to carry him past us to the open air. Our table was so near the side of the tent that only one person at a time could go between it and the canvas. H—— was standing in the way, just in the act of striking the ball with his cue, when one of the persons carrying the wounded man touched him with the request that he move to one side. He turned and saw the Mexican being supported by the legs and arms, the blood flowing from his neck; then with the coolest indifference he said, "Hold on, hold on, boys, till I make this shot," then, resuming his former position, he deliberately finished his shot.

These events occurred so constantly that residents of the place became callous, and although at the sound of the pistol crowds rushed forward, it was with no deeper feeling than curiosity.

Sometimes in the newer communities property as well as life was in danger. I remember that one night in West Point, Calaveras County, a party of roughs "cleaned out" the leading saloon because the proprietor would not furnish them free whisky.

A little later law and order began to assert their claims in the community. Several families from the East came in, and a protest was made against the sway of the gamblers. The result was that the card business did not pay so well; miners grew more careful of their money, and the professional "sports" left the place in great numbers. One of them as he packed up his chips remarked: "They're getting too partickler. If a feller pulls his pistol in self-defense and happens to blow the top of a miner's head off, they haul him up before a jury. The good old times are about over here, and the country's played out!"

How We Get Gold
in California
(1860)

HOW WE GET GOLD IN CALIFORNIA.

BY A MINER OF THE YEAR '49.

OF the thousands who note the semi-monthly arrivals of treasure, and who, from habit, have at last come to consider California a sort of gold-producing Croton, whence the supply is expected as a matter of course, comparatively few are acquainted with the methods by which these riches are drawn from the bowels of the earth. I have even found men who supposed that the primitive rocker or cradle of 1849 is still in general use in 1860. I believe that it will be

OUR CAMP ON THE STANISLAUS.

THE FIRST GOLD-HUNTERS.

a service to our friends in the Atlantic States to set them right on various points connected with the miners of California.

The old localities, such as the beds of well-known rivers and the adjacent "bars," being partially exhausted, it has been believed that mining could not now be followed so successfully as formerly, and that only gleanings remained for the future adventurer. But for ten years the great gold fountain of the Pacific coast has never failed; and instead of a decreased supply, each year's returns have shown that, with the improvements in machinery and contrivances for saving the gold, the yield is steadily augmenting; and this without a material increase in the number of workmen engaged. If the shipments are sometimes smaller, it is no evidence that the gold region is becoming exhausted, but rather proves that our resources have been so developed that many articles formerly imported, such as flour, beef, pork, hay, lumber, potatoes, bricks, grain, and coal, are now produced in the State, and consequently have not to be paid for abroad. Business being dull or brisk in San Francisco is not always a criterion of the prosperity of the extensive gold-producing regions, where the stalwart sons of toil pursue their labors, almost forgetting the existence of the distant emporium, which thousands of them who came across the plains never saw or desired to see. It is to the multitudes who labor in the mines and on farms that we must turn, to estimate the prosperity or decline of the State. The various methods of gold mining, and the important improvements which have been introduced since 1850, must prove of interest to all whose attention has been seriously directed toward the rapid development of the Pacific States since the conquest.

It was with the view of personally examining these improvements, as well as to renew old mining associations, that the writer of this joined a party who recently made the tour of the gold region. We laid out our course and left San Francisco early in May, when the great plains and rolling lands extending down from the spurs of the sierras were carpeted with flowers and clover, the sky cloudless, and the air clear as crystal. As the limits of this article will not permit the narration of every strange scene and adventure we met, I shall waive descriptions of towns and villages, and confine myself to illustrating, as nearly as possible, the various methods of mining in which some of the party had once been engaged, or which were explained to us during our journey.

When, in 1848, the news of the gold discovery by J. W. Marshall at Sutter's Mill became generally known, all the little world of California hastened into the mountains to hunt for gold. Those were indeed the primitive days of mining. Machinery had not then been invented, and the materials for constructing the rudest implements were with difficulty obtained. In many instances baskets or basins of willow twigs were used. The sand or earth supposed to contain gold was agitated in these, and so rich in many instances was the earth that, even with these imperfect appliances, a very short term of labor was cer-

"PANNING," ON THE MOKELUMNE.

tain to reward the adventurer. At that time gold was found in the crevices of the rocks, protruding from the banks of the streams, and dazzled the eye here and there in bright nuggets on the surface of the earth, as it reflected the sun's rays. Many gold-seekers used no other instrument than a common sheath-knife, with which to pry out these "*chispas*," and thus, as they averred, saved time and the expense of machinery. Thousands of dollars' worth were

WINNOWING GOLD, NEAR CHINESE CAMP.

CRADLE ROCKING, ON THE STANISLAUS.

thus collected long before the cradle was introduced.

As the wonderful news became more widely diffused the common washing-pan was brought into use. This was doubtless suggested by the Spanish-American *batea*, or bowl, as the method of using both is similar. The pan is filled with auriferous earth. The operator sitting or squatting upon the edge of the stream in which he submerges the load, holds the pan by the rims, and by an alternate gyratory and oscillating motion, with an occasional stirring and kneading of the mass with one hand, the earth is completely moistened. The largest stones are thrown out, and a flow of water is made to pass constantly around the inner circumference of the pan, by which the load is gradually reduced to a few pebbles and specks of black, metallic sand, among which the particles of gold, if there be any, will be found. The rotary movement by which the heavier pebbles or bits of gold are kept in the centre, and the lighter earth thrown rapidly over the edges, is acquired only by long practice; and very few Americans can rival the dexterity of the Sonorians in this art, which many of them have practiced from childhood in the gold regions of northern Mexico. The fine gold can not be separated from the black sand, which has nearly an equal specific gravity, until the whole has been dried in the sun or by a fire, when the sand is blown away with the breath.

Before going farther it will be as well to premise that the known fact of the superior specific gravity of gold over all known metals and min-

erals (except platinum) underlies the principle of *nearly* all gold-saving inventions. This will appear more prominently as we proceed.

At the middle bar of the Mokelumne River we found a few Sonorians engaged in this panning, a method now confined to them, and which, among Americans, is only used as an adjunct to more extended operations. Nevertheless, one of our party, who had a pan, scraped some "good-looking dirt" from the bottom of a deserted "hole," and squatting beside Don Antonio, the two had a trial of dexterity, in which our friend, though no novice, was "nowhere." He had, however, the pleasure of finding nearly half a dollar's worth of gold in his pan. Six years before two of our party had been among the company who inaugurated gold-digging at this place; but, with the exception of the immovable mountains and huge rocks on the opposite banks, all had been changed under the tireless hand of the miners. Whole acres of land had been upturned, and the earth and sand passed through a second and third washing, and apparently every particle of gold extracted; yet the less ambitious Chinese and Mexicans find enough in these deserted places to reward them for their tedious labors.

A volume would be required to perpetuate the fabulous tales still circulated of the former richness of the *placeres* along the banks of this river, and to which two of us could, in part, bear witness from personal experience. How the price of a common Irish potato, in 1849, was one dollar; a *pinch* of gold dust paid for a drink of bad whisky; the same for a "chaw" of tobacco; and a doctor did not look at you under twenty dollars. The Indians, when pressed with hunger, would occasionally hunt for gold, and often with astonishing success, though it was alleged that, until the arrival of the whites, they knew naught of the rich placers they were daily treading over. A Yankee had set up a small tent among the miners' cabins, whence he dispensed whisky, tobacco, physic, raisins, and other groceries. It is related that an Indian came to the tent with a handful of gold wrapped in a rag. This he placed in one of the scales, which the shop-keeper weighed down with raisins in the other, much to the satisfaction of the customer. He was so careful, however, to evince no imprudent haste in the transaction that the Indian, fearing the other might repent of his bargain, suddenly seized the paper of raisins, and disap-

peared into the woods with the speed of a deer. Of course our Yankee did not pursue him, the raisins costing him about five cents, and the gold amounting to more than thirty dollars.

The success of mining in California, as well as in all other gold districts, depends mainly upon a constant supply of water, without which the gold can not be separated from the earth. For this reason the earliest efforts of the miner were directed along the banks of the rivers. There were, however, many *placeres* discovered on ground too elevated for any running stream to reach; and here the gold had to be "packed" on the shoulders of miners or the backs of donkeys to the nearest water, often a distance of miles. Of course the earth must be unusually rich to warrant such an outlay of labor and time. Chinese Diggings in Tuolumne County was an instance of this. Here were seen troops of sturdy Chinamen groaning along under the weight of huge sacks of earth brought to the surface from a depth of eighteen feet, and deposited in heaps, after a weary tramp, along the banks of a muddy pool. These were washed by other parties stationed there for the purpose, and the day's proceeds equally divided. At Shaw's Flat, at the time of its discovery, similar means were used. A curious method was the "dry washing," or winnowing process, which was confined to places where water could not be obtained. Two Mexicans, partners of course, would collect a heap of earth from some spot where the ground contained grain-gold, and rejecting all the pebbles, the remainder, pounded to the consistency of sand, was placed upon a sheet or coarse cotton cloth, the corners of which were held in the hands of the operators, and the earth tossed to a height of three or four feet, somewhat in the style of Sancho Panza's treatment by the citizens of Segovia. The strong breeze carried away the light dust and particles of earth, while the superior gravity of the gold, if ever so fine, caused it to drop again

WASHING WITH THE LONG TOM, NEAR MURPHY'S.

RIVER OPERATIONS AT MURDERER'S BAR.

into the cloth. Bellows were sometimes used by solitary adventurers, and where these could not be obtained Mexicans could be seen here and there tossing little clouds of dust into the air from their wooden *bateas*.

These primitive methods soon gave way to the more practical rocker, or "cradle." The peculiar form of this useful machine is, doubtless, familiar to most readers. Rude and simple as it is, the California rocker has been the means of enriching thousands. It is not known who was the inventor, but its enlivening rattle began to be heard in the mines as early as 1848. At that time its form was, indeed, rough and

"HELLO, STRANGER! HOW'S DIGGINS?"

us to Sonora, the principal mining town of Tuolumne County, and situated about two hundred miles from San Francisco. Here, again, we found all changed; the town had been entirely destroyed by fire since our last visit, and was now rebuilt, with the addition of many fine brick stores. Not far from here, to the northward, is a bar or bend in the Stanislaus River, where, in the "days of '49," two of our party had rocked our cradles and lined our buckskin purses to some purpose. Here we resolved to locate on the old spot. The river tumbled and foamed along its rocky bed, and the loud voice of the rapids echoed far and near among the surrounding mountains. The bank was shelving and smooth like an ocean beach, and a tiny surf, caused by the swift

awkward. Before saw-mills or lumber were within reach the cradle was hewn out of logs and the trunks of trees; but it is safe to believe that, in those early days, these ungainly machines yielded a richer harvest than the neatly-finished ones of the present time.

Our journey from the Mokelumne River led

torrent, combed in miniature breakers upon an expanse of speckled sand, glittering with mica and smooth as a planed board. We placed our "bed pieces," set the rocker with the requisite pitch, and then attacked the long-deserted *placer*. After throwing aside a few tons of stones, and uprooting a dense undergrowth of shrubbery which

PACKING EARTH, AT CARSON'S.

QUICKSILVER MACHINE, IN MORMON GULCH.

nearly hid our old treasure-house, we came upon the place where our last efforts had been directed. This we had deserted some years before, after collecting from it several thousand dollars in coarse gold, and the "hole," now nearly filled with stones, had not since been appropriated. But times had somewhat changed since, in the plentitude of fortune, we had quit this for better diggings, and we now resumed the work with all the ardor of new miners. A large boulder, which had formerly discouraged us, was first pried out, revealing a long deep crevice filled with a tough clay, the lower part of which we found stuffed with the shining nuggets. A pan was soon filled with this, and when washed by G—— in the cold waters of the river, resulted in about eighty dollars of beautifully-rounded gold. Thus encouraged we commenced with the cradle.

This little machine consists of a box about three and a half feet long, by about twenty inches wide and eighteen inches deep. The top and one end are open : upon the back half of the top is fitted a closely-jointed box, with a sheet-iron bottom pierced with holes of a size sufficient to allow small pebbles to drop through into the machine. Into this box is thrown the earth designed to be washed, which is disintegrated and made to pass through by a rocking motion given to the machine, and for which it is provided with rockers like a child's cradle. The water is bailed by hand from the stream, near which the cradle must be placed. The gold thus separated from the earth is arrested in its passage through the machine by wooden cleets nailed along the bottom, while the lighter materials, such as earth and pebbles, are carried out of the open or lower end by the stream of water.

Rocking the cradle, digging, carrying earth, and bailing water were equally divided among the party. By night we had exhausted the lead, and returned to Sonora the next day four hundred and thirty dollars the richer for our adventure.

For the labors of one man the cradle is probably the most economical method of gold mining, as the several operations may be conducted without aid. It is now, however, mainly confined to Chinese and Mexicans, whose ambition seldom aspires to the later improvements.

A short distance north of Sonora is the town or diggings of Murphy's, once the most celebrated gold-mine in California, and still employing hundreds of workmen to advantage. The discoverer, a Missourian, after whom the place was named, is said to have enjoyed his good fortune alone for some time, trading with the Indians, afterward known as the Murphy tribe, and supplying them with cheap articles of finery in return for their labor in the mines. With his two sons he thus amassed an immense sum in a few months.

Here we saw the first improvement made upon the cradle. This came out in 1850, and at that time was regarded as the *ne plus ultra* of mining machinery. It is called the "long tom," and consists of a shallow trough from ten to twenty feet long, and generally about sixteen inches wide; one end, which slightly turns up like a shovel, is shod with iron and perforated like the sieve of a cradle. This trough is placed on slightly inclined ground, the sieve being at the lower end. A stream of water is then turned on at the upper end, and several hands supply the tom with water, which finds its way to the sieve, carrying with it the earth, which it washes and disintegrates in its passage. A man is stationed at the end to clear away the "tailings," or earth discharged from the machine, and also to stir up the earth accumulated in the tom. Directly beneath the sieve is placed a box, which is furnished with "riffles" or cleets, to catch the gold as it falls through the tom-iron. The machine differs little in principle from the cradle. Sometimes, where the gold is very fine and liable to be carried away by the force of the water, a box containing a quantity of quicksilver is attached to the end of the riffle, where the finer particles are saved by amalgamation. The long tom is calculated to wash ten times more earth than cradles employing an equal number of hands. The work is not performed in a more thorough manner, but there is a great saving of time and labor. When its value became generally appreciated the cradle began to disappear from many localities, and the long tom is now almost exclusively used by small companies.

Within a few miles of Auburn, a considerable mining town of Placer County, we visited a well known bend in the middle fork of the American river called Murderer's Bar, where one of the earliest attempts were made to turn the course of a large river with the view of exploring the bottom for gold. Every bend or shallow place in the numerous mountain streams of the gold region has been thus attacked, the waters diverted from their course, and made to pass through artificial channels, leaving the old course dry for mining operations. Works such as that shown in the illustration of Murderer's Bar, in El Dorado County, are carried on by large companies, who have among them carpenters, surveyors, engineers, and stout hands. Sometimes the water is taken into a strongly-built flume from above, and conducted in a long box through the old bed of the river, by this avoiding the necessity of a canal. The bed of the river thus laid dry, the company enter it and search in every crevice and pocket for the golden deposits which should naturally have accumulated by the action of the river against the bases of the adjacent hills. These enterprises often yield immense riches, every depression in the bed-rock holding its quota of brightly-burnished gold. The operations are frequently so extensive as to occupy several successive seasons before the whole can be explored. At others, the premature approach of the rainy season, and the consequent freshets, carry away the whole works in a night; but on renewing them the following year, the crevices and holes are often found to have collected an amount of gold almost equal to the original deposits brought down by the floods from the numerous diggings above. Frequently the place has been injudiciously chosen, and, after months of hard la-

FLUTTER-WHEEL, ON THE TUOLUMNE.

FRÉMONT MILL AND VEIN, MARIPOSA.

bor, the river proves entirely bare of gold. No amount of judgment can select with any certainty a favorable location for "jamming" or turning a river. The long space of still-water below a series of rapids will sometimes contain pounds of gold; but the same rule followed, in another instance, will perhaps result in a total failure, and the company who have located above the rapids be the fortunate adventurers. The river operations at Murderer's Bar are the property of a company of some seventy-five men, one of whom informed us that they employed nearly two hundred more during the dry season. As fresh deposits of gold are made each year, the place may be considered a perpetual investment. It is estimated that only one in three of these river enterprises proves remunerative.

One of the richest *placeres* of California was an extensive sloping flat near the centre of Calaveras County, at the foot of a range of quartz mountains, separating it from the valley of the Stanislaus, and known as "Carson's Flat." The gold deposits were first struck at this place in 1851. The discoverers sunk a small hole in the shallowest part of the flat where the bed-rock lay about ten feet below the surface. Here they panned out several thousand dollars during the first week; but though their labors were continued with great secrecy, they were speedily tracked and multitudes flocked to the place. A small town was built where Carson's Creek discharged into the Stanislaus, goods came pouring in, Jew clothiers, rum-dealers, and gamblers followed the crowds of working-men, and in a

month every foot of ground, supposed to be auriferous, was appropriated.

At a certain distance beneath the surface, throughout the gold region of California, a layer of rock is found, down to which the gold, by its superior specific gravity, has gradually worked itself, and here it has become wedged into the inequalities of this "hard pan." Long experience has taught the miner to discard the upper earth, which is generally valueless, and to seek for gold either in these cracks and "pockets," or in the earth or layer of clay covering the bed rock. The discovery of this fact gave rise to the method of "coyoteing" or drifting, which has since been superseded by the improvement of tunneling. The first received its name from its fancied resemblance to the subterranean burrowing of a little animal resembling the fox, and known in California as the "coyote." As the ledge, or bed-rock, at Carson's, and other diggings of this kind, is often found thirty or forty feet beneath the surface, and no gold can be got except within a few feet of it, the expense of shoveling away the upper earth is avoided by burrowing, and following the "leads," or crevices of the rock, in and around which the gold is deposited.

About six months sufficed to completely honeycomb the flat—an area of twenty acres—so that the workmen could pass through each other's claims for a distance of half a mile. These passages are made through a firm but sticky clay, and are only of a sufficient height for the workmen to sit upright in. Following the windings of the various leads they are as irregular as the intricacies of any labyrinth of mythology. A tallow candle stuck into a niche hewn into the damp wall serves to light the burrow. Descending into one of these holes we stood on a square space of rock at a depth of twenty feet from the surface. On the sides of this square were four arched entrances leading off into subterranean passages. We crawled into one and followed our conductor, "hitching" along in a sitting posture with an unhappy feeling of insecurity at hearing flakes of the moist clay fall from the low roof and partly impeding our progress. Here and there wooden stanchions had been placed to support the roof, but the immense weight had warped and bent these, while the superincumbent mass bulged on each side as if about to close down upon us forever. The muffled blows of other subterranean laborers were heard around us (for these diggings were still worked), and as we progressed we could discern the lights of dimly-burning candles shedding a ghastly glare upon cadaverous faces.

Our conductor led the way into a small chamber about six feet by eight and four feet in height, and, having lighted several other candles, we obtained a full view of our tomb-like apartment. On each side of this damp cave, as well as in the passages we had just crawled through, the stones and other refuse were piled up with the most scrupulous regard to economy of room. They had been carefully scraped to save any fine gold that might be contained in the clay adhering to them. On the floor of the cavern were two small picks, and as many short crow-bars of

tempered steel, which had been made of miniature size for the express purpose of "coyoteing."

The owner of the claim now directed our attention to a side of the cavern where we heard the blows of an adjacent miner, and, a moment after, the point of a pick came through the clay partition. A few more blows and the boundary between the two claims was broken away; a rough, bearded face looked through with the exclamation,

"Hello, strangers! How's diggins?"

We soon became on intimate terms with our underground acquaintance, and, when he had picked away the wall sufficiently to give us passage, we crept on hands and knees into his possessions, which rivaled, in size and richness, that of our *cicerone*. He had just found the end of a crevice, and had a pan filled with clay, earth, and pebbles, in which dozens of minute specks of gold glittered in the light of the candles. As the day was nearly spent we crawled out to the nearest shaft, whence we accompanied him to the creek and saw him wash out his day's work. There were nearly four ounces of coarse gold in his pan, valued at about sixty dollars.

Sometimes these coyote diggings cave in without warning, despite the subterranean supports placed by the miners for security. The earth thus undermined settles upon the bedrock, and so slowly and silently that the victims are buried in a living tomb unknown to the outside world.

Shortly after our arrival at Carson's a twelve-pound lump of gold, slightly mixed with quartz,

HELVETIA QUARTZ MILL, GRASS VALLEY.

EL RASTRA.

was found in the deepest part of the flat. This was valued at about two thousand dollars. The fortunate possessor walked leisurely along toward the store, bearing his glittering treasure in his hands, and followed by a crowd of admiring companions. He had been prying out of his lead a nest of smooth stones, which he scraped clean before throwing them into the heap. One of these struck him as being rather heavy, but the thought of its being gold did not occur to him, until, in scraping the supposed stone, the yellow metal reflected the rays of his candle. With that exception his claim had not yielded remarkably well. The earth taken from these diggings is either carted or carried in panniers, by mules or donkeys, to Carson's Creek, near by, and panned out in the usual manner. It is asserted that, counting the celebrated deposit found on the quartz mountain near by, more than four million dollars have been taken from Carson's.

One of the principal tributaries of the Stanislaus is the stream passing through Mormon Gulch, and running within a stone's-throw of Tuttletown. The diggings in this vicinity have been celebrated for their richness, especially toward the head of the cañon known as Mormon "Creek." Desirous of ascertaining if our old diggings had been worked out during our four years of absence, we purchased an old quicksilver machine at this place, which we stationed in a certain bend, half-way between Tuttletown and the river. The gold in the bed of this stream is so fine as to escape from the riffles of a

long tom, and can only be worked to advantage by the use of quicksilver. Minute particles, in the shape of flakes, are found adhering to the blades of grass in the shallow parts of the stream. Our machine, which resembled the "bumper," or Virginia rocker, consisted of a wooden trough, furnished with quicksilver riffles, placed in a frame-work, and so hung as to be rocked to and fro by hand. This motion was made by one man, and the machine was supplied with earth by the others, who shoveled it in from the bed of the creek. The water was led through canvas hose from a series of rapids above us; and the operation of shoveling and rocking was continued for a week without interruption. At the end of that time the amalgam was taken from the machine and retorted, when we found nearly three hundred dollars as the reward of our labor. Most of this gold was fine as snuff, and could only have been saved by coming in contact with the quicksilver, with which it instantly amalgamates. There were, however, many pieces from the size of shot to that of a pea.

The elevation of many rich mines has given rise to a variety of ingenious inventions for raising and supplying them with water. Among these is the "flutter-wheel," which the traveler will find erected in every conceivable manner and place; carried, in all cases, by the force of the river currents. It consists of a wheel, sometimes thirty feet in diameter, the paddles of which are furnished with large buckets, made to catch themselves full of water at each revolution, and to discharge into a trough, through which it flows to the tom, or sluice, where the mining operations are being conducted. This contrivance differs little from the common "undershot wheel." They may be seen by the dozens along the Tuolumne and Stanislaus rivers, and supply countless miners with the indispensable water. We saw many of them in the vicinity of Jacksonville, a mining town of considerable importance, standing at the junction of the Tuolumne River and Wood's Creek. Seven years of steady working have not exhausted the mines in this vicinity, and new *placeres* are constantly discovered.

Near here we witnessed an instance of the habitual gallantry of the California miner. A party, among whom were two ladies, were traveling through the mines, and visited a well-known claim near Jacksonville, to see how gold was dug. One of the ladies, a celebrated beauty, went by invitation into a formidable-looking tunnel, where she evinced so much *sang froid* that one of the proprietors, filling a pan with earth, promised her all the gold it might contain if she dared soil her hands by washing it out. She gayly consented, and went through the operation amidst the laughter of her companions. As the earth was gradually reduced so that the bottom of the pan could be seen, the rattling of gold could plainly be heard on the tin, and when thoroughly washed there remained nearly fifty dollars' worth of gold. This is the special prerogative of ladies, who are always at liberty to wash out a pan of earth at any claim they may honor with their presence, and the miners take special care that the labor shall be well rewarded.

Our tour of the mines carried us into the famous gold country of Mariposa—the far-famed region claimed by the pioneer Frémont. One of the largest mining counties in the State is that bearing this name, which is mellifluous Spanish for our word "butterfly." In the centre of its richest portion stands the picturesque town of Mariposa. This county ranks Number Four in the quartz-crushing interest, which has grown into an immense and lucrative business, despite the disaster and ruin attending it in 1850-'51. It employs millions of capital and thousands of miners, and has grown into the most important occupation in the State.

In every part of the mining region there are found veins of quartz rock, outcropping in many places, and often traceable through leagues of country. These generally contain gold: sometimes so fine as to be invisible to the naked eye; at others the quartz, when broken, is completely studded with the glittering particles. In some instances the proportion of gold is so small that the most economical methods of pulverizing it to extract the gold will not pay the necessary expenses; again the yield has been so large that costly mills carried by steam and water power have been erected, and with such astonishing results that *savans* have at last been compelled to admit that "quartz is the mother of gold;" and it is now generally believed that gold has been originally formed in, or together with, quartz, and that it is by the gradual disintegration of the latter by the action of water

OCEAN BEACH MINING, AT GOLD BLUFF.

GROUND SLUICING, AT GOLD HILL.

and atmospheric influences that the gold has been distributed over the country.

The mill situated at the Frémont vein, in Mariposa County, was among those visited during our journey. Like most of the principal ones this mill is carried by steam power; and some description of this, and another in Nevada County, will give the reader some idea of the great interest of quartz crushing. The quartz is conveyed to the works by carts or mule panniers from the vein, near which they are generally erected. The machinery is under the cover of a large shed; the apparatus consisting of a series of iron stampers, placed in a line, and made to fit into iron boxes, which receive the quartz, previously broken into egg size. The stampers are moved by cogs or cans, connected with a revolving wheel, which alternately lifts and lets them fall into the boxes containing the quartz. By this means from ten to fifty tons per day are crushed, according to the power of the mills—yielding, at Mariposa, from $30 to $80 per ton.

The quartz operations at Grass Valley, in Nevada County, have probably made the largest returns. Some of the richest veins in the State have been discovered in this vicinity, some of them yielding occasionally two hundred dollars to the ton, but by no means averaging as much. The Helvetia quartz-mill at this place is one of the principal, working thirty-four stampers, and crushing on an average thirty tons a day. The stamping-box, already described, is supplied with water by a hose or pipe. Through a hole made

for the purpose the quartz, as it is crushed, passes out in the form of a thick, milky water, carrying with it much of the fine gold, which is thus discharged upon a frame-work, across which are placed several quicksilver riffles, where the gold amalgamates in its passage. Any fine particles escaping the quicksilver are arrested below, as they pass over a hide or blanket stretched tightly across a frame. But even these careful preparations for saving the gold are not always successful; for the "tailings," or refuse from the mill, is found to pay nearly as well under a second process as by the original crushing. The question how to avoid this waste of gold has long been agitated among miners, and is apparently now as far from practical solution as ever.

Besides the quartz-mill proper there is the primitive Spanish-American *rastra*, or drag, which we saw in operation at Bear Valley, in Mariposa County, and other places. This consists of two heavy stones attached by a strap to a horizontal bar. These are dragged by mule-power slowly around a circular trough, paved at the bottom, and through which a small stream of water is constantly flowing. The gold-bearing quartz, previously broken into small pieces, is ground to paste in the trough, and flows away in the usual milky form, to which it is reduced by friction or crushing; and the gold amalgamates with quicksilver, which, at short intervals, is sprinkled into the trough during the grinding. After a certain time the water is turned off, the entire pavement of the trough taken up, and the amalgam carefully collected and retorted. A single ton of quartz often affords a day's work for one of these slow-jogging machines; but they do their work more effectually than the crushing-mills, as the quartz is more thoroughly pulverized by this constant friction and rubbing than by stamping; and in proportion as the stone can be thoroughly reduced to a paste, so much the more completely can the gold be extracted. Hence the *rastra* is used with success at veins which had been abandoned as profitless for the modern quartz-mill.

These machines are usually put up, worked, and owned by Mexicans, who take the grinding of quartz, by the job or ton, from mining companies who lack capital to erect steam mills.

In the more retired parts of California, where the distance and difficulties of access have hitherto prevented the rush of population, there are extensive gold regions which have as yet only begun to be known. Years must elapse before the mineral wealth of Siskiyou, Klamath, and Shasta counties can be fully developed, though mining enterprises of great importance have been successfully attempted in all. Not many miles north of the California line on the Pacific is an extent of sea-coast, called Gold Bluff from the extraordinary gold discoveries made there in 1851. An American officer, in pursuit of hostile Indians with a detachment of troops, discovered, on the ocean beach, small shining particles in the sand, which extended many miles along the coast. These, on examination, proved to be gold. In a few months the report reached San Francisco in an exaggerated form, and crowds flocked to Gold Bluff. The result was ruin and

death to many, and fortune to a few. This style of mining has since been pursued with great success. Whether this gold is thrown up by the surf from the bed of the ocean, or washed down from the inland bluffs, remains unexplained. It is found by throwing off the upper or white sand, which discovers a layer of smooth, round stones embedded in a bank of black sand, in which the gold dust literally sparkles in the sunlight. The stones are thrown aside, and the auriferous sand shoveled into a long trough, on the bottom of which is tacked a coarse blanket or hide. A stream of water is let on, which carries away the sand while the gold is caught in the furze of the blanket. If any escapes, it is secured below in a short series of quicksilver riffles at the end of the trough or sluice. Instances are known at Gold Bluff and at Cape Blanco, in Oregon, where parties of four men have made from five to ten thousand dollars by gold-beach washing in a single season.

A very popular method of mining is that called "ground-sluicing." This we saw in operation in hundreds of instances. I have already described the manner of getting at the "pay dirt" underneath a heavy layer of barren earth, by "coyoteing." Ground-sluicing accomplishes the same result with half the labor, and with the chance of obtaining from the upper earth some gold, which, did any exist, would be lost by the first plan. At Gold Hill, in Placer County, this operation was in very general use, and one of our party, during our short stay there, bought an interest in a company of ground-sluicers, by which he cleared three ounces of gold-dust, and,

TUNNELING, AT TABLE MOUNTAIN.

INTERIOR OF TUNNEL.

on our departure, sold out his share at an advance.

It has been found that the principal deposits of gold are on the great rocky ridge already referred to as the "bed-rock," and extending throughout the mining region, sometimes outcropping at the surface, and at others sinking to a depth of above a hundred feet. Where the bed-rock is not at too great a depth, the miners, instead of sinking a shaft to reach the deposits of gold, turn a heavy stream of water upon the bank which is to be removed, and with the aid of picks and spades reduce it so as to leave the lower or gold-bearing earth accessible to be worked. The force of the water is such as to carry away the *debris*, while any gold it may contain remains by its own gravity and is saved with the earth intended to be washed by the ordinary methods. Ground-sluicing is thus, to a certain extent, used as a substitute for shoveling, to remove heavy layers of earth from places where gold is supposed to be deposited, rather than to separate the gold, which is done by a style of sluicing hereafter to be considered.

Passing through Tuolumne County is a remarkable plateau about twelve hundred feet above the surrounding country, which, from its flat surface and peculiar form, has been named Table Mountain. A few years since, a miner (Mr. T. A. Ayres), while prospecting here, was led to believe that it had anciently been the course of a river—a conclusion which has since proved correct, by the alluvial deposit and fossils found there by the miners. Here had accumulated, in distant

ages, vast amounts of gold, which however could only be reached by shafts or tunnels. One of these had been commenced by the discoverer, and was abandoned; but others carried it through, and struck the interior basin or bed of an ancient river, in which were found deposits of gold of fabulous richness. The news spread, and the adjacent country was quickly "staked off" into claims, according to the local mining rules of that neighborhood.

One of the largest tunnels which have been driven into the mountain is on its western slope, about six miles from the town of Sonora, and has been worked entirely through a bed of talcose slate and vitreous volcanic matter. It has more than paid its way by the richness of the mass through which it passes, though the object was to reach as quickly as possible the interior deposits. The proprietor invited us to enter the tunnel, which was made with no small pretensions to skill in such work. It enters horizontally, and follows the uneven surface of the bedrock. On each side of us, as we entered, the damp walls reflected the light of our candles, while the roof, which was of sufficient height to allow us to walk upright, was strongly timbered at regular distances, and down the sides the water dripped from numerous subterranean springs, doubtless far above our heads. Passing along the middle is a railroad, upon which cars, loaded with earth, are run out by mule-power. Beneath this is a drain, carrying off, in a large stream, the accumulations of water from the works, and which affords enough for all mining purposes.

As the work progresses the quantity of gold increases. While we were exploring a lateral chamber leading off from the main tunnel one of the workmen came upon a pocket, or nest of gold, which had accumulated in a hollow place in the bed-rock. We held the candles, and watched with curious interest the process of gathering the gold. The hole, which was about the size of a common wash-bowl, was filled with a collection of black mud, clay, disintegrated slate, and some black vitreous matter which occurs, in alternate layers with sand and pebbles, in the body of the mountain. This substance yielded like clay to a few blows of the pick; and as the slices were turned carefully up, they resembled chunks of plumb-cake, the clay being stuffed in every part with the golden lumps. Upon breaking these pieces in the hand like bread, the interior was still found plugged with pellets of gold, and the whole mass was heavy with it.

When we had reached the end of the tunnel we were fifteen hundred feet into the solid heart of the mountain. The proprietor had invested the earnings of three years in this enterprise, and had been eighteen months patiently working toward the treasures which were certainly to reward his enterprise. This description, with slight variations, would answer for hundreds of such tunnels in the golden State—such as those at Michigan Bluff, Placerville, and Iowa Hill.

The very general mode of mining known as "sluicing" (which is quite distinct from "ground sluicing," already described) employs not far from one half of the entire mining population of California; and with the "hydraulic process" of which it forms a necessary part, is undoubtedly the chief method to which is due the enormous sums still obtained from the soil. With them are inseparably connected the great system of flumes or aqueducts, cobwebbing and interlacing the gold region, and leading to extensive and ingenious mining operations. The allusion to these I have reserved for the close of the article, not only because they constitute the latest improvements in gold mining, but because all improvements hereafter to be made, it would seem, must necessarily be based upon them.

As the rivers and creeks were gradually worked over, there remained to the miner only those localities which, though gold-bearing, had not become such depositories of the precious metal as the vicinity of rivers which had gradually collected the gold in their beds as they passed through the country. It was at first believed that the only available places for gold-washing were the river beds, bars, flats, and cañons, which were so generally attacked in 1849 and '50. As these were exhausted, the hue and cry was raised abroad that the mines were "worked out." California was then, as since, pronounced "played out." "She had gone up," it was said, "like a rocket, and come down like a stick." The bubble had burst—it had long been anticipated—and sagacious newspaper editors remembered that they had often warned their readers, and predicted all this long before. True, the monthly millions continued to pour in upon New York as before, and that staggered the doubts of some; but this, it was said, was only the natural draining of

HYDRAULIC MINING, AT FRENCH CORRAL.

FLUME, ON THE SHADY CREEK CANAL.

the great amounts still floating about the country; and California, after giving a new impulse to the world's commerce and prosperity, was about to be laid quietly on the shelf as a used-up concern.

It was now that intelligent miners began to realize that their operations must be extended to the districts which had thus far been neglected for the more immediate results to be obtained from the rivers. The gold region of California embraces a country equal in area to the whole of New England, and throughout this great space there is no part which does not contain gold; but in most places the amount is so small that, at the present rates of living, it will not pay for the working, except by some improved process, by which a much greater amount of earth could be washed than by the cradle. I have shown how this necessity was in part supplied by the long tom. The great inventions of hydraulic mining and the sluice-box formed the next step; and as it is merely executing in miniature a process which has been performed since the creation by the mountain streams, no very material improvements can be made upon the principle, though alterations in the manner of its application may be suggested.

At French Corral we visited every place of interest with the gentlemanly proprietors of the Shady Creek Canal, who have become identified with that section of the country. Here may be seen the various works of sluicing, canaling, fluming, and hydraulic mining.

A hill of moderate size, which is found to contain gold throughout its formation, but too thinly scattered for cradle-washing, is generally selected for the operation of hydraulic mining. A series of boxes, fourteen inches in length by about three feet wide, called "sluice-boxes," are fitted together at the ends so as to form a continuous, strongly built trough as long as may be desired, sometimes extending several thousand feet. This is made of the stoutest boards, and of sufficient strength to allow the passage of any amount of earth and stones forced through by a flood of water. It is lined on the bottom with wooden blocks, like the octagonal street pavement, for the double purpose of resisting the friction of the *debris* intended to pass through it, and to make place in the interstices for quicksilver which secures the fine gold. Sometimes the bottom is furnished with small transverse gutters or riffles charged with quicksilver for the same purpose. The sluice, thus prepared, is firmly placed in a slanting position near the foot of the hill intended to be attacked.

To *shovel* a mass of several million tons of earth into this sluice for washing would, of course, prove a profitless job. It is now that the art of hydraulic mining is called into play, by which the labor of many men is cheaply performed, and the hill torn down to its base. The operation is simply throwing an immense stream of water upon the side of the hill with hose and pipe, precisely as a fire-engine plays upon a burning building, and few who have not witnessed it can imagine the effect. The water is led through gutta percha or oftener double canvas hose, and generally from a great height above the scene of operations. It is consequently thrown with such force as to eat into the hill-side as if it were made of sugar or salt. Neither man nor beast can stand for a moment against the projectile power of the hydraulic hose; they become a weapon of defense, and a miner with a hose-pipe in his hand need not fear the advance of half a dozen adversaries. Several of these streams directed upon a hill-side bring down more earth than a hundred men with shovels and picks could throw. But the art of the miner does not rest here. It is his constant aim to undermine as well as to break down; he consequently works, in a single day, huge caverns into the hill-side with his "water-batteries," until by certain indications he knows that a "cave in" is about to take place. Then every body flies from the spot. The earth far above their heads begins to quake and crinkle, and slowly the face of the precipice topples over and falls to the earth with the noise of an avalanche. Thus the miner makes one of the simplest laws of nature subservient to his will, and hundreds of tons of earth are leveled down for washing.

Now they return and commence throwing into the sluice. Here again the water becomes their giant servant; for it not only carries the earth through the sluice, completely disintegrating it, and allowing the gold it may contain to lodge in the interstices of the octagonal pavement, but it acts the part of many shovels, and rushes the earth into the sluice with tremendous force. By these means a few men find it profitable to work earth, which, with the discarded, snail-paced rocker, could never have been advantageously washed.

When it is considered that in California there are at least one hundred million superficial acres of gold-bearing territory, from ten to two hundred feet deep, most of which may be profitably submitted to this hydraulic process, the folly of predicting the failure of the mines will be apparent. Vast as have been the sums already extracted from the soil, the mines are said to have been but "scratched over" as yet; and with all the quick-succeeding improvements, gold-mining is yet in its infancy.

But experience has shown that most of this earth will "pay" for a second process; and numberless are the "tailing companies," whose labors are confined to washing by a more careful method the "tailings" or refuse discharged from the end of the sluices, often with a success which leads one to doubt the efficacy of the original process.

So perceptible already have been the effects of this sluicing process, that the entire face of the country is being changed by the removing of hills and filling up of flats and cañons, while some of the larger mountain affluents of the Sacramento and San Joaquin rivers are becoming filled with the deposits constantly poured into them from innumerable sluices, each discharging its daily tons of earth. The muddy current extends the entire length of the Yuba into the Feather River, and thence into the Sacramento far below Marysville. The country papers have more than once sounded the alarm at this threatened invasion of their inland steam navigation, which the political theorists regard as the first spur of necessity toward forcing railroads into general use. Such is a brief outline of the arts of hydraulic mining and sluicing—twin sisters—the natural offspring of gold.

The one great mining interest which remains to be explained is that of the water-companies. It has already been shown that water is the grand desideratum, without which the richest mines are not available. Many of the most famous *placeres* have been discovered at elevations above the level of the adjacent water-courses, and the attention of enterprising companies was at once turned to obtaining an artificial supply by diverting the mountain streams from their channels through ditches and canals, following the sinuosities of the hills at a proper grade by means of flumes supported by stout pine tressel-work. To obtain the requisite level, it is often necessary to go back into the Sierra Nevada and tap some river near its head waters. Some of these aqueducts extend across valleys, through tunnels, and along the brows of mountains over leagues of country, and more resemble great public works than private enterprises. The water is supplied to the various mining companies by lateral branches, tapping the main trunk along its entire course, which in many instances exceeds fifty miles, and in a few is more than one hundred. Water is sold *by the inch;* that is, a price is charged for all the water that will flow by the day with a certain pressure through an aperture a given number of inches high and wide. Nearly all the hill diggings and hydraulic mining claims are thus supplied with their heavy batteries of water. The Shady Creek Canal, owned by Messrs. Pollard and Eddy, which receives its waters from a stream of that name in Nevada County, has proved one of the most successful, though not among the largest of these enterprises.

It is thus that gold mining is conducted in California. From a hap-hazard scrambling of uninitiated adventurers, scraping here and there among the rocks, it has grown into a well-organized and wonderful system, employing millions of capital and tens of thousands of stout hearts and strong hands, and bringing into action an amount of energy and inventive genius which must result in building up a great Pacific empire. With her boundless expanse of arable lands, her matchless climate, and the inexhaustible gold-mines, California invites the world to share with her the blessings of Providence.

Reader, when next you notice in your morning paper, among other "distinguished arrivals" from California, the little item of "$1,500,000 IN GOLD DUST!" think not of the youngest sister of the Republic as a creature of premature and unhealthy growth, but as a child blooming in her freshest charms, and smiling in the confidence of a glorious future. And, above all, when some pompous wiseacre tells you that California is "played out," ask him if he ever heard of "hydraulic mining."

The Outlook in Southern California (1891)

HARPER'S
NEW MONTHLY MAGAZINE.

Vol. LXXXII.   JANUARY, 1891.   No. CCCCLXXXVIII.

THE OUTLOOK IN SOUTHERN CALIFORNIA.

BY CHARLES DUDLEY WARNER.

FROM the northern limit of California to the southern is about the same distance as from Portsmouth, New Hampshire, to Charleston, South Carolina. Of these two coast lines, covering nearly ten degrees of latitude, or over seven hundred miles, the Atlantic has greater extremes of climate and greater monthly variations, and the Pacific greater variety of productions. The State of California is, however, so mountainous, cut by longitudinal and transverse ranges, that any reasonable person can find in it a temperature to suit him the year through. But it does not need to be explained that it would be difficult to hit upon any general characteristic that would apply to the stretch of the Atlantic coast named, as a guide to a settler looking for a home: the description of Massachusetts would be wholly misleading for South Carolina. It is almost as difficult to make any comprehensive statement about the long line of the California coast.

It is possible, however, limiting the inquiry to the southern third of the State—an area of about fifty-eight thousand square miles, as large as Maine, New Hampshire, Massachusetts, Connecticut, and Rhode Island—to answer fairly some of the questions oftenest asked about it. These relate to the price of land, its productiveness, the kind of products most profitable, the sort of labor required, and its desirability as a place of residence for the laborer, for the farmer or horticulturist of small means, and for the man with considerable capital. Questions on these subjects cannot be answered categorically, but I hope to be able, by setting down my own observations and using trustworthy reports, to give others the material on which to exercise their judg-

ment. In the first place, I think it demonstrable that a person would profitably exchange one hundred and sixty acres of farming land east of the one-hundredth parallel for ten acres, with a water right, in southern California.

In making this estimate I do not consider the question of health or merely the agreeability of the climate, but the conditions of labor, the ease with which one could support a family, and the profits over and above a fair living. It has been customary in reckoning the value of land there to look merely to the profit of it beyond its support of a family, forgetting that agriculture and horticulture the world over, like almost all other kinds of business, usually do little more than procure a comfortable living, with incidental education, to those who engage in them. That the majority of the inhabitants of southern California will become rich by the culture of the orange and the vine is an illusion; but it is not an illusion that twenty times its present population can live there in comfort, in what might be called luxury elsewhere, by the cultivation of the soil, all far removed from poverty and much above the condition of the majority of the inhabitants of the foreign wine and fruit producing countries. This result is assured by the extraordinary productiveness of the land, uninterrupted the year through, and by the amazing extension of the market in the United States for products that can be nowhere else produced with such certainty and profusion as in California. That State is only just learning how to supply a demand which is daily increasing, but it already begins to command the market in certain fruits. This command of the market in the future will depend upon itself, that is, wheth-

YUCCA-PALM AND DATE-PALM.

fruit-raising and fruit-curing, but it already knows that to compete with the rest of the world in our markets it must beat the rest of the world in quality. It will take some time yet to remove the unfavorable opinion of California wines produced in the East by the first products of the vineyards sent here.

The difficulty for the settler is that he cannot "take up" ten acres with water in California as he can one hundred and sixty acres elsewhere. There is left little available government land. There is plenty of government land not taken up and which may never be occupied, that is, inaccessible mountain and irreclaimable desert. There are also little nooks and fertile spots here and there to be discovered which may be preempted, and which will some day have value. But practically all the arable land, or that is likely to become so, is owned now in large tracts, under grants or by wholesale purchase. The circumstances of the case compelled associate effort. Such a desert as that now blooming region known as Pasadena, Pomona, Riverside, and so on, could not be sub-

er it will send east and north only sound wine, instead of crude, ill-cured juice of the grape, only the best and most carefully canned apricots, nectarines, peaches, and plums, only the raisins and prunes perfectly prepared, only such oranges, lemons, and grapes and pears as the Californians are willing to eat themselves. California has yet much to learn about

dued by individual exertion. Consequently land and water companies were organized. They bought large tracts of unimproved land, built dams in the mountain cañons, sunk wells, drew water from the rivers, made reservoirs, laid pipes, carried ditches and conduits across the country, and then sold the land with the inseparable water right in small parcels. Thus the region became subdivided among small holders, each independent, but all mutually dependent as to water, which is the *sine qua non* of existence. It is only a few years since there was a forlorn and struggling colony a few miles east of Los Angeles known as the Indiana settlement. It had scant water, no railway communication, and everything to learn about horticulture. That spot is now the famous Pasadena.

What has been done in the Santa Ana and San Gabriel valleys will be done elsewhere in the State. There are places in Kern County, north of the Sierra Madre, where the land produces grain and alfalfa without irrigation, where farms can be bought at from five to ten dollars an acre—land that will undoubtedly increase in value with settlement and also by irrigation. The great county of San Diego is practically undeveloped, and contains an immense area, in scattered mesas and valleys, of land which will produce apples, grain, and grass without irrigation, and which the settler can get at moderate prices. Nay, more, any one with a little ready money, who goes to southern California expecting to establish himself and willing to work, will be welcomed and aided, and be pretty certain to find some place where he can steadily improve his condition. But the regions about which one hears most, which are already fruit gardens and well sprinkled with rose-clad homes, command prices per acre which seem extravagant. Land, however, like a mine, gets its value from what it will produce; and it is to be noted that while the subsidence of the "boom" knocked the value out of twenty-feet city lots staked out in the wilderness, and out of insanely inflated city property, the land upon which crops are raised has steadily appreciated in value.

So many conditions enter into the price of land that it is impossible to name an average price for the arable land of the southern counties, but I have heard good judges place it at $100 an acre. The lands with water are very much alike in their producing power, but some, for climatic reasons, are better adapted to citrus fruits, others to the raisin grape, and others to deciduous fruits. The value is also affected by railway facilities, contiguity to the local commercial centre, and also by the character of the settlement, that is, by its morality, public spirit, and facilities for education. Every town and settlement thinks it has special advantages as to improved irrigation, equability of temperature, adaptation to this or that product, attractions for invalids, tempered ocean breezes, protection from "northers," schools, and varied industries. These things are so much matter of personal choice that each settler will do well to examine widely for himself, and not buy until he is suited.

Some figures, which may be depended on, of actual sales and of annual yields, may be of service. They are of the district east of Pasadena and Pomona, but fairly represent the whole region down to Los Angeles. The selling price of raisin grape land unimproved but with water at Riverside is $250 to $300 per acre; at South Riverside, $150 to $200; in the highland district of San Bernardino, and at Redlands (which is a new settlement east of the city of San Bernardino), $200 to $250 per acre. At Banning and at Hesperia, which lie north of the San Bernardino range, $125 to $150 per acre are the prices asked. Distance from the commercial centre accounts for the difference in price in the towns named. The crop varies with the care and skill of the cultivator, but a fair average from the vines at two years is two tons per acre; three years, three tons; four years, five tons; five years, seven tons. The price varies with the season, and also whether its sale is upon the vines, or after picking, drying, and sweating, or the packed product. On the vines $20 per ton is a fair average price. In exceptional cases vineyards at Riverside have produced four tons per acre in twenty months from the setting of the cuttings, and six-year-old vines have produced thirteen and a half tons per acre. If the grower has a crop of, say, 2000 packed boxes of raisins of twenty pounds each box, it will pay him to pack his own crop and establish a "brand" for it. In 1889 three adjoining vineyards in Riverside, producing about the same average

crops, were sold as follows: the first vineyard, at $17 50 per ton on the vines, yield-
ed $150 per acre; the second, at six cents
a pound in the sweat boxes, yielded $276
per acre; the third, at $1 80 per box pack-
ed, yielded $414 per acre.

Land adapted to the deciduous fruits,
such as apricots and peaches, is worth as
much as raisin land, and some years pays
better. The pear and the apple need
greater elevation, and are of better quality when grown on high ground than in
the valleys. I have reason to believe
that the mountain regions of San Diego
County are specially adapted to the apple.

Good orange land unimproved but
with water is worth from $300 to $500 an
acre. If we add to this price the cost of
budded trees, the care of them for four
years, and interest at eight per cent. per
annum for four years, the cost of a good
grove will be about $1000 an acre. It
must be understood that the profit of an
orange grove depends upon care, skill,
and business ability. The kind of orange
grown with reference to the demand, the
judgment about more or less irrigation as
affecting the quality, the cultivation of
the soil, and the arrangements for marketing are all elements in the problem.
There are young groves at Riverside, five
years old, that are paying ten per cent.
net upon from $3000 to $5000 an acre;
while there are older groves which, at the
prices for fruit in the spring of 1890—
$1 60 per box for seedlings and $3 per box
for navels delivered at the packing-houses
—paid at the rate of ten per cent. net on
$7500 per acre.

In all these estimates water must be
reckoned as a prime factor. What, then,
is water worth per inch, generally, in all
this fruit region from Redlands to Los
Angeles? It is worth just the amount it
will add to the commercial value of land
irrigated by it, and that may be roughly
estimated at from $500 to $1000 an inch
of continuous flow. Take an illustration. A piece of land at Riverside below
the flow of water was worth $300 an acre.
Contiguous to it was another piece not irrigated which would not sell for $50 an acre.
By bringing water to it, it would quickly
sell for $300, thus adding $250 to its value.
As the estimate at Riverside is that one
inch of water will irrigate five acres of
fruit land, five times $250 would be $1250
per inch, at which price water for irrigation has actually been sold at Riverside.

The standard of measurement of water
in southern California is the miner's inch
under four inches pressure, or the amount
that will flow through an inch-square
opening under a pressure of four inches
measured from the surface of the water
in the conduit to the centre of the opening through which it flows. This is nine
gallons a minute, or, as it is figured, 1728
cubic feet or 12,960 gallons in twenty-
four hours, and $\frac{1}{50}$ of a cubic foot a second. This flow would cover ten acres
about eighteen inches deep in a year; that
is, it would give the land the equivalent of
eighteen inches of rain, distributed exactly when and where it was needed, none
being wasted, and more serviceable than
fifty inches of rainfall as it generally
comes. This, with the natural rainfall,
is sufficient for citrus fruits and for corn
and alfalfa, in soil not too sandy, and it
is too much for grapes and all deciduous
fruits.

It is necessary to understand this problem of irrigation in order to comprehend
southern California, the exceptional value
of its arable land, the certainty and great
variety of its products, and the part it is
to play in our markets. There are three
factors in the expectation of a crop, soil,
sunshine, and water. In a region where
we can assume the first two to be constant, the only uncertainty is water.
Southern California is practically without
rain from May to December. Upon this
fact rests the immense value of its soil,
and the certainty that it can supply the
rest of the Union with a great variety of
products. This certainty must be purchased by a previous investment of money. Water is everywhere to be had for
money, in some localities by surface wells,
in others by artesian wells, in others from
such streams as the Los Angeles and the
Santa Ana, and from reservoirs secured
by dams in the heart of the high mountains. It is possible to compute the cost
of any one of the systems of irrigation, to
determine whether it will pay by calcu-
lating the amount of land it will irrigate.
The cost of procuring water varies greatly with the situation, and it is conceivable that money can be lost in such an investment, but I have yet to hear of any
irrigation that has not been more or less
successful.

Farming and fruit-raising are usually
games of hazard. Good crops and poor
crops depend upon enough rain and not

RAISIN-CURING.

too much at just the right times. A wheat field which has a good start with moderate rain may later wither in a drought, or be ruined by too much water at the time of maturity. And, avoiding all serious reverses from either dryness or wet, every farmer knows that the quality and quantity of the product would be immensely improved if the growing stalks and roots could have water when and only when they need it. The difference would be between say twenty and forty bushels of grain or roots to the acre, and that means the difference between profit and loss. There is probably not a crop of any kind grown in the great West that would not be immensely benefited if it could be irrigated once or twice a year; and probably anywhere that water is attainable the cost of irrigation would be abundantly paid in the yield from year to year. Farming in the West with even a little irrigation would not be the game of hazard that it is. And it may further be assumed that there is not a vegetable patch or a fruit orchard East or West that would not yield better quality and more abundantly with irrigation.

But this is not all. Any farmer who attempts to raise grass and potatoes and strawberries on contiguous fields, subject to the same chance of drought or rainfall,

has a vivid sense of his difficulties. The potatoes are spoiled by the water that helps the grass, and the coquettish strawberry will not thrive on the regimen that suits the grosser crops. In California, which by its climate and soil gives a greater variety of products than any other region in the Union, the supply of water is adjusted to the needs of each crop, even on contiguous fields. No two products need the same amount of water, or need it at the same time. The orange needs more than the grape, the alfalfa more than the orange, the peach and apricot less than the orange; the olive, the fig, the almond, the English walnut, demand each a different supply. Depending entirely on irrigation six months of the year, the farmer in southern California is practically certain of his crop year after year; and if all his plants and trees are in a healthful condition, as they will be if he is not too idle to cultivate as well as irrigate, his yield will be about double what it would be without systematic irrigation. It is this practical control of the water the year round, in a climate where sunshine is the rule, that makes the productiveness of California so large as to be incomprehensible to Eastern people. Even the trees are not dormant more than three or four months in the year.

But irrigation, in order to be successful, must be intelligently applied. In unskilful hands it may work more damage than benefit. Mr. Theodore S. Van Dyke, who may always be quoted with confidence, says that the ground should never be flooded; that water must not touch the plant or tree, or come near enough to make the soil bake around it; and that it should be let in in small streams for two or three days, and not in large streams for a few hours. It is of the first importance that the ground shall be stirred as soon as dry enough, the cultivation to be continued, and water never to be substituted for the cultivator to prevent baking. The methods of irrigation in use may be reduced to three. First, the old Mexican way, running a small ditch from tree to tree without any basin round the tree. Second, the basin system, where a large basin is made round the tree, and filled several times. This should only be used where water is scarce, for it trains the roots like a brush instead of sending them out laterally into the soil. Third, the Riverside method, which is the best in the world, and produces the largest results with the least water and the least work. It is the closest imitation of the natural process of wetting by gentle rain. "A small flume eight or ten inches square of common redwood is laid along the upper side of a ten-acre tract. At intervals of one to three feet, according to the nature of the ground and the stuff to be irrigated, are bored one-inch holes, with a small wooden button over them to regulate the flow. This flume costs a trifle, is left in position, lasts for years, and is always ready. Into this flume is turned from the ditch an irrigating head of 20, 25, or 30 inches of water, generally about 20 inches. This is divided by the holes and the buttons into streams of from one-sixth to one-tenth of an inch each, making from 120 to 200 small streams. From five to seven furrows are made between two rows of trees, two between rows of grapes, one furrow between rows of corn, potatoes, etc. It may take from fifteen to twenty hours for one of the streams to get across the tract. They are allowed to run from forty-eight to seventy-two hours. The ground is then thoroughly wet in all directions and three or four feet deep. As soon as the ground is dry enough, cultivation is begun, and kept up from six to eight weeks

before water is used again." Only when the ground is very sandy is the basin system necessary. Long experiment has taught that this system is by far the best, and, says Mr. Van Dyke, "those whose ideas are taken from the wasteful systems of flooding or soaking from big ditches have something to learn in southern California."

As to the quantity of water needed in the kind of soil most common in southern California, I will again quote Mr. Van Dyke: "They will tell you at Riverside that they use an inch of water to five acres, and some say an inch to three acres. But this is because they charge to the land all the waste on the main ditch, and because they use thirty per cent. of the water in July and August, when it is the lowest. But this is no test of the duty of water; the amount actually delivered on the land should be taken. What they actually use for ten acres at Riverside, Redlands, etc., is a twenty-inch stream of three days run five times a year, equal to 300 inches for one day, or one inch steady run for 300 days. As an inch is the equivalent of 365 inches for one day, or one inch for 365 days, 300 inches for one day equals an inch to twelve acres. Many use even less than this, running the water only two or two and a half days at a time. Others use more head; but it rarely exceeds 24 inches for three days and five times a year, which would be 72 multiplied by five, or 360 inches, a little less than a full inch for a year for ten acres."

I have given room to these details because the Riverside experiment, which results in such large returns of excellent fruit, is worthy of the attention of cultivators everywhere. The constant stirring of the soil, to keep it loose as well as to keep down useless growths, is second in importance only to irrigation. Some years ago, when it was ascertained that tracts of land which had been regarded as only fit for herding cattle and sheep would by good ploughing and constant cultivation produce fair crops without any artificial watering, there spread abroad a notion that irrigation could be dispensed with. There are large areas, dry and cracked on the surface, where the soil is moist three and four feet below the surface in the dry season. By keeping the surface broken and well pulverized the moisture rises sufficiently to insure a crop.

Many Western farmers have found out this secret of cultivation, and more will learn in time the good sense of not spreading themselves over too large an area; that 40 acres planted and cultivated will give a better return than 80 acres planted and neglected. Crops of various sorts are raised in southern California by careful cultivation with little or no irrigation, but the idea that cultivation alone will bring sufficiently good production is now practically abandoned, and the al-

there is no exception to the rule that continual labor, thrift, and foresight are essential to the getting of a good living or the gaining of a competence. No doubt speculation will spring up again. It is inevitable with the present enormous and yearly increasing yield of fruits,

IRRIGATION BY ARTESIAN WELL SYSTEM.

IRRIGATION BY PIPE SYSTEM.

the better intelligence in vine culture, wine-making, and raisin-curing, the growth of marketable oranges, lemons, etc., and the consequent rise in the value of land. Doubtless fortunes will be made

most universal experience is that judicious irrigation always improves the crop in quality and in quantity, and that irrigation and cultivation are both essential to profitable farming or fruit-raising.

It would seem, then, that capital is necessary for successful agriculture or horticulture in southern California. But where is it not needed? In New England? In Kansas, where land which was given to actual settlers is covered with mortgages for money absolutely necessary to develop it? But passing this by, what is the chance in southern California for laborers and for mechanics? Let us understand the situation. In California

by enterprising companies who secure large areas of unimproved land at low prices, bring water on them, and then sell in small lots. But this will come to an end. The tendency is to subdivide the land into small holdings—into farms and gardens of ten and twenty acres. The great ranches are sure to be broken up. With the resulting settlement by industrious people, the cities will again experience "booms"; but these are not peculiar to California. In my mind I see the time when this region (because it will pay better proportionally to cultivate a small area) will be one of small farms, of neat cottages, of industrious homes. The owner is pretty certain to prosper—that is, to get a good living (which is independence) and lay aside a little yearly—if the work is done by himself and his family. And the peculiarity of the situation is that the farm or garden, whichever it is called, will give agreeable and most healthful occupation to all the boys and girls in the family all the days in the year that can be spared from the school. Aside from the ploughing, the labor is light. Pruning, grafting, budding, the picking of the grapes, the gathering of the fruit from trees, the sorting, packing, and canning, are labor for light and deft hands, and labor distributed through the year. The harvest, of one sort and another, is almost continuous, so that young girls and boys can have, in well-settled districts, pretty steady employment—a long season in establishments packing oranges; at another time, in canning fruits; at another, in packing raisins.

It goes without saying that in the industries now developed, and in others as important which are in their infancy (for instance, the culture of the olive for oil and as an article of food, the growth and curing of figs, the gathering of almonds, English walnuts, etc.), the labor of the owners of the land and their families will not suffice. There must be as large a proportion of day-laborers as there is in other regions where such products are grown. Chinese labor at certain seasons has been a necessity. Under the present policy of California this must diminish, and its place be taken by some other. The pay for this labor has always been good. It is certain to be more and more in demand. Whether the pay will ever approach near to the European standard is a question, but it is a fair presumption that the exceptional profit of the land, owing to its productiveness, will for 'a long time keep wages up.

During the "boom" period all wages were high, those of skilled mechanics especially, owing to the great amount of building on speculation. The ordinary laborer on a ranch had $30 a month and board and lodging; laborers of a higher grade, $2 to $2 50 a day; skilled masons, $6; carpenters, from $3 50 to $5; plasterers, $4 to $5; house-servants, from $25 to $35 a month. Since the "boom," wages of skilled mechanics have declined at least 25 per cent., and there has been less demand for labor generally, except in connection with fruit raising and harvesting. It would be unwise for laborers to go to California on an uncertainty, but it can be said of that country with more confidence than of any other section that its peculiar industries, now daily increasing, will absorb an increasing amount of day-labor, and later on it will remunerate skilled artisan labor.

In deciding whether southern California would be an agreeable place of residence there are other things to be considered besides the productiveness of the soil, the variety of products, the ease of outdoor labor distributed through the year, the certainty of returns for intelligent investment with labor, the equability of summer and winter, and the adaptation to personal health. There are always disadvantages attending the development of a new country and the evolution of a new society. It is not a small thing, and may be one of daily discontent, the change from a landscape clad with verdure, the riotous and irrepressible growth of a rainy region, to a land that the greater part of the year is green only where it is artificially watered, where all the hills and unwatered plains are brown and sere, where the foliage is coated with dust, and where driving anywhere outside the sprinkled avenues of a town is to be enveloped in a cloud of powdered earth. This discomfort must be weighed against the commercial advantages of a land of irrigation.

What are the chances for a family of very moderate means to obtain a foothold and thrive by farming in southern California? I cannot answer this better than by giving substantially the experience of one family, and by saying that this has been paralleled, with change of details, by many others. Of course, in a highly developed settlement, where the land is mostly cultivated, and its actual yearly produce makes its price very high, it is not easy to get a foothold. But there are many regions—say in Orange County, and certainly in San Diego—where land can be had at a moderate price and on easy terms of payment. Indeed, there are few places, as I have said, where an industrious family would not find welcome and cordial help in establishing itself. And it must be remembered that there are many communities where life is very simple, and the great expense of keeping up an appearance attending life elsewhere need not be reckoned.

GARDEN SCENE, SANTA ANA.

A few years ago a professional man in a New England city, who was in delicate health, with his wife, and five boys all under sixteen, and one too young to be of any service, moved to San Diego. He had in money a small sum, less than a thousand dollars. He had no experience in farming or horticulture, and his health would not have permitted him to do much field work in our climate. Fortunately he found in the fertile El Cajon Valley, fifteen miles from San Diego, a farmer and fruit-grower who had upon his place a small unoccupied house. Into that house he moved, furnishing it very simply with furniture bought in San Diego, and hired his services to the landlord. The work required was comparatively easy, in the orchard and vineyards, and consisted largely in superintending other laborers. The pay was about enough to support his family without encroaching on his little capital. Very soon, however, he made an arrangement to buy the small house and tract of some twenty acres, on which he lived, on time, perhaps making a partial payment. He began at once to put out an orange orchard and plant a vineyard; this he accomplished with the assistance of his boys, who did practically most of the work after the first planting, leaving him a chance to give most of his days to his employer. The orchard and vineyard work is so light that a smart intelligent boy is almost as valuable a worker in the field as a man. The wife, meantime, kept the house and did its work. House-keeping was comparatively easy; little fuel was required except for cooking; the question of clothes was a minor one. In that climate wants for a fairly comfortable existence are fewer than with us. From the first, almost, vegetables, raised upon the ground while the vines and oranges were growing, contributed largely to the support of the family. The out-door life and freedom from worry insured better health, and the diet of fruit and vegetables, suitable to the climate, reduced the cost of living to a minimum. As soon as the orchard and the vineyard began to produce fruit, the owner was enabled to quit working for his neighbor, and give all his time to the development of his own place. He increased his planting; he added to his house; he bought a piece of land adjoining which had a grove of eucalyptus, which would supply him with fuel. At first the society circle was small, and there was no school. But the incoming of families had increased the number of children, so that an excellent public school was established. When I saw him he was living in conditions of comfortable industry; his land had trebled in value; the pair of horses which he drove he had bought cheap, for they were Eastern horses; but the climate had brought them up, so that the team was a serviceable one in good condition. The story is not one of brilliant success, but to me it is much more hopeful for the country than the other tales I heard of sudden wealth or lucky speculation. It is the founding in an unambitious way of a comfortable home. The boys of the family will branch out, get fields, orchards, vineyards of their own, and add to the solid producing industry of the country. This orderly, contented industry, increasing its gains day by day, little by little, is the life and hope of any state.

It is not the purpose of this paper to describe southern California. That has been thoroughly done; and details, with figures and pictures in regard to every town and settlement, will be forthcoming on application, which will be helpful guides to persons who can see for themselves, or make sufficient allowance for local enthusiasm. But before speaking further of certain industries south of the great mountain ranges, the region north of the Sierra Madre, which is allied to southern California by its productions, should be mentioned. The beautiful Antelope Plains and the Kern Valley (where land is still cheap and very productive) should not be overlooked. The splendid San Joaquin Valley is already speaking loudly and clearly for itself. The region north of the mountains of Kern County, shut in by the Sierra Nevada range on the east and the Coast Range on the west, substantially one valley, fifty to sixty miles in breadth, watered by the King and the San Joaquin, and gently sloping to the north, say for two hundred miles,

is a land of marvellous capacity, capable of sustaining a dense population. It is cooler in winter than southern California, and the summers average much warmer. Owing to the greater heat, the fruits mature sooner. It is just now becoming celebrated for its raisins, which in quality are unexcelled; and its area, which can be well irrigated from the rivers and from the mountains on either side, seems capable of producing raisins enough to supply the world. It is a wonderfully rich valley in a great variety of products. Fresno County, which occupies the centre of this valley, has 1,200,000 acres of agricultural and 4,400,000 of mountain and pasture land. The city of Fresno, which occupies land that in 1870 was a sheep ranch, is the commercial centre of a beautiful agricultural and fruit region, and has a population estimated at 12,000. From this centre were shipped, in the season of 1890, 1500 car loads of raisins. In 1865 the only exports of Fresno County were a few bales of wool. The report of 1889 gave a shipment of 700,000 boxes of raisins, and the whole export of 1890, of all products, was estimated at $10,000,000. Whether these figures are exact or not, there is no doubt of the extraordinary success of the raisin industry, nor that this is a region of great activity and promise.

The traveller has constantly to remind himself that this is a new country, and to be judged as a new country. It is out of his experience that trees can grow so fast, and plantations in so short a time put on an appearance of maturity. When he sees a roomy, pretty cottage overrun with vines and flowering plants, set in the midst of trees and lawns and gardens of tropical appearance and luxuriance, he can hardly believe that three years before this spot was desert land. When he looks over miles of vineyards, of groves of oranges, olives, walnuts, prunes, the trees all in vigorous bearing, he cannot believe that five or ten years before the whole region was a waste. When he enters a handsome village, with substantial buildings of brick, and perhaps of stone, with fine school-houses, banks, hotels, an opera-house, large packing-houses, and warehouses, and shops of all sorts, with tasteful dwellings and lovely ornamented lawns, it is hard to understand that all this is the creation of two or three years. Yet these surprises meet the traveller at

GRAPE-VINES ON THE GROUNDS OF MR. MAGEE, MONTECITO VALLEY, SANTA BARBARA.

every turn, and the wonder is that there is not visible more crudeness, eccentric taste, and evidence of hasty beginnings.

San Bernardino is comparatively an old town. It was settled in 1853 by a colony of Mormons from Salt Lake. The remains of this colony, less than a hundred, still live here, and have a church like the other sects, but they call themselves Josephites, and do not practise polygamy. There is probably not a sect or schism in the United States that has not its representative in California. Until 1865 San Bernardino was merely a straggling settlement, and a point of distribution for Arizona. The discovery that a large part of the county was adapted to the orange and the vine, and the advent of the Santa Fe Railway, changed all that. Land that then might have been bought for $4 an acre is now sold at from $200 to $300, and the city has become the busy commercial centre of a large number of growing villages, and of one of the most remarkable orange

and vine districts in the world. It has many fine buildings, a population of about 6000, and a decided air of vigorous business. The great plain about it is mainly devoted to agricultural products, which are grown without irrigation, while in the near foot-hills the orange and the vine flourish by the aid of irrigation. Artesian wells abound in the San Bernardino plain, but the mountains are the great and unfailing source of water supply. The Bear Valley Dam is a most daring and gigantic construction. A solid wall of masonry 300 feet long and 60 feet high, curving toward the reservoir, creates an inland lake in the mountains holding water enough to irrigate 20,000 acres of land. This is conveyed to distributing reservoirs in the east end of the valley. On a terrace in the foot-hills a few miles to the north, 2000 feet above the sea, are the Arrow-head Hot Springs (named from the figure of a gigantic "arrow-head" on the mountain above), already a favorite resort for health and pleasure. The views from the plain of the picturesque foot-hills and the snow peaks of the San Bernardino range are exceedingly fine. The marvellous beauty of the purple and deep violet of the giant hills at sunset, with spotless snow, lingers in the memory.

Perhaps the settlement of Redlands, ten miles by rail east of San Bernardino, is as good an illustration as any of rapid development and great promise. It is devoted to the orange and the grape. As late as 1875 much of it was government land, considered valueless. It had a few settlers, but the town, which counts now about 2000 people, was only begun in 1887. It has many solid brick edifices and many pretty cottages on its gentle slopes and rounded hills, overlooked by the great mountains. The view from any point of vantage of orchards and vineyards and semi-tropical gardens, with the wide sky-line of noble and snow-clad hills, is exceedingly attractive. The region is watered by the Santa Ana River and Mill Creek, but the main irrigating streams, which make every hill-top to bloom with vegetation, come from the Bear Valley Reservoir. On a hill to the south of the town, the Smiley Brothers, of Catskill fame, are building fine residences, and planting their 125 acres with fruit trees and vines, evergreens, flowers, and semi-tropic shrubbery in a style of landscape-gardening that in three years at the farthest will make this spot one of the few great show-places of the country. Behind their ridge is the San Mateo Cañon, through which the Southern Pacific Railway runs, while in front are the splendid sloping plains, valleys, and orange groves, and the great sweep of mountains from San Jacinto round to the Sierra Madre range. It is almost a matchless prospect. The climate is most agreeable, the plantations increase month by month, and thus far the orange-trees have not been visited by the scale, nor the vines by any sickness. Although the groves are still young, there were shipped from Redlands in the season of 1889-90 80 car loads of oranges, of 286 boxes to the car, at a price averaging nearly $1000 a car. That season's planting of oranges was over 1200 acres. It had over 5000 acres in fruits, of which nearly 3000 were in peaches, apricots, grapes, and other sorts called deciduous.

Riverside may without prejudice be re-garded as the centre of the orange growth and trade. The railway shipments of oranges from southern California in the season of 1890 aggregated about 2400 car loads, or about 800,000 boxes, of oranges (in which estimate the lemons are included), valued at about $1,500,000. Of this shipment more than half was from Riverside. This has been, of course, greatly stimulated by the improved railroad facilities, among them the shortening of the time to Chicago by the Santa Fe route, and the running of special fruit trains. Southern California responds like magic to this chance to send her fruits to the East, and the area planted month by month is something enormous. It is estimated that the crop of oranges alone in 1891 will be over 4500 car loads. We are accustomed to discount all California estimates, but I think that no one yet has comprehended the amount to which the shipments to Eastern markets of vegetables and fresh and canned fruits will reach within five years. I base my prediction upon some observation of the Eastern demand and the reports of fruit dealers, upon what I saw of the new planting all over the State in 1890, and upon the statistics of increase. Take Riverside as an example. In 1872 it was a poor sheep ranch. In 1880-1 it shipped 15 car loads, or 4290 boxes, of oranges; the amount yearly increased, until in 1888-9 it was 925 car loads, or 263,879 boxes. In 1890 it rose to 1253 car loads, or 358,341 boxes; and an important fact is that the largest shipment was in April (455 car loads, or 130,226 boxes), at the time when the supply from other orange regions for the markets east had nearly ceased.

It should be said also that the quality of the oranges has vastly improved. This is owing to better cultivation, knowledge of proper irrigation, and the adoption of the best varieties for the soil. As different sorts of oranges mature at different seasons, a variety is needed to give edible fruit in each month from December to May inclusive. In February, 1887, I could not find an orange of the first class compared with the best fruit in other regions. It may have been too early for the varieties I tried; but I believe there has been a marked improvement in quality. In May, 1890, we found delicious oranges almost everywhere. The seedless Washington and Australian navels are favorites, especially for the market, on account of

ORANGE CULTURE.
Irrigating an Orchard—Packing Oranges—Navel Orange-tree Six Years Old—Irrigating an Orange Grove.

their great size and fine color. When in perfection they are very fine, but the skin is thick and the texture coarser than that of some others. The best orange I happened to taste was a Tahiti seedling at Montecito (Santa Barbara). It is a small orange, with a thin skin and a compact sweet pulp that leaves little fibre. It resembles the famous orange of Malta. But there are many excellent varieties— the Mediterranean sweet, the paper rind St. Michael, the Maltese blood, etc. The experiments with seedlings are profitable, and will give ever new varieties. I noted that the "grape fruit," which is becoming so much liked in the East, is not appreciated in California.

The city of Riverside occupies an area of some five miles by three, and claims to have 6000 inhabitants; the centre is a substantial town with fine school and other public buildings, but the region is one succession of orange groves and vineyards, of comfortable houses and broad avenues. One avenue through which we drove is 125 feet wide and 12 miles long, planted in three rows with palms, magnolias, the *Grevillea robusta* (Australian fern), the pepper, and the eucalyptus, and lined all the way by splendid orange groves, in the midst of which are houses and grounds with semi-tropical attractions. Nothing could be lovelier than such a scene of fruits and flowers, with the background of purple hills and snowy peaks. The mountain views are superb. Frost is a rare visitor. Not in fifteen years has there been enough to affect the orange. There is little rain after March, but there are fogs and dew-falls, and the ocean breeze is felt daily. The grape grown for raisins is the muscat, and this has had no "sickness." Vigilance and a quarantine have also kept from the orange the scale which has been so annoying in some other localities. The orange, when cared for, is a generous bearer; some trees produce twenty boxes each, and there are areas of twenty acres in good bearing which have brought to the owner as much as $10,000 a year.

The whole region of the Santa Ana and San Gabriel valleys, from the desert on the east to Los Angeles, the city of gardens, is a surprise, and year by year an increasing wonder. In production it exhausts the catalogue of fruits and flowers; its scenery is varied by ever-new combinations of the picturesque and the luxuriant; every town boasts some special advantage in climate, soil, water, or society; but these differences, many of them visible to the eye, cannot appear in any written description. The traveller may prefer the scenery of Pasadena, or that of Pomona, or of Riverside, but the same words in regard to color, fertility, combinations of orchards, avenues, hills, must appear in the description of each. Ontario, Pomona, Puente, Alhambra—wherever one goes there is the same wonder of color and production.

Pomona is a pleasant city in the midst of fine orange groves, watered abundantly by artesian wells and irrigating ditches from a mountain reservoir. A specimen of the ancient adobe residence is on the Meserve plantation, a lovely old place, with its gardens of cherries, strawberries, olives, and oranges. From the top of San José hill we had a view of a plain twenty-five miles by fifty in extent, dotted with cultivation, surrounded by mountains—a wonderful prospect. Pomona, like its sister cities in this region, has a regard for the intellectual side of life, exhibited in good school-houses and public libraries. In the library of Pomona is what may be regarded as the tutelary deity of the place, the goddess Pomona, a good copy in marble of the famous statue in the Uffizi Gallery, presented to the city by the Rev. C. F. Loop. This enterprising citizen is making valuable experiments in olive culture, raising a dozen varieties in order to ascertain which is best adapted to this soil, and which will make the best return in oil and in a marketable product of cured fruit for the table.

The growth of the olive is to be, it seems to me, one of the leading and most permanent industries of southern California. It will give us, what it is nearly impossible to buy now, pure olive oil, in place of the cotton-seed and lard mixture in general use. It is a most wholesome and palatable article of food. Those whose chief experience of the olive is the large, coarse, and not agreeable Spanish variety, used only as an appetizer, know little of the value of the best varieties as food, nutritious as meat, and always delicious. Good bread and a dish of pickled olives make an excellent meal. The sort known as the Mission olive, planted by the Franciscans a century ago, is generally grown now, and the best fruit is from the older trees. The most suc-

IN A FIELD OF GOLDEN
PUMPKINS.

cessful attempts in cultivating the olive and putting it on the market have been made by Mr. F. A. Kimball, of National City, and Mr. Ellwood Cooper, of Santa Barbara. The experiments have gone far enough to show that the industry is very remunerative. The best olive oil I have ever tasted anywhere is that produced from the Cooper and the Kimball orchards; but not enough is produced to supply the local demand. Mr. Cooper has written a careful treatise on olive culture, which will be of great service to all growers. The art of pickling is not yet mastered, and perhaps some other variety will be preferred to the Old Mission for the table. A mature olive grove in good bearing is a fortune. I feel sure that within twenty-five years this will be one of the most profitable industries of California, and that the demand for pure oil and edible fruit in the United States will drive out the adulterated and inferior present commercial products. But California can easily ruin its reputation by adopting the European systems of adulteration.

We drove one day from Arcadia Station through the region occupied by the Baldwin plantations, an area of over fifty thousand acres—a happy illustration of what industry and capital can do in the way of variety of productions, especially in what are called the Santa Anita vineyards and orchards, extending southward from the foot-hills. About the home place and in many sections where the irrigating streams flow one might fancy he was in the tropics, so abundant and brilliant are the flowers and exotic plants. There are splendid orchards of oranges, almonds, English walnuts, lemons, peaches, apricots, figs, apples, and olives, with grain and corn—in short, everything that grows in garden or field. The ranch is famous for its brandies and wines as well as fruits. We lunched at the East San Gabriel Hotel, a charming place with a peaceful view from the wide veranda of live-oaks, orchards, vineyards, and the noble Sierra Madre range. The Californians may be excused for using the term paradisiacal about such scenes. Flowers, flowers everywhere, color on color, and the song of the mocking-bird!

In this region and elsewhere I saw evidence of the perils that attend the culture of the vine and the fruit tree in all other countries, and from which California in the early days thought it was exempt.

Within the past three or four years there has prevailed a sickness of the vine, the cause of which is unknown, and for which no remedy has been discovered. No blight was apparent, but the vine sickened and failed. The disease was called consumption of the vine. I saw many vineyards subject to it, and hundreds of acres of old vines had been rooted up as useless. I was told by a fruit buyer in Los Angeles that he thought the raisin industry below Fresno was ended unless new planting recovered the vines, and that the great wine fields were about "played out." The truth I believe to be that the disease is confined to the vineyards of Old Mission grapes. Whether these had attained the limit of their active life, and sickened, I do not know. The trouble for a time was alarming; but new plantings of other varieties of grapes have been successful, the vineyards look healthful, and the growers expect no further difficulty. The planting, which was for a time suspended, has been more vigorously renewed.

The insect pests attacking the orange were even more serious, and in 1887-8, though little was published about it, there was something like a panic, in the fear that the orange and lemon culture in southern California would be a failure. The enemies were the black, the red, and the white scale. The last, the *Icerya purchasi*, or cottony cushion scale, was especially loathsome and destructive; whole orchards were enfeebled, and no way was discovered of staying its progress, which threatened also the olive and every other tree, shrub, and flower. Science was called on to discover its parasite. This was found to be the Australian lady-bug (*Vedolia cardinalis*), and in 1888-9 quantities of this insect were imported and spread throughout Los Angeles County, and sent to Santa Barbara and other afflicted districts. The effect was magical. The vedolia attacked the cottony scale with intense vigor, and everywhere killed it. The orchards revived as if they had been recreated, and the danger was over. The enemies of the black and the red scale have not yet been discovered, but they probably will be. Meantime the growers have recovered courage, and are fertilizing and fumigating. In Santa Ana I found that the red scale was fought successfully by fumigating the trees. The operation is performed at night under a movable tent, which covers the tree. The cost is about twenty cents a tree. One lesson of all this is that trees must be fed in order to be kept vigorous to resist such attacks, and that fruit-raising, considering the number of enemies that all fruits have in all climates, is not an idle occupation. The clean handsome English walnut is about the only tree in the State that thus far has no enemy.

One cannot take anywhere else a more exhilarating, delightful drive than about the rolling, highly cultivated, many-villaed Pasadena, and out to the foot-hills and the Sierra Madre Villa. He is constantly exclaiming at the varied loveliness of the scene—oranges, palms, formal gardens, hedges of Monterey cypress. It is very Italy-like. The Sierra Madre furnishes abundant water for all the valley, and the swift irrigating stream from Eaton Cañon waters the Sierra Madre Villa. Among the peaks above it rises Mount Wilson, a thousand feet above the plain, the site selected for the Harvard Observatory with its 40-inch glass. The clearness of the air at this elevation, and the absence of clouds night and day the greater portion of the year, make this a most advantageous position, it is said, to use the glass in dissolving nebulæ. The Sierra Madre Villa, once the most favorite resort in this region, was closed. In its sheltered situation, its luxuriant and half-neglected gardens, its wide plantations and irrigating streams, it reminds one of some secularized monastery on the promontory of Sorrento. It only needs good management to make the hotel very attractive, and especially agreeable in the months of winter.

Pasadena, which exhibits everywhere evidences of wealth and culture, and claims a permanent population of 12,000, has the air of a winter resort; the great Hotel Raymond is closed in May, the boarding-houses want occupants, the shops and livery-stables customers, and the streets lack movement. This is easily explained. It is not because Pasadena is not an agreeable summer residence, but because the visitors are drawn there in the winter principally to escape the inclement climate of the North and East, and because special efforts have been made for their entertainment in the winter. We found the atmosphere delightful in the middle of May. The mean summer heat is 67°, and the nights are al-

ways cool. The hills near by may be resorted to with the certainty of finding as decided a change as one desires in the summer season. I must repeat that the southern California summer is not at all understood in the East. The statement of the general equability of the temperature the year through must be insisted on. We lunched one day in a typical California house, in the midst of a garden of fruits, flowers, and tropical shrubs; in a house that might be described as half roses and half tent, for added to the wooden structure were rooms of canvas, which are used as sleeping apartments winter and summer.

This attractive region, so lovely in its cultivation, with so many charming drives, offering good shooting on the plains and in the hills, and centrally placed for excursions, is only eight miles from the busy city of Los Angeles. An excellent point of view of the country is from the graded hill on which stands the Raymond Hotel, a hill isolated but easy of access, which is in itself a mountain of bloom, color, and fragrance. From all the broad verandas and from every window the prospect is charming, whether the eye rests upon cultivated orchards and gardens and pretty villas, or upon the purple foot-hills and the snowy ranges. It enjoys a daily ocean breeze, and the air is always exhilarating. This noble hill is a study in landscape-gardening. It is a mass of brilliant color, and the hospitality of the region generally to foreign growths may be estimated by the trees acclimated on these slopes. They are the pepper, eucalyptus, pine, cypress, sycamore, redwood, olive, date and fan palms, banana, pomegranate, guava, Japanese persimmon, umbrella, maple, elm, locust, English walnut, birch, ailantus, poplar, willow, and more ornamental shrubs than one can well name.

I can indulge in few locality details except those which are illustrative of the general character of the country. In passing into Orange County, which was recently set off from Los Angeles, we come into a region of less "fashion," but one that for many reasons is attractive to people of moderate means who are content with independent simplicity. The country about the thriving village of Santa Ana is very rich, being abundantly watered by the Santa Ana River and by artesian wells. The town is nine miles from the ocean. On the ocean side the

land is mainly agricultural; on the inland side it is specially adapted to fruit. We drove about it, and in Tustin City, which has many pleasant residences and a vacant "boom" hotel, through endless plantations of oranges. On the road toward Los Angeles we passed large herds of cattle and sheep, and fine groves of the English walnut, which thrives especially well in this soil and the neighborhood of the sea. There is comparatively little waste land in this valley district, as one may see by driving through the country about Santa Ana, Orange, Anaheim, Tustin City, etc. Anaheim is a prosperous German colony. It was here that Madame Modjeska and her husband, Count Bozenta, first settled in California. They own and occupy now a picturesque ranch in the Santiago Cañon of the Santa Ana range, twenty-two miles from Santa Ana. This is one of the richest regions in the State, and with its fair quota of working population it will be one of the most productive.

From Newport, on the coast, or from San Pedro, one may visit the island of Santa Catalina. Want of time prevented our going there. Sportsmen enjoy there the exciting pastime of hunting the wild goat. From the photographs I saw, and from all I heard of it, it must be as picturesque a resort in natural beauty as the British Channel Islands.

Los Angeles is the metropolitan centre of all this region. A handsome, solid, thriving city, environed by gardens, gay everywhere with flowers, it is too well known to require any description from me. To the traveller from the East it will always be a surprise. Its growth has been phenomenal, and although it may not equal the expectations of the crazy excitement of 1886–7, 50,000 people is a great assemblage for a new city which numbered only about 11,000 in 1880. It of course felt the subsidence of the "boom," but while I missed the feverish crowds of 1887, I was struck with its substantial progress in fine, solid buildings, pavements, sewerage, railways, educational facilities, and ornamental grounds. It has a secure hold on the commerce of the region. The assessment roll of the city increased from $7,627,632 in 1881 to $44,871,073 in 1889. Its bank business, public buildings, school-houses, and street improvements are in accord with this increase, and show solid, vigor-

OLIVE-TREES SIX YEARS OLD.

ous growth. It is altogether an attractive city, whether seen on a drive through its well-planted and bright avenues, or looked down on from the hills which are climbed by the cable roads. A curious social note was the effect of the "boom" excitement upon the birth rate. The report of children under the age of one year was in 1887, 271 boy babies and 264 girl babies; from 1887 to 1888 there were only 176 boy babies and 162 girl babies. The return at the end of 1889 was 465 boy babies and 500 girl babies.

Although Los Angeles County still produces a considerable quantity of wine and brandy, I have an impression that the raising of raisins will supplant wine-making largely in southern California, and that the principal wine-producing will be in the northern portions of the State. It is certain that the best quality is grown in the foot-hills. The reputation of "California wines" has been much injured by placing upon the market crude juice that was in no sense wine. Great improvement has been made in the past three to five years, not only in the vine and knowledge of the soil adapted to it, but in the handling and the curing of the wine. One can

now find without much difficulty excellent table wines—sound claret, good white Reisling, and sauterne. None of these wines are exactly like the foreign wines, and it may be some time before the taste accustomed to foreign wines is educated to like them. But in Eastern markets some of the best brands are already much called for, and I think it only a question of time and a little more experience when the best California wines will be popular. I found in the San Francisco market excellent red wines at $3 50 the case, and, what was still more remarkable, at some, of the best hotels sound, agreeable claret at from fifteen to twenty cents the pint bottle.

It is quite unnecessary to emphasize the attractions of Santa Barbara, or the productiveness of the valleys in the counties of Santa Barbara and Ventura. There is no more poetic region on the continent than the bay south of Point Conception, and the pen and the camera have made the world tolerably familiar with it. There is a graciousness, a softness, a color in the sea, the cañons, the mountains there that dwells in the memory. It is capable of inspiring the same love that the Greek colonists felt for the region between the bays of Salerno and Naples. It is as fruitful as the Italian shores, and can support as dense a population. The figures that have been given as to productiveness and variety of productions apply to it. Having more winter rainfall than the counties south of it, agriculture is profitable in most years. Since the railway was made down the valley of the Santa Clara River and along the coast to Santa Barbara, a great impulse has been given to farming. Orange and other fruit orchards have increased. Near Buenaventura I saw hundreds of acres of Lima beans. The yield is about one ton to the acre. With good farming the valleys yield crops of corn, barley, and wheat much above the average. Still it is a fruit region, and no variety has yet been tried that does not produce very well there. The rapid growth of all trees has enabled the region to demonstrate in a short time that there is scarcely any that it cannot naturalize. The curious growths of tropical lands, the trees of aromatic and medicinal gums, the trees of exquisite foliage and wealth of fragrant blossoms, the sturdy forest natives, and the bearers of edible nuts, are all to be found in the gardens and by the road-side—from New England, from the Southern States, from Europe, from North and South Africa, southern Asia, China, Japan, from Australia and New Zealand and South America. The region is an arboreal and botanical garden on an immense scale, and full of surprises. The floriculture is even more astonishing. Every land is represented. The profusion and vigor are as wonderful as the variety. At a flower show in Santa Barbara were exhibited 160 varieties of roses all cut from one garden the same morning. The open garden rivals the Eastern conservatory. The country is new, and many of the conditions of life may be primitive and rude, but it is impossible that any region shall not be beautiful, clothed with such a profusion of bloom and color.

I have spoken of the rapid growth. The practical advantage of this as to fruit trees is that one begins to have an income from them here sooner than in the East. No one need be under the delusion that he can live in California without work, or thrive without incessant and intelligent industry, but the distinction of the country for the fruit-grower is the rapidity with which trees and vines mature

to the extent of being profitable. But nothing thrives without care, and kindly as the climate is to the weak, it cannot be too much insisted on that this is no place for confirmed invalids who have not money enough to live without work.

The immense county of San Diego is on the threshold of its development. It has comparatively only spots of cultivation here and there, in an area on the western slope of the county only, that Mr. Van Dyke estimates to contain about one million acres of good arable land for farming and fruit-raising. This mountainous region is full of charming valleys, and hidden among the hills are fruitful nooks capable of sustaining thriving communities. There is no doubt about the salubrity of the climate, and one can literally suit himself as to temperature by choosing his elevation. The traveller by rail down the wild Temecula Cañon will have some idea of the picturesqueness of the country, and, as he descends in the broadening valley, of the beautiful mountain parks of live-oak and clear running water, and of the richness both for grazing and grain of the ranches of the Santa Margarita, Las Flores, and Santa Rosa. Or if he will see what a few years of vigorous cultivation will do, he may visit Escondido, on the river of that name, which is at an elevation of less than a thousand feet, and fourteen miles from the ocean. This is only one of many settlements that have great natural beauty and thrifty industrial life. In that region are numerous attractive villages. I have a report from a little cañon, a few miles north of Escondido, where a woman with an invalid husband settled in 1883. The ground was thickly covered with brush, and its only product was rabbits and quails. In 1888 they had 100 acres cleared and fenced, mostly devoted to orchard fruits and berries. They had in good bearing over 1200 fruit trees, among them 200 oranges and 283 figs, which yielded one and a half tons of figs a week during the bearing season, from August to November. The sprouts of the peach-trees grew twelve feet in 1889. Of course such a little fruit farm as this is the result of self-denial and hard work, but I am sure that the experiment in this region need not be exceptional.

San Diego will be to the southern part of the State what San Francisco is to the northern. Nature seems to have arranged for this, by providing a magnificent har-

SEXTON NURSERIES, NEAR SANTA BARBARA.

bor, when it shut off the southern part by a mountain range. During the town-lot lunacy it was said that San Diego could not grow because it had no back country, and the retort was that it needed no back country, its harbor would command commerce. The fallacy of this assumption lay in the forgetfulness of the fact that the profitable and peculiar exports of southern California must go East by rail, and reach a market in the shortest possible time, and that the inhabitants look to the Pacific for comparatively little of the imports they need. If the isthmus route were opened by a ship-canal, San Diego would doubtless have a great share of the Pacific trade, and when the population of that part of the State is large enough to demand great importations from the islands and lands of the Pacific, this har-

bor will not go begging. But in its present development the entire Pacific trade of Japan, China, and the islands gives only a small dividend each to the competing ports. For these developments this fine harbor must wait, but meantime the wealth and prosperity of San Diego lie at its doors. A country as large as the three richest New England States, with enormous wealth of mineral and stone in its mountains, with one of the finest climates in the world, with a million acres of arable land, is certainly capable of building up one great seaport town. These million of acres on the western slope of the mountain ranges of the country are geographically tributary to San Diego, and almost every acre by its products is certain to attain a high value.

The end of the ridiculous speculation in lots of 1887-8 was not so disastrous in the loss of money invested, or even in the ruin of great expectations by the collapse of fictitious values, as in the stoppage of immigration. The country has been ever since adjusting itself to a normal growth, and the recovery is just in proportion to the arrival of settlers who come to work and not to speculate. I had heard that the "boom" had left San Diego and vicinity the "deadest" region to be found anywhere. A speculator would probably so regard it. But the people have had a great accession of common-sense. The expectation of attracting settlers by a fictitious show has subsided, and attention is directed to the development of the natural riches of the country. Since the boom San Diego has perfected a splendid system of drainage, paved its streets, extended its railways, built up the business part of the town solidly and handsomely, and greatly improved the mesa above the town. In all essentials of permanent growth it is much better in appearance than in 1887. Business is better organized, and, best of all, there is an intelligent appreciation of the agricultural resources of the county. It is discovered that San Diego has a "back country" capable of producing great wealth. The Chamber of Commerce has organized a permanent exhibition of products. It is assisted in this work of stimulation by competition by a "Ladies' Annex," a society numbering some five hundred ladies, who devote themselves not to æsthetic pursuits, but to the quickening of all the industries of the farm and the garden, and all public improvements. To the mere traveller who devotes only a couple of weeks to an examination of this region it is evident that the spirit of industry is in the ascendant, and the result is a most gratifying increase in orchards and vineyards, and the storage and distribution of water for irrigation. The region is unsurpassed for the production of the orange, the lemon, the raisin grape, the fig, and the olive. The great reservoir in the Cuyamaca, which supplies San Diego, sends its flume around the fertile valley of El Cajon (which has already a great reputation for its raisins), and this has become a garden, the land rising in value every year. The region of National City and Chula Vista is supplied by the reservoir made by the great Sweetwater dam—a marvel of engineering skill—and is not only most productive in fruit, but is attractive by pretty villas and most sightly and agreeable homes. It is an unanswerable reply to the inquiry if this region was not killed by the boom that all the arable land, except that staked out for fancy city prices, has steadily risen in value. This is true of all the bay region down through Otay (where a promising watch factory is es-

tablished) to the border at Tia Juana. The rate of settlement in the county outside of the cities and towns has been greater since the boom than before—a most healthful indication for the future. According to the school census of 1889, Mr. Van Dyke estimates a permanent growth of nearly 50,000 people in the county in four years. Half of these are well distributed in small settlements which have the advantages of roads, mails, and school-houses, and which offer to settlers who wish to work adjacent unimproved land at prices which experience shows are still moderate.

In this imperfect conspectus of a vast territory I should be sorry to say anything that can raise false expectations. The country is very big, and though scarcely any part of it has not some advantages, and notwithstanding the census figures of our population, it will be a long time before our vast territory will fill up. California must wait with the rest. But it seems to me to have a great future. Its position in the Union with regard to its peculiar productions is unique. It can and will supply us with much that we now import, and labor and capital sooner or later will find their profit in meeting the growing demand for California products.

There are many people in the United States who could prolong life by moving to southern California; there are many who would find life easier there by reason of the climate, and because out-door labor is more agreeable there the year through; many who have to fight the weather and a niggardly soil for existence could there have pretty little homes with less expense of money and labor. It is well that people for whom this is true should know it. It need not influence those who are already well placed to try the fortune of a distant country and new associations.

I need not emphasize the disadvantage in regard to beauty of a land that can for half the year only keep a vernal appearance by irrigation. But to eyes accustomed to it there is something pleasing in the contrast of the green valleys with the brown and gold and red of the hills. The picture in my mind for the future of the land of the sun, of the mountains, of the sea—which is only an enlargement of the picture of the present—is one of great beauty. The rapid growth of fruit and ornamental trees and the profusion of flowers render easy the making of a love-

SWEETWATER DAM.

ly home, however humble it may be. The nature of the industries —requiring careful attention to a small piece of ground—points to small holdings as a rule. The picture I see is of a land of small farms and gardens, highly cultivated, in all the valleys and on the foot-hills, a land therefore of luxuriance and great productiveness and agreeable homes. I see everywhere the gardens, the vineyards, the orchards, with the various greens of the olive, the fig, and the orange. It is always picturesque, because the country is broken and even rugged; it is always interesting, because of the contrast with the mountains and the desert; it has the color that makes southern Italy so poetic. It is the fairest field for the experiment of a contented community without any poverty and without excessive wealth.

An Orange Empire
(1910)

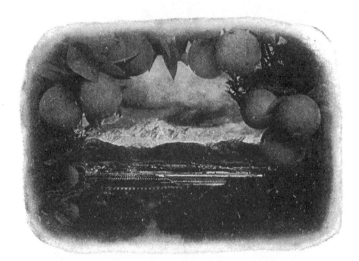

An Orange Empire

San Bernardino County, Where Gold Grows on the Trees—The Literal Blossoming of
the Desert—Attractive Towns and an Ideal Farm Life—The
Beauty of Damascus Among the Orchards

By A. J. WELLS

WHEN Daniel Webster was a boy on the farm he had trouble with his scythe one summer morning. It would not "hang" right. After fixing it two or three times his father finally told him to "hang it to suit himself." Young Daniel hung it on the fence and left the field. Would he have left a California orange grove? The city palled upon Webster as the years went on—he got a farm of his own, and "Marshfield" became a retreat to which he turned with increasing longing. "I find," he said, "better company among my cows and horses than in the Senate,"—and he died on the farm.

If anywhere in the world one hears the call of the country clearly and sympathetically, it is in this delectable region where the farm has become the orange grove, and one does not need to study catalogues to find out the difference between beets and beans, or read a handbook on "How to tell the Crops from the Weeds."

There will always be two opinions about the country—save in an orange grove. The average farm is ragged and dirty isolated and lonely, with its work never done, and its social hunger never appeased. The orange grove is the big ranch cut up into small farms—neighborhood made a fact and not an empty word, work confined to one crop, and clean tillage made a condition of success. Tidiness belongs to the situation, and the orange business becomes the very poetry of horticulture. Its fascination is many-sided.

The "mother lode" of the orange tree

The tree itself is handsome: when loaded with blossoms it is superbly beautiful: when full of ripened fruit it is a pile of golden globes, and satisfies another sense— that of the fitness of things. Yet an orange grove has about it no suggestion of Mammon, or of commercial greed. The very business discourages greed. If you try to raise some other crop between the rows you will soon cut it out. If you stimulate growth unduly, you will soon see the folly of that. If you economize in the matter of fertilizers, the

Alfalfa, a "long green" that rivals the gold of the orange

meager crop will rebuke you where you are most sensitive. The orange tree has its laws, and to learn them is to succeed. The orange tree cannot be ill treated, nor can it be whipped up and made to do its utmost at a time. And if the orange grower will repress his greed and be content with such acreage as he can readily cultivate, the aggregate of such acreage will make a real neighborhood. And this has been done. The bugbear of the country is not found here. There is no isolation and no loneliness. "Tempering their speculative instincts with love of home," the historian says, "they developed towns and surround-

ings of rare beauty and comfort and made them centers of high social and intellectual life." The attractions of the business drew a brainy class, and its exactions developed ability. There were original difficulties of growing, tilling, watering, of soil treatment and of marketing, and these men have solved every problem, and made the orange industry of California the most attractive country life in the world.

The industry is not a pastime for the rich. It is not play-farming nor a matter of sentiment as related to the country, the bacillus of back-to-the-soil, "the aroma of fields," the "nature hunger," and other gush. One coined a phrase some years ago: "California is the rich man's paradise and the poor man's hell." It was like an ax—it had a cutting edge which was true, and the heavy poll which weighted it was false.

No other country offers the rich so much, but it will share its bounty on equal terms with the man of thrift and energy who has his fortune yet to make. The very climatic conditions which make the Golden State attractive to those who can command leisure, tend also to make it the land of the common people. Less land is required to support a family in generous comfort, less fuel, less clothing, or cheaper clothing and less expensive shelter. At the same time the abundant sunshine and peculiar distribution of rainfall necessitates irrigation, and irrigation through a long rainless summer makes the farmer realize more perfectly the ideal of producing what is consumed.

Deposits of golden nuggets made by the San Bernardino sun in five years' time

Water, the partner of the sun in the all-powerful firm that has made a garden of San Bernardino County

The world-famous combination of orange groves and snowy Sierra in San Bernardino County

The Technical School at San Bernardino

Still a land of big things—of big ranches, of big enterprises, of big talk now and then—the true and final greatness of the great state will be found in its aggregate of small farms and an independent population living upon the soil. This is the strength of the orange belt of the south; this has made San Bernardino county rich—the many owners of orange groves—the many tillers of the ground.

The business returns yearly now about $7,500,000 in this county, and this, on the basis of the orange growing acreage, gives each acre credit for $250. That is a substantial average, is it not? To make it, what must be the maximum? We do not have to balance probabilities. Successful men range in this industry all the way from $500 to $800, and even $1,200 an acre, and when you have digested that you will not be surprised to know that the community as a whole is prosperous, and that it is not sentiment but business which pays $2,000 an acre for a bearing orange grove. The Dean of the College of Agriculture for the state, Prof. E. J. Wickson, says of our fruit growing districts that they have the busiest towns, the handsomest rural improvements, the largest assessment rolls, and are the most attractive to homeseekers; and what is true of fruit towns generally, is especially and emphatically true of the citrus towns of this region.

When we saw this district in the early '80's it suggested the biblical description of the desert—"a dry, thirsty land, where no water is." Much of the region was desert in fact. From the western borders of the county eastward to the lowlands of the San Bernardino valley was a barren plain, broken only by a little verdure at Cucamonga, where some springs breaking up made a "cienega," and where a vineyard was flourishing.

Over the hills where Redlands now sits amid orchards and gardens of flowers the writer traveled when they were worth perhaps $2.50 an acre for grazing sheep —a wide sweep of barren, rolling hills, sunburned and brown in early June and apparently hopelessly dry.

To-day, after three decades, the region blossoms with orange groves and vineyards, groves of lemon and orchards of apricots and prunes, and the traveler questions which is most apparent, beauty or bounty. If he has traveled widely, he reaches this conclusion, that California not only stands as the most remarkable state in the Union, but as the most noted division of land in the world, and that no part of California excels in beauty and evident prosperity this part of San Bernardino county redeemed from the desert. Here are nearly a dozen towns credited in the last thirty years, with no frontier airs about them or signs of pioneering. Poets have celebrated the beauty of Damascus

The Masonic Temple at San Bernardino, a Greek facade with a hint of the balconies of Spain

and the region around it—a maze
of bloom and fruitage, where
olive and pomegranate, orange
and apricot, plum and walnut
mingle their varied tints of green.
It is the miracle of irrigation in
the Syrian desert, and the rivers
of Damascus which Naaman
preferred to all the waters of
Israel, that make the life—the in-
estimable treasure of Damascus.
But Damascus is not more beautiful than some of these San
Bernardino towns — Redlands,
San Bernardino, Ontario, Upland
—or than they will be when
fully grown and mature. Seen
from some of the overlooking
heights, the whole region is a
vision of peace and plenty, of exuberant vegetation,
of endless orchards, vineyards and fields of alfalfa.

And it is all the miracle of irrigation in our
modern day, prosaic perhaps, and wearing a commercial aspect, because not ancient and historic,
and because lacking the poetic charm of a great
river. Here the fountains are hidden in the giant
hills and the life-giving streams are but irrigating
ditches, and steal through the orchards unobserved.
But back of the green luxuriance of plain and valley
and foothill, is a story of water development where
no water seemed to be, of flumes and ditches, pipe

The building of the Elks' Club at San Bernardino, suggesting the homes of
an earlier brotherhood

lines and canals, artesian wells, reservoirs, artificial
lakes with hundreds of miles of main canals and
thousands of miles of laterals and distributing ditches.

We need not discuss the problem of the market.
That has been solved by the California Fruit
Growers' Exchange. The railroads are co-operating
—the Southern Pacific having just built a great
pre-cooling plant at Colton, and the Santa Fe
another at San Bernardino; the two costing, perhaps,
a round million of dollars.

There is a great armorial sign on the shield of San
Bernardino valley—that huge, natural Indian arrow-

San Bernardino has the air of a modern city, with its library, other public buildings and busy thoroughfares

Gateway to one of the stately gardens that make San Bernardino County notable in Southern California

The Electric Heating Company at Ontario manufactures some thing prized by the housewife, a hot-point electric flat-iron. About one hundred and fifty persons are employed, and the many bicycles we saw outside the factory indicated the delightful way in which these factory people live among the trees.

This county is like Southern California in this, that only a fraction of it is tillable. Here are 20,160 square miles, and it will help the imagination to realize what these figures mean if we say that Massachusetts, Rhode Island, Delaware and New Jersey will go within the boundaries of this county. Its general surface is made up of mountains and *mesas*, or uplands, of fertile valleys and barren deserts. There are vast mineral deposits in the "waste places"; the sterile northern and eastern parts of the county will insure a dry air, no matter how much irrigation goes on in the orange groves, and the tillable lands, if not quite in one body, are so nearly continuous as to constitute a definite section that is highly cultivated.

head covering several acres of the mountain side. Directly under its point are great mineral hot springs, and connected with them for the use of patrons of the springs, a magnificent hotel. It is an attractive place on a bench of hills that form a dell in the higher range—a recess from which you look out over those gardens of Hesperides in the valley below. The elevation is two thousand feet, and an electric car runs from San Bernardino. The climate is Italian, and the scenery striking, while the hotel is equal to its setting.

These springs have a wide reputation, and for certain diseases are not excelled by any in this country or in Europe. When it ceases to be the thing to go to Europe, the invalid or the semi-invalid will find all here that they can find at the end of a sea voyage, with a better climate and with everything adjusted to American tastes. It is time Americans believed in the natural resources of their own country. Great is the god of tradition—if it is made in Europe. Infectious diseases and tuberculoses are not treated at Arrowhead. The treatment of diseases and morbid conditions for which these waters offer relief is under the direction of a resident physician or medical director of experience. The hotel is a good place of rest for well people. It must be enough to just live in an orange grove, and probably we poor beggars outside are the real patrons of Arrowhead Springs.

The topography includes an elevated plateau or plain, the lowest elevation of which is about nine hundred feet. This plain is traversed by a range of mountains with a northwest and southeast trend, rising to six thousand feet and starting up sharply from the level of the plain, so that foothills are

A residence overlooking the San Bernardino Valley, in keeping with the historical atmosphere of the region

hardly a feature. The highest peaks are respectively 11,800 and 12,600 feet, the latter rising from the desert, and from below the sea-level is one unbroken sweep. In this it is unique among the mountains of the world. This is Mount San Gorgonio, and it is perpetually snow-capped, furnishing much water for irrigation. The general range carries much snow at times, and the abundant orange groves at the base, seen with their perpetual green, or the gold of their fruit, or the

In the heart of a San Bernardino garden, where the green and blue of tropical foliage and California sky are mirrored in beauty

splendor of their blossoms against the background of snow, makes the land seem one of enchantment.

There is much timber on the range, save on the south sides, which yield only chaparral. These forests or forest covers hold back the water of rainfalls or melting snows, and give to the valley an artesian belt of vast value. The San Bernardino valley is one of the best watered valleys of Southern California.

The mountains on the north and east act as a shield from the heated air of the Mojave and Colorado deserts. These deserts are really one, being divided only by a low range of wavy hills, bare and dry as themselves. The Mojave is the northern portion, and is larger than Massachusetts. The southern portion, nearly as large, is the Colorado. To these encircling mountains and these arid

deserts we owe no small part of the charm of our climate and the chief industrial feature of the county.

That opportunities have not all gone by will be seen from the business activity within the county during the past year. It has moved up one in the rank within the year, and is now ninth in a total of fifty-eight counties. Its assessed valuation in 1908 was $33,040,625, a gain of over $3,000,000. The total valuation of the county's products for that period will reach close to $19,000,000.

A notable feature of the county's growth has been the activity in building circles, especially in the erection of homes and manufacturing plants. Every community reports large additions to its residence sections, while from The Needles, the bustling metropolis of the desert on the far eastern boundary of the county, to Ontario, Upland and Chino, on the western line, generous sums have been expended for manufacturing purposes.

An increased acreage is placed under cultivation. The desert region has not been behind the fertile valleys west of the San Bernardino mountains in this respect, having added large areas to the productive column. Water development for agricultural purposes has been widespread and uniformly successful, even in heretofore arid regions, thereby widening the field of productive husbandry and largely increasing the population of the county by attracting industrious homeseekers.

A luxurious, tree-embowered home where not many years ago the prairie-dog had his bare and unpretentious dwelling

The great Arrowhead on the mountain side above the famous springs named by this phenomenon

Development of the county's mining resources has kept pace with its agricultural expansion. Rich discoveries have stimulated interest, and throughout the county's vast mineral belt capital is being expended as never before, and the future of the mining interests never looked more alluring.

Population is steadily increasing, the total gain for the year noted being about 12,000. This expansion is based upon the principle of the "open door," and the man of thrift and energy will readily get a foothold.

These are hints of the resources and attractions of a great county, which run from borax mines to raisin vineyards; from alfalfa fields in the most barren deserts to orange groves at the foot of snowy mountains; from rugged mining camps to handsome cities and the most fascinating country life in the world. And the more you know of the climate and the industries it fosters, the more you will want a stake here in Southern California and in this imperial county.

It has not seemed wise to cover the resources in this sketch nor even to mention the various towns. These, with the single exception of San Bernardino, have been created by the orange groves, and are a part of its social fruitage. Taking the country itself, these towns are attractive, and if one prefers to be both urban and rural he can live in town while caring for his oranges a few miles away. Chino is a prosperous alfalfa center; Etiwanda and Cucamonga are among vineyards and oranges; Upland is between the main line of the Southern Pacific and the Santa Fe, and is handsome and growing with but few acres of oranges between it and Ontario. Ontario, Upland, Highland, Bloomington, Rialto, Chino, as well as Redlands and the county-seat, will send you booklets of their own on request.

This county has just issued an attractive booklet which may be had from the various chambers of commerce. It covers topography, climate, productions, resources and resorts, and is a study of conditions rather than a dry catalogue.

California
(1872)

CALIFORNIA.
HOW TO GO THERE, AND WHAT TO SEE BY THE WAY.
By CHARLES NORDHOFF.

VIEW FROM THE CLIFF HOUSE, SAN FRANCISCO.

THOUGH California has been celebrated in books, newspapers, and magazines for more than twenty years, it is really almost as little known to the tourist—a creature who ought to know it thoroughly, to his own delight—as it was to Swift when he wrote, in his description of the flying island of Laputa, "The continent of which this kingdom is a part extends itself, as I have reason to believe, eastward to that unknown tract of America westward of California, and north to the Pacific Ocean, which is not above a hundred and fifty miles from Logado," and so on.

California is to us Eastern people still a land of big beets and pumpkins, of rough miners, of pistols, bowie-knives, abundant fruit, green wines, high prices—full of discomforts, and abounding in dangers to the peaceful traveler. A New Yorker, inefficient except in his own business, looking to the government, municipal, State, or Federal, for almost every thing except his daily dollars; overridden by a semi-barbarous foreign population; troubled with incapable servants, private as well as public; subject to daily rudeness from car-drivers and others who ought to be civil; rolled helplessly and tediously down town to his business in a lumbering omnibus; exposed to inconveniences, to dirty streets, bad gas, beggars, loss of time through improper conveyances; to high taxes, theft, and all kinds of public wrong, year in and year out—the New Yorker fondly imagines himself to be living at the centre of civilization, and pities the unlucky friend who is "going to California." He invites him to dine before he sets out, "because you will not get a good dinner again till you return, you know." He sends him, with his parting blessing, a heavy navy revolver, and shudders at the annoyances and dangers which his friend, out of a rash and venturesome disposition, is about to undergo.

Well, the New Yorker is mistaken. There are no dangers to travelers on the beaten track in California; there are no inconveniences which a child or a tenderly reared woman would not laugh at; they dine in San Francisco rather better, and with quite as much form and a more elegant and perfect service, than in New York; the San Francisco hotels are the best in the world; the noble art of cooking is better understood in California than any where else where I have eaten; the bread is far better, the variety of food is greater; the persons with whom a tourist comes in contact, and upon whom his comfort and pleasures so greatly depend, are more uniformly civil, obliging, honest, and intelligent than they are any where in this country, or, so far as I know, in Europe; the pleasure-roads in the neighborhood of San Francisco are unequaled any where; the common country roads are kept in far better order than any where in the Eastern States; and when you have spent half a dozen weeks in the State, you will perhaps return with a notion that New York is the true frontier land, and that you have nowhere in the United States seen so complete a civilization—in all material points, at least—as you found in California.

If this seems incredible to what out there they call an Eastern person, let him reflect for a moment upon the fact that New York receives a constant supply of the rudest, least civilized European populations; that of the immigrants landed at Castle Garden the neediest, the least thrifty and energetic, and the most vicious remain in New York, while the ablest and most valuable fly rapidly westward; and that, besides this, New York has necessarily a large population of native adventurers; while, on the other hand, California has a settled and permanent population of doubly picked men.

"When the gold was discovered," said a Californian to whom I had expressed my wonder at the admirable *quality* of the State's population, "wherever an Eastern family had three or four boys, the ablest, the most energetic one, came hither. Of that great multitude of picked men, again, the weakly broke down under the strain; they died of disease or bad whisky, or they returned home. The remainder you see here, and you ought not to wonder that they are above your Eastern average in intelligence, energy, and thrift. Moreover, you are to remember that, contrary to the commonly received belief, California has a more settled population than almost any State in the Union. It does not change; our people can not move west, and very few of them return back to the East. What we have we keep, and almost all, except the Chinese, have a permanent interest in the State. Finally," added this old miner, who is now a banker, and whom you could not tell from a New Yorker, either in his dress or the tones of his voice, or in the manner in which he transacts business, and who yet has not been "home," as he calls it, for seventeen years—"finally, you must remember that of our immigrants who came from China, not a single one, so far as is known, but knew how to read, write, and keep at least his own accounts on his own abacus when he passed the Golden Gate. We are not saints out here, but I believe we have much less of a frontier population than you in New York." And my experience persuades me that he was right.

Certainly in no part of the continent is pleasure-traveling so exquisite and unalloyed a pleasure as in California. Not only are the sights grand, wonderful, and surprising in the highest degree, but the climate is exhilarating and favorable to an active life; the weather is so certain that you need not lose a day, and may lay out your whole tour in the State without reference to rainy days, unless it is in the rainy season; the roads are surprisingly good, the country inns are clean, the beds good, the food abundant and almost always well cooked, and the charge moderate; and the journey by rail from New York to San Francisco, which costs no more than the steamer fare to London, and is shorter than a voyage across the Atlantic, is in itself delightful as well as instructive. Probably twenty Americans go to Europe for one who goes to California; yet no American who has not seen the plains, the Rocky Mountains, the Great Salt Lake, and the wonders of California can honestly say that he has seen his own country, or that he even has an intelligent idea of its greatness. It is of this journey from New York to San Francisco that I wish to give here such an accurate and detailed account as will, I hope, tempt many who contemplate a European tour to turn their faces westward rather, sure that this way lies the most real pleasure.

The regular route runs from New York, by way of Philadelphia and Pittsburg, to

BIRD'S-EYE VIEW OF THE PACIFIC RAILROAD, FROM CHICAGO TO SAN FRANCISCO.

Chicago—this is called the Pittsburg and Fort Wayne road—thence to Omaha, either by the Chicago, Burlington, and Quincy, the Chicago and Northwestern, or the Chicago and Rock Island. At Omaha you take the Union Pacific road to Ogden, and thence the Central Pacific to San Francisco. If you wish to see Colorado on your way out, you may go also from Chicago to Denver, over the Chicago, Burlington, and Missouri and the Kansas Pacific roads; and at Denver you have your choice of diversions in Colorado, with Mr. Bowles's admirable book, the "Switzerland of America," to show you the way. When you are done you pass from Denver to Cheyenne by a road which is 105 miles long, and which makes close connection with the Pacific or overland trains. You are to understand that all these lines are connected; that, now that the great bridge at Omaha is completed, you might, if you desired it enough to charter a car, go through without change of cars; that you may buy your through-ticket in New York; and that the traveling time, from ocean to ocean, is seven days. Further on will be found tables of time, cost, and other particulars.

In practice the tourist bound to California will do well to stop two days in Chicago, and one day in Salt Lake City, in which case he would get to San Francisco in ten days, and with surprisingly little fatigue, and he will have seen several very remarkable sights on the way. For instance, though Chicago itself was burned and is not yet rebuilt, the ruin is worth seeing; and near at hand, accessible by frequent trains, he may find one of the most characteristic sights of our continent, the great Chicago stock-yards—a city whose inhabitants are cattle, sheep, and hogs, and where these creatures are so well cared for that many a poor human being supposed to have an immortal and amenable soul, living in a New York tenement-house, is neither so cleanly lodged nor so well protected against harm or cruelty.

This city of the beasts has streets, sewers, drains; it has water laid on; it is lighted with gas; it has a bank, an exchange, a telegraph-office, a post-office, an admirably kept hotel; it has even a newspaper—else it would not be an American city. It has very comfortable accommodations for 118,350 residents—namely, 21,000 head of cattle, 75,000 hogs, 22,000 sheep, with stalls for 350 horses. It contains 345 acres of land; and when all this is prepared for use, 210,000 head of cattle can be lodged, fed, and cared for there at once, and with the certainty that not one will suffer or go astray.

It has thirty-five miles of sewers; ten miles of streets and alleys, all paved with wood; three miles of water-troughs, all so arranged that the water may be stopped off at any point; 2300 gates, which are the front-doors,

so to speak, of the place; 1500 open pens, heavily fenced in with double plank; 100 acres are covered with pens for cattle, and all these are floored with three-inch plank; 800 covered sheds for sheep and hogs; and seventeen miles of railroad track connect this city of the beasts with every road which runs into Chicago. It has two Artesian wells, one 1032, the other 1190 feet deep, which, being spouting wells, send the water into huge tanks forty-five feet high, whence it is distributed all over the place in pipes. Fourteen fire-plugs are ready to furnish water in case of fire; immense stacks of hay and large granaries of corn contain the food needed for the beasts; and, I believe, a train of palace cattle cars now bears the emigrant animals from this their city comfortably to the Eastern butchers.

Of course, as the "lower animals" do not help themselves, a considerable force of men is needed to attend upon those gathered here. The company receives and cares for all animals sent to it. It has thus taken in, penned, fed, watered, littered, and taken account of 41,000 hogs, 3000 cattle, and 2000 sheep in a single day, and that without accident, hitch, or delay. From 175 to 200 men are constantly employed in this labor; and to accommodate these and their families numerous cottages have been built, while a town-hall for public meetings and lectures, a church, a Sunday-school, and a well-kept day-school provide for their instruction and amusement. The hotel, which has bath-rooms, and is in other respects well fitted, is for the use of the drovers and owners of cattle, whom business brings hither. At the Exchange sales are effected, and the news of a sale may be sent to Maine or Texas by a telegraph from the same room, while the money paid may be securely deposited in the bank, which is under the same roof. Thus you will see that this surprising enterprise is completely furnished in every part; and it will not be the least part of your surprise and pleasure to find that this whole business, which about New York often involves painful brutalities, is here conducted as quietly as though a Quaker presided over it, and with as much care for the feelings of the dumb brutes as though good Mr. Bergh were looking on all the time.

It will cost about two millions when it is completed; is a pecuniary success, as it deserves to be; and when you hear that so long ago as 1869 Chicago received and sent off 403,102 head of cattle, 1,661,869 hogs, and 340,072 sheep, and that it will probably remain for years one of the greatest cattle markets in the world, you will see the need for such elaborate arrangements as I have described, and, if you are a humane person, will be pleased that these immense droves of animals are kindly cared for and comfortably lodged and fed on their way to a market. Most of the people employed in the yards are Americans.

Among such a multitude of beasts as are here received Mr. Buckle's law of averages would tell you that there will be a certain few monstrosities; and you will probably be shown one or two Texas steers which look much more like elephants or mammoths than horned oxen; perhaps a two-headed sheep, or a six-legged hog; and, indeed, when I saw the stables they contained a collection which would have turned the face of a Chatham Street exhibitor green with envy.

The Union Stock-yards lie but half an hour from the centre of Chicago, and there is no reason why ladies and children should not visit them if the weather is fine. I do not know of a more instructive or remarkable sight for tourists. If you want to see how private enterprise and good taste can provide for the pleasant lodging of men and women, turn from this city of the beasts and go out to Riverside Park.

It always seemed to me that it would be the summit of human felicity to have a handsome house in the New York Central Park, and thus to seem to own and control, and to really enjoy as a piece of personal property, that fine pleasure-ground. When the Tammany Ring was in the height of its power this thought was also entertained by its chiefs, who for some time nursed and fondled a proposition that "a few eminent citizens" should be allowed, "under proper restrictions," to build themselves fine houses in the Park. It is not difficult to guess who would have been the eminent citizens to share among themselves this happy privilege; and New York may thank *Harper's Weekly*, the *Times*, and Thomas Nast that their ambitious scheme has come to naught. Their names would have begun with a T and an S and a C and an H.

Well, a company of capitalists in Chicago conceived the idea that it would be possible and profitable to buy a piece of ground near that city, lay it out as tastefully and improve it as thoroughly as the New York Central Park, and then sell it off in lots to people of taste and wealth. It needed some faith to begin such an undertaking; but if you go to Riverside you will see Central Park roads, drives, and paths; you will find gas and water supplied as though it were a city; you will find tasteful public buildings, a hotel, which was a place of refuge for multitudes of Chicago people after the great fire, and which is a favorite summer resort; and you will see a good many people living already with Central Park surroundings, and with all the comforts and social advantages of the city and the country combined.

Perhaps you will wonder whether co-operation is not a good thing for the wealthy as well as the struggling poor, and whether the many who prefer to live in the suburbs

of great cities would not do wisely and save money if they would—having found a region they like—unite to improve it upon some general and tasteful plan.

And whatever you may think of Chicago in ruins, or of the future of that stirring place, when you have seen Riverside and the Union Stock-yards you will acknowledge that Chicago capitalists have known how, in the words of the old tavern signs, to provide "first-rate accommodations for man and beast."

At Chicago the journey to California really begins. In the East we make journeys by rail; west of Chicago men live on the cars. In the East a railroad journey is an interruption of our lives. We submit to it, because no one has yet been ingenious enough to contrive a flying-machine, and the telegraph wires do not carry passengers by lightning; but we submit to it reluctantly, we travel by night in order to escape the tedium of the journey, and no one thinks of amusing himself on the cars. When you leave Chicago you take up your residence on the train. The cars are no longer a ferry to carry you across a short distance: you are to live in them for days and nights; and no Eastern man knows the comfort or pleasure of traveling by rail until he crosses the plains.

I suspect that part of our discomfort in making a railroad journey comes from its brevity. You are unsettled; the car, on a common journey, is but a longer ferry; and who ever thought of taking his ease on a ferry-boat? You can not fix your mind on the present; your constant thought is of when you will get there. Now the journey to San Francisco takes not a few hours, but a number of days; and when you are safely embarked on the train at Chicago, you leave care behind in the dépôt, and make yourself comfortable, as one does on a sea voyage.

Moreover, until you have taken this journey, you will never know how great a difference it makes to your comfort whether your train goes at the rate of forty or at twenty-two miles per hour. This last is the pace of the iron horse between Omaha and San Francisco; and it is to the fierce and rapid rush of an Eastern lightning express what a gentle and easy amble is to a rough and jolting trot. It would not be surprising to find that the overland journey will, by-and-by, create a public opinion in favor of what New Yorkers would call slow trains. Certainly a lightning express rushing through from Chicago to San Francisco would not carry any one, except an express-man, a second time. At thirty-five or forty miles per hour the country you pass through is a blur; one hardly sees between the telegraph poles; pleasure and ease are alike out of question; reading tires your eyes, writing is impossible, conversation impracticable except at the auctioneer pitch, and the motion is

INTERIOR OF A PULLMAN PALACE CAR, PACIFIC RAILROAD.

wearing and tiresome. But at twenty-two miles per hour travel by rail is a different affair; and having unpacked your books and unstrapped your wraps in your Pullman or Central Pacific palace car, you may pursue all the sedentary avocations and amusements of a parlor at home; and as your house-keeping is done—and admirably done—for you by alert and experienced servants; as you may lie down at full length or sit up, sleep or wake, at your choice; as your dinner is sure to be abundant, very tolerably cooked, and not hurried; as you are pretty sure to make acquaintances on the car; and as the country through which you pass is strange, and abounds in curious and interesting sights, and the air is fresh and exhilarating—you soon fall into the ways of the voyage, and if you are a tired business man, or a wearied housekeeper, your careless ease will be such a rest as certainly most busy and overworked Americans know how to enjoy.

I tell you all this in some detail, because it was new to me, and it is worth while to be spared the unpleasant forebodings of weariness and lack of occupation which troubled me when I was packing my trunk for Frisco.

You write very comfortably at a table in a little room, called a drawing-room, entirely closed off, if you wish it, from the remainder of the car, which room contains two large and comfortable arm-chairs and a sofa, two broad, clean, plate-glass windows on each side, which may be doubled if the weather is cold, hooks in abundance for shawls, hats, etc., and mirrors at every corner. Books and photographs lie on the table; your wife sits at the window, sewing and looking out on long ranges of snow-clad mountains, or on boundless ocean-like plains; children play on the floor, or watch at the windows for the comical prairie-dogs sitting near their holes, and turning laughable somersaults as the car sweeps by. You converse as you would in your parlor at home; the noise of the train is as much lost to your consciousness as the steamship's rush through the waters; the air is pure, for these cars are thoroughly ventilated; the heating apparatus used seems to me quite perfect, for it keeps the feet warm, and diffuses an agreeable and equal heat through all parts of the car. This is accomplished by means of hot-water pipes fastened near the floor.

As at sea, so here, the most important events of the day are your meals. The porter calls you at any hour you appoint in the morning; he gives you half an hour's notice of breakfast, dinner, or supper; and the conductor tells you not to hurry, but to eat at your ease, for he will not leave any one behind. Your beds are made up and your room or section swept and aired while you are at breakfast, or before, if you are early risers; you find both water and fresh towels abundant; ice is put into the tank, which supplies drinking-water at the most improbable places in the great wilderness; and an attentive servant is always within call, and comes to you at intervals during the day to

DINING-ROOM, UNION PACIFIC RAILROAD.

COOKING RANGE, PULLMAN PALACE CAR, UNION
PACIFIC RAILROAD.

ask if you need any thing to make you more contented.

About eight o'clock—for, as at sea, you keep good hours—the porter, in a clean gray uniform, like that of a Central Park policeman, comes in to make up the beds. The two easy-chairs are turned into a double berth; the sofa undergoes a similar transformation; the table, having its legs pulled together, disappears in a corner; and two shelves being let down furnish two other berths. The freshest and whitest of linen and brightly colored blankets complete the outfit; and you undress and go to bed as you would at home, and unless you have eaten too heartily of antelope or elk, will sleep as soundly.

Thus you ride onward, day after day, toward the setting sun, and unless you are an extremely unhappy traveler, your days will be filled with pleasure from the novel sights by the way. At Burlington you cross the Mississippi over a noble bridge, and will be surprised to see what a grand river the Father of Waters is nearly 1600 miles above its mouth. At Omaha you cross the Missouri, there a variable, turbid, but in the early spring a narrow river, which yet requires a bridge more than a mile long when the stream is bank-full. This new bridge at Omaha was built by the engineer to whom New York is indebted for the iron bridge at Harlem, T. E. Sickles, and it is a remarkable work to be done so far from the appliances of civilization.

From Chicago to Omaha your train will carry a dining car, which is a great curiosity in its way. I expected to find this somewhat greasy, a little untidy, and with a smell of the kitchen. It might, we travelers thought, be a convenience, but it could not be a luxury. But in fact it is as neat, as nicely fitted, as trim and cleanly, as though Delmonico had furnished it; and though the kitchen may be in the forward end of the car, so perfect is the ventilation that there is not even the faintest odor of cooking. You sit at little tables which comfortably accommodate four persons; you order your breakfast, dinner, or supper from a bill of fare which, as you will see below, contains a quite surprising number of dishes, and you eat from snow-white linen and neat dishes admirably cooked food, and pay a moderate price.

It is now the custom to charge a dollar per meal on these cars; and as the cooking is admirable, the service excellent, and the food various and abundant, this is not too much. You may have your choice in the wilderness, eating at the rate of twenty-two miles per hour, of buffalo, elk, antelope, beefsteak, mutton-chops, grouse—but it is better to give you a bill of fare from which I once ordered my dinner on such a car, and wondered where they kept their stores:

BROILED.

Porter-house Steak	$0 75	Spring Chicken	1 00
Do., with Mushrooms	1 00	Do., half.	75
Mutton-Chops, plain	50	Breakfast Bacon	40
Do., with Tomato Sauce	75	Broiled Ham	40
Veal Cutlets, breaded	50	Lamb Chops, plain	50

COLD DISHES.

Sliced Boiled Tongue	40	Sardines	40
Do., Ham	40	Pickled Lobster	40
Pressed Corned Beef	50	Spiced Oysters	40

OYSTERS.

Raw	50	Stew	50
Fancy Roast	75	Fried	60

EGGS.

Boiled Eggs	25	Shirred Eggs	30
Fried Eggs	25	Omelet, plain	30
Poached Eggs	25	Do., with Rum	40
Scrambled Eggs	30	Do., and Ham	40

VEGETABLES.

Green Corn	10	New Boiled Potatoes	10
New Green Pease	10	Fried Potatoes	10
Stewed New Potatoes	10		

RELISHES.

Chowchow	10	Worcestersh'e Sauce	
Mixed Pickles	10	Walnut Catsup	
Queen's Olives	15	Tomato Catsup	
Horse-Radish		French Mustard	

PRESERVED FRUITS.

Peaches	25	Apricots	25
Prunes	25	Damsons	25
Blackberries	25	Cherries	25
Pine-Apples	25		

BREAD.

Dry Toast	10	Hot Biscuit	10
Milk Toast	25	Corn Bread	
Buttered Toast	15	French Loaf	
Albert Biscuit	10	Boston Brown Bread	
Dipped Toast	15		

BREAKFAST WINES.—Claret and Sauterne.
CHAMPAGNE WINES.—Heidsick and Krug.

French Coffee, English Breakfast Tea, and Chocolate	15
French Coffee, Tea, Chocolate, without an order	25

GEORGE M. PULLMAN.

Beyond Omaha, unless you have taken seats in a hotel car, you eat at stations placed at proper distances apart, where abundant provision is made, and the food is, for the most part, both well cooked and well served. These hotel stations are under the supervision and control of the managers of the roads, and at many of them, especially on the Central Pacific road—in California, that is to say—your meals are served with actual elegance. Sufficient time is allowed —from thirty to thirty-five minutes—to eat; the conductor tells you beforehand that a bell will be rung five minutes before the train starts, and we always found him obliging enough to look in and tell the ladies to take their time, as he would not leave them.

There is a pleasant spice of variety and adventure in getting out by the way-side at the eating stations. We saw strange faces, we had time to look about us, the occasional Indian delighted the children, we stretched our legs, and saw something of our fellow-passengers in the other cars. Moreover, if you have a numerous party desirous to eat

together, the porter will telegraph ahead for you to have a sufficient number of seats reserved, and thus you take your places without flurry or haste, and do not have your digestion spoiled by preliminary and vexatious thoughts about pushing for a good place. In short, these trains are managed for the pleasure and accommodation of the passengers. The voyage would, I suppose, be unendurable else.

The sleeping car, but for which the journey to the Pacific by rail would be extremely uncomfortable, but by whose help it is made a pleasure-trip, owes its development and perfection to Mr. George M. Pullman, who is the inventor and patentee of most of the ingenious devices by which the traveler's comfort is secured in these cars. Of course he is an American. He began life poor; was once a miner in Colorado, and was, I believe, so poor when he began the experiment of his sleeping cars that it was with great difficulty he raised the means to build his first car. He is now president of the Pullman Car Company, which has five hundred sleeping, drawing-room, and hotel cars on different railroads, and is building more, at the rate of three finished cars for every week of the present year. The company are also building a new kind of day cars, to be put on such short routes as that between New York and Washington; and by the time you are reading this it will run a daily hotel car from Chicago to Ogden, in which you may sit and sleep and have your meals served at any time you may choose to order them. It is planning, and will fit up this year near Chicago, extensive car-works of its own on grounds large enough to contain also the cottages of the thousand workmen who will be there employed, and it is said that these grounds are to be planned with special regard to the convenience of the men and their families. The company has already found it expedient to keep and furnish, near the dépôts in all the great cities, rooms where conductors and porters may, at the end of a journey, bathe, change their clothes, make out their reports, and read, write, or amuse themselves. Mr. Pullman thinks that as he requires much from his men, and as they are picked men, trained with care, it is an advantage to the company to furnish them such a home at the ends of the great routes of travel, where they may make themselves comfortable and at ease. Certainly it is a humane thought, and likely, besides, to give him the command of responsible servants.

The Pullman cars are constantly improving. The Russian Grand Duke traveled last winter in perhaps the most commodious and

INTERIOR OF PULLMAN SLEEPING CAR, PACIFIC RAILROAD.

perfect manner in which any one ever traveled by rail. He had in one train a day car, in which he and his companions could sit at ease, read, write, or amuse themselves as in a parlor; a dining or hotel car, into which they walked to breakfast or dinner; and a sleeping car. No doubt the impressions he got of this kind of pleasure-traveling will facilitate Mr. Pullman's entrance into Russia, where, as well as in England, Germany, and France, the Pullman Company will within two years have placed their cars, as arrangements are now making for that purpose.

The superiority of the American sleeping cars is in their cleanliness, the perfection of their heating and ventilating contrivances, and the presence of every thing which can make a car convenient to live in. There is nothing like them in Europe, and all European travelers in this country have been surprised and delighted with them. The Pullman Company is successful, as it deserves to be. It now runs cars on nearly one hundred roads, the railroad companies generally owning one-half the stock of the cars they use, and thus having a mutual interest. The Pullman Company sells to the public what the railroad company in such cases does not furnish—the sleeping-car accommodations. You may now ride in Pullman cars over sixty thousand miles of railroad. The Pullman Company already employs over two thousand persons, and in its new car-shops will employ one thousand more, and all this vast business has grown from the smallest beginnings.

One of the pleasantest ways to travel across the continent, though not, I think, the way in which you will see most of the people, is to make the journey with a party of friends numerous enough to fill, or nearly fill, a car. To show you at what cost—exclusive of the regular railroad fare—such a company may journey, I give you here some extracts from a little book issued for the information of travelers by the company:

"The Pullman Palace Car Company is ready to furnish excursion parties with sleeping, drawing-room, and hotel cars for a trip to San Francisco or elsewhere on these terms:

"For a regular sleeping car, containing twelve open sections of two double berths each, and two state-rooms of two double berths each (in all twenty-eight berths), with conductor and porter, seventy-five dollars per day.

"For a drawing-room car, containing two drawing-rooms, having each a sofa and two large easy-chairs by day, and making up at night into two double and two single berths, three state-rooms having each two double berths, and six open sections of two double berths each (in all twenty-six berths), with conductor and porter, seventy-five dollars per day.

"For a hotel car, containing two drawing-rooms, as above described, one state-room having two double berths, and six open sections of two double berths each (in all twenty-two berths), and having also, in one end, a kitchen fully equipped with every thing necessary for cooking and serving meals, with conductor, cook, and two waiters, eighty-five dollars per day.

"The conductor, if desired, will make all arrangements for the excursionists with the railroads for procuring transportation of the car; and in the case of their taking a hotel car, will also act as steward, purchasing for them the requisite provisions for the table.

"The car is chartered, with its attendants, at a certain rate per day from the time it is taken until we receive it back again.

"We have no facilities for securing special rates of railroad fare, and would suggest that, in case an excursion is organized, application be made to any ticket agent who is empowered to sell through-tickets, and the best rates of railroad fare obtained from him to and from the terminal point of the proposed trip.

"We can forward a car from our head-quarters in Chicago to any point which the excursionists may designate as their starting-place."

The Pullman hotel car is one of the most ingenious as well as one of the most convenient of all modern arrangements for travel. It can seat forty persons at the tables; it contains not only a kitchen—which is a marvel of compactness, having a sink, with hot and cold water faucets, and every "modern convenience"—but a wine closet, a china closet, a linen closet, and provision lockers so spacious as to contain supplies for thirty people all the way from Chicago to the Pacific if necessary; its commissary list contains, as I ascertained by actual count, 133 different articles of food; it carries 1000 napkins, 150 table-cloths, 300 hand-towels, and 30 or 40 roller-towels, besides sheets, pillow-cases, etc., etc. And unless you are of an investigating turn, you would never know that the car contained even a kitchen.

Whenever a sleeping car arrives at the end of a journey, it is laid over for twenty-four hours. Thereupon the porter gathers up the soiled linen for the laundry, and a force of men and women enter the car and take out of it bedding, carpets, and every movable thing; all are beaten with rods and hung up to air; and meantime the whole car is aired, and the wood-work dusted, rubbed, and scrubbed in the most thorough manner. This is the manner of their housekeeping.

On the whole, a company of three or four can travel the most enjoyably across the continent; and there is no reason why a man should not take his children, if they are ten years old or over, as well as his wife. Four fill a drawing-room comfortably, four can be comfortable in a section on a sleeping car; and in California, if you have three or four in your party, you can travel as cheaply by private carriage as by stage to all the notable sights of the State which you do not reach by rail, and thus add much to the comfort and pleasure of such journeys. On the cars you are sure to make pleasant acquaintance, and probably to your advantage, for you will find persons who have been over the route before ready to point out curious objects to you. And from the hour you leave Omaha you will find every thing new, curious, and wonderful: the plains, with their buffalo, antelope, and prairie-dogs; the mountains, which, as you approach Cheyenne, lift up

ROUNDING CAPE HORN.

the rush and vehement impetus of the train, the whirl around curves, past the edge of deep chasms, among forests of magnificent trees, fill you with excitement, wonder, and delight.

When we had seen the Wasatch cañons we thought the glory of the journey must be over, but the lovely mountains about Salt Lake gave us new delight; and last, as though nature and man had conspired to prepare a series of surprises for the traveler to California, comes the grand stormy rush down the Sierra, followed, as you draw down to the lower levels, by the novel sights of men actually engaged in gold mining; long flumes, in which they conduct the water for their operations, run for miles near the track; and as you pass below Gold Hill you may see men setting the water against great hills, which they wash away to get out the gold from the gravel which bears it. The entrance into California is to the tourist as wonderful and charming as though it were the gate to a veritable fairy-land. All its sights are peculiar and striking; as you pass down from Summit the very color of the soil seems different and richer than that you are accustomed to at home; the farm-houses, with their broad piazzas, speak of a summer climate; the flowers, brilliant at the road-side, are new to Eastern eyes; and at every turn in the road fresh surprises await you.

On the plains and in the mountains the railroad will have seemed to you the great fact. Man seems but an accessory; he appears to exist only that the road may be worked; and I never appreciated until I crossed the plains the grand character of the old Romans as road-builders, or the real importance of good roads. We, too, in this generation are road-builders. Neither the desert nor the sierra stops us; there is no such word as "impossible" to men like Hunt-

their glorious snow-clad summits; the deep cañons and gorges which lead from Wasatch into Ogden, and whose grim scenery will seem to you, perhaps, to form a fit entrance to Salt Lake; the indescribable loveliness and beauty of the mountain range which shelters the Mormon capital; the extended, apparently sterile, but, as long-headed men begin to think, really fertile alkali and sage-brush plain; the snow-sheds which protect the Central Pacific as you ascend the Sierra; and, on the morning of the last day of your journey, the grand and exciting rush down the Sierra from Summit to Colfax, winding around Cape Horn and half a hundred more precipitous cliffs, down which you look out of the open "observation car" as you sweep down from a height of 7000 feet to a level of 2500 in a ride of two hours and a half. A grander or more exhilarating ride than that from Summit to Colfax on the Central Pacific Railroad you can not find in the world. The scenery is various, novel, and magnificent. You sit in an open car at the end of the train, and the roar of the wind,

ington; they build railroads in the full faith that population and wealth will follow on their iron track.

And they seem to be the best explorers. The "Great American Desert" which we school-boys a quarter of a century ago saw on the map of North America has disappeared at the snort of the iron horse; coal and iron are found to abound on the plains as soon as the railroad kings have need of them; the very desert becomes fruitful, and at Humboldt Wells, on the Central Pacific Railroad, in the midst of the sage-brush and alkali country, you will see corn, wheat, potatoes, and fruits of different kinds growing luxuriantly, with the help of culture and irrigation; proving that this vast tract, long supposed to be worthless, needs only skillful treatment to become valuable.

One can not help but speculate upon what kind of men we Americans shall be when all these now desolate plains are filled, when cities shall be found where now only the lonely dépôt or the infrequent cabin stands; when the iron and coal of these regions shall have become the foundation of great manufacturing populations; and when, perhaps, the whole continent will be covered by our Stars and Stripes. No other nation has ever spread over so large a territory or so diversified a surface as ours. From the low sea-washed shores of the Atlantic your California journey carries you to boundless plains which lie nearly as high as the summit of Mount Washington. Americans are digging silver ore in Colorado three thousand feet higher than the highest point of the White Mountains. At Virginia City, in Nevada, one of the busiest centres of gold mining, the travelers find it hard to draw in breath enough for rapid motion, and many persons, when they first arrive there, suffer from bleeding at the nose by reason of the rarity of the air. Again, in Maine half the farmer's year is spent in accumulating supplies for the other and frozen half; all over the Northern States the preparation for winter is an important part of our lives; but in San Francisco the winter is the pleasantest part of the year. In Los Angeles they do not think it needful to build fire-places, and scarcely chimneys, in their houses. And one people, speaking the same language, reading the same books, holding a common religion, paying taxes to the same government, and proud of one common flag, pervades these various altitudes and climates, intervisits, intercommunicates, intermarries, and is, with the potent help of the railroad, fused constantly more closely together as a nation. What manner of man, think you, will be the American of 1972, the product of so many different climes, of so various a range as to altitude?

I wrote that on the plains and on the mountains the railroad is the one great fact. Whatever you notice by the way that is the handiwork of man appears to be there solely for your convenience or safety who are passing over the road. On the Union Pacific you

OBSERVATION CAR.

EAGLE GAP, ON THE TRUCKEE RIVER.

see miles upon miles of snow-fences. On the Central Pacific thirty or forty miles of solid snow-sheds, thoroughly built, and fully guarded by gangs of laborers, make the passage safe in the severest snow-storms. Great snow-plows, eleven feet high, stand at intervals on the plains and in the mountains, ready to drive, with three or four, or even seven or eight, locomotives behind them, the snow out of the cuts. The telegraph accompanies you on your whole long journey. Coal miles are opened only to furnish fuel to your locomotive. At intervals of a hundred miles, night and day, you hear men beating the wheels of the train to see if they are sound. Eating stations furnish you your meals; ice is supplied on the way; laborers stand aside in the desert and on the mountains as the train sweeps by, and close up behind it to repair the track or keep it in order. There is a Chinaman and a half on every mile of the Central Pacific Railroad; and this road is not only a marvel of engineering skill and daring, running through a most difficult country, and abounding in deep rock

cuts, tunnels, and snow-sheds, but you will find its road-bed every where firm and solid, as though it had been laid for years, the cuts clean and clear, and on every part of the work an air of finish and precision, which show the confidence of its owners, and the thorough spirit in which it was conceived and completed and is maintained.

You reach San Francisco by passing through the great Sacramento plain, one of the famous wheat fields of the State, to Vallejo, whence you sail down the magnificent bay of San Francisco to the city; and thus you have to the last hour of your journey some new scene opening to your eyes, and when you go to sleep in your hotel at last, may dream of the Cliff House ride as a pleasure still to come.

I close this article with a few detailed directions to tourists, such as I should myself have been glad of when I first made the journey.

1. At Ogden your train will connect with the regular train for Salt Lake City, which place you reach the same evening. The Townsend House is kept by a Mormon, the

American by a Gentile. An omnibus conveys you to either. Go to Brigham Young's theatre in the evening, if you like, and see his rocking-chair in the aisle, and the large space set apart in the box tier for his children. Rise early the next morning and walk about for an hour, and you may see almost the whole place. After breakfast get a carriage and tell the driver to take you to the Tabernacle and the menagerie —the last contains a number of native animals well worth seeing—and to show you the principal objects of interest. You will have time for a leisurely dinner before the cars

SNOW-SHEDS ON THE PACIFIC RAILROAD.

start, and will yet have seen all that Salt Lake City affords to the traveler—for it is not easy for non-residents to see the inside of a Mormon house.

2. At Salt Lake City buy a little gold for California; they take greenbacks in Utah.

3. In San Francisco you can exchange your greenbacks for gold notes, which are more convenient than coin, and just as serviceable.

4. Eat only two meals per day on your journey, as you are not exercising nor working. After you enter California you will find both fruit and flowers for sale on the train—signs of civilization which do not attend you on an Eastern train.

5. From Ogden, when you start westward, telegraph to the Grand Hotel, the Occidental, or wherever you mean to stay in San Francisco, for rooms. The cost is a trifle, and it is a convenience to have your apartments ready for you when you arrive.

6. In planning your journey you will desire to know how much time is required, and what the expense of your trip will be. We give three schedules or time-tables for tours of various lengths, and a general estimate of expenses.

SNOW-PLOW ON THE PACIFIC RAILROAD.

INTERIOR OF SNOW-SHED.

FOR A FIVE WEEKS' TOUR.

	DAYS.
From Chicago to San Francisco	5
At Salt Lake	1
San Francisco and the surroundings	5
The San José Valley, to the Almaden Mine	3
The Geysers	2
The Yosemite and Big Trees. (This gives you one day in the Calaveras grove and five in the valley.)	12
Return to Chicago	5
Total	33

FOR A SIX WEEKS' TOUR.

	DAYS.
From Chicago to San Francisco	5
At Salt Lake	1
San Francisco and surroundings	8
The San José Valley and Almaden Mine	3
Santa Cruz, Watsonville, Pescadero, etc.	4
The Geysers	3
The Yosemite and Big Trees	12
Lakes Tahoe and Donner	2
Virginia City	1
Total	39

FOR A NINE WEEKS' TOUR.

Take the last, and add—

	DAYS.
To Los Angeles and San Diego	14
To Mount Shasta	6
Total	59

If you can spare more time, you should add a week to your Yosemite journey, which would give you opportunity to make the tour of the valley's outer rim, which can be done by ladies now without discomfort.

In going to the Yosemite, go in by way of Bear Creek, which, though a little longer ride, gives you Inspiration Point as your first view of the famous valley; and pass out the other way, as that leads, by way of Chinese Camp and Sonora, through one of the most famous of the "placer diggings," to the Calaveras Grove of Big Trees. Next I put the cost of the journey:

Fare by railroad from Chicago to San Francisco	$118
Return	118
To Salt Lake and return	5
To San José and return	10
To the Geysers and return	26
To the Big Trees, Yosemite, and return	38
Railroad and stage fares for five weeks' tour	$315
To this add, for sleeping cars, about $3 per day— ten days	30
	$345

Add, for hotel accommodations, $3 50 per day, which is the usual price; and for carriage hire in seeing the Almaden mines, $5; for horses and guides on the Yosemite, $5 per day; for meals on the railroad, $2 per day. In all, $125 will pay your hotel and carriage bills, horse and guide in the Yosemite Valley, railroad, meals, etc.; and this, added to $345, makes $470. This is a liberal and not a close estimate; and if you allow $500 for a five weeks' tour to California and back, you will have enough to pay the slight premium on gold, and to buy some curiosities to take home with you. And you will have stopped at first-class hotels every where, and used a carriage wherever it was convenient.

To see Lake Tahoe, Donner Lake, and Virginia City will cost you twenty dollars more, including hotel bills. These you should see on your way home, getting off the Central Pacific train at Truckee, and resuming your place at Reno, when you have made the trip, without extra charge. Allow three days, and engage your sleeping-car accommodations at Sacramento, for a given day, on your way to Truckee.

To Los Angeles you go by steamer; fare, $18 each way, which includes meals and state-rooms. The sail is a lovely one, with land in sight all the way. Try to secure a berth on the land side, as the coast affords continuously fine views. The steamer lands you at San Pedro. Thence by cars to Los Angeles the fare is $2 50. From Los Angeles you should drive to the Mission San Gabriel, where are the finest orange orchards. The drive will cost you from three to five dollars. At San Diego you see a fine bay and a growing city, which now waits for railroad connections.

To Santa Cruz, Watsonville, and Pescadero the round trip should cost you from twenty to twenty-five dollars, and ten dollars less if you start from San José, after having seen the New Almaden quicksilver mines, and thus save the return to San Francisco.

If you have three weeks more to spare after going the round above described, you should visit the Columbia River, where also there is magnificent scenery. This journey is not so often made as it deserves to be. The following schedule of time and expense will help you to determine if you will make it:

	Days.	Cost.
San Francisco to Portland	4	$30
In the Willamette Valley	3	15
Up the Columbia and back	4	20
The voyage around Puget Sound	7	30
Back to San Francisco	4	30
Total	22	$125

You will find good hotels every where, though often, in the country, plainly furnished. The bread is always good, food is always abundant, and generally well cooked, and the beds are always clean and almost always good. The stage-drivers, landlords, and others with whom a traveler has to do are civil and obliging, and there are no attempts at extortion.

In a succeeding article I shall attempt to give some more detailed account of the sights which are worthy of a tourist's attention in California.

A Santa Barbara Holiday
(1887)

HARPER'S
NEW MONTHLY MAGAZINE.

Vol. LXXV.　　　　　NOVEMBER, 1887.　　　　　No. CCCCL.

A SANTA BARBARA HOLIDAY.

BY EDWARDS ROBERTS.

IF Reginald Gray, young, lately married, and actively engaged in business at a little town in northern New York, had been told in October that he would pass the greater part of the coming winter in southern California, he would very likely have thought it impossible. And yet it was only early December when he decided to go to Santa Barbara for six months or a year.

His wife was not well. She was far from being an invalid, but had been having trouble with her throat ever since the end of July, when she had a violent cold. Instead of getting better, she grew rather worse, and old Doctor Kimball, who had known both the young people all their lives, told Reginald that he ought to take his wife to a warm climate for the winter. "It will cure her," he said; "and if she stays here, I won't answer for the consequences."

In deciding upon Santa Barbara, Reginald was influenced by William Good-

now, his friend and classmate, who had only lately returned from California, and was now enthusiastic in his praise of its climate and natural attractions. Because of their many agreeable qualities, Reginald had asked two cousins of Anna, Edith and Kate Maynard, to join the party.

Strangers seeing Kate and Edith together never imagined them sisters. The former was a blonde, and had never known an ache or pain. An excellent lawn-tennis player, skilful with the oar, a perfect rider and good walker, tall, lithe, strong, and even-tempered, she was universally popular. Edith was more slender than her sister and more quiet. She was clever, played and sang well, sketched a little, and was always happy, no matter what her surroundings. Everybody liked Kate and loved Edith. She wore her hair brushed carelessly back from her forehead, and had a glorious pair of eyes— dark, large, and wonderfully expressive.

Goodnow had graduated at Harvard without class honors, but in the athletic records his name was left opposite the best time made in hundred-yard and half-mile dashes, and he pulled on the 'Varsity. After graduation he went to California to see what business opening he could find. At Reginald's wedding he met the Maynards, with whom he at once became good friends.

It was at the beginning of winter when the long journey across the continent was begun, and the cold was intense. On reaching Los Angeles, however, perfect summer weather was found. The grass was green on all the hill-sides, and the gardens were filled with flowers. The city is the largest in southern California, and is surrounded by a rich fruit country.

There are two ways of reaching Santa Barbara from Los Angeles. One may go by boat up the coast, or by train to Newhall, and from there overland by a stage which makes daily trips to and from Santa Barbara. By this route the ride is nearly ninety miles long, but the road is through a beautiful valley and along the edge of the sea. Had Reginald been alone, he would have gone overland, but for Anna's sake he went by boat. Los Angeles, like Athens, is some six miles inland, and its Piræus port is San Pedro. A railway connects the two places.

Leaving Los Angeles early in the morning, the little party rode past a succession of groves, and later out upon wide salt-marshes, at the edge of which is the bay and town of San Pedro. The harbor is an exceedingly good one for California, but is at best a poorly protected and shallow haven. The larger steamers cannot come to the dock, but anchor about two miles from shore. On reaching the end of the railway Reginald and Goodnow re-checked the luggage, and then all boarded a small tug-boat, on which were gathered nearly a hundred other passengers. The confusion equalled that which marks the departure of an Atlantic steamer. In time, however, the starting whistle was blown, and the little boat began ploughing its way down the harbor. The day was perfect; not a cloud was visible, and the hills guarding the bay were all a deep green from wave-washed base to very top.

"Imagine its being December!" said Edith. "You have been in California before, Mr. Goodnow: is this a typical winter's day?"

"Yes, I think it is. Of course it is not always so bright and warm. There are heavy rains, but the 'wet season' is little understood. It rains hard at times, and often for a week, but there are more clear than cloudy days."

"How good it seems, not having to be wrapped up!" said Anna. "I feel better already. Is there anything about Eastern weather in the paper to-day?"

"Yes; there's a flood in Boston, a blizzard at Chicago, and a terrible snow-storm in New York," replied Reginald.

On reaching the steamer the passengers were transferred from the tug, after which the two boats separated, one returning to the San Pedro wharf, and the other making up the coast. "Is it far to Santa Barbara?" asked Kate.

"No; only eighty miles from San Pedro," said Goodnow. "We'll get there by early evening. They're not fast ships on this line, and don't make over ten miles an hour. Do you notice the coast-line? Not much like that along the Atlantic, is it?"

"No. Is it rough and hilly like this all the way?"

"Yes. There are only three or four harbors along the entire nine hundred miles of California's shore. The best and largest is that of San Francisco, next is that of San Diego, and you have seen the third—San Pedro."

From where Kate sat she could see, toward the west, the vast expanse of the Pacific. The boat had but little motion. Scores of sea-gulls followed the ship, and in the distance were white-sailed boats. Beyond the line of hills following the coast were the higher peaks of the Sierras. Some of these were capped with snow, and about all the dark blue slopes hung a filmy haze. Here and there appeared a cottage or two, or a flock of sheep could be seen feeding on the steep hill-sides. Kate tried to read aloud, but no one paid attention, and so she abandoned her book.

"It's all too beautiful to be neglected," said Anna. "I never saw more glorious colorings nor breathed such delicious air. What is the name of the range we see ahead of us?"

"That's the Santa Ynez," replied Goodnow. "It runs nearly due east and west, and forms the northern boundary of the Santa Barbara Valley. Southern California is covered with a net-work of these minor ranges. They run in every con-

THE ARLINGTON VERANDA.

ceivable direction, and form an infinite variety of valleys. You will know the Santa Ynez Mountains thoroughly before leaving Santa Barbara. Everybody visits them, and they are one of the attractions of the place. Not every resort has the sea and mountains together."

It was well into the evening before the red light at the end of the Santa Barbara wharf was seen. The mountains made long dark marks against the starlit heavens, and the light was invisible until the steamer was within two miles of where it shone out over the waters of the harbor. Nearing the wharf, where there could now be seen the dim outlines of waiting hacks and a long storehouse, the wharf bell rang out a welcome to the new arrivals, and the cannon which was discharged from the bow of the boat sent thunder-like echoes rolling along the hill-sides. It was a novel landing. No other ships were at the wharf, and the town was still hidden from view, since the dock extends for nearly a mile out into deep water. In half an hour the tired travellers were safely domiciled at the Arlington, a large home-like hotel, in which every Santa Barbaran takes much pride. Wood fires were burning brightly in open fireplaces, and the wide veranda surrounding the hotel was filled with promenaders, who eyed the strangers with that air of superior wisdom and experience always worn by those who happen to be one's predecessors in a new place by a fortnight or less. Supper was being served, and after it our friends sought their beds, Anna tired out, Reginald rejoiced that she could now rest, Edith quiet and satisfied, Kate anxious for daylight, and Goodnow happy to be once more in the American Mentone.

The morning sun flooding the valley sent a stray beam into Kate's room, and waked that heavy sleeper into the full consciousness that she had a new world to conquer. Drawing aside the curtain, she looked out upon the town. Beyond the few house-tops and trees which lined the long street leading to the wharf she could see the ocean, and in another direction the Santa Ynez range. Between the mountains and the sea, and occupying a long narrow valley, lay the town of Santa Barbara, a quiet, listless little village, its face turned southward, and its cottages surrounded by trees. The birds were holding a carnival of song that morning, and the air was filled with the perfume of flowers. High up the mountain-side the

ROWS OF EUCALYPTUS.

grass was green and velvety, and the low hills that separate a part of the town from the bay were covered with rank grass. Kate had seen many an Italian village, and knew Naples thoroughly, but as she looked down on Santa Barbara she thought it prettier than any place she had ever seen. "You can't describe it," she wrote home that first day. "It suggests other places, but has charms peculiar to itself. Here it is the last of December, and yet the weather is exactly like that of June at home. The town is full of people. I'm glad I have both summer and winter dresses. I need the light ones during the day, and the others at evening. Mr. Goodnow has made many plans for us. He is delighted to get back, and this morning half a dozen picturesque old Mexicans called to see him. He speaks Spanish, and so these men like him. Anna is so happy; and so is Reginald."

The first morning in Santa Barbara was passed in utter idleness by all excepting Reginald, who went down town to interview a real estate agent regarding a furnished cottage. After breakfast Anna and the two girls sat on the "Arlington" veranda reading the letters they had found waiting their arrival, while Goodnow went to call on some old friends. A strangely quiet and beautiful place was the "Arlington" veranda. It was wide and long, and extended along the entire northeast side of the hotel. A thick mass of vines had grown over the pillars and sides and formed high Gothic arches, through which was had a view of the lawn and deer park. The walk that led from it to the street was bordered with rose-bushes, and on the lawn were broadleafed palms and ornamental trees. Everybody visits the veranda after breakfast —the old men to consult the thermometer, the young people to talk, and the ladies to sew or read.

Reginald had little trouble in finding a cottage. It stood near the head of the valley, and commanded a clear view of the bay, and of the mountains that stretch along the coast. The house was plainly but comfortably furnished, and the garden surrounding it contained a profusion of flowers, vines, and trees. To the right stood a gnarled old pine which had been brought across the Isthmus in '55, and was now nearly twice as high as the house. Just beyond its shadow was the garden, divided into different beds by a series of walks that radiated from a fountain. By the side of the latter, shading and half hiding it, grew a banana-tree; and at different corners of the beds were orange and lemon trees. North of the house there was an elm, brought from New England. As soon as they were fairly settled, Anna moved her easy-chair out upon a balcony overlooking the garden.

SANTA BARBARA.

CASTLE ROCK.

"I like the air here," she said to Reginald, "and the view can never grow monotonous. I have been enjoying it all the morning. Did you ever see anything more perfect?"

And Reginald, looking in the direction she indicated, thought he never had. The balcony answered every purpose of a lookout tower. From it the town and valley were visible; and beyond was the ocean, with the islands of Santa Rosa and Santa Cruz rising above the placid waters like huge mountains. Skirting the edge of the bay ran a crescent beach of yellow sand, extending from Castle Rock, near the wharf, to Review Hill, twenty miles away. From the balcony, too, the waves could be seen rolling in upon the beach, while the mountains that overlook the valley were visible for many miles as they stood clearly outlined against the sky.

In a week the family were settled, and at once began to look about the place which they had selected as a winter home.

To Reginald, accustomed to an active business life, it seemed a very quiet little town; and indeed it is. The population is not above 5000, and there is not a manufacturing establishment anywhere to be found. Attempts have frequently been made to establish a fruit cannery, but no one has ever been successful in doing so, and to-day Santa Barbara has quietly ac-

cepted the alternative of being known as a health resort. Every year sees an increased number of visitors attracted by the climate, and the town is the American Nice. It occupies the centre of a narrow sheltered valley, guarded by the sea and mountains, and overlooks a bay that bears a striking resemblance to that of Naples. A long wide street extends through the village from the wharf to the Mission, and facing this are the shops, banks, and hotels, around which is whatever of activity there may chance to be. From this thoroughfare other streets run at right angles toward the mountains on the northwest, and to the range of low green hills that rise abruptly from the water's edge on the southeast. Bordering these streets, never without their long rows of eucalyptus or pepper trees growing by the road-side, are vine-clad cottages and houses half hid behind a dense mass of shrubbery. To walk past such homes on a midwinter morning, when the air is soft and clear and the birds are singing, instantly compels one to admire Santa Barbara. Reginald was delighted when he made his first tour of inspection. It is a New England village transplanted, he thought. As for quiet Edith, she was silent with admiration when she saw the flowers and breathed their rich perfume. Choice varieties of roses were hers for the asking. The bushes grew higher than her head, and were set out in hedges along the walks. Every shrub grows in Santa Barbara. Plants that require careful attention in the East—geraniums, fuchsias, and the more tender roses—grow vigorously and without care. Edith gathered great baskets of choice flowers every morning, and yet the garden seemed as full as ever after she had visited it, and the different beds were masses of beautiful colors. Juan Valento, the gardener, noticing her fondness for his roses, smoked fewer cigarettes than was his custom, and displayed an energy in taking care of the beds that was surprising. He was a walking encyclopædia of information. It was not only during the winter, he told Edith, that the roses were in bloom; it was the same in July as in December. He could not understand her love for the geraniums. They were a pest, he thought; they grew so high and rank. But the roses he liked, and was always trimming and pruning. In some of the beds Juan had hollyhocks twelve feet high, and marigolds that were masses of gold. In others were pinks and calla-lilies and mignonette.

Life at Santa Barbara is mostly an outdoor one. Up to the present time the decrees of fashion have not begun to restrict and restrain one, and as a result the resident is free to do as he pleases. In no other village in America is housekeeping reduced to such a minimum of care as at Santa Barbara. The open hospitality of the people is proverbial. Friends "drop in" to luncheon without invitation and as a matter of course. Conventional rules are observed, to be sure, but do not restrict one in his enjoyment. People live quietly. Nature compels placidity of temperament, and invites good-will and pleasure.

Before two weeks had passed both Anna's and Reginald's attention was diverted from all that was humdrum or prosaic. They had had one honey-moon, and were now having another, sitting beneath the pine or orange trees together, gathering flowers, taking long walks about the garden. It was delightful to see how rapidly Anna improved. Reginald noticed with wonder the sudden loss of her former weakness and pallor. She looked ten years younger than she did on her arrival, and said that she felt so. There was a stable connected with the house, and Reginald had bought a steady-going horse and a low phaeton, so that Anna might be driven about the town. As she grew stronger he took her down to the beach every pleasant day, and for an hour drove up and down the stretch

SANTA BARBARA HARBOR.

of sand which extends for miles along the bay. There were little boats always anchored near the end of the wharf, and curiously rigged Chinese junks were often seen cruising about. By eleven o'clock the beach was the scene of much animation. Horseback parties galloped over its hard yellow sands, and groups of idlers sat on the dunes, reading, or gazing seaward upon the blue expanse of waters.

To Kate the beach was a never-failing attraction. She and Goodnow had many a horse-race from Castle Rock to the wharf, a good half-mile, and often rode as far as Ortega Point, an extension of the hill dividing the valley of Carpenteria from that of El Montecito. It is only possible to take this ride at low tide, for when the water is high the various points extending into the bay are impassable. A mile beyond the wharf the beach is bordered by a series of low sand heaps, over which one looks far up the valley to the Mission. Beyond these, again, are high bluffs which rise abruptly from the water's edge to a height of fifty feet. Their face is scarred and yellow, but their tops are carpeted with grass, and in spring with patches of yellow mustard and wild flowers. Two people were never better fitted to enjoy this beach ride than were Kate and Goodnow. Both were appreciative and observant. The deep coloring of the bay, the dull yellow of the beach and bluffs, the green tufts of grass and the wild flowers creeping over their edges, the distant hazy islands, the long stretch of curved coast, mountain-guarded, were always noticed and admired. As they cantered over the shining sands the waves softly broke in snowy masses of foam, and the waters often bathed the horses' feet. It is possible to ride all the way to Carpenteria by way of the beach at low tide, a distance of eleven miles. There is a constant succession of coves and crescents, and at the western edge of Carpenteria begins a line of sand-dunes, low and rolling, and fringed with low-growing reeds and bushes.

There was still another beach ride that all liked. It began at the wharf and extended westward along the beach, past steep bluffs, to a foot-path that turned inland through a narrow opening among the coast hills. Half a mile beyond the wharf a rocky headland, known as Castle Rock, projects across the beach, and over this the road led. Kate always rested her horse on reaching the top, and took a good long look at the prospect it commanded. The view across the valley to the mountains, and along-shore to Carpenteria, Ruicon, and Ventura points, was unobstructed. This headland is thirty miles from Santa Barbara, and forms a narrow neck of land that at first is only a few feet above the water's edge, but which soon merges into a mountain. Edith, who rarely rode, always liked to visit Castle Rock. Making a seat there, she would sit for hours looking out upon the wide, beautiful bay or upon the mountains, and watching the riders cantering over the smooth, shining beach. To where she sat there came no noise; only the murmur of the waves breaking upon the rocks at her feet disturbed the perfect quiet. It was the middle of January now, but the air was warm, the sky was a cloudless blue, and among the grasses growing along the edge of the cliffs were brightly colored wild flowers. Tiring of the sea, she had only to turn her head to see the valley, or could look on both at the same time. Old Juan came with her one day, and told what he knew of the neighborhood. The Point, he said, used to be called La Punta del Castillo, and when the Spaniards were the only people living in Santa Barbara there was a strong fort on the level ground back of the rock—a fort of earth mounted with four brass cannon. When a ship sailed into port, laden with goods from Spain, and bringing many a lover to his sweetheart, the soldiers fired the cannon and the ship returned the salute. On hearing the noise the people ran down to the beach, and waded into the surf to pull the boats ashore. Among those who one day went down to meet the ship was old Tomaso. He expected a certain señorita from Spain to be his bride. When all the boats had landed, and she did not appear, they told him the truth. She whom he sought had died on the voyage, and was buried at sea. Poor Tomaso! He fell on the sands, and was as one dead. From that time his mind was gone. After a long illness he came every day to the beach, watching for his beloved one. For many years he waited, running down to help haul in every boat, and looking long into each face, but never saying a word. He died watching, too, for one day they found him dead on the beach, his face turned toward the sea and his eyes wide open.

THE HIGH WALL OF THE MISSION.

Just to the left of Castle Rock, at the edge of the beach, is a low rounded hill called Burton's Mound. When the Spaniards first sailed into the Santa Barbara channel they found the coast and islands inhabited by a race of Indians living in large villages. On Burton's Mound was one of their largest towns. All traces of it have now disappeared, but the ground is still filled with the stone and earthen articles made by the forgotten people. On the crest of the mound is a low adobe house surrounded by a wide veranda overgrown with vines. Near it is a sulphur spring, the water from which is pumped into heated tanks, and used for bathing. Anna took regular baths, and was greatly benefited. The place is a favorite picnic resort, and will some time be a hotel site.

It makes little difference how one enters the Santa Barbara Valley, for the Mission which overlooks it is the first object that attracts attention. It occupies an elevated site at the head of the valley, and is clearly outlined against a background of hills. The church was begun in 1786, and finished in 1822. In 1812, and again in 1814, it was nearly destroyed by earthquakes. It was intended by Father Junipero Serra to build the Santa Barbara Mission long before it was really begun, but he died before doing more than select its location and consecrate the ground. From 1822 until 1833, when the act of secularization was passed, the building was the centre of great wealth and power. The fathers were temporal as well as spiritual rulers of the land, and their church was the best and largest in California. The walls were of stone six feet thick, and plastered with adobe; the roof was covered with bright red tiles, and in the towers was hung a trio of Spanish bells. In the rear of the Mission the fathers had their garden—a shrub-grown half-acre completely isolated from the outside world. From the west tower a long L extended at right angles to the body of the church, and facing this was an open corridor. The Indian converts lived in huts, and the fathers raised large quantities of grapes and olives. When war was made upon the Franciscans, the Santa Barbara brothers were the only ones who dared remain at their posts. That they did so is due the excellent preservation of the old building. Time has changed it

somewhat, to be sure, but has mellowed and softened rather than destroyed. The stone steps leading to the façade are cracked and moss-grown; only one of the original six fountains is left; the Indian cabins have disappeared. A few Franciscans, shaven, and dressed in long coarse robes girded at the waists, still inhabit the bare narrow cells, and loiter about the corridors and garden, and regular service continues to be held.

To Edith there was no road more attractive than that leading to the gray-walled church. The Mission fascinated her, as, indeed, it does all who see it. There was hardly a day that she did not visit it. Sometimes she sat on the rim of the fountain basin dreamily gazing past the town to where the blue waters were glistening in the strong sunlight, or wandered about the olive grove, and rested in the shade of the trees to read. One day, while absorbed in her book, and only stopping now and then to glance about her, she was aroused by the sound of some one coming. Looking up, she saw one of the fathers. He had thrown back his hood, and his clean-shaven face was suffused with a deep blush at thus coming

THE MISSION FOUNTAIN.

GARDEN OF THE MISSION.

unexpectedly upon so delightful a vision as that of a young girl seated on a grassy mound beneath an olive-tree.

"You are a daughter of our Church, child?" asked the padre.

"No, father, not a daughter, but a lover of it."

"Would there were more children belonging to our Mission!" the old gray-haired man said. "I fear Father Junipero would grieve to see the California missions now. It is little we can do to-day."

At Edith's request the old man seated himself at her side, and after telling of the life he and his brothers led, asked if she would like to go with him to the church. On her accepting, they both left the orchard, and passing the fountain, entered the dimly lighted interior. Directly above the entrance was the choir, and before it stretched a long nave, the walls of which were set with rows of small windows, and hung with paintings of saints and apostles. A few of the pictures were admirably executed. The largest and best was "Heaven and Hell."

"Many were painted in Spain," said the father, "and others were done by the Indians."

There was a decidedly musty smell to the church, and both the visitors spoke in whispers. Edith's guide showed her all the paintings, and gave the history of each—who this was done by and when, how it came to Santa Barbara, and other facts of interest. Just beyond the choir were two small chapels, each with its altar pictures and ornaments, and a few steps from that on the right of the nave the father stopped before a high double doorway, and began unlocking the heavy doors. When he had thrown them open he crossed himself, and leading the way, asked Edith to follow. Doing so, she found herself in a walled enclosure overgrown with rank grasses and rose-bushes. Above the doorway Edith saw three whitened skulls set in the wall, while under the eaves of the church, which projected upon thick buttresses, the swallows were flitting back and forth from their nests of sun-baked mud.

"This is our cemetery, señorita," said the father at last.

"Are the skulls real, father?" asked Edith.

"Yes, child."

"And are many people buried here?"

"Oh yes, very many. We do not use it now. There is not room, to tell the truth. You need not dig deep to find skulls and bones in here."

It was not a pleasant thought to Edith to feel that she was walking over the last resting-place of she knew not how many pious fathers and Indians. It was very quiet. A high wall completely hid the road to Mission Cañon, and on the west was the church, above which rose the towers. There were several vaults, and each had its wooden cross and vines. Doves were cooing on the eaves, and the swallows chatted incessantly.

On leaving the cemetery the father and Edith returned to the church, and passed up the long nave to the altar, which was covered with a snowy cloth, and decorated with tall candlesticks and other ornaments. Behind it, filling the end of the room, was a wooden reredos, elaborately carved, and having fine life-sized colored statues before each panel. On either side of the altar, set on white pillars, were two other statues, and between them was a large cross, with the Christ upon it. To the right Edith noticed a curiously shaped hat hanging upon the wall, which was covered with dust.

"It belonged to Garcia San Diego, the first Bishop of California," said the father, when he saw Edith looking at it. "His body is entombed here, as the tablet says. He was a patient worker and a godly man. Would I could be buried here, in the very walls of the church I serve!"

To the left of the altar a narrow doorway leads into the sacristy. With her guide Edith entered the small room, and saw directly opposite her another doorway opening upon a garden, or what seemed to be that.

"Yes, it is our cloister—our garden," said the padre. "I wish you could step into it, child, but no woman is allowed there. When the Princess Louise was here an exception was made, and she was shown our quiet walks and flowers."

"Can I look in?" asked Edith.

"Oh yes, but do not step outside the door."

With this permission Edith crossed the sacristy, and stood for some time looking through the open doorway. It was almost as though she stood within the garden, for her position commanded a view of nearly the entire place. In speaking of it afterward she said she could not well describe it. "There was perfect quiet, and the sunlight made beautiful shadow patches on the walks. There is a deep corridor along the south side, made by a row of stone pillars supporting a tiled roof. Some of the fathers were seated in its shade. I wish I could have painted it, but fear I couldn't give the true coloring, it was so varied and deep. In one of the arches hung a queer old bell from Spain. From where I stood I could see down the path to the corridor, and to the old building that forms one side of the garden. An old padre came out and struck the bell three times. It had a beautiful, low, deep tone. On hearing it the old men all went to their rooms to pray, and my friend went back into the church and left me alone."

On returning from his devotions the father found Edith still looking upon the scene, and was greatly pleased at her enjoyment.

"Is it beautiful?" he asked at length.

"It is more than that, father; I never saw so lovely a place. How happy you must all be, having such a garden!"

"So we are, child. It is our home, and some of us could not live without it now."

There was not much to see in the sacristy. In a chest of drawers were the vestments used when high mass is said, and on the bare white walls were a few statues of saints and apostles. In a smaller room the father showed Edith some curious copper vessels fashioned by the Indians a century ago. He also showed

THE CORRIDOR OF THE MISSION.

her the brass candlesticks used on Corpus Christi and other fête-days, and a little forge at which the fathers repair anything that may become broken.

On leaving the Mission the father walked with Edith to the end of the olive grove, and there said good-by. Turning to look back toward the Mission, Edith saw him standing on the steps of the church, his tall, heavily robed figure clearly outlined against the white façade.

When Reginald and Goodnow visited the Mission for the first time, they made a much more thorough examination than Edith had been allowed to do. Their first exploit was to climb the belfry of one of the towers. From where the bells hung they could see far down the valley; in one direction to Gaviota Pass, forty-five miles westward, and in another down the coast to Ventura. As it nears Gaviota Pass, the Santa Barbara Valley loses its width, and becomes a mere neck of land crowded down between the sea and the mountains. From where they stood the

two men could look far up the narrow vale to farms and orchards. In many of the fields grew dark green live-oaks, and in others nothing but waving grain. They watched the shadows grow fainter and the colorings begin to change as the sun sank low toward the sea, and at last was hid from sight behind the watery horizon. When the light was entirely gone, the bells in the towers rang for evening mass, and as Reginald and his companion returned to the body of the church, the fathers had already gathered at the altar, and were busy with their prayers.

The two men were free to go where they pleased. Both made friends with the padres, and were always welcome. Reginald liked the garden best, but Goodnow was more interested in seeing the cells where the fathers slept, and in visiting the corridor, with its view between the arches, of the town and bay. It extends the entire front of the Mission wing, and is fully a hundred feet long. Opening from it are the living apartments, and above are the bare and narrow cells in which the brothers sleep. To the left of the Mission are a small corral and stable, where the padres keep their few cattle and sheep. Reginald always went there, if he happened to be at the church late in the afternoon, to see Father G—— milk the cows. The old man was an adept, and handled his robes most gracefully. If a cow forgot to behave, he forgot his meekness in a moment, and pounded her with his stool. The young calves were his particular care. He led them tenderly about, but when refractory, pulled hard at the rope, reminding Goodnow of the picture of the refractory ass and the angry friar. Edith made several sketches of the church. It was her great delight to study it in all its details, and she found many of its features as picturesque as those of cathedrals in Spain. In fact, one is constantly impressed with the idea, while he is at the Mission, that he is in Spain. For at noonday the shadows are as dark and clearly defined as they are at the Alhambra; and at evening the gray-white walls are suffused with a softening light such as one expects to find only in the countries across the sea.

In their rides about the country Goodnow was never an idle wanderer. It had been his desire, ever since seeing Santa Barbara, to find a ranch that would return a fair per cent. on his investment. He and the girls always rode, while Reginald and his wife drove. Kate had at first worn a black habit and stiff hat, but had discarded these in time, and adopted a costume that made her figure a conspicuous object wherever she went. Her hat was light straw, like those worn by college oarsmen, and her jacket was a bright flannel Norfolk. Edith wore a broad-brimmed felt hat, and was always as fresh-looking after a long ride as when she started. Goodnow had bought a Mexican sombrero.

At first Goodnow was tempted to buy a place in El Montecito Valley, which lies near Santa Barbara, and is only separated from it by a low ridge of hill extending nearly to the beach, and between which is a view of Ruicon Peak and a bit of the bay. The valley faces the sea, and runs back to the mountains. It is in reality a suburb of Santa Barbara, and contains a score or more beautiful residences, erected by those who have been attracted to the region by its delightful climate and su-

perior natural attractions. The valley has a quick slope from the sea to the range, and is dotted with groves and live-oaks. The first time Goodnow piloted his friends there he took them to the base of the mountains, and bade them look upon the country at their feet. The view was like a picture. There lay the ocean, pressing upon yellow sands; westward rose the low hills, oaks growing on their sides, and behind which was Santa Barbara; eastward ran a higher ridge, tree-grown and covered with fields of grain; in the valley were red-roofed cottages surrounded by luxuriant groves of orange and lemon trees. Summer and winter the Montecito never loses its verdure or its freshness. It is literally the home of an eternal summer.

Goodnow would have bought one of the places offered him, but could not obtain land enough to make a profitable farm. His next hope was to find something at Carpenteria—a valley separated from El Montecito by the Ortega Hill. It is a productive region, and contains large ranches and small farms, on which oranges, walnuts, beans, and almonds are grown. It occupies a long, narrow neck of land lying between the mountains and the sea. At its extreme eastern end is Ruicon Peak, over and by the sea edge of which extends the stage road to Ventura and Newhall. The fields are all cultivated, and scattered over them are numerous cottages. Goodnow and his friends made several trips to the valley, as all do who wish to see everything of interest around Santa Barbara. But he could not decide what to purchase, and there was not much property offered for sale. They invariably took their lunch and were gone all day, resting for a few hours at some Carpenteria grove, and returning home late in the afternoon.

In the western part of the Santa Barbara Valley, however, Goodnow found what he wanted. When Kate saw the place she said at once it was just what they had long been seeking. The property comprised a tract of 160 acres, and was one-half level and one-half rolling land. But little of the land had been improved, and the house was not worth considering. From the higher parts of the ranch Goodnow could see across the valley to the sea; in another, had a glimpse of Santa Barbara; and in still another, looked far away to Gaviota Pass. Over the level fields were scattered live-oaks, and the rolling land

IN GAVIOTA PASS.

extended into the range through winding cañons choked with shrubs and sycamore-trees. There was not a prettier spot in the country than up these cañons. Good-now began immediately to plant his olive and nut trees, and rode out nearly every day to superintend affairs, and see that the men did good work on the cottage he was building. Later, he and the girls, leaving Reginald and his wife to rest beneath the trees, rode into the cañons for a mile or more. The trail followed a creek that ran over a rocky bed in the deep shadow of the leafy sycamores, and led to an elevated spur of the range, from which the country for miles around was seen. Very often Reginald and Anna followed the riders a short distance up the gorge, taking their luncheon on a bit of level ground by the stream.

A short distance beyond Goodnow's new ranch were those of Glen Anne and Ellwood. Both of these famous places are well known and very valuable. They are respectively twelve and sixteen miles west of Santa Barbara, and extend from the

sea-shore far into the cañons. At Glen Anne, owned by Colonel W. W. Hollister, a California pioneer, who has done much to make Santa Barbara attractive, the chief business is orange-growing, stock-raising, and general farming. But on the ranch may be found trees and shrubs of almost every known variety. Leading to the house is an avenue of tall palms, and beyond there are olive, orange, lemon, banana, date, peach, apple, nectarine, and fig trees, with here and there acres of wal-nut, almond trees, and vineyards. The grounds are carefully kept, and the flow-ers were such as to fill the soul of Edith with a joy which she could not express.

"Here you see the sort of place I shall have," said Goodnow, as he conducted the party through the Glen Anne grounds.

"Yes, in the future," replied Kate.

"In the future, of course," answered Goodnow. "And yet it will not be very long before I can show some progress. There are no hard, long winters in Cali-fornia, remember. Next year I'll have wheat, flowers, and all my orange and olive cuttings out; in twelve months more, my vineyard growing. In six years my income from the place will be worth having, and in ten years I can live like a nabob on what my ranch produces."

"Provided nothing goes wrong," said Kate.

"Oh, well, I am not too sanguine; but you can see as well as I, of how much this soil is capable, and what the climate is. I wish I could give ten acres of land in this State to every man in New York who works in an office all day for a thousand a year. He only gets a bare living there, and here ten acres would give him that, and sunshine, good air, and independence besides. 'Get land,' is my motto. Our cities are over-full, and our professions crowded. We must begin to cultivate our country more carefully. California is equal in size to France, and yet has only a million inhabitants."

At Ellwood, Reginald found much to interest him. The land is planted with olives, English walnuts, almonds, and wheat. The nuts are superior to those imported. From the olives is made a finely flavored oil. It has a wide reputation in the East, and is in great demand. The various orchards are planted with great care, and the trees are set out in long rows that extend for a great distance over the gently rolling ground. The home at Ellwood is a small, vine-covered cottage standing in the shadow of some huge, wide-branching oaks. Near the grove are the packing-houses, drying-furnaces, and a garden filled with choice varieties of flowers gathered from nearly every part of the world.

Beyond Ellwood the country highway follows the beach past the Sturges ranch, occupying the upper end of an oak-grown cañon, and to Gaviota Pass, a wild, narrow passage crossing the Santa Ynez range. High ledges of rock rise on each side of the road, and from the mouth of the pass one may look far down the valley in the direction of Santa Barbara.

By the time Goodnow's house was completed the California spring had come. The rainy weather was over. Day after day the sun rose in a cloudless east and set in a cloudless west. Every shrub was in bloom, and the violet beds in Reginald's garden were blue with blossoms. Out in the country the almond, peach, and apricot trees were all a mass of delicate color, and with the oranges still

weighing down the branches were pure white blossoms whose perfume filled the air with a delicious fragrance. Fields were a velvety green; the leaves of the oaks were washed bright and fresh; the sycamores had sent forth new leaves and branches, and birds were busy building their nests. By the side of country roads the wild mustard grew higher than one's head, golden and delicate, a rich contrast to the blue of sky and ocean; and in many of the meadows were long wide patches of blue-flax. Farmers were planting their corn and beans; gardeners were spading their flower beds for the last time. Old Juan and Edith were all day pruning, raking, and watering slips and seedlings. There was no dust and no mud. The air was soft, warm, and fragrant. Riding parties, improving every hour left them before their departure from Santa Barbara, scoured the country in search of new places of interest, or went once more to the cañons and other favorite haunts. By the first of May the "winter season" was over. The hotels had room at last for those who came, and one by one the rented cottages were given up.

But still there was not utter desertion. All who could stay did so, well knowing that beautiful as Santa Barbara is during the winter, one should know her in her summer dress to realize how great is her charm.

"I prefer the months from May until autumn," said Goodnow. "You have seen for yourself what May is, and June is nearly its equal. As for July and August, they are wonderfully cool and comfortable. There is never a night that a blanket isn't necessary. Of course it's dusty. There's no rain, and all the fields are parched. But you'll get used to that, and I like the brown hills as well as the green."

Before their departure, Reginald had planned a week's trip to the Ojai Valley, a park-like retreat about forty miles from Santa Barbara, nestled among the mountains of the Santa Ynez. Its elevation is nearly one thousand feet above sea-level, and the climate is radically different from that of Santa Barbara, being drier and more bracing. Many whose health does not improve at the sea-side go to the Ojai, and are quickly benefited. The mountains entirely surround the valley, which is about thirty miles long by from three to six wide, and the only entrance to the

IN THE VALLEY OF THE OJAI.

beautiful amphitheatre of oak-grown fields and long grassy levels is by the Casitas Pass, which leads from Carpenteria over the range to the little town of Nordhoff, the only village there.

To save trouble, Reginald engaged the regular four-horse stage that runs between Santa Barbara and the Ojai. Early in the season as it was, the day when they started was June-like in its bright freshness — clear, mild, and beautiful. For the first two hours the way led down the coast through El Montecito and Carpenteria. The fields of green grain and blue-flax, the live-oaks and wild flowers, the orange groves and nut orchards, gave, with the sea and sky, a coloring rich and varied. In Carpenteria the road ran near the beach, past a line of sand-dunes, now overgrown with trailing vines and flowers thrown into bold relief against the background of ocean. To the left, reaching the mountains, were open fields, some frilled with walnut orchards and fruit trees, others freshly ploughed and ready for their crop of Lima-beans, of which the Carpenteria Valley is the home. At the mouth of the pass the road turned abruptly northward and entered a narrow, winding cañon, guarded by steep hill-sides overgrown with oaks and tangled brushwood. Down the centre of the ravine flowed a noisy creek; and on both banks was a net-work of ferns and morning-glory vines. Before reaching the steepest part of the pass an hour's rest was taken in a spot shaded by large oaks, a short distance from which ran the brook. In every direction there was nothing but verdure—the green of the ferns intensified by the oaks, and that of the trees by the shrubs on the mountain slopes.

As the top of the pass was neared the oaks disappeared, and in their place were wild wastes of sage and chaparral, and patches of wild flowers of a hundred different shades—blue, gold, and red. Some of the distant hills appeared on fire, so thickly were they carpeted with the flowers, and so brilliant was their hue. Edith counted over seventy different varieties without leaving the wagon. When the crest of the range was reached the driver halted, and the little party gazed upon the mountains whose broken contour extended as far as the eye could see. Northward, guarded by tree-grown hills, and resting in the very lap of rugged mountains, lay the Ojai, a filmy haze softening

its outlines, and groves of live-oak. But most admired was the pass itself, winding in narrow coils around the many hills, and the view beyond it of the Santa Barbara Valley, blue, softly outlined and girded by the yellow beach, upon which the waves could be plainly seen breaking in masses of foam. With a glass the houses were visible, and with the naked eye all could see a steamer ploughing its way across the bay to the wharf. Few, perhaps no other passes in California, have the varied beauty of the Casitas; none, certainly, has its views of mountain, valley, and ocean combined in one harmonious whole.

It was nearly sundown when the Ojai was reached, and the tired but delighted travellers alighted at the Oak Glen cottages. The last half of the ride was as interesting as the first. The road led down the mountain-side by easy grades, and through dense forests of oak and sycamore. Several streams were crossed— wide, shallow rivers of clear water into which men were casting their flies for trout. Beyond the last ford in the Ojai the wild flowers grew thicker than ever, and the air was of the mountains, crisp and invigorating. None, save Goodnow, who had made the trip before, had ever seen such oaks, so many, or so large, as those which now were passed. They made veritable forests, and beneath their wide-spreading branches, festooned with swaying clusters of gray Spanish-moss, were groups of resting cattle. Years ago all the southern California valleys were choked with oaks. But to-day many have been cut down, and it is only in the Ojai that one can find them in abundance.

There is little to do in the Ojai but to admire and study nature. The little town of Nordhoff is as quiet as the grave. The Oak Glen cottages stand by themselves just off the highway, and are equally as quiet. For a day after her arrival Anna sat on the veranda, shaded by a large oak, gazing listlessly down the valley beyond its trees and fields to the chain of mountains at the western end. But after she had rested there followed days of exploration. Kate was in her element. The horses were low-spirited beasts, but the country was too beautiful to ride across rapidly, so no one complained. The first excursion was down the valley to the Matilija Cañon, which extends several miles into the range, and from being wide and brush-grown, soon becomes a narrow pathway bordered by rough, rocky cliffs, washed by a swift little stream dashing headlong over a bowlder-strewn bed. At the extreme end of the cañon is a spring of strong sulphur water. Kate and Goodnow rode on to this, but the others halted at an interval for luncheon. Reginald of continual summer, but now I think I never should."

What Edith's opinion of California life was, Goodnow had not been able to discover. That she enjoyed all she saw, he felt positively sure. But she was never enthusiastic in her expressions, and it was only lately that Goodnow had tried to

ADOBE HOUSE.

went trouting, and after an hour's casting returned with a basket of fish, which Goodnow cooked over a bed of coals.

"It's like Colorado here," said that young man of general information. "Shouldn't know it from a cañon of the Rocky Mountains. Wonderful variety of scenery we have in California. Half an hour's ride from this cañon, and we're in a park of trees."

"Spoken like a true Californian," said Edith.

"Yes; but then I am one now, you know. It's dangerous staying long in this State. There's an old legend about seeing the Rio Grande. See it once, and you'll never rest until you see it again, or live near its waters; the same might be told of California. Come, now, does any one here think he will ever be satisfied without coming back to the scenes we've been enjoying so long?"

"I should never be," said Kate. "I'm sure never to cease thinking what a California winter is like. I might get tired

fathom her thoughts. But since one quiet evening alone with her he had found that his regard had changed to love. She had read much and talked well, and to be with her gave Goodnow mental refreshment. He always asked her opinion now, and came to her with all his doubts. Reginald had noticed the change in his friend, but said nothing.

While at the Ojai, Edith and Goodnow were more often thrown together. Kate rode with them, to be sure, but was generally rushing off into side paths or dashing far ahead of her two soberer companions. She was the life of the party, and her red jacket was sure to be seen on all the highest hill-sides and isolated peaks. Reginald intended to leave the Ojai sooner than he did, but Kate had heard of Sulphur Mountain, and said she would not go away until she had climbed it.

"Perhaps you won't be able to leave then," said Goodnow, "for there isn't much of a trail, and the climb would be hard even if there were."

"But isn't the view grand from the top?"

"Oh yes, wonderfully so. We may as well try it. I know the way, and will be responsible for our safety."

Just back of the cottages a high ridge of land runs across the valley, dividing it into two nearly equal parts, known as the Upper and Lower Ojai. Making an early start, Goodnow and the girls rode over this to the Upper Ojai. The road led through a succession of wide fields of grain and past groves of orange-trees, now putting forth fresh young leaves. The region was like a bit of Scotland, not too wild or rugged, nor yet lacking in grandeur. To the right of the valley were densely wooded hills, and high above them the bare crest of Sulphur Mountain. For hours the trail was through the forests that covered the steep sides of the peak. At times it seemed impossible to proceed. Deep ravines and beds of soft asphaltum, thickets of live-oaks and chaparral, blocked the way. But Kate, determined and persevering, would stop at nothing. Goodnow rarely left Edith's side.

"I can manage," Kate had said. "You look after Edith."

Once the trail was utterly lost. High overhead towered the mountain; below was a deep wide gorge. Edith was tired out, and Goodnow insisted upon her resting. Kate pushed on ahead, and in a few moments was lost to view among the wild-growing bushes. Presently, however, Goodnow caught the bright gleam of her jacket. She had reached a point high above her companions. Her voice as she called to them could scarcely be heard, but Goodnow understood that he and Edith were to go in the direction she pointed. Riding in a zigzag course up a slope that grew steeper every moment, Kate was reached at last, and the three, getting off their horses, sat down by the side of a hardy oak.

"We can see the top now," said Kate, "and it can't be far off. What air this is! I could climb all day and not be tired."

When the crest of the mountain was reached, the country seemed to the delighted lookers-on to lay spread at their very feet. Southward, thirty miles away, but seemingly not a quarter of that distance, was the ocean, with its islands and curving shore of yellow sands; the Santa Clara Valley, watered by a river that shone in the sunlight like a thread of silver; and nearer at hand, the sharp bare hill-tops, reaching upward like fingers of a giant hand, and holding miniature levels in their strong embrace. To the north was the Ojai, now a mere depression among the mountains; and in the distance, their slopes a deep dark blue and their summits capped with snow, rose the peaks of the Sierra Madre range. There is a small lake on the top of Sulphur Mountain—a shallow pool left by the rains of winter. It disappears in summer, but was now full of water. By its side Kate spread the luncheon which Goodnow had brought in his saddle-bags, and while they rested the tired party ate, and studied at their leisure the beauty of the view. After luncheon Edith read aloud and Goodnow smoked, while Kate, restless as ever, roamed about the place, trying from what point she had the better view. When Edith finished reading, she and Goodnow walked to where they could look afar off to the Santa Barbara Valley. It was flooded with sunshine, and its coloring was exquisite. Under the inspiration of the moment Goodnow spoke. It was a simple question that he asked, and it was as simply answered. Kate had not heard it, but knew when she came to where they stood what had been said.

"Enraptured with the view?" she asked, laughingly.

"Yes; and is our sister pleased?" said Goodnow.

"Immeasurably. But what *would* have happened, Edith, if you couldn't have answered 'yes'? Think how disagreeable the going home this afternoon would have been!"

That night the news was told Reginald and Anna. "You have my permission only on one condition," said Anna. "You must invite us to visit you at least once a year."

By the middle of May the summer season at Santa Barbara is well under way. On their return from the Ojai the bath-houses, near the wharf, were open, and every day a gay party of lookers-on gathered beneath an awning stretched over the sands to see the bathers go in. There is no better bathing in the world than that at Santa Barbara. The beach slopes gradually into deep water, and there is little surf; the temperature of the sea is much warmer than that of the Atlantic, and there is rarely any undertow. Goodnow

SCENE IN HOPE RANCH.

had bathed at least once a week all through the winter, and Kate had gone in at Christmas. She now took a swim nearly every day, going with Goodnow to the end of the wharf, or taking Edith, not so strong as her companions, to the raft which is anchored a short distance from the shore. There were always twenty or thirty people in at once, and the beach was the liveliest part of the town from eleven until twelve o'clock in the morning.

Whatever Santa Barbara had done for the others, it had certainly cured Anna. No one would have recognized her in May as the woman whom they had seen in December. In his report to Dr. Kimball, Reginald said that her cough had entirely disappeared, and that she had gained strength and flesh ever since her arrival. "In fact," he wrote, "the climate of Santa Barbara is phenomenal. I have heard of many remarkable cures. Of course every one coming here is not benefited, but the majority are. All miasmatic and pulmonary diseases are greatly helped, and the place is gaining a wide reputation as a natural sanitarium. The air is wonderfully dry for a sea-side resort, and the temperature varies but slightly throughout the year, the average being about 70° for winter and 80° for summer. From May to November there is never any rain, and during the so-called 'wet season,' lasting from November to the middle of April, the rains are only occasional, and stormy days are succeeded by clear, bright, warm ones, during which it is a delight to be out-of-doors. The town has been full of invalids all winter. Many have come to stay. The accommodations—hotels, boarding-houses, and rented cottages—are excellent; in fact, there is every modern comfort. The cost of living is very reasonable; the climate excels that of Nice; the scenery is varied and beautiful. If you have any more such patients, send them out. I'll guarantee they have the best time they ever had, and will get well as rapidly as Anna has."

In nearly the centre of Santa Barbara is a quarter known as Spanishtown, which was once a good copy of villages in Spain. So late as 1836, when Richard Henry Dana, then a sailor before the mast, visited Santa Barbara, the Spaniards were almost the only people in the valley, and their thick-walled adobe houses with red-tiled roofs were huddled closely together midway between the beach and the Mission. To-

day the quarter has been relegated to side streets, and a part of it given over to the Chinese.

It was not long before Kate found Spanishtown. Her first visit was made alone, but on the second she went with Edith and old Juan, the one to sketch and the other to show the more interesting features of the settlement. Juan was in his element, acting as guide and interpreter, and returned the Spanish salutations with much grace and dignity, and consumed any number of cigarettes as he walked through the narrow streets. His first stop was made before the remnant of an old thick adobe wall still standing. "It is the only part of the old presidio left," he said. "I can remember when the whole wall was up. It was too high to climb over, and inside was a large square which the soldiers used, and where there was a chapel and barracks. At the four corners were four brass cannon. And outside the walls, protected by the guns, were the houses of our people. There was nothing then between here and the beach, so that we could sit in our doorways and look out upon the bay and the mountains."

Then he told of the fête-days, when mass was said at the Mission, and there were races on the beach and dancing at the presidio. Every one had work then, for the rich Spaniards owned large ranches and had many servants.

"Sometimes it does not seem Santa Barbara any more—the new houses and strange people and hotels. Some of us have little to do now, and our own town is no longer beautiful or gay. Even our houses are being pulled down, as you can see, and in a few years, I think, there will be no Spanishtown."

One of the houses visited was that which Dana describes as the scene of the wedding festivities that took place when he was at Santa Barbara. It answers perfectly to his description, and is still owned by the same family whose daughter Dana saw married. Juan took the girls into its large court-yard and to the veranda. Near the De la Guerra Mansion, as the house is called, Juan pointed out the old Noreaga garden, once a famous place, but now overgrown with grass, and containing only a few scrubby peach-trees and neglected grape arbors. On one side of it was found the best preserved Spanish house the girls had yet seen. It was a long low building, one story high, and had a roof of bright red tiles. Around the house extended a deep veranda, shaded by overhanging eaves which rested on a row of time-stained pillars. It was still inhabited by Mexicans, whom Juan knew, and who invited him and his party in. The garden fronting the little cabin was filled with rose-bushes, and in its centre was an old well, its wooden frame nearly hid by vines.

It requires several visits to know Spanishtown thoroughly. There are many interesting corners and by-ways, and in all are pictures of a life gradually dying out in Santa Barbara. Some of the cottages are in groups, and face upon the street; and others are by themselves, and have their own bit of garden and vineyard.

Chinatown always seemed an incongruity to Edith, who disliked finding the Spanish adobes peopled by so foreign a race; yet she often went there, in company with either Goodnow or Reginald, and visited the shops of Chung Wah and Sing Lee for Chinese curios. On the days when their New-Year is celebrated Chinatown is overrun with visitors, who are expected to call at the different stores and partake of the refreshments that are there spread out upon little tables. All the houses are decorated with lanterns, and long strings of Chinese crackers and bombs are exploded at regular intervals.

The marriage of Edith and Goodnow was to take place at Christmas, so that Edith might return to Santa Barbara for the last half of the winter. The two sisters, with Goodnow and other friends who might happen to go, rode nearly every day. There was nothing about Santa Barbara which they did not see. One of their rides was through El Montecito Valley to the Hot Springs Cañon. From the bath-house at the head of this gorge is a view of all Montecito and the bay, and from a spur of the range near by one can see for miles up and down the coast. The springs contain strong sulphur water, which is drank and bathed in with great bodily benefit. They have been known for years, and were widely famous among the Indians who inhabited the region. Still another ride was over the hills of the Hope Ranch to a tiny lake lying in a grove of oaks. The trail follows the edge of the cliffs after leaving the beach, and for a few miles before the lake is reached commands a view of the channel, valley, and mountains of which Kate never tired.

"But you can't decide which ride you like best," she wrote home. "Never was there such a place as this. We are always finding something new. There are a dozen or more cañons among the mountains, and we go first to one and then to another, spending the day, or just riding up the trails and home again, in time for luncheon or dinner. Last week we rode over to the San Marcos Pass, which crosses the range to the west of Santa Barbara, and went to the Santa Ynez Valley. In it are many farms and an old church, something like the one we have here, only not nearly so well preserved. The San Marcos is not so beautiful a pass as the Casitas, but is wilder, and from its top you can see from one end of the Santa Barbara Valley to the other. I like the cañons: they are always so cool and green. When we get tired of the sea or the town, we go into the mountains. Everybody tries camping for a week, and we have done as the rest.

The night before all except Goodnow were to say good-by to Santa Barbara, Kate gave a picnic on the beach. Twenty or more young people rode out to the place of meeting, while others came in carriages. Supper was served on the veranda of an old weather-beaten bath-house standing under the brow of the cliffs a mile to the east of the wharf. Some of the men built a fire of drift-wood, and as darkness came on all gathered around it, and listened to Edith, who played on the guitar and sang some quaint old Spanish songs which Juan the gardener had taught her. As she sang, the moon came up, out of the sea it seemed, and its light, with that of the fire, threw a weird soft glow over the long stretch of sands, and the faces of the picturesquely grouped listeners. It was hard to realize that this was the last evening at Santa Barbara. The time had passed all too rapidly. And when the farewells had been said on the following day, and Goodnow, the picture of woe, was left standing alone on the wharf, Edith was the only one who, looking back upon the beach, did not think of the picnic of the night before—that perfect ending of a perfect time. In her mind was present the memory of Sulphur Mountain. There, she knew, had been found the perfection of her winter's happiness; the music of the words said there was sweeter than that of the guitar she had played, and was more full of brightness than were the moonbeams on the waters.

Tenderfeet on Tiburon
(1912)

THE "WANDERER" LYING OFF SERILAND RECEIVING VISITORS

TENDERFEET ON TIBURON

BY MICHAEL WILLIAMS

Photographs by the Author

A Trip That Exploded the Old Myth of a Race of Bloodthirsty Cannibals in the Gulf of California

WE were going to Tiburon Island. We were really going to Tiburon! Like the burden of a song ran the thought of it in our minds and in our talk. We were to visit mysterious, romantic, legendary Seriland—the home and haunt of the least known, most feared, and almost the most inaccessible tribe of Indians in America. Throughout the Southwest, especially in Mexico, to say "Tiburon," or "The Seris," is to conjure up innumerable tales of the most wild and wonderful description.

The Seris are said to be cannibals. As big physically as the giants of Tierra del Fuégo, they are the prototypes of the Brobdingnagians of Swift and of the Amazons of Spanish-American legends, who guarded on their shark-surrounded, mountainous, semi-mythical island, the richest of gold and silver mines and pearl oyster beds. They have never been Christianized. A hundred and fifty years ago they killed the one missionary who ever reached the island. None has ventured again the task of their conversion, even in Mexico, where the soldiers of the Cross gained fame for daring.

They have never been conquered in warfare, though now and again defeated in single battles. The terror of their poisoned arrows, of their stone clubs, and of their mode of fighting with teeth and sharp-nailed hands, as wild animals fight, for hundreds of years has been active in Mexico, and still is very much alive in Sonora. According to J. W. Powell, director of the Smithsonian Institution's Ethnology Bureau, "among aborigines known to Caucasians, the Seri Indians appear to stand nearly or quite at the foot of the scale."

The telegram, ardently hoped for, ar-

rived from Guaymas, telling us that all
was in readiness and to come at once.
And at once we went. There was a
revolution going on in Mexico—but
what did we care? We were obliged
to travel several hundred miles through
the war zone on a railroad along the line
of which bridges were being dynamited
and towns were being captured and re-

A BOWMAN OF THE SERIS

captured and many fierce little battles
fought.

"If nothing worse happens, such as
being shot, or held for ransom by some
bandit gang, you're quite likely to be cut
off in Mexico," said our friends in Tucson, Arizona, where we were staying
when the unexpected chance came to
visit Tiburon. Indeed, according to our
friends (not all of them, be sure!—for
many were aching to go themselves), we
were likely to get into all kinds of
trouble. To go to Seriland at any time
was a risky business at best, but to go
during a revolution, when the land was
seething and boiling with discontent
and hostility to foreigners, was—Oh,
well, why enumerate all its kinds and

degrees of risk, and foolishness, etc.?
Especially since it all went in one ear
and blew out the other, without even
jolting our minds to attention in its passage.

We were going to Tiburon, you see.
We were really going to Tiburon! And
when you go adventuring, something
happens in your brain cells, or coils, or
neurons, whatever you call them. Your
mental processes undergo a subtle and
profound change. You don't hear or
see or think or reason about things as
do your friends who stay home and hold
down chairs at roll-top desks and seek
romance in bridge whist. The way we
figured the situation, we felt that so
long as the *revoltosos* didn't blow up any
more bridges until we had reached Guaymas, the port from which we were to
set forth on our voyage up the Gulf of
California, we really didn't care about
what might happen afterwards.

And if Señor El Presidente Porfirio
Diaz couldn't keep his insurgent citizens from blowing up the bridges until
we were safe in Guaymas, why, then,
Señor El Presidente Porfirio Diaz had
better betake him to the tall timber, or
up Salt Creek, or down South, or to
Paris—wherever it is that has-been
rulers of Latin-American republics do
betake themselves. Usually it is Paris,
when they can beat the revolting patriots
to the treasure box.

Wasting no more thought on the revolution, we packed our suit-cases and
took the next train leaving Tucson for
the West Coast of Mexico—the line
that runs through Nogales on the border, via Hermosillo, the capital of the
state of Sonora, and Guaymas, and Cul-
iacan, and Mazatlan, southward to
Yago, in the state of Tepic, not far from
Guadalajara, to which point it will be
extended to connect with a line to the
City of Mexico and thus open up a wonderful and wealthy country for commerce, sport and travel.

The next morning we were in Guaymas. The only thrill—a very mild one
—supplied by the revolution was a
glimpse of a rebel command marching
in the brush below Hermosillo and the
presence of Federal soldiers on the
train.

SERIS COMING OFF TO WELCOME THE WHITE INVADERS

We drove to the hotel where we were to meet the head of our expedition, Mr. E. A. Salisbury, a rancher with a hundred thousand acre ranch in the Yaqui Valley, and a celebrated big game hunter, fisherman, and yachtsman. On his motorboat, the *Wanderer,* for the last four or five years he had been hunting, fishing, and exploring in the Gulf of California, making a special study of Tiburon Island. He had managed to get on friendly terms with the Seri In-

"That's just why I want to go!" replied the Señora. "It's perfectly delightful to think I'll be the first white woman to set foot on Tiburon!"

Señor William Robinson—otherwise "Billy" Robinson—former Prefect of Guaymas, and, despite his name, which descends to him from an ancestor, a Mexican of courtly manners and Castilian aplomb, being one of those who heard the Señora so declare herself, rose to the occasion gallantly by remarking:

JUAN TOMAS, CHIEF OF THE SERIS AND THE ONLY MAN AMONG THEM WHO
SPEAKS ANY SPANISH

dians and was recognized by the tribe as its one white friend.

The *Wanderer* was lying at the pier a hundred feet from the hotel taking on board the last of the gasoline and provisions. Jumping into a cab, we left the water-front for a hurried, exciting hour or two of shopping for minor necessaries, fruit, vegetables, and the like, among the quaint stores and shops of the city. Salisbury was known everywhere, and the news that he was making another trip to Tiburon excited no especial interest—but when it became known that the Señora also was going, there was excitement galore, very much to the enjoyment of the Señora.

"But never has a white woman ever ventured to Tiburon," was said, again and again.

"And the foot of the Señora will leave a mark which, though tiny, will never be forgotten!"

"*Ah, Dios, si, si!*" remarked somebody else. "If only the cannibals do not devour it!"

"Well, if they do they'll find it tender—like her husband's as well!" laughed Salisbury, and hurried his tenderfeet guests away from the croakers and prophets of evil to the motorboat. While the tenderfeet changed their clothes in the cabin, everything was made ship-shape and snug, and when we came on deck again the trip to Tiburon was under way.

It was nearing noon. It was a bright-skied April day. A light breeze was blowing across the water from the west, here and there touching with white foam the blue of the gently-swelling waves. Running out of the sun-splendid, island-studded harbor into the Gulf of California, we cruised along the shore line in a northwest direction.

Big, grotesque pelicans were doing an awkward-looking but effective fishing business all about. So also was a small fleet of boats from Guaymas. The fishermen, however, were no longer met with after we passed the Lighthouse Point. The pelicans retained a mon-

resistance of the cruise, but there were plenty other good things on the bill of fare. We had gasoline, water, and provisions aboard sufficient for a week, and we meant to make the most of our time.

We felt that if we were not precisely marking a sea-trail that would soon be followed by many others to the hunting and fishing and yachting pleasures of almost inexhaustible possibilities that abound in the Gulf, at any rate we were among the very first pioneers.

THE GATHERING IN THE TRIBAL HUT WITH THE ONLY WHITE WOMAN WHO EVER VISITED TIBURON

opoly. We were now beyond the last point of ordinary navigation in the Gulf. There is no other lighthouse after you pass Guaymas.

Except for turtle-hunters and gull-egg gatherers, and now and again a smuggling craft, or the vessel of some adventurer looking for gold, or pearls, or landing Chinese on their way into the United States, the Gulf of California beyond Guaymas is unfrequented and almost unknown. Few places in the world to-day are so little known as this mysterious, desert-islanded, desert-bordered gulf.

Tiburon lies about one hundred and thirty miles north of Guaymas. It was Salisbury's plan to reach it at dawn next morning. We were in no hurry. Tiburon, to be sure, was the *pièce de*

Sportsmen often ask: "Where are the great game fields of the world to-day?" Few can give an answer. Alaska—a very old story! Except, of course, for its real interior, which is more difficult than interior Africa to-day. And Africa itself is rather stale except for the far regions that cost a small fortune to penetrate.

Generally speaking, the sportsman of to-day faces a world rapidly growing short of sport. Hunting and fishing and out-of-door life nearly everywhere have been so systematized and commercialized that their adventurous tang, their romantic qualities, have been pretty well lost. Yet here, right in the back-yard of the United States, so to speak, is a place in which to play to your heart's content, on waters and lands that are

THE SQUALLING, SQUABBLING MOB OF SEA BIRDS

PRACTICALLY THE WHOLE TRIBE ASSEMBLED IN FRONT OF ONE OF THE HUTS

ONE OF THE MANY STRANGE, SCULPTURED ROCKS ALONG THE SHORE OF THE GULF

still largely unexplored, with mountains to climb and deserts to conquer, and literally swarming with game.

Back from the shore-line of the Gulf you can get grizzly and brown bear and mountain lions. Antelope roam certain of the regions in bands of two and three hundred. The big horn mountain sheep are plentiful. Tiburon Island is crisscrossed with deer tracks till the ground resembles the trodden trails about the home corral of a cattle ranch. To give a list of the fish and birds and other game would be to turn this article into a sort of dictionary of sport.

Here's just a sample paragraph: Besides bear, antelope, and several kinds of deer, there are mountain lions, wild hog, and bob cats. For feathered game— there is wild turkey and ducks of all kinds in incredible numbers. Admiral Dewey, who, when a commodore, mapped the Gulf, told Dr. D. T. MacDougal, director of the Carnegie Desert Laboratory and himself a hunter and explorer of sorts, that he, George Dewey, would take his affidavit that he saw a raft of wild duck coming out from the mouth of the Colorado River that was more than two miles long and half a mile wide! (I give the names on which this little anecdote rests, for you can't be too careful in this hunting story business. Modern pump and magazine guns

haven't by any means altogether superseded the good old long bow!) Then there are edible parrots, Sonora pigeons, sandhill crane, geese, brant, curlew, snipe, plover, and quail—quail—quail.

Fish—well, I'll go light concerning fish, just mentioning turtle (if the turtle goes in the fish class), jew fish, tuna, yellow tail ranging as high in weight as seventy-five pounds, with fifty-pounders common; cabrillo (golden, striped, and pinto), running in weight up to two hundred, and a first rate fighting fish. Time after time on our trip a cabrillo would be caught, and while being drawn in, by rod or hand, would be swallowed by a monster cabrillo, who usually broke the line, though once we got a hundred-and fifty-pounder.

Often, too, one would jump for the log when it was thrown out and its brass was all dented with teeth marks.

Once when sounding with the lead in unknown waters, we were puzzled by the fantastic variations of depth the lead would record until we discovered that a big school of bass was under the boat and that the lead was resting on its almost solidly-packed mass most of the time. And I could tell you others—all true, at that! I'll refer you to the Señora if you don't believe me, for she's from New England, the place that made the conscience famous.

SERI WICKIUP, A CRUDE STRUCTURE OF POLES, BARK AND BRANCHES

Then there is a rooster fish, something like a yellowtail, only with a blunter, bull-dog kind of head and with fins sticking out on its back like the tail of a rooster, a vicious fighter from strike to gaffing. There is the tartuva, a fish resembling a white sea bass, something rather like a cross between a jew fish and a white bass. As high as seven dollars gold a kilo (about two and one-fifth pounds) is paid by the Chinese for its bladder, for it is esteemed by them a great delicacy. The bladder looks like a piece of transparent tallow. Add just about a hundred-odd other kinds that also run to and fro in those wonderful waters—and whales, and sharks, and tinteros, or sting-rays, some said to weigh a ton or more, all of which are hunted by those who like a liberal spicing of danger in their sport.

All the afternoon we slipped through a smooth sea in a leisurely fashion, keeping close to the shore, down to which the foothills of the Sierra Madres marched in fantastic array, looking as if they had been cut out by Rodin and a company of Japanese carvers and then colored by Maxfield Parrish. Here and there in the canyons were groves of palm trees, of a dull bronze-green, stiff in the windless sunshine like decorations of metalwork. The great gulf was like a smoldering blue flame in the flood of

ardent sunshine. Flocks of tern sprinkled it with dots of white. Huge turtles swam by. Whales appeared, to spout and sound again.

Clouds of fish, or solitary ones, came and passed in the calm depths below the boat, like strange emotions and curious thoughts passing through the meditative soul of a hermit. There were rocks near shore that looked like lions and sphynxes, or broken bridges, shattered columns, and architraves of ruined cities. Mountains of mirage suspired from the water like the dreams of a poet taking form and lifted their wavering peaks of amethyst, mauve, lilac and rose in altitudinous aspiration toward the sky, only to tremble back into oblivion as though shriveled by the sun.

As the sun neared the western sea horizon—for at this point the gulf is about one hundred miles wide and the other shore was invisible—there began that vesperal miracle of color transmutation,—that silent symphony of changing, dissolving, blending, harmonic weaving and interweaving hues—as though the secret shrine of night was being protected by veil after veil—which evening after evening is repeated but is never the same.

The level light splashed back from the cliffs along the shore and filled the water with gold and purple, darkened here and there by patterns of sea-weed and touched with scarlet by schools of vivid red fish. Black cormorants, with snaky heads, and pelicans with long bills crossed and criss-crossed from rock to rock, and the noise of the water on the shore and the thud-thudding of the *Wanderer's* screw and the splash of leaping fish and the cries of the water-fowl, emphasized the profound silence and solitude in which we moved, as people praying on the floor of a cathedral indicate its immensity.

Shortly after six o'clock we sighted the mountains of Tiburon dead ahead and sixty miles away, the faintest possible bluish blur against the sky.

It was Captain Salisbury's intention to run slowly all night and arrive at Tiburon at daybreak, at the southwestern end of the island, near Willard's point.

I stayed on deck throughout the night, now sleeping, now waking. The water was calm as a mill pond. Fish broke its surface with flashes and whirlpools of phosphorescent flame, and at our bows we carried two spreading wings of blue fire—blue as the light sparkling from a dynamo.

The air was warm and balmy,— balmy, and balmy! And all about us,

on the shore or on strange desert islands, loomed the apparitional shadows of the mountains.

At one o'clock Salisbury half-whispered, "Look at the fire yonder!" I looked and saw a great still flame far away—and then the rest of the huge moon followed the crimson upper rim into sight. Arising out of the sea and half veiled by a cloud, it looked for all the world like the bulging sail of some strange ship of dream.

I knew the night could give me nothing greater than the moonrise and I slept. Shortly after four o'clock I was awake again and Monument Point, the southeastern end of Tiburon, appeared as a black silhouette against the dim beginning of the dawn, and the first of the pelicans were clumsily heaving themselves from the shore-line toward the sea.

"If the early bird gets the worm, on shore, what does the early pelican get?" somebody wanted to know, but at 4 A. M. your wit does not work readily, and the best that anybody could suggest was that perhaps they got oyster cocktails. But we took coffee.

We ran close in and skirted the westward shore of Tiburon. Hilly, dusky, slumbrous, and mysterious did it seem,

A SERI FAMILY GROUP—TENDER AND AFFECTIONATE TO EACH OTHER

THE SERI WICKIUPS ON THE SAND DUNES

emerging from behind the curtain of night. The atmosphere of all the legends and romances—the treasure hunts, the battles, the tragic disappearances of prospectors and explorers in its recesses —all this seemed to hang about it like a palpable veil of mystery.

On our port beam appeared the island of San Estevan, taking the colors of the coming day before they reached Tiburon. It glowed like a huge gem of carved topaz and molded amber and sculptured rose-marble on the indigo-blue floor of the calm water. Then the sunbeams reached Tiburon and its tall, grim hills donned cloaks of .imperial purple and gold and violet.

"In one of the bays of Tiburon, or on the mainland near it," said Salisbury, "there is supposed to be a great treasure of pearls, gold coin, and the loot of Spanish churches and ships and cities, gathered together by the brother of Oliver Cromwell, who was a pirate, according to the legends of the Gulf, and made Tiburon his haven. He captured a good many Spanish ships in or near the Gulf, but at last was himself defeated and destroyed, with ship and crew, by a French frigate on the Baja California coast, opposite Guaymas. But the Frenchmen did not get his treasure. It has been for centuries a part of the lore that attracted adventurers here.

"Another part of Tiburon's magnetic faculty is the story, widely credited on the West Coast, that there is a bed of pearl oysters of immense richness somewhere in its waters. Many of the early Spanish chroniclers mention it, and it is alluded to by Lieutenant Hardy and other voyagers. But so far nobody has succeeded in securing the secret of its location from the Seris, who have driven away or killed many companies of adventurers who came here to discover the pearls. And in the hills of the island are thought to be rich mines of gold and copper.

"During the last three centuries more than fifty recorded attempts to subjugate the Seris have been made, and the various fights and encounters with them are innumerable. They killed two San Francisco newspaper men who landed on Tiburon some years ago and were accused of having eaten them as well, but that was false. And not long ago they killed a curio hunter named Johnson, together with a companion, who were sailing in a Chinese junk from San Diego up and down the Gulf. When I came here for the first time I had two Mexicans with me in a small motorboat. I literally had to fight them to compel them to run the boat in to the shore when I said I meant to land on Tiburon. And all the while I was on shore I was in a funk lest they run away with the boat."

"How did the Seris receive you?" I asked.

"As an object of great suspicion, and things looked pretty squally all the while," said Salisbury. "But I gave them some presents and made my get-away, and on repeated visits since I have made it a rule not to trade with them and always to bring them cigarettes, or old clothing, or cooking utensils, or something of the kind, and now I'm welcomed—though, just the same, I always go well armed when I am among them."

First White Woman on Tiburon

Running into a pretty little bay, we anchored and lowered the rowboat and went ashore. As the bay was unnamed on the maps, Salisbury declared that we would give it the name of "Peggy's Landing," in honor of the first white woman to land on Tiburon. Map-makers, take notice! We did not expect to see the Seris, but were after deer for the larder. The Seris' main village is on the mainland opposite the northeast end of the island, across the Boca Inferno, or Mouth of Hell—the narrow, treacherous strait that separates Tiburon from the Sonoran coast. At certain seasons of the year the Indians migrate to the island and hunting and fishing parties are continually crossing and recrossing.

Having made the first landing of a white woman on mysterious Tiburon, however, the Señora remained on the shore near the boat, while Salisbury and I, accompanied each by a Mexican sailor, went inland after deer.

We did not go far. Within a quarter of a mile from the beach Salisbury killed a fat buck. We saw eight big white-tail deer almost as soon as we began to hunt, and could have killed at least six if we had been so minded. But we were merely after meat, and we soon were afloat again with the larder well supplied and deer liver and bacon on the bill of fare for next morning's breakfast.

All that day we leisurely coasted Tiburon, arriving early in the afternoon at Patos Island, about thirty miles from Peggy's Landing and fifteen from the Seri village. Seen from a distance, Patos Island looks singularly like an Egyptian pyramid, as there is a hill whitened with guano standing in its midst that is shaped

very much like one of the ancient monuments by the Nile. We landed on Patos despite the clamorous, squalling, agitated mob of gulls that live there. Here and there we found the ruined walls of old fortifications erected by guano gatherers to protect themselves from the Seri. We came upon old iron wheelbarrows buried in the sand.

The wind freshened as the day wore on so considerably that, as the Seri village is on the open roadstead, it was decided not to go there until next morning, as we had good anchorage in shelter where we were. That night the tender-feet had little sleep, though we were rocked soothingly and gently by the calm water in which the *Wanderer* lay. Our proximity to the Seris, no doubt, exerted too exciting an influence. Speaking for myself, I know that all the tales I had ever heard or read—and their name is legion!—came into mind, with appropriate illustrations supplied by mental pictures of cannibal feasts and poisoned arrows hurtling in flights.

We were awakened early, and after the deer liver and bacon breakfast, we left Patos Island for the Seri village just as the sun came up. We ran close in to the Tiburon shore at this point in order to see the big valley that opens there—the valley which an imaginative recent writer on Tiburon said contained an immense stone idol worshipped by the Seris,—but which doesn't.

As we approached the mainland we ran up our flags—all in honor of Juan Tomas, the chief of the Seris. The stars and stripes and the Mexican flag and the pennants of various yacht clubs and motorboat associations made a brave showing. At seven o'clock we were well up with the coast. Preparations were begun for the landing. Mrs. Williams, Salisbury, myself, and one of the sailors were to go ashore, while the engineer, an American, and the rest of the crew, two Mexican sailors, were to guard the *Wanderer*.

Loaded rifles were dealt out to them, with instructions to keep us under observation all the time we were in on shore and to cover our retreat if a retreat should be found necessary. We of the landing party did not take rifles, contenting ourselves with six-shooters. Big canvas bags were filled with cigarettes and boxes of matches as gifts. All loose articles on deck were put away—to remove temptation from the path of the Seris.

Presently we approached the sandy, desert looking shore close enough to discern the huts of the Seris—desolate patches of brush and turtle shell amid the sand dunes and organ-pipe cactus. We blew a bugle and saw the Seris appear and race down the sandhills to the beach and begin to launch their canoes. Dropping anchor, we quickly launched our rowboat and pulled toward shore. The Seris, seeing that we would land before they could reach the *Wanderer,* turned their canoes and paddled back.

"They know the *Wanderer* and want to be Johnny on the spot when the cigarettes appear," said Salisbury.

As soon as our boat's keel touched the sand the Seris swarmed about us and assisted us to land and haul the boat up. Decidedly—and especially for tenderfeet!—they were a wild-looking lot. And never had we heard such strange sounds from human beings as issued from the Seris as they jabbered excitedly. Lieutenant Hardy, who visited Tiburon a hundred years ago, said that their language reminded him of that of the Tehuelche tribe of Patagonia. Some ethnologists have ascribed it to an Arabian, others to a Welch, and others again to a Patagonian, origin—but nobody really knows the origin of this tribe, that is so strangely different from all others in this part of America.

When Maldanado, a Spanish conquistador, one of Coronado's officers, saw the Seris, he wrote that they were so large and tall that "the best man in the Spanish tribe reached only to their chests." Certainly they are even yet well built and strapping men compared to most of the Mexicans and Indians of Mexico, but if there were really giants in Seriland in those days, their descendants have degenerated.

Juan Tomas, the chief, was soon shaking hands with us. He is the only man among the Seris who speaks any Spanish, and his vocabulary is very limited. But he has made a trip or two across the desert that guards Seriland on the east to Hermosillo, the capital of Sonora, and concluded a formal treaty of peace with the Mexican government which has been maintained for a number of years. Like most of the men of the tribe, there is something Chinese in the cast of Juan Tomas' features. The women, however, have a more Caucasian look and some of them are pretty, even according to our standards.

Men, women and children, and dogs—more dogs, apparently, than humans—swarmed about us and reached out eagerly (that is, the humans did!) for the cigarettes and matches, and soon everybody, down to year-old babies, were smoking. We were led to the biggest hut in the village—which did not contain more than a dozen wickiups all told. They were very proud of this largest hut, which was a new one and used as a sort of tribal headquarters. We were seated on the ground in a circle, the Señora having the post of honor by the chief's right hand, and smoked cigarettes and talked, as well as we could, to Juan Tomas. Incidentally, we took a rough-and-ready census of the tribe.

A Dying Race

Various reports in the outside world had estimated the number of the Seris at anything from two hundred to a thousand. But Juan Tomas caused a young man of the tribe to make a mark in the sand as he repeated the name of each male member of the tribe, and they numbered fifty-five. There are about thirty women, or possibly forty, so that the entire Seri tribe numbers less than one hundred. And soon there will be few of these left. They are dying rapidly. There are few young children. Their days are numbered.

A few months ago there appeared a magazine article purporting to be a truthful account of its author's adventures on Tiburon with the Seris—how he landed to get water from a certain spring (which happens to be on the other side of the island from where the article places it), and how the Seris came down upon him and his party and opened rifle fire and engaged them in a bloody fight,

And in another magazine recently there was an equally thrilling account of the flights of poisoned arrows shot around the author and his companion by the Seris.

Though it seems rather a pity to shatter romantic illusions and myths in a world from which romance (of that kind, anyway) is fading rapidly, yet it must be said that there are only two old, useless rifles in the hands of the tribe, and, at the time of our visit, only two bows and a couple of quivers full of arrows, not one of which was headed. And now they haven't those, for we bought them for souvenirs.

Among themselves, at any rate, however they may have behaved to strangers in the past, the Seris were as kindly and even affectionate a lot of people as I have ever had the good fortune to encounter. Never did we see a mother or father slap a child. Never was anger displayed, or irritation. They were continually sharing with each other the little gifts we made them. Really, you know, when you see a group of alleged cannibals sharing chewing gum (the first they had ever tasted) from mouth to mouth, and enjoying themselves hugely, respect for travelers' tales of blood and thunder goes down a peg or two.

And yet, it is true that the tales are not all false. In the sunset time of their lives, the Seris seem placidly and gently passing away from the mysterious land they have held inviolate for centuries of recorded history, with their blood unmixed with outland blood and unaffected by the civilization that has conquered all other portions of America. They are dying as they have lived—never having emerged in the slightest from barbarism, dependent upon fish and bird eggs and an occasional deer for food, and when we brought our visit to an end and chug-chugged away in our up-to-date motorboat, into the dream-like waters of the great Gulf, the experience seemed like an emergence from a dream —a dream of the long-dead past and the ancient peoples of a by-gone world.

Hunting Sheep & Antelope in Lower California (1902)

OUTING

VOL. XXXIX.   FEBRUARY, 1902.   No. 5

HUNTING SHEEP AND ANTELOPE IN LOWER CALIFORNIA

By Charles B. Slade

THE sparsely settled wilderness comprising the peninsula of Lower California extends short of a thousand miles between the Gulf of California and the Pacific, with an average width of over one hundred miles. Scattered here and there at isolated points gold and onyx mines are being worked, and a few small cattle ranches are hidden in the interior. The necessity of having a permanent point of ingress and egress for supplies, materials, etc., to and from the mines and ranches, accounts for the presence of San Quintin, the little lost settlement by the sea.

Picture to yourself a clustered dozen of small frame houses, sheltering a population of not more than twenty-five, one hundred miles from any other civilized community; with the vast ocean before and an all but impenetrable desert-land behind—and you see San Quintin. Here we arrived after a five days' sail from Ensenada, just over the border line between Lower California and the United States.

The next day, Duarte, followed by a fat mongrel cur called Fino, appeared with the mules. He brought with him his son Marguerito and a swart Mexican from Guadalajara, called Ignatio O'Rosco whose deftness in the culinary art was demonstrated later to our entire satisfaction.

The morning passed in packing the train. There were eighteen animals in all, nine pack mules, seven saddle animals, the bell

mare, and one spare mule. Flour, rice, bacon, coffee, sugar and other provisions of all sorts, which we had brought with us, were soon stowed away. In all, nearly half a ton of supplies were distributed; an average load weighing two hundred pounds. Owing to previous experience, and with a keen, not to say pointed, recollection of sleepless nights passed on jagged rocks and amid spiny cactus beds, we came provided with two folding cots, together with four stout but light mattresses and eight heavy blankets. These awkward impedimenta tried the very soul of Duarte and tested to the utmost his skill as a packer. One mule was selected to carry these and other odds and ends which were difficult to pack, and when the bedding, kitchen utensils, etc., had been loaded upon it the beast presented an absurd appearance. The principal thing in view was a pair of wing-like ears, to which was attached a confused, misshapen mass about as wide as long, from the general appearance of which there seemed to be no particular reason why it should progress in any one direction more than another. However, a closer inspection discovered four legs and a head protruding, and a wisp of a tail, hanging from the after section of the pile like the frayed end of a rope.

And thus we set out.

The spectacle of a pack-train in action is interesting if amusing. In the lead the old bell-mare stalked along to the jangling accompaniment of a rusty cow-bell hanging

249

from her scrawny neck. Next in line came the ludicrous odds and ends mule. Other hump-backed, wing-eared animals followed in close order, and from a distance one might be pardoned for mistaking the train for a caravan of camels.

We laid a trail parallel to the coast for a couple of miles, then turned almost due east and rode for five miles over the level plain leading to the mountains. An hour before sundown we reached Santa Maria, where our first camp was made. The next day we pushed on to Cypress, twenty-four miles away. Our journey was mainly up hill now, and the country became wild and rugged, a succession of terraces or mesas leading to the higher ground like a rough, giant stairway. The table-like mesas are cut and slashed by deep cañons, radiating in every direction, some of the great gorges being over a thousand feet deep. The more shallow cañons, with rather sloping sides, are called arroyas, and at the bottom of one of these Camp Cypress was made.

While Duarte and his men unpacked the animals, we—F. L. Lowndes, R. Crewe-Reid, G. S. Hamilton and I, who constituted our party—climbed out of the arroya upon the mesa. The big tableland, eighteen hundred feet above tide-water, afforded a grand view of the massive stairway by which we had come. Step by step the uneven ridges sank lower and lower for thirty miles, until at last the final step was lost beneath the placid waters of the mighty ocean. Looking eastward we saw an apparently impenetrable barrier or rather an interminable succession of barricades and obstructions which seemed to forbid our farther progress. Huge hills rose on every hand. Here a high ridge, there a jagged peak, lapping and overlapping, banked one upon another, until mountains and clouds commingled in an indistinct, irregular outline upon the horizon, many miles away.

The third day we pushed on to El Alamo, about thirteen miles away, and camped in the bend of a cañon on a sand drift beside a stream of water. This, by the way, was the only running water we discovered during the trip. Our future water supply was wholly dependent upon pools and natural basins which collected the rain in the cañon beds. The little stream followed the course of the cañon floor until three miles below our camp, where it disappeared into the ground. After traversing a subterranean passage for twenty miles, we were told that it reappeared in the bed of the same gorge and followed it to the sea. That night we were lulled to sleep by the musical discord of a thousand frogs. Save for this choir, led by the melancholy hooting of an owl and a whippoorwill's plaintive call, there was naught to disturb the immense silence of the wilderness. At daybreak I was awakened by songs of many birds. The earliest risers seemed to be the little warblers of a rich, golden yellow hue, which flitted in and out among the foliage of the alamo trees. From my couch I could see a handsome oriole with its gorgeous arrangement of rich yellow and black, making it conspicuous whenever present. Many varieties of dainty fly-catchers darted to and fro in the thick foliage. A quail was heard whistling in the distance. Overhead a dove flew noiselessly in and alighted upon a dead limb. The bright sunshine percolated through the trees, throwing latticed shadows upon the ground and the entire scene had a charm irresistible. My reverie was ended abruptly by a call from Rosco who had prepared breakfast. After the meal we broke camp.

It was a source of never-ending interest to watch the process of getting the pack-train under way. At night in making camp the packs were removed one by one and placed in a semi-circle upon the ground. The mules were then hobbled and left to forage for themselves. In the morning, the first effort was to catch the old bell-mare, and this feat apparently required the assistance of many vivid Spanish oaths. With the bell-mare tied to a nearby tree it was no difficult task to gather in the other animals. The subsequent behavior of the mules was uncertain. Sometimes they would stand like dusty brown statues, while the packs were being securely strapped to their backs. Again, they acted like a lot of small boys afflicted with the collywobbles after a raid in an apple orchard, pacing off a few yards and deliberately lying down for a period to grunt and groan in a way that would arouse sympathy in the hearts of one unfamiliar with their tricks, but which Duarte treated with a liberal application of small stones plied vigorously against their ribs.

The train moved at a gait of perhaps three miles an hour, now laboriously climbing a steep and rugged hillside, to follow along the crest of an uneven ledge jutting out

IN LINE ON THE CREST.

from some cañon side, again plunging abruptly down a seemingly vertical wall in an altogether alarming manner. The sagacity of the bell-mare was astonishing. Often only the faintest ghost of a trail was visible, yet she picked the way with marvelous accuracy. A well-bred hound could not have followed the trail of a fox with greater certainty. Leaving the crest of a ridge we were confronted with an almost vertical descent along the wall of a deep cañon. Without a pause the train plunged downward. On the brink we hesitated. I glanced at Crewe-Reid questioningly. He nodded with an assumed lightheartedness, and shouted "Come on!"

"Mules are sure-footed. Nice, sure-footed mules. Sure-footed mules never slip;" I repeated mentally, and followed by Hamilton, went after Crewe-Reid. Lowndes,

A FAMILY CHAPEL.

who was always kind-hearted, especially to dumb beasts, slipped out of the saddle and employed his legs and arms in the descent, "to save the mule's back!" he explained when we reached the bottom. Half way down the declivity, the trail abruptly fell three feet in a sort of terrace. In a moment my mount had made the step, but with its fore legs only. The rear legs were still on the elevation and the beast was apparently going to rest standing on its head. Meanwhile I lay back, stretched along the creature's spine, parallel with its body, my feet in the stirrups sticking up besides its ears. It was a trying moment. A slip meant a fall of perhaps five hundred feet; "Sure-footed. They never slip!" I murmured prayer-like to, myself, and the next instant my faith was justified by a cautious movement beneath me, and the mule had passed the terrace and was picking its way safely along the trail.

Some ten miles had been covered when we entered a forest of cactus trees. What the conifer is to northern latitudes the cactus is to Mexico. Here we saw the biggest specimens of the one hundred varieties of the prickly vegetation. The huge pulpy trunk and limbs, covered with sharp spines, grew in many instances to the height of fifty and sixty feet. Others were round masses of prickly, pale green vegetation lying on the ground like a porcupine rolled into a ball. The spines of some were three and four inches in length and hard and sharp as needles. The fantastic appearance of a cactus forest is difficult to express. The general impression was that of a submarine scene. Many of the trees looked like huge coral growths. Others extended tentacle-like arms in all directions. The porcupine balls resembled sea urchins resting on the ocean bed, and are found in abundance throughout the mountain country. They constitute food for the sheep, that use their big horns to knock off the outer rind with its spines, thus exposing the soft, pulpy heart which is eaten with avidity.

We covered twenty miles that day, and were glad to rest when Duarte led us to a sandy bar on the floor of an arroya amid a clump of palm trees, near which a number of alamo trees growing beside a pool of water served to name the camp, Los Alamos. We were now close to the big game country and rivalry keen among us to achieve the honor of first sighting sheep.

Early one morning, we entered the Puerta Suela (single gate) cañon, which, as its name implies, is the only gap leading into the heart of the high hills. Traversing this gap, we headed toward Matami, the loftiest peak in the range, and the very center of the big game region, and camped at La Huerte in a clump of palms beside a spring of clear, cold water—a most unusual find on the peninsula.

At dawn next day Duarte and I left camp to hunt the hills and bottoms for sheep. We found it extremely rough going for the first two miles and though there were many tracks of sheep, none was fresh, so we kept on up and down and around the precipitous shelves projecting from the mountain sides. Four hours later, during which time we had traveled about ten to twelve miles without sighting game, a warning from Duarte brought me to a sudden halt.

"*Dos blancos, boregas,*" said he, looking steadily toward a shelf three quarters of a mile away.

Following the direction of his gaze, I saw

ONE OF THE GIANT CACTUS WE SAW.

two sheep feeding lazily up the steep rocky sides of a ragged hill. After picking our way cautiously through a cañon bed with much difficulty for a quarter of a mile, around a promontory we saw three of the wary animals. They were feeding gracefully and unconscious of our presence, yet while we watched, they suddenly disappeared over the crest and gained a mesa beyond. We were now obliged to make a detour of a mile and a half to the leeward side of the mesa, where, from between two big boulders, I espied three fine rams not one hundred yards away. Out of breath and still shaking from the exertion, I raised my rifle. It was too good a chance to lose. A moment I hesitated, to steady my aim.

"Quick!" urged Duarte. At the sound of his voice, the ram I had covered, turned and looked straight into my eyes. Now was the time. I fired. The report echoed and re-echoed through the surrounding valleys and among the high peaks. At the same instant the three sheep bounded swiftly away over the sloping mesa. After running a hundred yards the foremost ram stumbled to its shoulders and rolled over dead. My bullet had penetrated the heart. I hurried after the others, pausing at intervals to shoot. A final dash of two hundred yards brought me to the last margin of the mesa. A wounded ram was ascending the opposite hill. A quick shot ended its life. The last one of the trio disappeared among the hills.

One of the sheep was three and the other five years old, and they were beautiful specimens, with creamy white coats instead of the dingy gray which they carry later in the season. We covered the carcasses with large flat stones to protect them from buzzards and coyotes, and returned to camp well satisfied. In the morning Marguerito and I started on mule back to bring in my kill, and on approaching the caché we discovered several old rams on the very ground where the day before we had sighted the others. They evidently saw us and were moving about uneasily. One big fellow, the leader, faced us for a moment. Immediately dismounting and uncasing my rifle, I fired at him, and in less time than it takes to write it, the entire band was lost to view among the boulders, although they soon reappeared near the top of the hill, with the same big ram in the lead. On the summit he stood with proud dignity holding aloft the mighty horns. It was an inspiring picture and sharply outlined against the sky he made a fine target. In another moment I levelled my rifle and fired. Then followed a scene to send the warm blood to the heart of any sportsman. There, on the crest, two hundred and twenty yards above me, the old monarch faltered, swayed from side to side, limbered and fell, striking another member of the band, and the others quickly stepping aside, the dead ram rolled helplessly down among the rocks for forty yards. The other sheep were missed by a volley of shots and disappeared.

The dead ram was a king of his kind, about twelve years old. My first bullet had traversed the abdomen, without apparently inconveniencing him, the second entered the back of his neck lodging at the base of the skull, causing almost instant death. We rolled the heavy carcass to the foot of the hill and loaded it, together with two other sheep, upon the mules, which made a heavy load to carry back to camp.

Meanwhile Lowndes and Crewe-Reid had been out into the hills to the southward. Toward dark they came in with one ram and a deer, so that we now had plenty of meat in the larder. At first the flesh of the big-horns was rather tough, but after hanging a few days it became a tender morsel indeed, having a delicate flavor somewhat resembling that of young beef, and with no suggestion of domestic mutton.

We enjoyed the sport at this location for ten days, and then pushed southward to San Juan de Dios, where, at Espanosa's ranch, we left the heads and hides of our game to be picked up on our return, and then went on to an abandoned habitation known as the Stone Corral. We were now approaching the antelope country, and it was a parched and desolate region indeed. Our guides said no rain had fallen in ten years in nearby sections of the country, which we could readily believe as we had been out nearly a month and it had rained only once. Our water supply at the Corral was abominable. It was obtained from a half dried pool found in a dark cave in a cañon wall; the cave was the haunt of numerous bats, and the water in the basin was alive with myriads of insect life. But boiling made the water harmless if not palatable.

After a day of enforced inactivity, because of a strong wind which forbade venturing among the crags, I went out one morn-

OUR PACK TRAIN IN ACTION.

ing looking for antelope, and determined to bring in a pair of horns or resign all pretensions as a hunter. Following a cañon bed some three hundred yards, I ascended to a mesa five hundred feet above. From this view point the outlook was a picture of desolation. On all sides were ever-extending mesas, bare and lifeless. The horizon to the north and west was serrated by the irregular outline of the mountains in the distance. The mesas averaged about one mile in width and were of unequal height, separated by irregular, ragged,

one hundred and twenty yards in front. I halted at once, and they did likewise. One of the three stepped aside, apparently to get a better view of me, and presented a broadside target of which I took quick advantage. At the report the antelope fell in his tracks while the others bounded away, their black horns glistening in the sunshine and their manes floating lightly in the wind.

From the Corral we moved onward ten miles to La Tinaja, so-called because of the presence of a natural cistern of stagnant water, where we enjoyed the opportunity to

"THE DEAD RAM WAS A KING OF HIS KIND."

cliff-walled gorges. It was on these table-lands I hoped to find the object of my search. Toward noon I came to a small pool of water, a mere puddle standing in the bottom of a tinaja, as the water catch-basins are called by the Mexicans. Stooping over to drink I heard the thunder of galloping hoofs along the ground. Near at hand, under a dead juniper tree, with tracks leading from the pool, I found a yet warm bed. The click of my rifle butt against the rocks had evidently frightened the animal. Following the tracks, I suddenly caught sight of three buck antelope. They saw me at the same moment and were trotting away

use soap and towels. Thence we trailed due south twenty-five miles to the plains of St. Augustine within twenty miles of the coast and completed thirty-one days of travel and an estimated two hundred and eight miles since leaving San Quintin.

The return journey was begun by striking west as the crow flies to San Fernando, twenty-two miles, then northwest twenty-one miles to San Juan de Dios, thus making an irregular parallelogram. From thence, we retraced our outward bound trail, reaching San Quintin on the forty-first day of the trip, having covered two hundred and ninety-seven miles in all.

Wheeling Through
the San Joaquin
(1899)

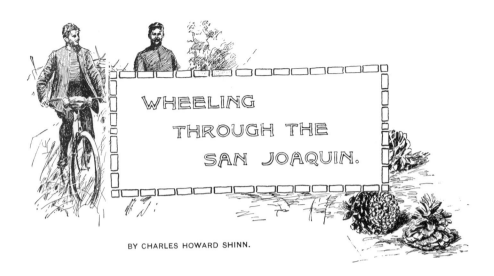

WHEELING THROUGH THE SAN JOAQUIN.

BY CHARLES HOWARD SHINN.

CALIFORNIA offers many attractions to wheelmen, and the stories of the Coast Range, the foothill valleys, the warm southlands of Los Angeles and Santa Barbara, have often been told in verse and prose. The great San Joaquin Valley, however, has received little or no attention from tourists, although at some seasons of the year its charm is unsurpassed.

Late autumn, winter and spring are the times to see the San Joaquin Valley at its best, when the air is clear and the lofty Sierras fill the whole eastern horizon. Sometimes in winter snow lies on both the Coast Range and the Sierra chains, sixty miles apart from rim to rim of the wide valley, and the wheelman, riding along avenues of golden-fruited orange trees, looks both east and west, through cloudless Italian skies, upon vast, gleaming battlements, rose-red at sunrise and sunset, pale and shining under the full moon, white and cold all day with the whiteness of Alps or Pyrenees. At such times, the broad, level expanses of orchards, vineyards, fields, farms and wild-flower-haunted wastes seem to lie in a land enchanted.

But it takes time to conquer the San Joaquin, excellent though the wheeling is, especially after the first autumnal showers. Two hundred miles from San Francisco hardly carried one to the heart of the valley ; a thousand miles of travel can easily be used in circling the round to Bakersfield and along the foothills on either side of the valley axis, visiting the most fruitful of the colonies.

Then, too, there is much to see at various places along the route, and excursions can be made into the foothills, and with few exceptions the roads are fairly good.

Many wheelmen go from San Francisco to Stockton by boat, and spend a day or two in that busy little manufacturing town. The broad sloughs or bayous of blue water, the islands and tree-shaded levees, the orchards and gardens, are all attractive to the stranger. Outside of the city one learns soon that the black, heavy adobe soils offer superb wheeling, for they are hard, free from dust and smooth. Even a cattle trail can be followed with great rapidity through a wide field in this adobe soil.

But really one finds in California that people wheel anywhere. A ditch-tender of my acquaintance in the Sierra foothills is accustomed to ride, often at full speed, along a foot-wide cattle path upon the bank of the ditch. The bank itself is narrow and overgrown with bushes. On one side it always descends five to twenty feet to the swift, deep current ; on the other side it sometimes looks down on the tops of pine forests, or on jagged rocks a hundred feet below. Down in the valley irrigation ditches overgrown with sunflowers, teazels and willows, nearly always have an excellent though narrow pathway on top of their bank, which constitutes the best short cut across lots from town to town, sometimes saving half the distance. A drove of half-wild black Berkshires may start up with sudden grunt-

259

ings from under the oaks or from the edges of the scanty rivers, and so meet the luckless wheelman full tilt on his narrow trail. Worse than this, a sharp-horned, aggressive steer may take it into his head to investigate the intruder, and if he happens to have a point of vantage where irrigation ditches divide or cross, or where the trail dives under a barbed-wire fence, the wheelman will possibly have an adventure worth the telling. Time was when the whole San Joaquin Valley was one vast range for Spanish cattle, and no man was safe unless he was on horseback.

San Joaquin, Stanislaus, Merced, Madera, Fresno, Kings, Tulare and Kern—these are the eight imperial counties that fill the great valley. Even the smallest is large, equal in size to some of the lesser States of the Union, while one or two contain upwards of five million acres. As a whole, these counties are but thinly populated, and are still in the pioneer stage, but there are centers of horticultural development so full of active life and so attractive to every visitor that they are worth as long a journey to see as are the famous fruit and vine districts of France or Spain. One of these is Fresno, where the raisin industry can best be studied.

In the town, and scattered through this portion of the valley, are immense raisin-packing, fruit-drying, canning and wine-making establishments. Eight million pounds of dried fruit, eight million more pounds of fresh fruit, eight million gallons of wine and brandy, sixty million pounds of raisins —such, in round numbers, are some of the astonishing statistics of horticultural Fresno, which, twenty-five years ago, was a sandy desert where wheat did not grow. Now the district has a thousand miles of irrigation ditches capable of irrigating half a million or more acres.

Out from this prosperous town, in the heart of the San Joaquin, one wheels towards the mountains or towards the colonies and the lowlands. Let us turn eastward to Fancher Creek, through a smiling land overflowing every autumn with such fruitage as all of Europe cannot surpass. The broad, hard road is crowded with teams hauling late fruit to the canneries, grapes to the canneries, new-made raisins to the packers. All along the roadside lie waste and unnoticed

grape clusters; the vineyards and orchards are open and unfenced. From olive avenues hang the dark, shining berries, and drop to the footpaths to be crushed by the wheel. A little farther are avenues of white Adriatic figs, for half a mile or so, and the ground is red and green with the fruit. Over and over again one passes tall palm trees, some the dates, some the beautiful desert palm, so common in Southern California. There are olive groves, too, and nurseries, where half a million or more of young olive trees stand close together. There are deciduous orchards of pear, plum, peach, prune, almond and apricot, with leafage swiftly growing golden and scarlet. There are lemon trees, and, more attractive to most persons than anything else, there are avenues and orchards of oranges, increasing in numbers as one rises to the foothills of the Sierras. Pomegranate hedges, too, illuminate the scene with their glistening globes of red and purple. Japanese persimmons, one occasionally sees, bending nearly to the ground with tomato-shaped or pointed fruits of brilliant, waxen orange.

Between these manifold orchards and home acres lie the broad vineyards, occupying the greater part of the land. By the very roadside one sees a purple-hued stream several feet wide, the waste from a huge winery, going down to the rivers and the sea. The musky breath of crushed grapes fills the air for miles, mingling with the smell of olives, of fig leaves, of orange boughs, and of avenues of slate-hued eucalypts. Among the semi-tropical growths are clumps of pines, Deodar cedars, anaucarias and sequoias, swiftly becoming splendid trees to give the valley fame centuries hence. Long, yellowing lines of great Lombardy poplars planted by the pioneers extend across the plain. Many of the farms are planned and carried on upon an exceedingly generous scale. It is a land where there is enough of everything, and something to spare besides. Tenfold its present population could live in comfort upon the products of its rich soil.

Abundant irrigation is the secret of the prosperity of this region. Hundreds of miles of ditches form a network across the country. The main canals are like rivers, and they divide and subdivide until the whole land is under their influence, either by seepage or by direct application of water to the surface. Indeed, the temptation of the horticulturist is to use too much water and so lower the quality of his products. In many cases crop after crop is taken from the soil to the extent of at least two, and with alfalfa four or five crops a year. As the story is told to strangers, a man who has a Fresno alfalfa field and tries to stack the hay in the field will need to rent an additional

to one and a half tons of raisins per acre. The profits range from $20 to $50 per acre, according to yield and prices. Raisin making on a large scale has built brick blocks and laid the foundations of fortunes, but it is most interesting on the average scale, as practiced in the colonies where only ten or twenty acres belong to each family.

One can go on and on along these pleasant roads and lanes to the Sierra foothills, and thence, ascending by sun-

SUNNING THE RAISINS.

piece of ground, for the stack will more than cover the original tract.

Raisin making has become perhaps the greatest single industry of the Fresno region. Irrigation is seldom or never needed for vines, and the grapes are better without it, often containing 25 per cent. of sugar by saccharometer test when ready for picking. The district ships about 75,000,000 pounds of raisins annually, which represents about 250,000,000 pounds of fresh grapes. It costs from $25 to $50 per acre to grow the grapes, gather them and cure them into raisins, and the yield is from one

ny, sheltered valleys, as far as the season permits. But the trip, if extended beyond an altitude of 3,000 feet, must be made in summer. The roads are no more difficult than those to the Yosemite, and carry one into the finest parts of the high Sierras, and to the sequoia groves that have no equals elsewhere. Thievish lumbermen are encroaching upon the Government forest reservations, and unless punished by the authorities are likely to destroy some of the largest trees of this rare species, Sequoia gigantea, left in the world. Sequoia lumber is being brought down

A FLOCK OF 7,000 SHEEP—" WHILE IN THE GROWING TWILIGHT."

the flume and sold in the market at Madera.

The southern sequoia groves of the Sierras can perhaps best be reached by a wheelman from Visalia or Porterville, but this, as I have said, is a summer, not a winter, journey. Every one who visits California, however, should see the Sierra forests at some point, partly because of their wonderful beauty, partly in order to better understand the need of forest reservations and of properly enforced laws to protect the forests.

But the valleys, in the time of fruitage and harvest, have their own especial charm, and every wheelman in the San Joaquin will acknowledge its witchery.

In Stanislaus, Fresno, Tulare, Kern, and Merced, one finds the large ranches on every hand. Here the industry is wheat-raising, on a scale which is not surpassed anywhere in the United States. One property of 112,000 acres is now being sold in subdivisions. In the season one can sometimes see five or six of the great harvesters, such as the one illustrated, circling slowly and cutting twenty-six feet in each swath, around a ten-thousand-acre field. Each machine cuts, threshes and sacks the golden grain, at the rate of seventy-five acres a day. It takes thirty horses to draw such a harvester. Some farmers still use header wagons and stationary

"IT TAKES THIRTY HORSES TO DRAW SUCH A HARVESTER." (*p. 593.*)

threshers—great, clumsy, powerful, out-door machines driven by steam, throb-bing with dust and heat under the sul-try summer skies of the San Joaquin.

One can wheel out into the harvest fields in the adobe soils by taking a "dead furrow," or the hard, unplowed headland next to a fence. On the sandy soils, wheeling in the fields is next to impossible. Vast stretches of the San Joaquin, however, contain alkali salts, which, though invaluable when not in excess, are sometimes so abundant as to greatly injure or prevent vege-tation. Such soils are usually of es-pecial excellence for wheeling. A path on heavy black alkali soil is smooth, solid, spongy, free from dust, and slight-ly damp, even in midsummer ; it forms a natural race-track. When there is no pathway, such areas are either barren or hard, or else covered with short, turf-like "alkali grass," over which the wheel can speed rapidly. Hummock, hog-wallow and hard-pan soils offer serious disadvantages, and the red slate soils of the foothills are extremely dusty. All the black soils, whether alkaline or not, give excellent going, not only on the roads and sidepaths, but often across lots. The heat of the semi-tropic sun bakes and hardens the whole surface, and the trade winds sweep almost free from dust, every trail, and often the highways. Sometimes the sand-stretches are made passable by a coating of straw which has been matted down by passing wagons. The sand one finds is very sel-dom loose like sea sand ; it is rather a sandy loam, with some surface crust, and if not too much cut up by teams, can be managed. Local inquiry will enable a wheelman to avoid the worst stretches of sand, and cling as closely as possible to the harder soils.

One finds in the San Joaquin types and illustrations of many sorts of out-door life. I have already spoken of the large wheat farms such as once existed in all parts of California, but which have often been divided into lesser tracts and used for orchards, vineyards, nurseries, gardens, town sites, and similar pur-poses. One also finds the pastoral age represented. Sometimes in alfalfa fields so large that the fences are merely dark lines on the horizon, are herds of fine Durhams and Herefords being fatted for market ; sometimes one sees a thou-sand head of horses and colts in a love-ly lowland region of willows and water grasses. Sometimes, too, the wheel-man, climbing late in the afternoon one of the ridges marking the division be-tween watercourses such as the Stanis-laus and the Merced, will observe, far off in the unfenced, rolling plain, bands of sheep, red-shirted shepherds and frisking collies, converging from the rim of the horizon toward a group of tents, a rude corral, a solitary white oak. Slowly they come together until in some cases four or five thousand sheep are swept into one bleating mass, white in the growing twilight. Crack goes a rifle away at the edge of the flock, where a sheep herder has tried to shoot a coyote which was lying almost concealed in a hollow beneath the dry grass, hoping to pick up a lamb. The fulvous brown fox of the West slips scatheless up the low ridge, gleams against the twilight sky, sends back a mocking cry and returns into his wilderness.

If you want an experience, wheel up to the tents, through the lines of sheep that pass into their brush-built corrals, and take pot-luck with the shepherds. They are good-natured enough, nor do they live at all badly, but there is no poetry about their business. All night long the shrill, monotonous noise of the sheep ebbs and flows, and the soft pat-ter of their moving feet keeps a stranger awake. The stolid Mexican and Portu-guese herders sleep like pebbles on a beach.

All about the plain where the sheep have been, and far beyond, are little, moving gray dots. Ride closer, and you see that each one is a huge "jack rab-bit," or California hare. The bands of sheep have disturbed them, and they are on the move, too. If one could take a census of the jack rabbits on this one sheep range, it would go far into the thousands. The farmers of a single county have killed 20,000 rabbits by "drives" in only one summer, and have poisoned and shot as many more.

It is a land of wild fowl and small game, so wide and uncultivated are the river bottoms, so extensive the marshes and lowlands, and so vast the great pastoral districts. From November to March the plains often seem white with wild geese. The watercourses and swamps swarm with teal, spoonbill, widgeon and mallard, not to mention the long-billed gentry so dear to the heart of a sportsman. The wheelman, to whom the roads of the upper San Joaquin prove easy all winter (since there is no snow and a very slight rainfall), is able to reach many villages distant from the railroads, where unspoiled hunting remains—such hunting as the men of a generation ago were permitted to enjoy. The jack rabbits cannot be called game, according to the Californian view, but they afford excellent practice. As for quail, the round-tufted quail of the valley, they abound in the river-edges and foothills of the whole San Joaquin country.

Visalia, the present east-side terminus of the new Valley Railroad, is an oasis of wonderful beauty. Imagine an oak forest islanded in gray plains, near the mountains, under deep blue skies. This forest, in pioneer days, must have been nearly fifteen miles square, watered by many beautiful streams, glowing with wild flowers, green with perpetual grass, the chosen home of deer, elk and bear. Some of the oaks remain, in groves of from fifty to two hundred and fifty acres, pastured down to turf and full of cattle, horses, sheep and hogs. The old oak-openings and many more recent clearings are occupied with famous orchards,

fields and gardens. As one wheels along the well-kept roads of this part of Tulare, the whole land is glowing with color, scarcely less in winter than in midsummer. White asclepias, golden sunflowers and other compositæ, purple-bordered daturas, willows, poplars, bamboos, palms, cedars of Lebanon—native plants and exotics mingle without law or license ; and some of the finest oaks in America, trees a hundred feet high with trunks that girth twenty and even twenty-five feet, give their own strength and predominance to the landscape.

In these rich lands of the San Joaquin one sometimes finds deserted orchards or vineyards run wild, open to animals, wild or domestic, and to every passerby. Sad places these, for they tell of loss and failure. There the weeds grow as high as a man's head ; the soil has long lain unplowed, yet the grapes are as sweet and as beautiful as in the carefully tended vineyards, though smaller and less abundant. The tramps camping in the cottonwoods carry off a few ; emigrants with white-canvased wagons slowly moving northward to Oregon, or southward to Arizona, pause, and, gathering basketfuls, spread them in the sun to dry, and camp to wait till their wild

"ABUNDANT IRRIGATION IS THE SECRET."

raisins are ready to pack away. Seldom indeed does any one raise an objection, for this is still a land of much freedom and generous impulses.

South of the town of Tulare lies one of the experiment stations, established in California under the Hatch Law by the University of California. It has collections of hundreds of varieties of grapes and fruits, it has introduced many useful cultures to the valley, and its chief problem is the reclamation of strong alkali soils. Visitors from all parts of the world, and experts from the agricultural bureaus of Austria, Italy, Russia and other countries deeply interested in the alkali question, have been here on many occasions. Every wheelman who passes through Tulare should visit this experiment station.

The heart of Kern, in the rich Bakersfield district, is such another vast expanse of well-watered lands as the Fresno region, but its development has been later. In time, no part of the valley will present more charming rural pictures of peace and prosperity, or more highly cultivated colonies. There, as elsewhere in the San Joaquin, the pastoral and the agricultural exist side by side with modern intensive horticulture. The land is too vast to be conquered except by degrees. It is an inland empire into which a few thousand men have gone to break the way for millions.

Such, indeed, is the valley as a whole. Man has taken possession; and in a few places a fresh, bold, young civilization is established. For the most part, however, the valley is like the valley of the Euphrates when the Accadian tribes, descending into its fertile expanses, began to make cities there. Years of toil must be spent here, and at last the fame of the gardens and cities of the well-watered San Joaquin will go to the ends of the earth. Now, in the days of its beginnings, when even orchard-hidden Fresno is less than a quarter of a century old, the observant tourist wheeling through its roads and villages sees in its wastes and crudenesses the hidden promise of imperial futures. More than the valley of the Rio Grande, or the Arizonian Colorado, this land of the San Joaquin is like another Assyria.

An Old Village
on the Pacific Coast
(1909)

AN OLD VILLAGE ON THE PACIFIC COAST

BY CLIFTON JOHNSON

ILLUSTRATIONS BY THE AUTHOR

OT for a long time had I been in a place that so filled me with delight as did Capistrano in southern California. Such a dreamy, easy-going community — no hurry, no worry—such a luxuriant valley, such lofty environing hills with the turf clothing every rounded outline! The village itself was a queer huddle of primitive homes, some no more than board shanties, and none of them large or in the least pretentious. However, the feature that gave especial distinction to the hamlet was the ruin of an old Mission, still impressive, calm and beautiful, and appealing powerfully to the imagination. One apartment is even yet used as a church, the chime of four bells performs its accustomed service, and there is a fine corridor in an excellent state of preservation.

The village was charmingly pastoral. The insects thrummed, the children laughed and called at their play, the roosters crowed in endless succession, the dogs barked, and the cattle lowed from the luscious hill-slopes. And what throngs of birds there were! I saw them flitting everywhere, and the air was athrill with their songs.

On the noon when I reached Capistrano the main street was full of teams tied to the wayside hitching rails, and yet the place seemed mysteriously devoid of human beings. At last I discovered the male inhabitants of the region gathered at the far end of the street in and about an adobe justice court. The wide doorway was jammed full of men peering over each other's shoulders, and the case was evidently of the most absorbing and vital interest. At length, however, the gathering broke up, the village became populous, and one after another the teams were unhitched and driven away. The excitement, it seemed, concerned two individuals, one of whom had said the other was a "liar," and the latter had responded that the former was a "son of a gun" and likened him to a variety of similar obnoxious things. But the court failed to get together a jury, and the judge had dismissed the case. As a clerk in a local store explained it, "The two fellers remind me of my school days

269

An Indian family at home.

In the old Mission.

when one of us kids 'd sometimes go an complain to the teacher saying, 'Jimmy's been a-callin' me names.'

"'What's he been callin' you'? she asked him.

"'I don't like to tell you,' the boy says. 'It's awful bad things.'"

While I was in the store a fat old Indian entered. He had short hair, wore overalls, and except for his color was not much different in dress and appearance from a white workingman. The clerk introduced him as the best sheep-shearer in the country. He shook hands and said, "Me good man! You good man?"

In the season he had about fifty other Indians working under him, got five dollars a day himself and two dollars for his wife, who did the cooking for the gang. The wealth he acquired did not stick to him. He gambled it away. Gambling was a common recreation among the villagers, and the place supported four "blind pigs," or unlicensed saloons. There were always loafers hanging about their porches and a noisy crowd inside playing pool. One of the Capistrano experts at poker was a Chinaman who had a ranch just outside the village. He lived in a dirty little hut there and kept his horse under a pepper tree with only the shelter afforded by the leafage. For ten miles around the people depended on him for vegetables. Some of the poorest families in the village bought of him, rather than take the trouble to raise their own vegetables, though they had the finest kind of land right at their doors.

"He can't speak hardly three words of English," I was told, "but he'll sit down and play poker all right with any of us. Perhaps he'll lose fifty dollars or more at a single sitting and not go home till the small hours of the morning; and yet he'll be at his work that day as usual without batting an eye.

"This was a much bigger place years ago," my informant continued. "In 1870 there were nearly two thousand inhabitants. Now there are less than four hundred. But in those days they were practically all Mexicans and Indians, and they didn't work any more than was necessary to exist. A few watermelons and a sack or two of beans will suffice a Mexican family for a year. They take no thought for the morrow and are content to half-starve rather than exert themselves. Why, an energetic American will raise a crop of walnuts and clear in a single season four or five thousand dollars, which is more than a Mexican would clear in four or five thousand years.

"Most of the Indians have drifted off to the reservations to get the benefit of Uncle Sam's coddling. We've managed to pauperize nearly the whole race. If some one else will support them they quit doing anything for themselves and are just loafers. Work is plenty, but most of our poorer class, if they take a job, are soon tired, or get too much money and lay off. A Mexican with five dollars will spend it like a lord. He is very apt to get drunk on Saturday night, and you never know whether he will be back to his work Monday morning or not. Some families are so shiftless we are obliged to support 'em. The county allows such from five to ten dollars a month. But they don't consider themselves indigents. They are, rather, indignants. We have no paupers. They call themselves 'pensioners,' and think it an honor to get public aid."

English walnut growing had chief place among the local industries, and there were a number of extensive groves. The trees spread out like apple trees, but have a smooth, light-gray bark. In the walnut harvest time the school closes for six weeks to give the children a chance to help gather the crop. Some of the nuts fall of themselves, but a large proportion is thrashed off with poles. A sack is the usual receptacle carried by the gatherers, but the women use their aprons. Back of my hotel were a number of the great slatted racks on which the nuts were dried. A few nuts were still left on the frames and I often loitered there and feasted. If I chose I could supplement this repast with oranges picked from trees in the garden.

The hotel was an old-time stage-route tavern—a big, long two-story building with a piazza and balcony on both front and rear. It had been built about three decades ago. There was then no railroad, and, as the landlord said, "In those times, by golly, the hotel was jammed all the time. The daily stages, one going south one going north, met here at midnight, and we always had hot coffee ready for persons

The local court is a center of interest.

that wanted it. You've noticed how the village people go and hang around the depot to see the trains come in. Well, they used to gather at our hotel just as thick to see those midnight stages arrive.

"You ought to be here the last day of Lent—Judas Day, we call it. The night before, it is customary for the Mexicans to ransack the village and steal buggies and tools and anything they can carry off, and they make a big pile of all this plunder just outside the fence in front of the old Mission. Then they take a worn-out suit of clothes and stuff it full of weeds, and stick it up on top of the pile, and that is Judas. Next thing they get an old dress and stuff that full of weeds and set it up side of Judas to represent his wife. In the morning when we wake up we find all the vehicles and loose things that were around our yards stacked up over by the Mission, with those two scarecrow figures on top. But the best of the performance comes in the afternoon when the Mexicans bring to the village two half-wild bulls from the hills. They tie Judas to one, and Judas's wife to the other and chase the creatures up and down the street till the two figures are torn to tatters."

The landlord paused in his remarks and one of his listeners asked, "Who was the man that was here to dinner and went away just afterward on the train?"

"It was a doctor," the landlord replied. "He had some thought of settling here; but I told him he'd starve to death. You see the people avoid callin' a doctor till the sick person has one foot in the grave and the other following after. The old women think they can cure most any one with herbs and weeds, and they keep dosing the sick person till he's nearly dead. Then, if the doctor can pull him through things are all right; but if the doctor has his patient die on him, they'll never pay for his services.

"One of the most interesting institutions of the village is its school. The seventy-five pupils are an odd mixture of whites and Mexicans and Indians and various combinations of the races. A generation ago the place had no school and its establishment was due to the energy of Judge Bacon, the local justice of the peace. He was one of the Argonauts of '49, and the ability to read and write was about the extent of his book-learning. His home was an old adobe without a floor, and yet," said my informant, "he was rich—oh, heavens! he had money galore. The school was Bacon's hobby, and he got a building put up and painted it himself—spent three weeks at it. He laid out the grounds around with the notion of having a sort of park, and he urged that there should be put on the post at each corner of the fence a big globe having the entire world mapped on it. Then, inside, on an arch over the teacher's alcove he wanted a motto painted—'The poorest child may tread the classic halls of yore.'

"But there were two other trustees, and they wouldn't agree to these things. They didn't see much sense to 'the classic halls of yore,' and were afraid it would only get them laughed at. So, instead, they finally had an eagle and some stars painted on the arch. As soon as he got the school building done he put in a seventy-five dollar chandelier to light up so they could have dances. He paid for it—plumked up every nickel himself, and he furnished the oil, and he hired a dancing master to come from Los Angeles, and they had a dance every Wednesday night.

"One day he happened to ask a woman why her daughter hadn't been to the last dance, and she said the girl couldn't go no more because she was wearin' out her Sunday gaiters with the dancing.

"'Buy her a pair of gaiters, and I'll pay for 'em,' says he; and after that he had to buy gaiters for every girl in town, you bet-cher!'

Then they got to asking for other things until the Judge got tired of the experiment and the weekly dances came to an end. Many other quaint incidents came to my knowledge, but I have repeated enough to indicate the picturesque charm of life in this old village both of the past and of the present.

In a Redwood Logging Camp (1882)

NOONDAY AT THE LOGGING CAMP.

IN A REDWOOD LOGGING CAMP.

ALL forest trees show a tendency to dispose themselves in groups or in strata. The usual cause, or at any rate a coincident of this, is the lithological character of the region where they grow, or else it is a matter of altitude. Thus in mountains you may see a regular stratification of trees from the base to timber-line. The case of the Californian redwoods of both species is a very marked one in respect to this characteristic. The "big trees" proper (*Sequoia gigantea*) are confined to certain groves on the western flank of the Sierra Nevada, whose boundaries are well known, and where even the individual trees have been counted in some cases. The other species, distinguished by the name "redwood" (*S. sempervirens*), is confined to that portion of the Coast Range between Santa Cruz and the northern line of California—a narrow belt about three hundred miles in length, which is said to be defined strictly by the outcropping of the metamorphic limestones left more or less uncovered by the lava currents from the coast volcanoes of former days.

The general history of the sequoias (the name is a compliment to that enlightened chief who first reduced the Cherokee language to writing) need not be retold here with much detail. The genus is coniferous, and is more nearly related to the cypresses than anything else, but its allies are scattered—one in Japan, one in the Himalayas, and another in the Gulf States of America, all reaching unusual stature. It is a group remarkable for its antiquity, too, remaining as the representative of almost the earliest period when trees grew upon the earth.

The redwoods in this coast belt stand in an unbroken forest along the base of the range—a forest whose height you appreciate only when you note how low a cleared hill seems beside its wooded fellows. It is difficult when in the forest to understand how tall the trees really are, since the spruces, etc., with which they are associated are far beyond the ordinary, and there is nothing to guide the eye. Where the redwoods grow, heavy fogs roll in from the Pacific during all the rainless

OLD CHAPEL AT FORT ROSS.

months. Entangled in the dense and clustering foliage of the tall and crowded trees, they are condensed by the cool air which is held in the pockets of shade under the matted twigs and needles, and fall in misty showers, constantly refreshing the soil. Thus it happens that the redwood forests are particularly rich in a great variety of other trees and bushes; and a perfect jungle of undergrowth, shrub-like and herbaceous, flourishes there, among the rest vast quantities of poisonous plants (especially rhus), so that it is the worst of places for any person to go a-rambling who is susceptible to harm from that source.

The trunks of all the coniferous trees, and especially of the sequoias, stand as straight as though turned in a lathe and set by a plummet, rising usually a great distance without large limbs, but sometimes hirsute with stubby boughs spirally attached all the way down. In specimens of healthy growth and sound heart the stem tapers gently to a stiff though slender top spray; but in the majority of trees you will see no tapering top, but a sudden squaring off, which looks like a deformity, and which the chopper will tell you betokens an unsound trunk.

Again they will bend off at right angles into a plume-like branch, which *is* a deformity. In windy places, like the exposed sea-front, all the boughs are twisted into a single plane landward, and great picturesqueness results; but it is always a stiff, motionless, statuesque picture, in the darkest tone foliage can assume, for there is nothing wavy or pliant anywhere from root to topmost leaf.

Such were the stern autochthonous trees whose downfall, at the hands of the lumbermen, we went up from San Francisco to witness.

Fully a century ago the pleasant vales leading up into the Coast mountains had been penetrated by the frontiersmen of Mexico, of which country this whole great region was an ill-defined province under the name of Alta California. These men were herdsmen or farmers. Early in the present century a colony of Russians and

Indians from Alaska, under the leadership of Alexander Koskoff, landed at Bodega Bay, and began farming where now is the village of Bodega. Not satisfied with this place alone, however, they travelled northward some forty miles, and established a permanent trading post and agricultural station near Salt Point, the site and many of the buildings of which are now occupied as the village of Fort Ross—an anglicized abbreviation of *Fuerte de los Rusos*, as the post was called by the Spaniards.

The occupancy of this strip of coast—for their hold extended all the way between Point Arenas on the north and Point Ruges on the south—by the Muscovites from 1811 until 1840, when they abandoned their station, left its impress upon the names of the region, and especially clings to the principal stream watering this portion of the redwood belt—the Russian River.

This river, which flows southward from sources close to the foot of Mount Shasta, turns suddenly to the west, forces its way through the Coast Range, and pours a swift flood into the Pacific—a matter of ambition to the stream, perhaps, but of not the slightest moment to the ocean, which does its best, in fact, to prevent the sacrifice. Seven miles above the mouth of the river, just where it escapes from the clutch of the hills and the forest, stands the two small settlements of Moscow and Duncan's. Both owe their existence to the presence of mills, and from each small branch railways run back into the forest

OLD BLOCK-HOUSE, FORT ROSS.

for the purpose of bringing out the logs. Duncan's, on the northern bank of the river, is the terminus of the North Pacific Coast Railway, and there we took up our quarters, a very comfortable hotel furnishing us bed and board.

Before we went back into the woods, however, circumstances and the tender of good horses led us to some excursions which taught us "the lay of the land," and enriched our sketch-books with some notes worth telling.

FORT ROSS—VIEW FROM THE LANDING.

A BIT OF DRIFT-WOOD.

Upon the high hill west of Duncan's stand splendid groves of varied trees, accented by thickets of the red-limbed madroña. Between lie open spaces of lush pasture, where cattle and horses loiter with contented eyes and rounded bellies.

"The men who own these uplands," said our neighbor, "live like lords—at least in respect to their lack of care. They buy calves when a few weeks old, adding to the produce of their own herds, turn them out, and never see them again till the butcher calls to buy beef. Right here," he added—with an appropriateness to place rather than talk—"three of us last spring tried to head off a single man who had just robbed the stage at the foot of the hill; but as he was coming up the gully there," pointing to a densely thicketed ravine, "something told him he ought to run. He crossed this open space, and was just in the edge of those woods when we came up. He got away that time, but a few months after he was caught on another charge, and proved to be notorious as a road agent."

A sudden escape from curtaining oak branches brought us full upon the summit, where the other side fell away precipice-like, but unbrokenly turfed, and there before us was all the grand expanse of the Pacific, the fretting of its surf coming as a continuous, far-away deep music,

"Like the great chords of a harp in loud and solemn vibrations."

But the shore was miles away, and its high horizon, rising to meet our point of view, made the interspace seem the deeper.

Through this interspace, avoiding skillfully the protruding headlands pushed out by the opposite hills to try what dovetailing would do toward stopping its course, wound the double S of the river.

Hurling its current against the rock-faced piers of the hills on this side and then on that, one bank always rising sheer from the water, leaving the other low and flat, the elbows of its sinuous course inclosed stretches of sand with coarse grass and willows, marshy islands and shallows where herons fed, and wandering cormorants alighted to rest their paddles, half-submerged ledges of rocks, and fertile areas of alluvial soil just above the reach of the freshets. Never was seen such a collection of drift-wood as the huge forest relics cast up here! I rode my horse up beside one short hollow log, high and dry on the beach, and could not look over its top as I stood in my stirrups. Its interior would have sheltered a picnic party.

All the hills were free from woodland near the river, save where occasional gullies sheltered thickets of small stuff, but through the turf here and there protruded the rocky frame-work, gray, splintered, and lichen-painted under the weather's hand. It was all green then that lay before us, save the sinuous band of blue river and its fringe of yellow sand-flats, but a green mottled and blending with yellow and orange, red, purple, and brown; a verdancy universal, yet nowhere uniform, broken, as a whole, only by the blues of the sky and the changing sea and the flashing stream, yet having as many expressions and touched with hues as various as the different points upon which your eye might rest. It was a landscape of the simplest elements—rounded hills, a water-course, the sea, a cloudless arch,

"High over all the azure-circled earth"—

yet its quiet beauty was satisfying, with a charm far beyond the reach of words to interpret.

Chiselled out of the steep hill-side, near the river-level, the stage-road ran upon a sort of shelf, giving it lodgment where otherwise not even a goat could have kept its foot-hold. Leading our horses down to this road by a series of zigzags, crushing sweet-fern and brilliant flowers under our feet at every step, we followed it along the river toward the shore. Here and there farm-houses and ploughed land were to be seen, but nearly all the wide expanse of open uplands was devoted to pasturage, hundreds of cattle being constantly in sight, gazing at us with frightened eyes from the road-side, or crawling about like ants on the lofty ridges. In several little nooks on the southern bank stood small shanties, which were the homes of Indians and half-breeds—mongrels left between the Diggers, who were natives of this region before the whites came, and the Kodiaks or Russians. They cultivate small tracts, and otherwise eke out a contented existence by fishing and working upon the ranches, chiefly as herders.

The cow, indeed, is the strong point of ranch industry here, and the only stables we saw were intended for her. Turning in through a high swinging gate, past a barn where the two species of resident swallows were quarrelling loudly over rights of possession, we entered one of the dairy-houses. There are a dozen or so of dairies about here, almost wholly in the hands of Swiss people, and the butter they make is of the most excellent kind, fragrant and yellow with the rich herbage of the hills. The cows, nevertheless, are of ordinary stock, and their owners profess contempt for the "fancy" breeds as something very pretty to play with, but of no real value to the farmer. Certain it is that these Swiss can get more milk out of a scrub cow than any of their neighbors are able to.

This dairy was a small frame building of three rooms. In the largest the pans were set upon racks against the wall, and kept at the proper temperature. In a second room were water-heaters and arrangements for washing pans, etc. The third room was a sort of shed where the butter was made. Here, between two upright posts, was hung upon trunnions a square pine box, like a Saratoga trunk, so as to revolve with a rapidity depending upon the speed with which a blindfolded pony in the neighboring yard walked around the set of cogs that kept the gearing in motion. This box was the churn, and we were just in time to get a dipperful of the

THE LUMBER MILLS AT DUNCAN'S.

buttermilk, which was drawn off by pulling a plug in the bottom when the butter had "come." We looked into the churn, and saw it partly filled with a foamy mass of yellow granules as rich as gold and fragrant as flowers. After this had been repeatedly washed with spring water, the dairyman drew near to the churn a heavy fan-shaped table, glistening with its cold bath. Here was heaped the sixty or seventy pounds of sticky pellets, to be "worked" under a stout roller-mallet until suitable for market. This done to his satisfaction, the man took up a pair of heavy brass calipers in whose jaws were fixed the two halves of a cylindrical wooden mould, the length and calibre of which shaped the size of the standard two-pound roll customary in this market. One powerful grasp compressed into this mould all it would hold; the surplus was cut off, the roll released and folded in its cool linen wrapping, and it only remained to stand it on end with the similar cylinders filling the shallow shipping case, and to cart it away to the train. The whole operation was deft and neat and genuine; and the heated gold broker at the Bohemian Club tasted in his crisp mouthful next day all the subtle juices of the herbs upon Sonoma hills.

The mouth of the river, when we had gone near enough to have a good view of it from a headland, made a very noble picture. The green hills on the south slope gradually to a well-turfed base, hiding the beach, but showing a long sand-spit running out almost across the very entrance of the little bay, behind which are calm shallows. The northern headland, on the other hand, stands in bold outline—a point of sheer cliff jutting between the ocean and the river. Yet the charge of those waves rolling from the spicy archipelagoes of the great South Sea, or from the bleak coasts of Tartary, is met, not by this mole, but by an outer row of gigantic isolated rocks, overtopping the tide as the stones of Carnac rear their heads above the level plain, and the imagination can easily believe some giant of old, more powerful than the Druids, to have planted them there as a breakwater guarding the harbor. Around their base curls the angry foam of swift-charging, impotent breakers, and they glory in the snowy clouds of spray that envelop their flanks, for thus the rage of the mightiest of oceans is proved ineffectual, and the tamed waves sink behind them into sullen peace upon the weedy shore.

Such was the broad landscape of the region where we cast our lot these pleasant June days, and watched the cutting of the big trees.

Tradition says that credit for the very first attempt to make lumber with a saw in this region (for the Russians hewed all their beams and planks) belongs to John Dawson, of Bodega. Dawson was one of three sailors who abandoned their ship at San Francisco as early as 1830, preferring the free and easy life of the Californians. In two or three years they became citizens under the Mexican government, and took up granted ranches hereaway, Dawson marrying the daughter of a Spanish dragoon officer. She was only fourteen when she went to live as mistress of the Cañada de Pogolome, and only seventeen when she found herself the richest widow in Northern California. Dawson's lumber was cut over pits by means of a rip-saw, which he handled without help. Not half a century later steam mills in this district are turning out two hundred thousand feet of lumber daily.

The centre, or at least one centre, of this lumbering is here at Duncan's, where the Russian River receives a tributary named Austin's Creek. A wonderful railway follows its banks half a dozen miles back into the hills to supply the mill with logs.

Never was seen so unshipshape and disreputable a locomotive as that on duty here. A stubby black boiler, with a trifling amount of upper gear, makes steam, turning four small wheels by means of a cog underneath. There is no cab, or place to put one, no pilot, head-light, or any other appurtenances of an ordinary locomotive, and the wire bonnet of the smoke-stack is worn on one side with such a "What-d'ye-soye?" air that the smutty little machine declares itself a very hoodlum among locomotives. Nevertheless, it accomplishes wonderful feats of pulling.

Free of the load of logs brought down, it is going back in the coolness of the early morning, and we go with it. The track is of the usual gauge, but the cars are platforms of only half the ordinary length, and are fastened together by ropes, shortened up when the train is empty, but lengthened so as to separate loaded cars by six or eight feet, in order that the protruding ends of the logs shall not interfere.

The track is rudely built and rickety, the rails being heavy strap-iron bolted upon string-pieces. It runs shakily through tunnels of infinitely varied verdure, curves along ledges blasted out of the brown and fern-hung rocks of the creek shore, traverses low ground upon causeways of ties and stringers, each as big as a hogshead, ventures out upon some precarious bracket-trestle whence it might plunge directly into the stream. Almost from the first we have entered the old forest, where (now that the choppers have passed on) we revel in the beauty of unhindered plant luxuriance: in the lofty spires of kingly redwoods, and of pines and spruces ambitious to equal them; in the glossy masses of erect pepper-woods, whose leaves look like oleander, smell of bay-rum, and tingle upon the tongue like curry; in the awkward form of the half-flayed madroña; and in the grace of the light-toned masses of maple, alder, and small shrubbery along the water-side. Enjoying this green wilderness, and with interest freshened by the sight of huge pedestals that once bore trees, and by increasing signs of the choppers, we reach the logging camp.

Here, however, no cutting is being done to-day, so we walk across the ridge to the next gulch, up which a branch of the railway diverges, and whence came at intervals the dull explosions knelling the downfall of some forest patriarch—

"A murmuring, fateful, giant voice, out of the earth and air—
Voice of a mighty dying tree in the redwood forest dense."

Thoreau once speaks of hearing "the rare, domestic sound" of the wood-chopper's axe. Echoing across

LOGGING CAMP ON AUSTIN'S CREEK.

A LOGGER.

the frozen rim of Walden Pond, it perhaps bore well these adjectives; but here no such impression is conveyed, and the thought suggested is a sad rather than a pleasing one, as the sharp strokes come to our ears with quick repetition. Shaping our course by such signals—

"A measured beat, a ringing sound,
A hardened resonance of sound"—

we presently learn our proximity to the scene of the chopping by the roaring profanity coming up from sources invisible as yet.

This gulch, like the other, proved a narrow ravine, down which dashed a trout brook, where once had grown two or three ranks of gigantic trees, the stumps remaining, like small Martello towers, to attest their greatness of girth and proud height. Yet these were by no means large examples, for whereas none of the stumps here measured more than a dozen feet across the top, specimens twice that diameter have been cut. Nor would the latter giants be unexampled among trees. Several of the members of the "big-tree" groves of the Sierra Nevada surpass any example of the *sempervirens* ever seen; the Douglas spruce of the mountain for-

ests often exceeds three hundred feet in length, and eleven hundred layers have been counted in a Lambert pine. Such a growth of vegetable fibre, toughening through many centuries, and rearing hundreds of cubic feet of solid substance, excites our astonishment, and has been well defined in the phrase, "A monument of accumulated and concentrated force."

To see the prostration of a column like that would be something to remember; and following two men who, axe in hand, were making their way up toward one of the larger-sized redwoods upon the steep hill-side, we watched their attack.

"The first question, sir," said the leading axe-man, politely, "when we are going to fall a big tree, is where she'll lay; because unless a man cares [*i. e.*, is careful] to fall her right, she'll break all up, and the bigger the trunk the more liable she is to break. You can see down across the creek there how that one snapped."

We looked where he pointed, and saw that a bole fully six feet in diameter had broken squarely across; the brittleness of this timber, nevertheless, is not excessive, compared with other soft woods. Meanwhile the chopper was holding his axe in front of his upturned face, letting it hang, head down, between his thumb and finger, like a plummet, while he squinted past it at the top of the tree, upon whose perfect shaft no branches grew below the upper quarter.

"I can tell by this whether she leans out of the perpendic'lar. If she does, you've got to allow for it; but this one don't, and I guess, Joe, we'll drop her right along that knoll just to the east'ard o' that oak stump—see it? But we'll have to roll that there log out of the way a little, or she'll break her back acrost it, sure."

Having made this simple preparation (sometimes hours are spent in dragging logs to fill gullies, or in levelling knolls and getting stumps out of the way), the men returned and began chopping out some mortise-holes in the trunk about four feet above the ground. These were intended for the insertion of their iron-shod "spring-boards"—pieces of flexible planking about four feet long and six inches wide, upon which they were to stand while chopping at a height too great to reach from the ground.

The undercut was made first, and it was a fine sight to watch these stalwart men perched upon their strips of springy board, hurling their axe-heads deep into the gaping wound, and never missing the precise poiht at which they aimed. I do not know any attitudes more manly or motions more muscularly graceful than those of the chopper; but perhaps the noble surroundings may count more largely than we think in this estimate.

In about an hour the undercut had approached the heart of the tree, and the men desisted from their work, which must now proceed on a scientific basis.

"As I said afore," the chopper explained, "we must fall a tree straight and true where we've fixed for it, or else she'll go to pieces. In order to do this we've got to measure it this way."

As he speaks he picks up from near where his coat and saw and water caddy are lying, two sticks about four feet in length—one a square stiff lath, the other switch-like. Going to the tree he lays one end of the lath upon the partially exposed stump in the undercut, its extremity resting against the heart of the wood at the exact centre of the bole. Then stooping and sighting along it, he moves the outer end of the lath until it points exactly along the line where the trunk is intended to be thrown.

"Joe, go out there about a hundred feet or so and set a stake; I want to show these gentlemen how nicely we can drive it in with this big sledge we're goin' to let loose directly."

"Do you mean to say you will drop your tree as accurately as that?"

"You bet—hit that stake plumb; 'n' it 'll take more mumble-te-peg 'n you're worth, I reckon, to pull it out afterward!"

Meanwhile he went on with his mathematics. Having aimed the lath, he measured with his switch from its outer end to the "corner" at each side of the undercut, and finding one side a little shorter than the other, chopped in until he had equalized the hypotenuses of the two right-angled triangles whose straight sides were back to back in the line of the lath. The object and importance of this was to make sure that the limit of the undercut, where the strain and breakage controlling the fall of the tree (and marked by the line of upright slivers in a stump) would finally come, should be at right angles to the intended direction of that fall.

"How tall do you think this tree is?" I ask.

"Well, I should say pretty nigh on two hundred feet; but it is easy enough to find out exactly."

Taking his axe the chopper cut a straight stake, sharpened its end, and placed it before him while he stood very erect. Then with his knife he cut a notch just four inches above the point on the stake which came squarely opposite his eyes—this extra four inches being an allowance for planting the stake in the ground. Walking away to a point on the hill-side level with the base of the tree, and about the right distance, as he guessed at it, he planted the stake and lay down on his back behind it, with his heels against its foot, and his eye trying to bring the notch on the stake in range with the topmost plumelet of the redwood. One or two slight shiftings of position enabled him to get this

A SAWYER.

range, and thereby to construct an equal-sided triangle. It only remained to measure with his five-foot rule the distance from his eyes to the base of the tree to learn the height of the tree, representing the other side of the triangle. The fact in this case was 180 feet.

This practical triangulation finished, the

THE BLACKSMITH.

Out of its stalwart trunk and limbs, out of its
foot-thick bark,
That chant of the seasons and time—chant not
of the past only, but the future."

So Walt Whitman—himself a sequoia
in the forest of poets—sets to fitting music in my grateful memory the ominous
crackings of tense fibre I think I hear, the
partings of well-knit rind, and the hushed commotion of shocked branches and
crowded leafage overhead. Then comes
the final stroke of the axe, severing the
last slender stay, and, with a mingled roar
and scream of frightened despair, the huge
mast, carrying all its lofty spars and well-set rigging, slowly leans to its fate, gathers
headway, spurns with giant heel the faithless stump which hitherto has borne it
proudly against every gale and torrent,
and so, stately to the last, "rustling,
crackling, crashing, thunders down."

Picking our way through the settling
dust and débris of crushed branches which
lie in a thousand splinters of red and green
around the head of the prostrate chief, we
look for the stake with which Joe challenged our credulity, but fail to find it, for
it has been driven "plumb through to
China," as Joe avers.

"Accidents must happen pretty often
in this business," we remark.

"Yes, right often, both to men and animals. Sometimes a tree is weak, and
topples over before you're ready for it ;
or, instead of lying still when it strikes,
it sort o' picks itself up and takes a long
jump forward, which is unexpected, and
liable to hurt somebody. Then the worst
of all is where the butt breaks off and
shoots back behind the stump like one o'
them darned big battering-rams you read
about, and worked by sheet-lightnin' at
that. Yes, a heap of men gets killed in
the woods every year. We never had
none killed dead right here, but a mighty
curious thing happened last September
was a year. One of the men went to
work in the mornin' 'long with the rest
—good, solid man he was, too, with heaps
of sand in him. He didn't come in to dinner, nor when night come. Then we begun to question round, and found none of
the boys had saw him since mornin'. We
found his coat and tools, but nary hide nor
hair of him then nor no time afterward.
We rather looked for a sheriff to be comin'
round the next day or two, thinkin' the
fellow might have got wind he was onto
his trail (though we knew nothin' agin

axes were laid aside, and the spring-boards
inserted in new mortises behind the tree,
and a big two-handed saw set at work to
make the overcut. Soon the crevice begins to open a little, and then a little more,
until the cautious woodmen begin to cast
their eyes aloft, watching carefully the
signal that the next stroke would be the
last, cutting the one remaining tendon
that holds the mighty column up, for already there are sudden strange shivering
motions in the densely bushy thickets of
foliage that adorn its lofty crown, and
dead twigs rattle down, snapped off by
thrills of approaching destruction.

"Riven deep by the sharp tongues of the axes,
there in the redwood forest dense,
I heard the mighty tree its death-chant chanting.

"The choppers heard not, the camp shanties echoed
not,
The quick-eared teamsters, and chain and jack-screw men, heard not,
As the wood-spirits came from their haunts of a
thousand years to join the refrain ;
But in my soul I plainly heard,

"Murmuring out of its myriad leaves,
Down from its lofty top, rising over a hundred
feet high,

him—but you can't 'most always tell, you know), but none came."

"What was your conclusion as to this strange disappearance?"

"Well, we just allowed that one of these big trees had got the drop on that fellow, as it were, and druv him clean into the ground. Cigar? No, thank ye; I'll stick to my pipe."

The wastefulness of this lumbering is one of the striking features of the scene. Only the largest trees are cut, those measuring less than two feet in diameter rarely being touched, and the axe is laid, not to the roots (though they are not thick and widely divergent, considering the height and weight they support), but some distance above, so that in very large specimens the massive stump, upon whose flat top you might build a comfortable house, stands ten or twelve feet above the ground, and contains hundreds of feet of sound lumber, which must be left to rot or burn. Then many trees are broken by their fall, so that large parts of them are useless; other parts may be knotty, or crooked, or inconvenient to drag out, and so only half of a great trunk will be utilized. Huge logs are consumed, also, in road-making and bridge-building in the hills, and dozens of small trees are crushed by the fall of their greater companions. Then, when a district is pretty well cleared of its best timber, fire is set in the brush and prostrate trunks. Feeding eagerly upon the resinous wood, half dried and broken, it gathers so much heat that the saplings are nearly all killed, and the flaky, tinder-like bark of the larger trees is singed in a way which must greatly injure and often destroy them. Moreover, these fires, fanned by the gusty breezes rushing in every afternoon from the ocean, often get beyond control, and sweeping through the oily tops and brittle trunks, spread blackened ruin over miles and miles of precious forest. *Precious*, however, it seems never to occur to the lumberman these forests are; yet he is probably no more wasteful and careless here than elsewhere, and finds his match for heedless extravagance in nearly every pursuit that deals in what nature furnished us at the outset in abundance, but replaces only very slowly, giving abundant leisure for our repentance. The spendthrift lumberman is bad enough, but no worse than the wasteful oysterman or buffalo-hunter, reckless of the future. It is, or ought to be, a matter of rejoicing to everybody that the Forestry people, under Mr. Sargeant's guidance, are paying especial attention to preserving as far as possible the magnificent forests of the Coast Range.

It is interesting to observe how speedily Nature re-asserts herself the instant the lumberman leaves her undisturbed. Every redwood stump that escapes the fire is at once surrounded and crowned by a dense thicket of sprouts, which in two or

THE COOK.

three years conceal it under a cone of vivid green. Meanwhile innumerable bushes, briers, evergreen saplings, and vines have grown up among the many trees left standing, so that an inexperienced person, not noting the absence of large trees, might never suspect that the lumberman had marched through the district, sparing nothing he cared to take, only a few months ago.

An example of this swift and pleasant renewal was a large ravine close to the mills whither we used often to go, partly to escape the intensely chilly wind that swept up the valley of the Russian River during the whole month of May, but chiefly for enjoyment of its loveliness.

This ravine was a circular basin, a quarter of a mile in width, surrounded by hills of considerable height, forested, except at one place where a promontory rose above the rest into a huge pile of crimson rocks and purple heather surmounting lower slopes of gold and green, where the long yellow plush of the turf rippled under the wind like the surface of the river itself. Into this basin, through a rift in the hills behind, poured a stream, expanding into a marsh here, but a marsh so choked with flags and coarse grass, or hidden under such a variety and luxuriance of trees and bushes, that it was no easy matter to see any water.

From end to end of this basin, and right through its centre, ran an old bridge or causeway, broken now and useful only for the small foot-travel which might go that way, but plainly once the avenue to the mill of thousands of logs, whose places the forest had hidden so bravely that we never missed any trees out of the still crowded ranks. Here was sketching material to last a whole summer through— backgrounds of hills near and remote; glimpses of white cottages to accentuate the middle distance; trees dark and massive, with drooping boughs and pinnacled tops, or carrying rounded, dense thickets of olive foliage far above the hill horizon; rounded heaps of willowy bush foliage, feathery maples, alders, and the like, some in blossom, with a foreground of lichen-painted and flower-studded rocks, ruined platforms of grass-grown logs, or the irregular perspective of the old causeway making a lane straight into the heart of your composition.

As I sit watching the making of a sketch it is hard to realize myself in California.

Looking one way, I might easily think a cypress swamp in Louisiana my hospice; looking another, any Eastern mountain scene is duplicated, from North Carolina to the Adirondacks. Of course a minute glance detects differences at once, but the general impression is about the same one would gather from a wild bit of wet woodland in the hills of any Atlantic State. Always on the lookout for my friends the birds, I see that a stranger would scarcely notice the difference between California and the Catskills in this respect. The scream of woodpeckers, the short whistle of the plumed quail—knightly bird!—the loud click and chatter of a blazing, bee-like hummer, would excite his question; but one hears here the same kind of melody, and recognizes the songs of old friends in a new brogue, as is to be expected of cousins living on this side of the big continent. Among these low bushes, for instance, a finch is bobbing about, chirping in a metallic manner perfectly familiar; and from another bush comes a joyous roundelay telling me at once that it is a song-sparrow that is the performer. The blackbirds, nestling in the willows so well moated by the sluggish creek, carol above their treasures in just the happy-go-lucky strain one hears in an Ohio "swale," but, improving on it, have converted the old cheery roulade into the sharp jingling of an armful of small sleigh-bells. Chickadees and wrens squeak and chatter at you, the solemn wail of the dove comes from the dark cliff, the coarse scream of the jay (here bluer and with more swagger than at home), and the pretty prattle of many a warbler, all suggest, if they do not precisely tally with, the familiar bird-notes of Eastern woods and swamps. I have heard it said that the birds in California do not sing. It is a wicked libel. They are more musical, on the whole, I believe, than those of the Atlantic coast, and richer melody was never heard than drops from their happy throats during all these sunshiny May days.

But let us return to our redwoods, and the second stage of their degradation from trees to logs, and from logs to lumber.

The tree having been felled, men proceeded to trim away its top, and to split off its thick coat of bark. This can often be pried away almost without breaking it, except on top, so that a great cast, as it were, of the trunk is left in the bark, which lies there, after the logs are removed, like

"SNAKING OUT" LOGS.

a huge ruined canoe. I have seen masses of redwood bark fifteen inches in thickness; the tree which it clothed, if straight and sound, would be worth a thousand dollars. It does not follow, however, that the biggest trunks are the most valuable, since it often happens that very large trees prove unsound or completely hollowed.

The stripping of top branches and bark having been effected, the trunk is sawed into logs fifteen or twenty feet in length. A path is now cleared to them from the nearest road sufficiently good to take in six or eight yoke of oxen. This does not require to be a very good path either—though in some cases much labor and rough engineering is required for these wood roads—since the agility of the little oxen is quite wonderful when one notes what barriers of fallen trunks and what almost vertical slopes of hill-side are surmounted. Near the lower end of the log an iron hook, called a "dog," is driven in, where the drag-chain is attached. Then, under a shower of such "good mouth-filling oaths" as would have satisfied Falstaff, under resounding thwacks and proddings of an iron-tipped goad, the slipping and stumbling cattle snake the log endwise down the hill. But a single log must be of extraordinary size to content the driver. Having arranged them in line at the head of the little gully which previous draggings have smoothed out, he chains together two, three, even five or six logs, and starts up the slow-moving cattle with a train behind them four or five rods long. Though the pitches they scramble down are too smooth and steep for us to follow, sure-footed they stay upon their legs, and keep out of the way of the logs; thus all goes well, yet the shouts and imprecations of the bull-whacker never cease. He curses the logs, which are trailing along without a fault; he hurls vile but vivid epithets at the exemplary oxen collectively and individually; he swears at the meek Chinaman who travels ahead diligently wetting the ground to make it slippery; he damns everything all the time, yet is suave and polite and mild-mannered to us as we scramble alongside, for his profanity is purely professional, and his objurgations to be taken wholly in a Pickwickian sense.

The snaking out of these logs is another source of casualty to the lumberman, arising not so often from the logs, however, as from the big round butts which in many cases are sawed off from the original trunk. These are like huge solid cart-wheels, and of great weight: if one of them gets loose upon the steep hill-side, whatever stops it must stand stiff and high. We were taking breakfast with Charlie Nolan, the wide-awake foreman at the camp, one day, Nolan sitting where he could look out of the open door and up the mountain. Suddenly he dropped his knife, grabbed up a small boy in each

hand, and shouting, "Get out of this!" made for the door. Nobody waited to inquire what was the matter, but followed the injunction, turning, when the open air was gained, just in time to see the stoppage by a firm stump of an immense butt, which had come thundering down through the thinned woods, aiming directly at our cottage, whose frail walls would have offered no obstacle whatever to its progress. Breakfast tasted much better after this escape from losing it altogether.

The railway having been reached by the bull-team and their train, the logs are laid lengthwise upon a sloping platform or bank strengthened by buried skids, where a white foreman and two or three Chinese laborers easily roll them down upon the cars, aiding themselves with cant-hooks, jack-screws, and consonantal expressions in two languages designed to relieve the feelings.

Having been placed upon the cars, the logs are secured by ropes and dogs so that they can not fall, and then are taken at a break-neck pace down to the mill, and tumbled over upon a slanting platform, whence they can easily be rolled upon the small car which carries them up into the mill by stationary engine-power.

The men who do this work are an interesting lot: *lot*, however, if it implies that it is a collection of like articles, is a bad word, for the striking thing about the Californian lumbermen is their diversity, and their habit of frequently changing from one kind of work to another, or from this camp to the next one, in endless succession. At Duncan's camps almost every European nationality was represented—French, German, Norwegian, Spanish, English, Scotch, and Irish, not to speak of Americans, Chinese, and "Indians not taxed." The Americans employed are very often graduates of the Maine woods, or "Bluenoses" from Lower Canada. These Maine men are likely to become foremen, or sub-foremen, and form a nucleus around which the floating crowd is gathered. It often happens that a man will hire himself to labor in the redwoods who is fitted for a far better kind of work, but has met with misfortune. You would think all of them had at one time possessed great wealth—or at any rate had had the opportunity of independent riches—to hear their stories; and if you believe them all, you are more strongly than

AT THE LANDING.

ever reminded of the "slip 'twixt the cup and the lip" so likely to happen. There is a kindly emulation among Californians to prove one's self to have been more unfortunate than one's neighbor, by magnifying the prize just missed. This is perhaps consoling to the unfortunates, but it is confusing to the credulous historian.

It is a curious social life existing in these forest communities, the membership of which is constantly changing, and whose scene is annually shifted. At this camp there were only two families, but they had nothing to do with the housing or feeding of the sixty or more men (half Chinese), who messed by themselves, and slept in slab shanties near by, the Chinamen having a group of well-mottoed houses to themselves.

John Chinaman is in force here, as everywhere, for all help-work. His slight, wiry frame, with its shoulder under the lever, shows as much tough strength as that of his burly white neighbor, and he grinds all day at the feed-cutter, or totes kegs of water, balanced across his neck, up and down the rough declivities from morning till night, without seeming to tire out or ever thinking of a holiday. His it is also to manage the kitchen of the camp.

"John, where can we get something to eat?" we ask, as the sun begins to send level beams between the ruddy pillars of the soldierly sequoias.

"Heap catchum cook-house," he answers, and following his beck, our experience shows him a capital bread-maker and beef-roaster, but *not* a careful washer of dishes.

The men had gathered in the long wooden shed for supper, eating on wooden tables, but with an abundance of furniture and a plentiful bill of fare. Supper was hurried through this evening, for the men had on hand a frolic which had also the serious purpose of ridding the camp of an obnoxious old boar that had acquired a troublesome taste for the blood of Mongolian shanks, whose shrunken lines could ill spare the commodity. Re-enforced with great heartiness by the Chinese contingent, the whole camp therefore turned out on a boar hunt, assisted by several dogs even more diverse in breed than their masters. The approved weapons for this sort of chase, I understand, are rifles, spears, and knives; but here were to be seen only a club or two and some ropes looped with lassos, except that a valiant wielder of the brush brought up the rear with a six-shooter tightly clutched in his red right hand. The advance was not incautious. That pig had long made himself respected to the extent that when he appeared every man not only gave him the right of the road, but hastened to climb upon a stump, so as to run no risk of incommoding his swineship in the least by his presence.

It was not long, however, before a series of energetic grunts was heard ahead, and the army stopped, the artist mounting a very high stump. He said he thought they had stumbled on a bear, and he wanted to be where he could fire over the heads of all the men. Though only a black and bristling pig, a bear of the biggest kind could not have held the army at bay more thoroughly. If he had charged, I tremble to think what might have happened; but he rushed away into the bushes and ran into a corner, where he became the victim of strategy, and was presently bound and led forth in degrading captivity, followed by a procession of one artist, a score of grinning lumbermen, and a mob of chattering and dancing Chinese, for the intention was not to kill him, but only to eradicate his pugnacious propensities.

This done, the painter put up his pistol, and we all adjourned to the big shanty, where some of the men pulled off their boots and stretched themselves in restful ease upon their bunks, while others shuffled the cards for "a little game," or did odd jobs of tinkering.

It was a strange and interesting picture the interior of the big shanty made as the darkness of the outside withdrew all the light from within, and left the walls and the faces illumined only by a great fire of resinous redwood chunks built upon a raised earthen hearth that occupied the whole centre of the cabin, and the smoke of which escaped up a big bell-hooded flue in the ceiling.

The talk fell upon the enemy ignobly conquered; upon their work, and the probable plans of "the old man," meaning their employer; upon some men who had just departed, which carried it away to Frisco, and drifted it upon the familiar ground of reminiscences of the dance-house, the poker table, and the men who were always waiting to "get the drop" on somebody, or watching that somebody didn't get the drop on them. Stirring stories some of them, but as unreportable as the vigorous metaphors in which they were portrayed. Many of these men did not know the names of their mates beyond a Sam or Jake to call them by; and they had no especial curiosity to know, this atmosphere making a man tender about asking his neighbor personal questions, being shy of disturbing the pleasant *status quo* which rests upon careless ignorance. Would "old Folinsbee's daughter" have enjoyed the ball at Poverty Flat, think you, any the better for knowing all about her partner, when she

"danced down the middle
With the man that shot Sandy McGee"?

I think not. In California one lays his course by Mrs. Partington's philosophy, no longer trite:

"Where ignorance is bliss,
'Twere the height of folly to be otherwise."

Down at the mills on the river, however, the men employed were largely those having families. For these the company had built a series of pretty cottages which were set in small gardens, kept in neat order, and held an air of solid home comfort that was very pleasing.

The mills here are essentially like all the rest in the redwood belt. I had hoped to see some wonderful boards, a dozen feet broad, cut out, but I was disappointed. If the log is of large size, it is sent at once against a "muley," or straight rip-saw, working perpendicularly, which splits it in two, after which the halves are often quartered. The smaller logs and these quarters are then hauled and rolled, with the help of steam-tackle, to the opposite side of the building, where they are cut up by a circular saw of large size. Lest its width should not suffice in all cases, however, there is rigged just over the circular saw a second one, working to meet it; between both, very wide boards might be turned out, but it is not often done, since there is no demand for them.

The capacity of these mills is from twenty to forty thousand feet of lumber a day, and to them are attached planers, shingle machines, picket headers, and so on. Next to boards, fence posts are made in largest quantity, and after these the rough split fence pickets so commonly used in this part of the State, the great durability of the wood, when unpainted, recommending it for service in fences and as roofing. Redwood shingles last like the cedar and cypress our grandfathers chose as the thatch of those old houses whose stability is our admiration. As this timber grows scarce it will doubtless be applied to uses far more varied and ornamental than at present, particularly in the way of "finishing," where the grain

IN THE BIG SHANTY.

of the wood is to be preserved in view, and for cabinet-work. The bedstead and bureaus of the room where I am writing are made of varnished white pine, and were no doubt imported from Michigan. The redwood treated in the same way, or by other methods to which pine and ash are subjected, would have produced a handsomer result, and in a more agreeable tone. I am reminded, however, that redwood lumber for fine uses must be seasoned with extraordinary care to save it from shrinking *lengthwise*—a fault in which, I believe, it is unique.

A final day at Duncan's was spent in Azalea Gulch, just opposite, than which nothing more lovely is hidden in the depths of the redwood gloom. It is reached by crossing the river in a boat, and walking through long galleries, canopied with flowers and foliage, chiselled out of the overhanging cliff. The vale is broad at first, with open glades carpeted in Persian pattern—the varied greens of grasses, the sulphur dots of innumerable asters, the purple dashes of wild pea, the warm orange of the eschscholtzia, and the bloody stains of the wide-spread sorrel, combined

in Nature's rough loom. There are hillocks sown thick with ferns; red-stemmed, white-crowned thickets of madroña climbing the sheltered hill-side through billows of emerald shrubbery; there are solid pyramids of bay as impenetrable and smooth as close-cropped hedges, or as the mossy ledge near by, where the dwarf oaks grow scraggy and gale-bent atop; and caves of indigo darkness in the face of the forest wall, half hidden under fringes of Spanish moss catching silver from the sunlight. These things and more, like them and different from them in degrees of beauty, chain the eye as you slowly ascend the glade, hearing ceaselessly the musical splash and gurgle of the trout water so well hidden under those dense alders— alders like a delicate lace-work, worked in an intricate pattern of emerald leaves and white branches and twigs; but the strangest of all pictures is in the groves of bay; borne down and contorted ever since they were saplings by floods in the creek, they display the most grotesque tree forms ever seen. The trunks become of great size (some of them are two and three feet in diameter), but all lie prostrate, or nearly so, upon the ground, and join together two or more tree-like growths of huge erect branches, or arch here and there in fantastic curves which resemble nothing so much as a crowd of huge snakes writhing about in a cave. Nor is the impression of a cave distant from the truth. The foliage of this tree, whenever it takes the dwarfed form, is borne only upon the tips of the branches, that terminate in great bunches of twigs. Each thick-crowding limb thus carries outwardly an umbrella-like mass of leaves, through which very little light can enter; and as here these branches are not only overhead, but are drooping upon all sides to the very ground, a complete canopy of shade results, unobstructed by interior twigs or foliage, through which the fat, distorted, smooth-skinned trunks and recumbent limbs seem to crawl and writhe in uncanny fashion.

When the glade began to narrow into a cañon the redwoods appeared—magnificent specimens standing all about the scant level of the bottom, two by two, and rising straight two hundred feet, as though trying to look over the hill-tops.

Between the buttresses of their great roots the soil is damp and black, and innumerable cushions of moss hide the ledges of rock, and feed upon the soft remains of logs half hidden in masses of ferns and weedy vegetation-loving shade, and endless dews of the deep coniferous woods. Half a mile further the cañon becomes too steep and narrow for much large timber, though choked with smaller growth; and at its head is a most picturesque cataract—a bit of music, a flash of green and white water, a veil of glistening verdure, and a background of splintered rocks.

Northern California
(1873)

NORTHERN CALIFORNIA.

By CHARLES NORDHOFF.

MENDOCINO AND CLEAR LAKE.

WATER-JAM OF LOGS.

SOME of the most picturesque country in California lies on or near the coast north of San Francisco. The coast counties, Marin, Sonoma, Mendocino, Humboldt, Klamath, and Del Norte, are the least visited by strangers, and yet, with Napa, Lake, and Trinity, they make up a region which contains a very great deal of wild and fine scenery, and which abounds with game, and shows to the traveler many varieties of life and several of the peculiar industries of California. Those who have passed through the lovely Napa Valley, by way of Calistoga, to the Geysers, or who have visited the same place by way of Healdsburg and the pretty Russian River Valley, have no more than a faint idea of what a tourist may see and enjoy who will devote two weeks to a journey along the sea-coast of Marin and Mendocino counties, returning by way of Clear Lake— a fine sheet of water, whose borders contain some remarkable volcanic features.

The northern coast counties are made up largely of mountains, but imbosomed in these lie many charming little, and several quite spacious, valleys, in which you are surprised to find a multitude of farmers living, isolated from the world, that life of careless and easy prosperity which is the lot of farmers in the fat valleys of California.

In such a journey the traveler will see the famous redwood forests of this State, whose trees are unequaled in size except by the gigantic sequoias; he will see those dairy-farms of Marin County, whose butter supplies not only this Western coast, but is sent East, and competes in the markets of New York and Boston with the product of Eastern dairies, while, sealed hermetically in glass jars, it is transported to the most distant military posts, and used on long sea-voyages, keeping sweet in any climate for at least a year; he will see, in Mendocino County, one of the most remarkable coasts in the world, eaten by the ocean into the most singular and fantastic shapes; and on this coast saw-mills and logging camps, where the immense redwood forests are reduced to useful lumber with a prodigious waste of wood. He will see, besides the larger Napa, Petaluma, Bereyessa, and Russian River valleys, which are already connected by railroad with San Francisco, a number of quiet, sunny little vales, some of them undiscoverable on the map, nestled among the mountains, unconnected as yet with the world either by railroad or telegraph, but fertile, rich in cattle, sheep, and grain, where live a people peculiarly Californian in their habits, language, and customs, great horsemen, famous rifle-shots, keen fishermen, for the mountains abound in deer and bear, and the streams are alive with trout. He may see an Indian reservation—one of the most curious examples of mismanaged philanthropy which our government can show. And finally, the traveler will come to, and, if he is wise, spend some days on, Clear Lake—a strikingly lovely piece of water, which would be famous if it were not American.

For such a journey one needs a heavy pair of colored blankets and an overcoat rolled up together, and a leather bag or valise to contain the necessary change of clothing. A couple of rough crash towels and a piece of soap also should be put into the bag; for you may want to camp out, and you may not always find any but the public towel at the inn where you dine or sleep. Traveling in spring, summer, or fall, you need no umbrella or other protection against rain, and may confidently reckon on uninterrupted fine weather. The coast is always cool. The interior valleys are warm, and even hot, during the summer, and yet the dry heat does not exhaust or distress one, and cool nights refresh you. In the valleys and on much-traveled roads there is a good deal of dust, but it is, as they say, "clean dirt," and there is water enough in the country to wash it off. You need not ride on horseback unless you penetrate into Humboldt County, which has as yet but few miles of

wagon-road. In Mendocino, Lake, and Marin the roads are excellent, and either a public stage, or, what is pleasanter and but little dearer, a private team with a driver familiar with the country, is always obtainable. In such a journey one element of pleasure is its somewhat hap-hazard nature. You do not travel over beaten ground and on routes laid out for you; you do not know beforehand what you are to see, nor even how you are to see it; you may sleep in a house to-day, in the woods to-morrow, and in a sail-boat the day after; you dine one day in a logging camp, and another in a farm-house. With the barometer at "set fair," and in a country where every body is civil and obliging, and where all you see is novel to an Eastern person, the sense of adventure adds a keen zest to a journey which is in itself not only amusing and healthful, but instructive.

Marin County, which lies across the bay from San Francisco, and of which the pretty village of San Rafael is the county town, contains the most productive dairy-farms in the State. When one has long read of California as a dry State, he wonders to find that it produces butter at all; and still more to discover that the dairy business is extensive and profitable enough—with butter at thirty-five cents a pound at the dairy—to warrant the employment of several millions of capital, and to enable the dairy-men to send their product to New York and Boston for sale. Marin County offers some important advantages to the dairy-farmer. The sea fogs which it receives cause abundant springs of excellent soft water, and also keep the grass green through the summer and fall in the gulches and ravines. Vicinity to the ocean also gives this region a very equal climate. It is never cold in winter nor hot in summer. In the milk-houses I saw usually a stove, but it was used mainly to dry the milk-room after very heavy fogs or continued rains; and in the height of summer the mercury marks at most sixty-seven degrees, and the milk keeps sweet without artificial aids for thirty-six hours. The cows require no sheds nor any store of food, though the best dairy-men, I noticed, raised beets, but more, they told me, to feed to their pigs than for the cows. These creatures provide for themselves the year round in the open fields; but care is taken, by opening springs and leading water in iron pipes, to provide an abundance of this for them.

The county is full of dairy-farms; and as this business requires rather more and better buildings than wheat, cattle, or sheep farming, as well as more fences, this gives the country a neater and thriftier appearance than is usual among farming communities in this State. The butter-maker must have good buildings, and he must keep them in the best order.

But besides these smaller dairy-farms, Marin County contains some large "butter ranchos," as they are called, which are a great curiosity in their way. The Californians, who have a singular genius for doing things on a large scale which in other States are done by retail, have managed to conduct even dairying in this way, and have known how to "organize" the making of butter in a way which would surprise an Orange County farmer. Here, for instance—and to take the most successful and complete of these experiments—is the rancho of Mr. Charles Webb Howard, on which I had the curiosity to spend a couple of days. It contains 18,000 acres of land well fitted for dairy purposes. On this he has at this time nine separate farms, occupied by nine tenants engaged in making butter. To rent the farms outright would not do, because the tenants would put up poor improvements, and would need, even then, more capital than tenant-farmers usually have. Mr. Howard, therefore, contrived a scheme which seems to work satisfactorily to all concerned, and which appears to me extremely ingenious. He fences the farm, making proper subdivisions of large fields; he opens springs, and leads water through iron pipes to the proper places, and also to the dwelling, milk-house, and corral. He builds the houses, which consist of a substantial dwelling, twenty-eight by thirty-two feet, a story and a half high, and containing nine rooms, all lathed and plastered; a thoroughly well-arranged milk-house, twenty-five by fifty feet, having a milk-room in the centre twenty-five feet square, with a churning-room, store-room, wash-room, etc.; a barn, forty by fifty feet, to contain hay for the farm horses; also a calf-shed, a corral or inclosure for the cows, a well-arranged pig-pen; and all these buildings are put up in the best manner, well-painted, and neat. The tenant receives from the proprietor all this, the land, and cows to stock it. He furnishes, on his part, all the dairy utensils, the needed horses and wagons, the furniture for the house, the farm implements, and the necessary labor. The tenant pays to the owner twenty-seven dollars and a half per annum for each cow, and agrees to take the best care of the stock and of all parts of the farm, to make the necessary repairs, and to raise for the owner annually one-fifth as many calves as he keeps cows, the remainder of the calves being killed and fed to the pigs. He agrees also to sell nothing but butter and hogs from the farm, the hogs being entirely the tenant's property.

Under this system 1520 cows are now kept on nine separate farms on this estate, the largest number kept by one man being 225, and the smallest 115. Mr. Howard has been for years improving his herd; he prefers short-horns, and he saves every year the calves from the best milkers in all his herd, using also bulls from good milking strains. I was told that the average product of butter on the whole estate is now 175 pounds to each cow; many cows give as high as 200 and even 250 pounds per annum. Men do the milking, and also the butter-making, though on one farm I found a pretty Swedish girl superintending all the in-door work, with such skill and order in all the departments that she possessed, so far as I saw, the model dairy on the estate. Here, said I to myself, is now an instance of the ability of women to compete with men which would delight Mrs. Stanton and all the Woman's Rights people; here is the neatest, the sweetest, the most complete, dairy in the whole region; the best order, the most shining utensils, the nicest butter-room—and not only butter, but cheese also, made, which is not usual; and here is a rosy-faced, white-armed, smooth-haired, sensibly dressed, altogether admirable, and, to my eyes, beautiful Swedish lass presiding over it all; commanding her men-servants, and keeping every part of the business in order. Alas! Mrs. Stanton, she has discovered a better business than butter-making. She is going to marry—sensible girl that she is—and she is not going to marry a dairy-farmer either. I doubt if any body in California will ever make as nice butter as this pretty Swede; certainly every other dairy I saw seemed to me commonplace and uninteresting, after I had seen hers. I don't doubt that the young man who has had the art to persuade her to love him ought to be hanged, because butter-making is far more important than marrying. Nevertheless, I wish him joy in advance, and, in humble defiance of Mrs. Stanton and her brilliant companions in arms, hereby give it as my belief that the pretty Swede is a sensible girl—that, to use a California vulgarism, "her head is level."

For the coast journey the best route, because it shows you much fine scenery on your way, is by way of Soucelito, which is reached by a ferry from San Francisco. From Soucelito either a stage or a private conveyance carries you to Olema, whence you should visit Point Reyes, one of the most rugged capes on the coast, where a lighthouse and fog-signal are placed to warn and guide mariners. It is a wild spot, often enveloped in fogs, and where it blows at least half a gale of wind three hundred days in the year. Returning from Point Reyes to Olema, your road bears you past Tomales Bay, and back to the coast of Mendocino County; and by the time you reach the mouth of Russian River you are in the sawmill country. Here the road runs for the most part close to the coast, and gives you a long succession of wild and strange views. You pass Point Arena, where is another light-house; and finally land at Mendocino city.

Before the stage sets you down at Mendocino, or "Big River," you will have noticed that the coast-line is broken at frequent intervals by the mouths of small streams, and at the available points at the mouths of these streams saw-mills are placed. This continues up the coast, wherever a river-mouth offers the slightest shelter to vessels loading; for the redwood forests line the coast up to and beyond Humboldt Bay. There are even mills which offer no lee to vessels loading; and here the adventurous schooner watches her opportunity, hauls under a perpendicular cliff, receives her lading in the shortest possible time, and her crew think themselves fortunate if they get safely off. I am told the insurance companies charge very high rates to insure the lumber droghers, and in some cases entirely refuse to take risks on them. A number are lost every year, in spite of the skill and courage of their masters and crews. "Big River" is one of the best of the lumber ports; but even here vessels are lost every winter. One of the old residents told me he had seen ₋₋₋ore than one hundred seamen perish in the twenty years he had lived here; and I saw the strange and terrible cave into which a schooner was sucked in a sudden gale before her crew could escape to the shore. She broke from her anchors, the men hoisted sail, and the vessel was borne into the cave with all sail set. Her masts were snapped off like pipe-stems, and the hull was jammed into the great hole in the rock,

where it began to thump with the swell so that two of the frightened crew were at once crushed on the deck by the overhanging ceiling of the cave. Five others hurriedly climbed out over the stern, and there hung on until ropes were lowered to them by men on the cliff above, who drew them up safely. It was a narrow escape; and a more terrifying situation than that of this crew, as they saw their vessel sucked into a cave whose depth they did not know, can hardly be imagined outside of a hasheesh dream.

Yankee ingenuity and mechanical dexterity have been strained to contrive means to support the slides on which lumber is let down from the steep cliffs. To throw the lumber down would be to shatter it to pieces. It must be gently handled: hence the wire-rope slides, lined and covered with smooth plank, and suspended at their outer ends from huge derricks which butt against the lower parts of the cliffs. These spider-web structures, which appear too frail to stand a gale, have, of course, to bear no heavy weight. The vessel anchors under one of them; a man stands by with a convenient and simple compress or brake to check the too rapid descent of the board or scantling; and above, a man shoves the pieces down from a car or lumber pile, keeping tally as they descend.

A large part of the lumbering population consists of bachelors, and for their accommodation you see numerous shanties erect-

COAST VIEW, MENDOCINO COUNTY.

SAW-MILL.

ed near the saw-mills and lumber piles. At Mendocino city there is quite a colony of such shanties, two long rows, upon a point or cape from which the lumber is loaded. I had the curiosity to enter one of these little snuggeries, which was unoccupied. It was about ten by twelve feet in area, had a large fire-place (for fuel is shamefully abundant here), a bunk for sleeping, with a lamp arranged for reading in bed, a small table, hooks for clothes, a good board floor, a small window, and a neat little hood over the doorway, which gave this little hut quite a picturesque effect. There was, besides, a rough bench, and a small table. It seemed to me that in such a climate as that of Mendocino, where they wear the same clothes all the year round, have evening fires in July, and may keep their doors open in January, such a little kennel as this meets all the real wants of the male of the human race. This, I suspect, is about as far as man, unaided by woman, would have carried civilization any where. Whatever any of us have over and above such a snuggery as this we owe to womankind; whatever of comfort or elegance we possess, woman has given us, or made us give her. I think no wholesome, right-minded man in the world would ever get beyond such a hut; and I even suspect that the occupant of the shanty I inspected must have been in love, and thinking seriously of marriage, else he would never have nailed the pretty little hood over his doorway. So helpless is man!

And yet there are people who would make of woman only a kind of female man!

As you travel along the coast, the stage-road gives you frequent and satisfactory views of its curiously distorted and ocean-eaten caves and rocks. It has a dangerous and terrible aspect, no doubt, to mariners, but it is most wonderful viewed from the shore. At every projection you see that the waves have pierced and mined the rock; if the sea is high, you will hear it roar in the caverns it has made, and whistle and shriek wherever it has an outlet above through which the waves may force the air.

It is in the logging camps that a stranger will be most interested on this coast; for there he will see and feel the bigness of the redwoods. A man in Humboldt County got out of one tree lumber enough to make his house and barn, and to fence in two acres of ground. A schooner was filled with shingles made from a single tree. One tree in Mendocino, whose remains were shown to me, made a mile of railroad ties. Trees fourteen feet in diameter have been frequently found and cut down; the saw-logs are often split apart with wedges, because the entire mass is too large to float in the narrow and shallow streams, and I have even seen them blow a log apart with gunpowder. A tree four feet in diameter is called undersized in these woods; and so skillful are the wood-choppers that they can make the largest giant of the forest fall just where they want it, or, as they say, they "drive a stake with the tree."

A CHOPPER AT WORK.

at first a sharp crack; the cutter labors with his axe usually about fifteen minutes after this premonitory crack, when at last the huge mass begins to go over. Then you may hear one of the grandest sounds of the forest. The fall of a great redwood is startlingly like a prolonged thunder-crash, and is really a terrible sound.

The Maine men make the best wood-choppers, but the logging camp is a favorite place also for sailors; and I was told that Germans are liked as workmen about timber. The choppers grind their axes once a week—usually, I was told, on Sunday—and all hands in a logging camp work twelve hours a day. The government has lately become very strict in preserving the timber on Congress land, which was formerly cut at

The choppers do not stand on the ground, but on stages raised to such a height as to enable the axe to strike in where the tree attains its fair and regular thickness; for the redwood, like the sequoia, swells at the base, near the ground. These trees prefer steep hill-sides, and grow in an extremely rough and broken country, and their great height makes it necessary to fell them carefully, lest they should, falling with such an enormous weight, break to pieces. This constantly happens in spite of every precaution, and there is little doubt that in these forests and at the mills two feet of wood are wasted for every foot of lumber sent to market. To mark the direction line on which the tree is to fall, the chopper usually drives a stake into the ground a hundred or a hundred and fifty feet from the base of the tree, and it is actually common to make the tree fall upon this stake, so straight do these redwoods stand, and so accurate is the skill of the cutters. To fell a tree eight feet in diameter is counted a day's work for a man. When such a tree begins to totter, it gives

random, and by any body who chose. Government agents watch the loggers, and if these are any where caught cutting timber on Congress land their rafts are seized and sold. At present prices it pays to haul logs in the redwood country only about half a mile to water; all trees more distant than this from a river are not cut; but the rivers are in many places near each other, and the belt of timber left standing, though considerable, is not so great as one would think. Redwood lumber has one singular property—it shrinks endwise, so that where it is used for weather-boarding a house, one is apt to see the butts shrunk apart. I am told that across the grain it does not shrink perceptibly.

Accidents are frequent in a logging camp, and good surgeons are in demand in all the saw-mill ports, for there is much more occasion for surgery than for physic. Men are cut with axes, jammed by logs, and otherwise hurt, one of the most serious dangers arising from the fall of limbs torn from standing trees by a falling one. Often such

SHIPPING LUMBER, MENDOCINO COUNTY.

a limb lodges or sticks in the high top of a tree until the wind blows it down, or the concussion of the wood-cutter's axe, cutting down the tree, loosens it. Falling from such a height as 200 or 250 feet, even a light branch is dangerous, and men sometimes have their brains dashed out by such a falling limb.

When you leave the coast for the interior, you ride through mile after mile of redwood forest. Unlike the firs of Oregon and Puget Sound, this tree does not occupy the whole land. It rears its tall head from a jungle of laurel, madrone, oak, and other trees; and I doubt if so many as fifty large redwoods often stand upon a single acre. I was told that an average tree would turn out about fifteen thousand feet of lumber, and thus even thirty such trees to the acre would yield nearly half a million feet.

The topography of California, like its climate, has decided features. As there are but two seasons, so there are apt to be sharply drawn differences in natural features, and you descend from what appears to you an interminable mass of mountains suddenly into a plain, and pass from deep forests shading the mountain-road at once into a prairie valley, which nature made ready to the farmer's hands, taking care even to beautify it for him with stately and umbrageous oaks. There are a number of such valleys on the way which I took from the coast at Mendocino city to the Nome Cult Indian Reservation, in Round Valley. The principal of these, Little Lake, Potter, and Eden valleys, contain from five to twelve thousand acres; but there are a number of smaller

vales, little gems big enough for one or two farmers, fertile and easily cultivated. A good many Missourians and other Southern people have settled in this part of the State. The better class of these make good farmers; but the person called "Pike" in this State has here bloomed out until, at times, he becomes, as a Californian said about an earthquake, "a little monotonous." The Pike in Mendocino County regards himself as a laboring-man, and in that capacity he has undertaken to drive out the Indians, just as a still lower class in San Francisco has undertaken to drive out the laboring Chinese. These Little Lake and Potter Valley Pikes were ruined by Indian cheap labor; so they got up a mob and expelled the Indians, and the result is that the work which these poor people formerly performed is now left undone. As for the Indians, they are gathered at the Round Valley Reservation to the number of about twelve hundred, where they stand an excellent chance to lose such habits of industry and thrift as they had learned while supporting themselves. At least half the men on the reservation, the superintendent told me, are competent farmers, and many of the women are excellent and competent house-servants. No one disputes that while they supported themselves by useful industry in the valleys where were their homes they were peaceable and harmless, and that the whites stood in no danger from them. Why, then, should the United States government forcibly make paupers of them? Why should this class of Indians be compelled to live on reservations? Under the best management which we have ever had in the Indian Bureau—let us say under its present management—a reservation containing tame or peaceable Indians is only a pauper asylum and prison combined, a nuisance to the respectable farmers, whom it deprives of useful and necessary laborers, an injury to the morals of the community in whose midst it is placed, an injury to the Indian, whom it demoralizes, and a benefit only to the members of the Indian ring.

Round Valley is occupied in part by the Nome Cult Reservation, and in part by farmers and graziers. In the middle of the valley stands Covelo, one of the roughest little villages I have seen in California, the gathering-place for a rude population, which inhabits not only the valley, but the mountains within fifty miles around, and which rides in to Covelo on mustang ponies whenever it gets out of whisky at home or wants a spree. The bar-rooms of Covelo sell more strong drink in a day than any I have ever seen elsewhere; and the sheep-herder, the vaquero, the hunter, and the wandering rough, descending from their lonely mountain camps, make up as rude a crowd as one could find even in Nevada. Being almost without exception Americans, they are not quarrelsome in their cups. I was told, indeed, by an old resident that shooting was formerly common, but it has gone out of fashion, mainly, perhaps, because most of the men are excellent shots, and the amuse-

ment was dangerous. At any rate, I saw not a single fight or disturbance, though I spent the Fourth of July at Covelo; and it was, on the whole, a surprisingly well-conducted crowd, in spite of a document which was given me there, and whose directions were but too faithfully observed by a large majority of the transient population. This was called a "toddy time-table," and I transcribe it here, for the warning and instruction of Eastern topers, from a neat gilt-edged card:

TODDY TIME-TABLE.

6 A.M.	Eye-Opener.	3 P.M.	Cobbler.
7 "	Appetizer.	4 "	Social Drink.
8 "	Digester.	5 "	Invigorator.
9 "	Big Reposer.	6 "	Solid Straight.
10 "	Refresher.	7 "	Chit-Chat.
11 "	Stimulant.	8 "	Fancy Smile.
12 M.	Ante-Lunch.	9 "	Entire Acte (sic).
1 P.M.	Settler.	10 "	Sparkler.
2 "	A la Smythe.	11 "	Rouser.

12 P.M. Night-Cap.

GOOD-NIGHT.

My impression is that this time-table was not made for the latitude of Covelo, for they began to drink much earlier than 6 A.M. at the bar near which I slept, and they left off later than midnight. It would be unjust for me not to add that, for the amount of liquor consumed, it was the soberest and the best-natured crowd I ever saw. I would like to write "respectable" also, but it would be ridiculous to apply that term to men whose every word almost is an oath, and whose language in many cases corresponded accurately with their clothes and persons.

ANOTHER COAST VIEW.

From Round Valley there is a "good enough" horseback trail, as they call it, over a steep mountain into the Sacramento Valley, but a pleasanter journey, and one, besides, having more novelty, is by way of Potter Valley to Lakeport, on Clear Lake. The road is excellent; the scenery is peculiarly Californian. Potter Valley is one of the richest and also one of the prettiest of the minor valleys of this State, and your way to Lakeport carries you above the shores of two pleasant mountain lakelets—the Blue Lakes, which are probably ancient craters. Two days' easy driving, stopping overnight in Potter Valley, brings you to Lakeport, the capital of Lake County, and the only town I have seen in California where they keep dogs in the square to worry strangers entering the place. As the only hotel in the town occupies one corner of this square, and as in California fashion the loungers usually sit in the evening on the sidewalk before the hotel, the combined attack of these dogs occurs in their view, and perhaps affords them a pleasing and beneficial excitement. The placid and impartial manner with which the landlord himself regards the contest between the stranger and the town dogs will lead you to doubt whether his house is not too full to accommodate another guest, and whether he is not benevolently letting the dogs spare him the pain of refusing you a night's lodging; but it is gratifying to be assured, when you at last reach the door, that the dogs "scarcely ever bite any body."

Clear Lake is a large and picturesque sheet of water, twenty-five miles long by about seven wide, surrounded by mountains, which in many places descend to the water's edge. At Lakeport you can hire a boat at a very reasonable price, and I advise you to take your blankets on board, and make this boat your home for two or three days. You will get food at different farm-houses on the shore, and as there are substantial, good-sized sail-boats, you can sleep on board very enjoyably. Aside from its fine scenery, and one or two good specimens of small Californian farms, the valley is remarkable for two borax lakes and a considerable deposit of sulphur, all of which lie close to the shore.

At one of the farm-houses, whose owner, a Pennsylvanian, has made himself a most beautiful place in a little valley hidden by the mountains which butt on the lake, I saw the culture of silk going on in that way in which only, as I believe, it can be made successful in California. He had planted about 2500 mulberry-trees, built himself an inexpensive but quite sufficient little cocoonery, bought an ounce and a half of eggs for fifteen dollars, and when I visited him had already a considerable quantity of cocoons, and had several thousand worms then feeding. It was his first attempt; he had never seen a cocoonery, but had read all he could buy about the management of the silk-worm; and as his grain harvest was over, he found in the slight labor attending the management of these worms a source of interest and delight which was alone worth the cost of his experiment. But he is successful besides; and his wife expressed great delight at the new employment her husband had found, which, as she said, had kept him close at home for about two months. She remarked that all wives ought to favor the silk culture for their husbands; but the old man added that some husbands might recommend it to their wives. Certainly I had no idea how slight and pleasant is the labor attending this industry up to the point of getting cocoons. If, however, you mean to raise eggs, the work is less pleasant. This farmer, Mr. Alter, had chosen his field of operations with considerable shrewdness. He planted his mulberry-trees on a dry side-hill, and found that it did not hurt his worms to feed to them, under this condition, even leaves from the little shrubs growing in his nursery rows. His cocoonery was sheltered from rude winds by a hill and a wood, and thus the temperature was very equal. He had no stove in his house, the shelves were quite rough, and the whole management might have been called careless if it were not successful. I believe that the country about Clear Lake and in the Napa and Sonoma valleys will be found very favorable to the culture of the silk-worm; but I believe also that this industry will not succeed except where it is carried on by farmers and their families in a small way.

Boat life on Clear Lake is as delightful an experience as a traveler or lounger can get anywhere. The lake is placid; there is usually breeze enough to sail about; you need not fear storms or rainy weather in the dry season. If it should fall calm, and you do not wish to be delayed, you can always hire an Indian to row the boat, and there is sufficient to see on the lake to pleasantly detain a tourist several days, besides fine fishing and hunting in the season, and lovely views all the time. Going to the Sulphur Banks on a calm morning, I hired an Indian from a rancheria upon Mr. Alter's farm to row for us, and my Indian proved to be a prize. His name was Napoleon, and he was a philosopher. Like his greater namesake, he had two wives. Of the first one he reported that "Jim catchee him," by which I understood that he had tired of her, and had sold her to "Jim;" and he had now taken number two, a moderately pretty Digger girl, of whom he seemed to be uncommonly fond. As he rowed he began to speak of his former life, when he had served a white farmer.

"Him die now," said Napoleon; adding, in a musing tone, "he very good man, plenty

AN INDIAN RANCHERIA.

money; give Injun money all time. Him very good white man, that man; plenty money all time."

Napoleon dwelt upon the wealth of his favorite white man so persistently that presently it occurred to me to inquire a little further.

"Suppose a white man had no money," said I, " what sort of a man would you think him?"

My philosopher's countenance took on a fine expression of contempt. "Suppose white man no got money?" he asked. "Eh! suppose no got money—he dam fool!" And Napoleon glared upon us, his passengers, as though he wondered if either of us would venture to contradict so plain a proposition.

The sulphur bank is a remarkable deposit of decomposed volcanic rock and scoria, containing so large a quantity of sulphur that I am told that at the refining-works, which lie on the bank of the lake, the mass yields eighty per cent. of pure sulphur. The works were not in operation when I was there.

Several large hot springs burst out from the bank, and gas and steam escape with some violence from numerous fissures. The deposit looks very much like a similar one on the edge of the Kilauea crater, on the island of Hawaii, but is, I should think, richer in sulphur. Near the sulphur bank, on the edge of the lake, is a hot borate spring, which is supposed to yield at times 300 gallons per minute, and which Professor Whitney, the State Geologist, declares remarkable for the extraordinary amount of ammoniacal salts its waters contain—more than any natural spring water that has ever been analyzed.

There is abundant evidence of volcanic action in all the country about Clear Lake. A dozen miles from Lakeport, not far from the shore of the lake, the whole mountain-side along which the stage-road runs is covered for several miles with splinters and fragments of obsidian, or volcanic glass, so that it looks as though millions of bottles had been broken there in some prodigious revelry; and where the road cuts into the side of the mountain you see the obsidian

INDIAN SWEAT-HOUSE.

lying in huge masses and in boulders. Joining this, and at one point interrupting it, is a tract of volcanic ashes stratified, and the strata thrown up vertically in some places, as though after the volcano had flung out the ashes there had come a terrific upheaval of the earth.

The two borax lakes lie also near the shore of Clear Lake; the largest one, which is not now worked, has an area of about three hundred acres. Little Borax Lake covers only about thirty acres, and this is now worked. The efflorescent matter is composed of carbonate of soda, chloride of sodium, and biborate of soda. The object of the works is, of course, to separate the borax, and this is accomplished by crystallizing the borax, which, being the least soluble of the salts, is the first to crystallize. The bottom of the lake was dry when I was there; it was covered all over with a white crust, which workmen scrape up and carry to the works, where it is treated very successfully. My nose was offended by the fetid stench which came from the earth when it was first put in the vats with hot water; and I was told by the foreman of the works that this arose from the immense number of flies and other insects which fly upon the lake and perish in it. Chinese are employed as laborers here, and give great satisfaction; and about eight days are required to complete the operation of extracting the borax in crystals. Earth containing biborate of lime is brought to this place all the way from Wadsworth, in the State of Nevada—a very great distance, with several transhipments—to be reduced at these works; and it seems that this can be more cheaply done here than there, where they have neither wood for the fires nor soda for the operation.

Clear Lake is but twelve hours distant from San Francisco; the journey thither is full of interest, and the lake itself, with the natural wonders on its shores, is one of the most interesting and enjoyable spots in California to a tourist who wishes to breathe fresh mountain air and enjoy some days of free open-air life.

The visitor to Clear Lake should go by way of the Napa Valley, taking stage for Lakeport at Calistoga, and return by way of the Russian River Valley, taking the railroad at Cloverdale. Thus he will see on his journey two of the richest and most fertile of the minor valleys of California, both abounding in fruit and vines as well as in grain. As there are two sides to Broadway, so there are two sides to the Bay of San Francisco. On the one side lies the fine and highly cultivated Santa Clara Valley, filling up fast with costly residences and carefully kept country places. Opposite, on the other side of the bay, lies the Russian River Valley, as beautiful naturally as that of the Santa Clara, and of which Petaluma, Santa Rosa, Healdsburg, and Cloverdale are the chief towns. It is a considerable plain, bounded by fine hills and distant mountains, which open up, as you pass by on the railroad, numerous pretty reaches of subsidiary vales, where farmers live protected by the projecting hills from all harsh sea-breezes, and where frost is seldom if ever felt. As you ascend the valley, the madrone, one of the most striking trees of California, becomes abundant and of larger growth, and its dark green foliage and bright cinnamon-colored bark ornament the landscape. The laurel, too, or California bay-tree, grows thriftily among the hills, and the plain and foot-hills are dotted with oak and redwood. This valley is as yet somewhat thinly peopled, but it has the promise of a growth which will make it the equal some day of the Santa Clara, and the superior of the Napa Valley.

Wintering in California
(1890)

OUTING.

Vol. XV.   JANUARY, 1890.   No. 4.

Wintering in California

BY CHARLES HOWARD SHINN.

The range and variety of winter resorts and winter amusements in California are far greater than American sportsmen and tourists have as yet discovered. Over a very large part of the State outdoor life is especially delightful from November to April, and travel is comfortable, even for the most confirmed invalid. Californians themselves are often apt to think that the time from April to June is usually the best part of the year, but even old Californians acknowledge the subtle charm of the soft, Italian winters, the green grass, the singing birds, the orange flames of wild poppies on the December hillsides, the clear blue skies that often hang for weeks without a flaw above the frostless fields and purple mountains, from which September showers have swept aside the veils of smoke of summer's forest fires. As a rule there are early rains which lay the dust and clear the atmosphere; then come many successive weeks of perfect and June-like weather, during which one can visit the seaside resorts, the famous beaches and bays where surf bathing and fishing can be enjoyed, and the old Spanish towns and missions may be studied; or one can see the fertile valleys and foothills of the interior at the season when they have peculiar charms.

The chief things for which tourists visit California—climate, beautiful scenery, picturesque outdoor life, fishing, hunting and the pleasure of discovering untrodden byways—are things which belong in a greater or lesser degree to the entire State. Those who know the twelve hundred miles of coast line, the mountain counties, as large as the whole State of Connecticut, whose names, even, are seldom heard east of the Rockies, and who have seen California at all seasons and under all conditions, know that, although a few localities are especially famous as health resorts, whole districts have mild, warm, open winters, and offer varied attractions to the visitor. All winter long, except during a few heavy rainstorms, the operations of field and farm work go on ; gardeners are harvesting their crops, men are plowing and sowing and planting new orchards, yellow lemons and red-gold oranges are being gathered by thousands of boxes. By January 1 the fragrant willow catkins are in bloom along the rivers and the irrigation canals ; by February almond and apricot blooms whiten the valleys for miles on miles, and yellow daffodils flood the old-fashioned gardens with sunlight. The great orange groves, fragrant and bright all winter with flowers, are in those splendid southern counties of San Diego, Los Angeles, San Bernardino and Santa Barbara, where orange culture began and has become an immense industry ; but all through the sheltered valley and foothills of the central and northern counties orange trees have b e e n planted, in many places on a large scale, so that the beautiful tree is beginning to be recognized as a part of the landscape of almost the entire State.

California is a land of hills and great mountains, protecting an immense number of valleys and high, warm plateaus. The Japan current, the winds, the mountain barriers, the cañons and many infinitely complex local causes all combine to give the State a multitude of local climates. San Francisco is often windy, foggy and cold, but eight or ten miles from San Francisco, either north, south or east, there are sheltered v a l l e y s and warm, frostless heights, where the lemon and orange ripen fruit, and heliotropes, roses and camellias bloom all winter in the open air. At Redding, near the head of the Sacramento Valley, about t w o

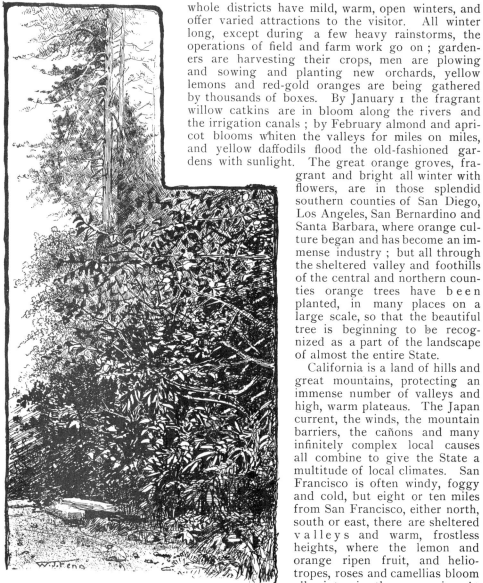

IN THE REDWOODS.

hundred miles north of San Francisco, there are avenues of palms and many young plantations of bearing orange trees, and the winter climate is delightful ; but in the mountains not twenty miles west, north or east, the winter rains are almost tropical in their downpour, and the higher peaks that lie against the distant horizon are covered with snow for more than half the year. At Santa Monica, over four hundred and fifty miles south of San Francisco, surf bathing goes on all winter, while the snow-crowned mountains of San Bernardino are seemingly but a few miles east. Everywhere throughout the immense extent of California, from Oregon to the Mexican boundary line, such sharp contrasts as these are found in the same counties, and often within the same townships. I have a friend in Butte County who owns two ranches ; twenty miles of distance and 5,000 feet of altitude separate them. On one ranch he can grow the fruits of Florida, on the other the fruits of Vermont. From

A LINE IN THE SANTA CRUZ.

CAMELLIAS.

the one he can push his boat out on a broad river in December and come back with a bag of wild fowl; on the pine-clad ridges of the other are deer, cinnamon bear, grizzlies, "catamount," foxes and lynxes.

The hard-beaten routes of travel and the places which ordinary tourists find most pleasant for a winter in California are mostly near or within easy reach of San Francisco and southward along the coast or in coast range valleys to San Diego. The railroad is at present in that beautiful Naples of the West, Santa Barbara, and in the ancient mission town of San Buena Ventura, and is pushing south from Santa Margarita, in San Luis Obispo, to complete the last important link of what is to be the favorite route for tourists, since along its line will be strung like pearls the seaside towns from Pescadero to Tia Juana. In the San Francisco region San Rafael, San José, Santa Cruz, Monterey, the Napa Soda Springs and many other coast and inte-

rior towns have the hotels, the drives, the climate and all the other attractions which please the winter tourist. Farther south in the region which still contains more of the old Spanish element than any other part of the State, and which has more slowly changed from the immense cattle ranges of the past, are the now easily-accessible valleys and seaside resorts scattered throughout the counties of San Luis Obispo, Santa Barbara and Ventura, all mild, healthy and beautiful districts, with many fine hotels, excellent hunting and fishing and safe beaches for winter bathing. Valleys such as the Ojai, the Montecito, the Carpenteria and the Santa Clara of the south lie between the parallel ridges of the Coast Range, sheltered, peaceful and lovely as the vales of Thessaly. Still farther south, and still even better provided with hotels of every grade, and with facilities for tourists, are the innumerable towns of the three coast counties of Los Angeles, Orange and San Diego, and of the great interior county of San Bernardino, all together forming the region that is probably better known abroad than any other part of California.

For the sportsman, and for men and women who enjoy new types of frontier character, magnificent valley, mountain

CRAWFISHING IN SANTA YSABEL CREEK.

HOTEL DEL MONTE, MONTEREY.

PERCHING ON WILD MUSTARD SPRAYS.

scenery, and the broader studies of Pacific Coast life, there are many parts of California suitable for a winter sojourn that are as yet seldom mentioned in any guide book. For the majority of tourists the famous resorts and easily accessible towns will probably always retain their position as favorites, but every year the State at large is more thoroughly traversed by visitors. The history of summer travel into New England and the Provinces is being repeated in the history of winter travel over California. The sleepy little villages, the old mining camps and the Spanish *embarcaderos*, or landing places along the bays, are being explored, and out of it all a new literature of outdoor California is finding expression. Many persons discover in the foothill regions of the State, north as well as south, some especial attractions of scenery and a winter climate which, while different from that of the more famous resorts of the coast, is, in essential respects, none the less attractive and invigorating. In the favored hill districts, after the September showers and warm early rains, the grass starts up everywhere and is often six inches high by Thanksgiving Day ; many garden flowers bloom all winter ; meadow larks sing and swing on the wild mustard stalks ; robins, linnets and mocking birds abound among the yellows, browns and purples of the leafless orchards of peach, pear, plum, cherry and apricot, and through the avenues of evergreen olives, loquats and magnolias. Quail rise from every cañon, and wild doves sweep across through the dark oaks, buckeyes and maples beside the streams, while every now and then one finds lagoons or broad swamps of cat tail and tulé, where the winter shooting includes snipe, curlew, a dozen species of ducks and an occasional wild goose.

In regions such as I have described the botanist discovers forty or fifty species of plants blooming in winter ; the naturalist finds the winter life of birds and animals especially busy and interesting, and the geologist can spend almost every day out of doors, as nearly all the rains of the winter fall during the night, and sink at once into the soil. December is usually the worst month for rains, but even in December in the foothills there are very few days when one must remain indoors. A gentleman living at Niles, in the frostless foothill belt of Alameda County, thirty miles from San Francisco, tells me that for ten years some member of his family has gone daily to the post office, a mile distant, but that he has seldom had an umbrella in the house. The annual rainfall of the region has been sufficient to insure excellent harvests, but most of it has fallen during the night, and every day has had its share of sunshine. My own observation, during several years of travel on the Pacific Coast, is that there are literally hundreds of villages in California which have an admirable winter climate and innumerable possibilities, some latent, some more or less developed, in the way of walks, drives and interesting occupation. Since I wish to write in the broader spirit of including in this paper sketches from the field of the unknown, as well as from that of the already famous, I shall briefly describe some of the districts that lie remote from the beaten highways that lead to the great hotels and watering places of Caliornia.

The great San Joaquin Valley plains, sloping toward each other and to the ocean, are at their best from January to March. Here the farmers have winter "rabbit drives," and often kill twelve or fifteen hundred hares that have been destroying their crops. I have driven along Bear Creek in February and have seen several hundred large hares moving about on a " flat " of perhaps fifty acres, between the willows of the stream and the rolling foothill pastures ; it was a poorly-harvested wheat

CATKINS.

field, and the hares were gleaning the aftermath. If one wishes to become a good rifle shot there is hardly anything better "to practice on," as an old hunter tells me, than these great, swift, gray-brown hares of the San Joaquin. "When ye can fetch them on the run," he says, "'tis time to go deer huntin'."

The foothills of Yolo, Napa, Solano and Sonoma, warm, sheltered, oak clad and picturesque, are as well worth visiting in winter as in the harvest season. Greater in extent, however, and of even more varied interest, are the counties of the Sierra foothill belt, the old mining camps of 1849, many of which are now being planted with grapes, olives, figs and oranges, and are rapidly becoming winter resorts for a large part of Central California. On December 12 last year I attended the annual "Citrus Fair" in the foothill town of Oroville, on the Feather River. The southern counties of the State have held many and very beautiful citrus fairs, but it is only of late years that the central counties have had the oranges to exhibit. This Oroville fair, however, was held in a large canvas pavilion, under the bluest of California skies. There were chrysanthemums, roses, lilies, sweet peas, fresh from the gardens, and wild flowers gathered from the forests. Oranges were displayed in wagon loads, and among other exhibits of the season were ripe raspberries, strawberries, melons, peppers and tomatoes, besides green peas and new potatoes. The climate during the week I was in Oroville appeared as mild and warm as a week of May weather in the rolling hill country of Maryland. All these old mining towns of the Sierras are well within reach of good hunting grounds. Smartsville, Oroville, Newcastle, Penryn, Ophir, Pla-

UNDER THE PALMS.

cerville, Lancha Plana, Jenny Lind, Cherokee and dozens of other "camps" lie in a region as healthful as, and far milder than, any of the most widely-known resorts of the southern Alleghanies. They are situated on vast, sheltered mountain promontories stretching out into the plain from the vaster mountain wall of the Sierra, and behind them are the snow peaks, miles distant, with immense forests of sugar pine and oaks to temper the air between.

WINTERING IN CALIFORNIA.

BY CHARLES HOWARD SHINN.

THE foothills still farther north, around the head of the Sacramento Valley, are easily reached by rail. The river and its tributaries are swarming with fish, and although the days when the Indians killed hundreds of salmon at the rapids near Redding are gone for ever, there are enough left to satisfy any reasonable master of the rod. The upper counties of the Sacramento are but thinly settled, and much of the land is held in large tracts, while a great area of rough hills is still Government land. A few years ago flocks of wild geese covering several acres on the open plain were a common sight, and they still destroy a great deal of grain for the farmers, as do the wild ducks and the mountain quail on the ranches in the foothills. The red " bench land " soil is easy to travel on all winter, and the whole life of the various little communities is essentially outdoor. The larger towns and county seats have reasonably good hotels. Workingmen on the railroad extensions, wood choppers and miners in the foothills often " camp out " in tents all winter. There is more rainfall than in the foothills farther south, and a double canvas tent with a stove in it is what a hunter should have. As the spring comes on in this foothill region, about the head of the great valley, one can push farther and

farther into the mountains, and explore the wildernesses that lie north about Mount Shasta, east about the Twin Peaks of Lassen, and west about the Yalloballa and the Trinities.

In the northern part of Napa County lies one of the more notable northern winter resorts of California. The district is called the Howell Mountain region, and more particularly the La Jota Rancho, a very impressive mountain plateau, surrounded by lesser hills and by a chain of sunny valleys dedicated to the grape and the olive. In height this plateau ranges from 1,600 to 2,000 feet, and it was originally clothed with a dense pine, fir and redwood forest, much of which remains and from which several streams flow. There are many cottages for summer or winter residence, built by Eastern and San Francisco people, and several good hotels. The drives extend along the four or five thousand acres of the mountain, over its adjacent ridges, and across the lovely surrounding valleys. Calistoga and St. Helena are the leading resorts of the Napa Valley below. A gentleman who has spent several winters at La Jota Villa, on the top of the mountain, writes that the noon temperature ranges from 60° to 85°. The nights are cool, but frostless. During some winters there have been one or two days of snow—not more than an inch falling—" just enough to give the children fun and make rabbit and deer tracks perceptible." There are many vineyards

CYPRESS POINT.

CACTUS.

on the mountain and a charming waterfall on Anguin Creek, where it falls into the ravine above El Nido.

A very attractive winter region is in the upper Salinas Valley, some two hundred miles south of San Francisco, extending from the Naciemiento River and the Estrella, past the old Mission San Miguel, to the ancient hot sulphur springs of Paso Robles and those of the Santa Ysabel. I have ridden on horseback over the country for a circle of twenty miles radius about Paso Robles, and it is a magnificent foothill region, well wooded, warm and possessing all the requirements of a great inland sanitarium, especially during the winter season. It is a valley of oaks, and oaks and pines crown the ravines. The pioneer settlers and stockmen are giving way to farmers and fruit growers, and the great ranches are being divided into smaller tracts, but it will be many years before the region loses much of its present wild and fascinating freedom. One can ride only a few miles west and find a log schoolhouse still standing among the oaks, and settlers living in log cabins or "oak shake" huts, not unlike those one sees in the East Tennessee Mountains. The upper Naciemiento and its branches are famous trout streams and there is a great deal of game in the Coast Range, especially in the Santa Lucia ranges along the borders of Monterey and San Luis Obispo. Paso Robles, one of the first hot springs known in California, was frequented by the Indians and much in favor with the Spaniards. The springs include hot and cold sulphur and mud baths. The waters resemble those of Aix-la-Chapelle and many invalids go there. Numbers of persons have built winter cottages at Paso Robles and the town has good hotel accommodations.

Santa Ysabel is a new and very promising winter resort, situated near Paso Robles, about one thousand feet above the sea.

One spring yields the immense flow of 20,000 gallons per hour of sparkling salino-sulphuretted water, of a temperature of 96°. There are several other hot and cold sulphur springs, all closely resembling the waters of the Arkansas Hot Springs.

Del Monte Club House.

LAWN TENNIS HEADQUARTERS ON THE PACIFIC.

A large lake has been made on the stream, near where the remains of a prehistoric dam of earth show that the

GARDEN AT MONTEREY.

THE DEL MONTE BATH.

is the county of Santa Cruz. The most of it is a very attractive and mountainous land, full of trout streams, deep gorges and splendid scenery. The forests are chiefly of giant redwoods, some of them measuring from forty to sixty feet in girth and 300 feet in height. The oaks, madrones, laurels, wild lilac, and all the shrubs and trees of the Californian coast are found in great luxuriance. Snow is never seen except upon a few of the bare rock peaks, where perhaps once in four or five years a slight snowfall occurs. Old mountaineers still dwell in their cabins in the fastnesses of these mountains, and deer and bear will long remain in the wilder cañons.

The heart of the Santa Cruz covers it may be two hundred square miles of forest, rocks and wilderness. It is crossed by a railroad, and dotted here and there with camps, villages, mountain farms, saw mills and colonies of fruit growers. It is a famous region for summer campers and tourists, who go thither by hundreds every year. The portions

Indians, ages ago, must have formed an enormous bathing pond in the ravine. Santa Ysabel, like San Miguel, has remains of the Spanish period in its old adobes and ranch houses, all of which are carefully preserved. The soil of most of this region absorbs the rain as fast as it falls, so that the winter drives are always excellent. The flora is in some respects unique, flowers that belong to Mexico and San Diego having been found wild in this district, and one or two pines grow only on the Santa Lucias. The old settlers, hardly twelve years ago, used to live on venison and bear meat, and there are plenty of deer left in the "back country," fifteen or twenty miles away from the railroad and the Salinas. Near the coast, extending from the Pacific Ocean to the Santa Clara and San Mateo valleys, and from Monterey Bay to the lowlands that border the bay of San Francisco,

SANTA MONICA BEACH.

which are frequented in winter are the towns, such as Los Gatos, on the eastern slope, and the sheltered towns along the beaches of the west—Santa Cruz, Soquel, Aptos and Capitola. Santa Cruz is not only a summer watering place, but one of the most restful and beautiful of winter resorts, having charming drives in the woods and along the beaches and wave-carved rocks, and natural bridges. The gardens of Santa Cruz are wonderful in their color and the variety of their flowers. The most delicate plants bloom freely in the open air all winter, and the little cottages are covered with vines. The mountain drives from Santa Cruz are over roads that are in excellent order, summer and winter. Botanists say that in

to the noble beaches and high promontories grouped about old Monterey, the ancient Spanish capital, the centre of petty revolutions, the heart of that courtly dominion of padre and hidalgo long before the Americans had crossed the Mississippi. Like Santa Barbara and San Diego, Monterey has become one of the great pleasure resorts of the entire Pacific Coast. It is here, at the Hotel Del Monte Club House, that the lawn-tennis players of the coast have their headquarters. Summer and winter alike the high and pine-clad peninsula protects the beach and town from every harsh sea wind. Sand hills and rocks shut off the winds that sweep the length and breadth of the Salinas. The Monterey pines and cypresses, which are found in a native state nowhere else in such luxuriance, clothe the otherwise naked heights and make the famous forests so often painted and de-

SHOT IN THE FOOTHILLS.

hardly any other part of the State can so long a list of December blooming plants be found as along the streams and roads near Santa Cruz.

If one follows the great curve of Monterey Bay southward, across Pajaro Valley, across the sand hills of forgotten seas and across the broad "bottoms" along the Salinas, with its stormy and mighty river which drains more than five thousand square miles of territory, he comes at last

scribed. Skill and capital have created a resort at Monterey which has no equal on the Pacific Coast for beauty of scenery, for groves and lakes and natural gardens extending over nearly two hundred acres, and for drives which reach many miles down the coast, along the bays and beaches, far in the interior to the famous Mission El Carmelo, and over the cypress-clad cliffs where storm-twisted trees stand that were old when Padre Junipero Serra planted his cross at Monterey. Cypress Point and Midway Point are promontories that jut out into the Pacific from the bold coast line below the town. Pacific Grove and its fine sheltered beach, Carmel Bay, six miles south of Monterey, and many lesser but equally beautiful beaches, noted for pebbles, shells or seaweed, belong to the Monterey group and help to make the fame of the district. Much of the old town remains as it was a century ago, and the ancient Spanish *régime* can be studied here as well as anywhere

All the places I have been describing are easily accessible from San Francisco. The metropolis itself becomes the winter home of large numbers of Eastern and Australian tourists, on account of its fine hotels and places of amusement and the cheap excursions into the country. Four hours' journey takes one to Santa Cruz, or the entire length of the nearer coast valleys. Monte Diablo, Mount Tamalpais and Mount Hamilton are all within easy reach for winter expeditions. Across the bay are Oakland, Alameda, Berkeley and the State University. Down the San Mateo peninsula is Palo Alto, the site of the future Stanford University. At least a dozen mineral springs of repute and health resorts, open all the year

NEAR SAN FRANCISCO.

in California. Old town Monterey is haunted by the sketcher and the amateur photographer, and so are the old whaling station and the Chinese fisher village.

Monterey has a most delightful climate. The temperature is very seldom lower than 24° in midwinter, nor higher than 80° in midsummer. The difference between the mean temperature of January and July is not more than 6°. Bathing goes on throughout the year. On the beach, near the Del Monte Hotel, are four immense tanks constantly supplied with pure salt water, heated and graduated to different degrees of temperature. Most bathers prefer these tanks in winter, but many enjoy the open surf outside. The lake, the old oaks, ivy clad and picturesque, the Arizona garden, and the immediate surroundings of Del Monte are very attractive to tourists, and the hotel itself is one of the largest and most widely known on the Pacific Coast. I am told that the deep-water fishing off Monterey is attracting many sportsmen to the place.

around, are available within half a day's journey from San Francisco.

Three great bays, San Francisco, San Pablo and Suisun, form the chain of inland waters extending to the tule islands and vast marshes at the union of the two interior rivers. The bays sweep into the valley lands with deep inlets and wide "creeks," such as Louisianians call bayous. For more than fifty miles eastward one can sail with even a large yacht, and, counting in the broad "sloughs" and the bays, the region is like another Chesapeake, with higher, rockier shores and wilder promontories between the wide green valleys. So abundant are wild fowl along these inland waters that farmers often poison wild geese in their grain fields, and hunting parties are always welcome on the islands and in the settlers' cabins in the great hollow pastures of the dyke-defended tule region. There are many shooting clubs in San Francisco renting or owning shooting grounds, but large areas of country are unoccupied. To the sportsman one of the chief charms about San Francisco is that so much good winter shooting is to be obtained within easy reach. Besides the wild fowl there is good quail shooting in the brushy ridges of Tamalpais and along the lagunitas, hardly two hours' travel from the city. Marin, Alameda and San Mateo, the three counties nearest to San Francisco, still contain a great deal of lively quail shooting.

South, and well beyond the range of the central counties, a group of winter resorts and sheltered sea beaches lie about San Luis Obispo, another of the old mission towns. Port Harford is the seaport, and there is excellent winter fishing here, as well as in Estero Bay, about Moro and Cayucas. There is a superb hunting region up the coast, back of San Simeon and Piedras Blancas; but few persons ever go so far. There are fine mineral springs just coming into notice and an extremely wild coast line between the quiet beaches. Still south comes Santa Barbara, of which I have spoken, a place to which some of the best people go winter after winter, buy homes and settle down for life, because of the charm of

the sea at Santa Monica, Newport, Redondo Beach and Wilmington, and looks across at Santa Catalina Island. Los Angeles also looks inland to Pasadena, Sierra Madre, Monrovia, and half a hundred colonies and prosperous settlements in and around the San Gabriel Valley. All these are "winter resorts," well provided with hotels, sanitariums and the conveniences of modern life. I have been in Southern California almost every year, and beyond a doubt a person can find any climate that he desires between the seacoast and the San Bernardino valleys. The great orange country is at Riverside and Redlands, and about Pomona and the highest part of the San Gabriel Valley. Horticulturally the region is delightful, and a great pleasure to visit. It has been photographed and described over and over, until there is little left to say, except that it deserves its reputation for winter climate.

The San Diego shores have many fine bathing beaches, but none that compare with the sandy peninsula of Coronado, opposite the city of San Diego. The bathing here is fine the whole year round. In the winter it is about as warm as it is at Old Orchard Beach, Me., in June and July; in the summer it is much the

the region. The Cooper Olivarium, the Hollister homestead, the rose festivals of Santa Barbara, the old Spanish town and mission, and a thousand things in and around the pleasant and beautiful city have been written down in books without end.

Los Angeles looks down to

ADOBE HOUSES.

same as at Cape May in the season. Fishing off San Diego is not, as a rule, equal to that in and around Jupiter Inlet, Fla., and near Charlotte Harbor ; but from April to September the surface fishing, such as Spanish mackerel and barracuta, is fully as good, fishermen catching as high as from five hundred to one thousand pounds in a day, the only bait required being a piece of white canvas on the hook. Coronado is about a mile from San Diego, across the bay, and is connected by steam ferry and a motor railroad. The rarest of tropical plants grow out of doors. The temperature of air and sea is about the same in winter as in summer.

The rocky Coronado Islands are just over the Mexican line. The landlocked bay of San Diego, with its daily breeze, is fairly alive with sail boats and yachts, winter and summer. The weather is suitable for boating, riding, driving and outdoor exercise "for three hundred and sixty days in the year."

With the Humboldt Trappers
(1891)

OUTING.

VOL. XIX.   NOVEMBER, 1891.   No. 2.

WITH THE HUMBOLDT TRAPPERS.

BY CHARLES HOWARD SHINN.

THE Humboldt country is a heavily timbered region something more than two hundred miles north of San Francisco Bay. It is entirely off the line of any railroad and is only reached by coast-line steamers or by stage from Ukiah, Redding or Southern Oregon. It has magnificent forests, open glades and prairies, extensive marsh islands, great rivers and high mountains. Game of every kind known in Northern California is especially abundant, and there is no district of the Pacific Coast that offers greater inducements to the sportsman. The Adirondacks, much as they were a half century ago, but on a very much larger scale, can be found here in the "Humboldt back country." Here, too, is the district where the last of the famous trappers and hunters of the West have made their homes and are waiting for the end. They have tramped westward all the way from the Pecos and the Missouri; they fought with long-forgotten tribes of Indians on the plains and in the Rockies; they trapped beaver in the valley of the Sacramento before it held an American settlement; they were the pathmakers whose footsteps were followed by Bidwell, Reading and Fremont. They were

boys with the famous trapping expeditions of the early years of the century, and their heroes are such men as Lewis and Clarke, Saint Vrain, Kit Carson, "old man" Bridger and the Ashleys. They belong to an older and greater group of frontiersmen than the Buffalo Bills.

Here are some brief chapters of early exploration. About 1820 California was first reached by wandering trappers. In 1823 the Ashleys, with their comrades, hunted on the Merced, Stanislaus and Tuolumne. In 1825 Jedediah Smith, with forty trappers, explored the whole San Joaquin and Sacramento region. In 1830 the Ewing Young party trapped in the same districts and over much of the Northern California coast. In 1832 Michael Laframboise, with a number of Hudson Bay trappers, spent a year in Northern California; that company for ten years or more kept about fifty trappers at work within the present limits of the State. Many of the early trappers, entering California from the south, settled down in the Spanish settlements, married well and became large land owners. The Northern trappers gave their names to rivers and mountains and gradually sought shelter in the wildest parts of the Coast Range. They rarely or never "went to the mines," settled in the rich valleys or helped to found cities. Some of them married Indian wives; others found helpmates among the early Missourian immigrants to California. Those of them that still remain live in rugged old age on small "mountain ranches," miles removed from the towns, in what is still the heart of the wilder-

THE CABIN OF THE TRAPPER.

ness, and must so remain for many years to come.

Only a few years ago Stephen Hall Meek was still living on Scott Creek, north of Humboldt, in the Siskiyou country, but within the same timbered and wild district. Meek was with a party of trappers that first visited California in 1833 and wintered on Tulare Lake. I think that Meek is still alive, one of the oldest of the whole group of trappers. He was born in 1807 in Washington County, Virginia, and was, I believe, a cousin of President Polk. He was with Captain Bonneville and joined the Walker expedition that discovered the Truckee, Carson and Walker rivers. His whole career is full of the free picturesque elements ; he and his rifle belong together in the front with wild nature. Like Bridger, he only once or twice visited a city, and highly disapproved of civilization and " them deep city cañons " in which he invariably managed to get lost.

The horseback trail west from Junction City on the Trinity River leads presently into the wild country that the old trappers love. I say the horseback trail, for there is no wagon road for thirty miles or more, and when you again reach settlements the roads are barely passable until you come to the rich valleys and farm lands or to the logging camps, which need good highways for hauling their supplies. But in the region of horseback trails you will occasionally come across an old man with his pack mule and rifle, slowly climbing some steep pine-covered ridge. You can see at a glance that he is no prospector nor cattleman nor even a sheep herder moving to another district. All these have pots and pans, weighty luggage and various impedimenta. The old trapper has only blankets, match box, pipe and rifle. He will live in the woods for months, and go back to his cabin with a mule load of dried venison. He never needlessly destroys game ; the instincts of a true sportsman are his, and if he saw a city dude aiming at a doe with fawns he would probably break the dude's gun across a pine stump and order him to " git back to San Francisco." Though he is all hunter now, he is something more besides ; the long years of his trapper training have given him a close and accurate knowledge of the ways of many birds and beasts that ordinary hunters think beneath their notice. For this reason, if for no other, the best possible guide over the vast Mendocino, Humboldt, Trinity and Siskiyou mountain land is an old trapper. His beaver traps that were set in the Snake and Shoshone in the midst of savage foes in days of old now lie rusting, forgotten in the gulch by his cabin, but that perfect training of every sense that came from those years of outdoor life still remains the marvel of young men.

I hardly know how to describe the fullness and variety of nature - knowledge that one finds in the best men of this old trapper type. Let a simple illustration suffice. A friend of mine once collected butterflies and moths for several years. He became quite an authority on the subject and his carefully-labeled specimens were very attractive. He removed to a town in the mountains, and making the acquaintance of an old trapper asked him to the house to " look at the butterflies." He pulled out drawer after drawer without eliciting a word of comment from his guest. Suddenly the latter pointed to a small and obscure butterfly, saying, " That is a scurce kind."

" It's extinct," said my friend.

" What's that ? "

" All dead ; no more of them anywhere."

" Not much they ain t. But, as I told yer, they is scurce. I only noticed that sort once, in a cañon about half a mile across. As you went up the gulch first was that kind," pointing to another species ; " then this sort that you say is petered out, then that other sort. I noticed them all in one little ' flat,' but I was trailin' a grizzly and so I didn't stop long."

My friend got a county map, and the old trapper leaned over it.

" Up Mad River, so far —Wild Cat Creek comes in about thar ; not on this map. Follow up Wild Cat about three miles ; thar's an oak bottom, the first of any size. Two gulches

comes down on the left hand ; take the second, and somewhere about the middle of it, if you hit the butterfly season, ye'll find them yellow speckled ones that you said was all ' extinct.' "

The next year my friend made a trip to the back country, and found the lost species in the identical pocket of the hills that the old trapper had described. It has never been found anywhere else.

The botanists owe some of their most important " discoveries " of new plants in the Humboldt region to these forest trackers, who could tell them where to look for rare forms. I once knew a country school teacher who spent his vacations botanizing in the mountains and hunting up every old trapper. He told me that it was a common experiment of his to place his specimen book of dried plants before one of them, and have him say something like this : " Well, young man, there's a plant on a ridge about *so* far north that you ought ter gather."

" What is it like ? "

" Sort of mountain lilac, only different from any you've got. Scarce up here ; may be lots of it somewhere else." Then a terse, vivid description followed, from which the species could often be determined.

The cabin of the trapper may be of logs or of stakes riven out of oak or pine. In a few cases it is built of slabs of limestone broken f r o m ledges, but usually the only use made of these natural walls, w h e r e the stone lies already quarried, is to furnish the materials for the h u g e outside chimneys that often fill o n e

THE LAST OF THE EIGHT.

TREED, AND HOBSON'S CHOICE.

Douglas City now stands. In 1852 Kinman helped to explore the Humboldt region, and in 1853 became the hunter fort For Humboldt, at Bucksport, near Eureka. The fort was one of the most popular posts on the coast, and many distinguished officers were stationed there at one time or another. Lieutenant, afterward General, Crook, the Indian fighter, shot his first bear under Kinman's guidance. Lieutenant U. S. Grant was one of the most popular of the young West Pointers at the fort, and the pioneers tell many stories of his hunting trips.

Seth Kinman became a well-known character when James Buchanan was elected President. He was much stirred in soul over the election of a Pennsylvanian, and so he made an armchair of splendid Humboldt County elk horns, fastened together with clamps of Pennsylvania iron. This he took to Washington and gave to the newly-elected President on May 23, 1857. Much to his own surprise, the chair and himself were the subjects of extended newspaper comment; the leading New York dailies devoted several columns to interviews with the old trapper. At that time Kinman was in the prime of life, over six feet high and extremely massive. His dress was buckskin throughout, and he carried a heavy bowie knife and rifle. When he reached San Francisco on his way to New York, he explained his errand in the following terms:

"Anybody can make a cheer, but I take a little credit for the elk horns. My range is from Bear River Valley to Oregon, an' this winter I killed and stored more meat than usual, so I thought I would take it easy, an' I sot about makin' this cheer for 'Old Buck.' After I got

gable of the cabin. Where stone is scarce these chimneys are made of sticks laid in clay, and a huge box of puddled clay forms the fireplace. Unlike the "shanties" that one finds in the "second-growth" forests of the Atlantic slope, these pioneer cabins of the far West are large, comfortable and picturesque. They stand in sunny glades of the unruined forests of redwoods and oaks ; the mountains rise high above them, and wide, clear rivers flow past. I have slept many a night in such hospitable shelters, and made my breakfast on trout fresh from the brook and quail from the chapparal. The old trappers live on the fat of the wilderness.

There has been no more remarkable trapper in the Humboldt region than Seth Kinman, the "maker of Presidential chairs." Kinman was born in Union County, Pennsylvania, in 1815, and when a lad left his home to seek adventures in the Western country. He trapped and hunted with many exploring parties, until in the spring of 1850 he joined Major Reading's noted company that prospected the Trinity basin, and "took mule loads of gold" out of Reading Bar, where

it done, the boys in our parts thought it would do to travel on, so I thought I would go on with it myself, and started with my rifle and powder horn. Nobody has ever sot in this cheer and never shall till after the President does."

In due time the trapper and the chair reached Washington. General Denver introduced Kinman, and "in the midst of loud applause," to quote from the newspaper reports of the time, "the President sat down in the elk-horn armchair." Kinman enjoyed his trip so much that he made a similar chair and gave it to Lincoln. He sent Andrew Johnson a grizzly-bear chair, one of the strangest combinations imaginable, and in 1876 President Hayes was the recipient of another elk-

at Rich Bar, on the upper Trinity, without sufficient provisions and poorly clad; they determined to reach the coast instead of returning to the Sacramento Valley, as the rest of the miners were doing. They started November 5 with only ten days' provisions, and the weather was so bad that they had a horrible time of it. After reaching Humboldt Bay, on December 20, they tried to go down the coast to reach some settlement. They divided into two parties, and it is hard to say which suffered most. Captain Gregg died of starvation, another man was badly torn by a grizzly, and all were mere wrecks of their former selves by the time they reached the towns. They were in a game country, but they were poor in

THERE STOOD VAN DUZEN, RELOADING HIS RIFLE (FOR THE FOURTH TIME).

horn chair. Up in Humboldt he is known as the Presidential chair maker, and it is the fond belief of his old cronies in the backwoods that the results of Seth's labors are veritable chairs of state and the proudest possessions of the White House.

One of the most disastrous of the early expeditions into the Humboldt region was that of the Gregg company of placer miners from Trinity County in the winter of 1849. These miners found themselves

woodcraft, and it was the rainy season, when it was next to impossible to keep their ammunition dry.

One of the party, however, a miner named Van Duzen, made a bear record early in December that is hard to beat, even in the days of repeater rifles. L. K. Wood, the historian of the party, writes: "I heard the report of a rifle, then two more in quick succession. I hastened to his assistance and shall not soon forget what I saw. There stood Van Duzen, reloading his rifle (for the fourth time); near by lay three grizzly bears, two dead and one with his back broken. Two smaller ones stood near, looking first upon their fallen comrades and then upon us." Wood was ready and shot one of them, and a third member of the party, named Wilson, killed the last of the grizzlies. This shooting was done with old-fashioned Kentucky rifles at very close range—not more than fifteen paces. Van Duzen's remark, as reported, was: "Well, boys, I'm glad you come up ; but I was good for one more."

Presuming too much upon their good fortune and hungry enough to "eat fried boot leather," Wood and three others, a month later, attacked eight grizzlies in a forest glade ; they shot one bear, but the others treed them instantly. One poor fellow was forced to take an exceedingly small sapling, it being Hobson's choice, and as it bent over with his weight two of the bears clawed him down and mauled him to their satisfaction for an hour or more. He was a badly used-up hunter, but his companions carried him to the settlements and eventually he recovered.

This article would be incomplete without a few words about the mountaineer in his "hours of ease." Scattered through the great northern wilderness of California are "post-office corners" and small towns that nestle in bends of rivers or in fertile mountain valleys. The stage roads are the connecting links, and the stage driver is still the hero of the epic. At intervals, where horseback trails that lead to lonely cattle ranches meet the highways, are wayside inns, overgrown cabins, where some pioneer of a thrifty turn of mind will care for one's horse and dispense a rude but lavish hospitality at very reasonable rates. How picturesque these frontier wayside inns appear may be seen in the illustration from a photograph taken last year. All sorts of curiosities seem to drift naturally to such a place, and the old trappers haunt it in their times of recreation. Though they are a sober folk when afield, most of them know how to "even up" during the rainy season.

But, after all, these weaknesses can easily be forgotten. It was a strange, strong race of pathmakers whose trail across the continent ends under the mighty redwoods. These, who rank among the last of the trappers, heroes of many a nameless fight, soldiers of many a forlorn hope, have cities and states as their monuments. They led the way before the gold seekers ; they crossed the continent the advance guard of the man with axe and plow; they still walk the forests, rifle in hand, heedless of the woodchopper, the land speculator, the planter of vineyards and orchards. Pretty soon the last one of the old trappers will be gone, and his rifle, his chair, his fallen cabin will be relics of a departed age. Then, as all the memories of the trappers fade and move farther and farther into the past, strange legends will cluster about them and a new race of giants will dwell at last in some vast world mythology whose foundations are being laid even now.

THE MOUNTAINEER IN HIS "HOURS OF EASE."

California on Horseback
(1890)

CALIFORNIA ON HORSEBACK.

BY CHARLES HOWARD SHINN.

L D pioneers, of Virginia and Kentucky stock, who have ridden their thousands of miles, have been heard to say that California is the paradise of the horseman. If history and tradition count for anything, there ought to be a race of superb riders here. Before the Americans came the country belonged to men who lived in the saddle. The land, for hundreds of miles, was unfenced and untilled. Horses and cattle were so abundant that in years of drought they were sometimes killed to save pasturage. Whoever found his horse tired turned him loose and caught another, and ordinary mustangs were sold for one dollar apiece.

Gen. John Bidwell, one of the first Americans in the Sacramento Valley, has told me that the California of 1845, before the discovery of gold, was the most beautiful country to ride over that ever existed in the world. The wild oats, as tall as a man's head, covered all the valleys and even the foothills. Wild flowers, of species now almost extinct, bloomed in masses of many acres. To this day, when the pioneers get together, they talk of this picturesque early California of the horseman, when every settler was more or less of a vaquero and lived outdoors most of the year. General Bidwell once rode up the Napa Valley with several native Californians. It was in April, and the grizzly bears were so numerous that ten or twelve were often seen in a single day. Half a dozen Mexican vaqueros were more than a match for the fiercest of

grizzlies in the open. They would lasso him from all sides and hold him still, while one of them slipped from the saddle with a knife and put a period to the story.

The California of fifty years ago has disappeared, but it is still the land of the horseman as much as those Upper Alleghany regions where a wheeled vehicle is seldom seen. Its great mountain wildernesses are crossed, to be sure, by beaten highways, but back and forth between them is woven the network of horseback trails from house to house and ridge to ridge. The wonderful forests of redwood and sugar pine, called by Professor Sargent the finest coniferous forests on the face of the earth, are unfenced for hundreds of miles. The country is still unspoiled for the horseman. The people, too, are frank, friendly and hospitable, ready to guide one to the best trout stream or to the likeliest ravine for deer. There is no place in America better than California for the man who wishes to escape the beaten paths and who enjoys grand scenery, new character studies, botany, hunting or fishing. But railroads and stages only carry one into the desired region. No one except the horseman is made free of the whole realm of the Californian wilderness.

There are several distinct courses open to a horseback traveler who starts from the vicinity of San Francisco. He can go south into the Santa Cruz redwoods among the campers and the vineyards. Within seventy-five miles of San Francisco is the heart of these great redwood forests, which the railroad only crosses at one point. He can arrange for a far longer and more varied journey, northward along the coast, or somewhat inland through the first range of valleys. Either route carries one across Marin, Sonoma, Mendocino, Humboldt and Siskiyou counties, four hundred miles to the boundary of Oregon. Thence one might go along the Cascades, or by the shores of the Pacific to Puget Sound and the tree-clad islands of that huge inland sea. It is a marvelously interesting journey, past pioneer cabins and growing towns, past cool, dark rivers bordered with blossoming azaleas, past acres of ripe salmon berries, where the cinnamon bears revel in the delicious fruit. There are great lumber mills, smoky and grim, standing in ravines by the ocean, by iron wharves over the cliffs. There are hundreds of loggers at work in the redwood forests, the last and the greatest of the native trees of the United States.

But the most comprehensive journey to be made in California, starting from San Francisco, would begin by making a dash for the Sierras. This route would first cross to the east shore, then thread the Coast Range foothills and descend upon the broad Sacramento-San Joaquin plain or valley. Crossing this, the horseman ascends the long, equable slopes of the Sierra to the old gold-mining camp districts and the counties that represent more than the rest of the State, the California of "'49." His course must then lie north, exploring the width of the range from valley to snow, as far north as Lassen and Shasta, and making the ascent of these two grand mountains. Magnificent is all this Sierra region, for its forests of pine and cedar, its lakes, its deep cañons, its waterfalls and mountain torrents as yet unphotographed. Then, if after the ascent of Shasta the horseman wishes to complete his summer in the saddle with absolute splendor, so that its rounded circle shall seem in subsequent life a supreme inspiration, he can cross to the Siskiyou ranges west and thread the wildest ravines of the Coast Range, across Trinity and along the Gualala and beneath the rhododendron copses and redwood forests of Noyo and Navarra.

As I have said, California is still the land of the horseback traveler whenever one escapes from stage and railroad. There are hundreds of cattle trails in the mountains where wagons cannot go. The farther one goes from the valley the more people he finds who use the saddle habitually, less for pleasure than for business. Drovers and speculators, young farmers, hunters, prospectors, all are apt to prefer a saddle horse to a wagon. As yet there are no tourists, no professional pleasure seekers, on the unfrequented horseback trails. I once spent the best part of a summer in the saddle and rode over some twelve large counties without meeting a single person who was taking a similar journey "for nothing but the fun of the thing."

When I first rose to the conception of cutting loose from the burdens and complexities of city life and living a sort of nomadic existence until I had seen the greater part of central and northern California, the thought was very attractive. To spend a summer in the saddle was a scheme worthy of Thoreau. But it soon became evident that success depended upon close attention to all the details. First and most important, the horse ; second, the outfit ; third, the route to be taken. I went to one of the ranches and picked out a strong young American horse, who did excellent service and never lost a day from sickness or otherwise. I invested in a Spanish saddle and a pair of saddle bags. A leather roll behind the saddle for a blanket completed the outfit. It is surprising with how little baggage a man can travel half across the continent. The less he has the better it is for his horse and for himself. He can get some of his meals at village hotels or farm houses or pioneer cabins, and he can sleep under a roof nearly every night if he chooses. But the best plan is to have a stake rope and let your horse feed all night and during the hot part of the day, while you lie rolled up in your blanket under an adjacent tree. A man who has had training and is master of woodcraft will manage to cook his own game, on a pinch, without taking along enough baggage to load a pack mule. But, since no two people will plan for the same outfit, it is useless to discuss this point any further.

The valley farm where the story of my journey properly begins is in the heart of southern Alameda, thirty miles from San Francisco, in the midst of orchards, vineyards and fields of wheat. It was sunrise, I remember, when I started and rode toward the hills, past a placid lagoon, where a red-shirted Portuguese boy was paddling toward a flock of ducks in the farther end by a clump of willows. Four miles brought me to the vineyards of the old Mission San José. Here are crumbling adobes, all that are left of the Spanish Mission establishment of a century ago. Here are groves of orange, fig and olive and palms tall in the sun. From the Mission a winding cañon leads into the Stockton Pass, and that into Sunol Valley. East of this is a broad range of hills, beyond which the San Joaquin lies, and the Sierra snow peaks are on the far eastern horizon.

The foothills of eastern Alameda are large enough to be called respectable mountains in many States. The forest growth is sparse and chiefly deciduous. Masses of oaks cling to the northern slopes, and spotted trunks of sycamore gleam through tangles of blackberry vines and wild clematis. But even in these hills there are byways worth exploration, narrow trails which only a horseman can follow, leading to wood camps and trout streams. On one of these hilltops is a Russian colony, whose leader and founder is an old exile from the Ukraine. Over the door of his home he has placed in bold letters the Russian word "Svboda," liberty. " That is she whom I worship " he once said to me. The old man has a garden of grapes, oranges and olives on the crest of a hill. Here he sits under his trees and brews Russian beer, and tells stories of adventure and political intrigue that would make a novelist's fortune. On the side of the ravine below is a limestone cave fronting the west and overlooking the whole valley and bay. Here, in a sepulchre of stone, the old Russian freedom lover expects to rest from his labors.

From the summit of the Coast Range one obtains a wonderful combination of hill and bay, of cultivated lowland and wild upland, of village, town, meadow, grain fields, orchards and vineyards, stretching to the blue San Mateo hills in soft undulations and under the golden haze of the Californian atmosphere. South rise Mission Peak, Mount Hamilton, where the Lick Observatory is situated ; north is Monte Diablo and northeast is Tamalpais. San Francisco is in full sight, crowned on its peninsula, and the broad bay fills the distance with color.

As one rides down the eastern slopes of the Coast Range, after having explored its recesses thoroughly, almost the first thing he notices is the wonderful color of the San Joaquin plains. It is from the acres of wild flowers that grow in great colonies of purples and golds, of blues and crimsons. The whole plain for miles is brilliant with lilac-hued gillias, pale-cream cups, scarlet-flushed gold of wild poppies, ultramarine blue of larkspurs, the clear heaven blue of nemophilas—these and multitudes of others, all woven into a Persian carpet pattern, of which the separate figures are acre-wide splashes of color.

In many respects the San Joaquin is now an old story, monotonous to cross, and interesting only because of the immense extent of country now being irrigated and turned into gardens and vineyards. But there is an unknown land of the lower San Joaquin, near the mouth of the river, along the Sacramento and around the innumerable tule islands. Take a duck-hunter's punt and push into the winding channels of these fresh-water sloughs. Here are blue marsh lakes, lonely and lovely, as beautiful as the expanses of the Louisiana bayous. Over them lean borders of wild sunflowers, tules, reeds, cat-tails, grasses in blossom and purple marsh flowers. Clumps of ancient willows, as hoary as those that grow by the rivers of Holland, cover Indian mounds on these green islands. In a slough one sometimes finds the decaying hulk of a schooner that once sailed to forgotten towns, and to deserted river landings, or "embarcaderos," as they were once called. Stern-wheel steamers pass with deck loads of grain, hay and firewood. Italian and Chinese fishermen drag their nets in the deeper channels. Dredgers lie beside the fertile islands that money and energy have reclaimed, building the levees still higher against the yellow April floods from the Sierras. I once had my horse and myself ferried across from island to island and rode through the heart of this Holland of California, that extends for fifty miles along its central rivers. The reclaimed islands have prosperous dairies, broad wheat fields, acres of vegetables and small fruits ; but the reclaimed territory is only a small part of the whole area of the tule lowlands. It is the great centre of the wild-fowl hunting in California after the first November rains.

From the lowlands one reaches the foothills of the Sierras by an almost imperceptible ascent. The finer horticultural developments are near the hills, and the interest of the journey increases as one leaves the valley. Along the creeks are immense masses of the wild grapevine of California. They grow on the bottoms and climb over the tallest trees, trailing down to the water's edge, forming leafy domes and arches, and mingling with oaks, laurels and sycamores. The ordinary tourist never sees them ; but in such valleys as Napa, Sonoma and Santa Clara, and especially along the upper Sacramento, they are superb, and the pride of all the old settlers. Sometimes one can ride for hours past vines of this fragrant wild grape, and under its shelters.

A great deal has been said about the California Missions—those adobe churches and priest gardens of the last century, whose picturesque ruins are found in the coast counties south of San Francisco. But a man who rides over California finds many adobe ruins of a different sort—the remains of the private residences of the Spanish era. These occur in the most unexpected places. One is riding up a cañon in the foothills and comes upon an adobe ruin, fast crumbling into a mound of black clay. Perhaps it stands beside a giant white oak or pine. There is always a spring or a stream near, and often, too, there are fig trees or grapevines, neglected, run wild, trampled by wandering cattle, but still bearing fruit. The traveler who studies California from the accustomed routes will seldom have a chance to see these old adobes in the foothills ; they have not even been listed and described by local antiquarians.

I remember some of the rivers of the Sierras—the Cosumnes, the Calaveras, the Stanislaus, the Mokelumne, the American, the Cloud—along whose banks the landscape painters of half a continent might wander and find inspiration. Tracing the course of such a river as the Mokelumne upward from the valley, one finds low mounds of gray gravel in the recesses of the grass - green hills, over which thousands of miners toiled in the brave days of "'49." There are knolls blue as the sky and white as sea foam, with flowers and wild shrubs, and out of deep ravines dark promontories lift abrupt rocks and silver-needled pines above the river. Across a mountain tributary that foams down between walls of brown and yellow a rude bridge extends, and a pioneer's cabin nestles in the manzanita bushes and under tall oaks beyond, while

through his rocky hillside garden flow fertilizing streams from an old flume built by the Argonauts of California.

All summer long I rode through the Sierras, under forests of Douglas spruce, sugar pine, Lawson cypress and sequoias. I rode in happy and careless freedom by mountain roads, by trails of old prospectors, through valleys as yet peopled by only a pastoral community. Sometimes for a week I was on one of the great Sierra highways that bind the mountain counties together—a highway throbbing with life, cloudy with dust of freight teams, bustling with travel of every sort. Old toll gates stand by bridges across the rivers ; old wayside inns look from under apple and peach trees. Now and then I found a town deep hid in the quartz-veined hills, and changing from the mining era to the still more golden era of horticulture. And all along the great highway a wise horseman reins his horse to talk with shepherds driving their flocks to higher pastures, with miners going with pick and drill to work their claims, with hunters riding down from the mountains with their game slung behind their saddle.

Half a mile away from the great highway and all grows still. Loneliness broods in the forest. I followed narrow bridle paths, "short cuts" from farm to farm. Sometimes the cabin to which they led had been deserted, the door broken in, the leaves drifted on the floor, the tracks of wildcat and coyote everywhere. In these wildernesses human life ebbs and flows. Nature is so strong that she soon obliterates the feeble traces of men, and takes back a part of her domain from the careless hands of the pioneers. Then come the hunters, the fishermen, the botanists, the pleasure seekers, and rediscover it all. That is what will happen with that high hill country of California which is now so unknown a region.

Fishing & Fishermen
in Southern California
(1903)

FISHING AND FISHERMEN IN SOUTHERN CALIFORNIA

By CHARLES FREDERICK HOLDER

Mrs. A. W. Barrett and Her 416-Pound Black Bass.

ODS are not put away during the winter in Southern California, for there are the whitefish, the sheepshead and the rock bass always to be had offshore; but as spring comes on there is greater activity, and the best fishing, the real sport, is in the spring and summer, where the black current that sweeps down the coast is tempered by the semi-tropic sun, and the shore is swarming with bait.

The mainland Pacific Coast presents many anomalies. Harbors, coves and bays it has only to a limited extent, the coast between San Francisco and San Diego being, in the Eastern sense, with one exception, without protected bays for the fishermen. The wind blows freshly every day, and the sea rolls in eternally upon long sandy beaches, broken here and there by rocky headlands. To fish with a small boat rigged with a chair, and the con-

veniences one finds on the St. Lawrence, is almost impossible. The professional fisherman goes offshore in his heavy sailboat from one mile to three, and trolls for barracuda or yellowtail, or sets trawllines along the rocky points. In Southern California the water in the morning is often smooth, but in the afternoon the wind rises and the sea comes in. To enable fishermen to reach the fishing and retain their equipoise, many towns and resorts, as Santa Monica, Long Beach, Redondo, Ocean Park, Terminal and Coronado, have built long and expensive piers, which are well patronized by anglers, who fish with long bamboo poles, stout enough to lift a heavy fish, and hand-lines, and catch surf fish, mackerel, and other small fishes. At Redondo, because of the setting in of a deep channel, yellowtail and sea bass are caught from the high pier, and occasionally a black sea bass. At Coronado the fishing at the pier is for yellow-fin, surf fish and small shore fishes. To obtain larger game the angler goes offshore from one to three miles with the professional fishermen, or to the entrance of the fine bay.

This wharf-fishing is eminently satisfactory to the angler whose piscatorial fancy is whetted by small fry, yellowfin and surf fish, which can be lifted in by the pole; but California has a series of large game fishes which afford all the sport of the salmon, the maskalonge, the bluefish and the tarpon; and to take them in a sportsmanlike manner, with the lightest lines and rods, requires smooth water and small boats, and to find these one must go to the Southern Californian islands, where the equipment and environment are perfect. These islands, beginning north of Santa Barbara, are San Miguel, Santa Rosa, Santa Cruz, Anacapa, San Nicolas, Santa Catalina and San Clemente. All lie parallel to the coast, forming a lee to the north and east, where the angler finds almost perfect conditions. San Miguel, Santa Cruz and Santa Rosa are reached from Santa Barbara. All are private property, and permission must be obtained to camp. This and the fact that bait is uncertain, there being no professional fishermen resident upon the islands, and no regular boat, has tended to discourage anglers. One hundred miles to the south, off Los Angeles County, lie two large islands— San Clemente and Santa Catalina—about which nature has done her best for the angler. The location seems to be a favored one, a common ground for all fishes. The islands are about twenty miles in length, Santa Catalina being about seventeen miles from the mainland, and San Clemente, a Government reservation, about forty. The former has fifteen miles of good lee, affording water as smooth as a lake, in a number of bays and coves formed by the cañons. The water is deep along shore, intensely blue, and the fishing on the line of fringing kelp.

Santa Catalina is the only island having a town and regular daily communication with the mainland, Avalon being well equipped with hotels and cottages—a unique spot, possessing everything required by the angler. The bay is filled with boats and small launches equipped and furnished with every appliance for the capture of the great game fishes of the region.

The peculiarity of this Californian angling is the large size of the fish, their great numbers, the remarkable equipment for the accommodation of anglers—the boatmen being provided with the best rods, lines and reels—and finally the climatic conditions, which afford the angler pleasant weather, without storms, from May to November. The tuna is the tarpon of the Pacific Coast, and is caught only at this island, between Avalon Bay and Long Point, a distance of about five miles. It is an oceanic fish, which explains its absence from the mainland shores. The season is from June to August.

Tuna rods are not less than six feet nine inches, and often seven or eight feet in length; the line not over 24 thread; the tip of the rod, or that portion from reel seat to tip does not weigh more than sixteen ounces. The short rods of noibe or split bamboo are for tuna and black sea bass, the longer ones for yellowtail; and for the latter up to thirty pounds a No. 12 line is the proper thing, at least to my

mind. The reels are strong and good; in point of fact, cheap tackle is the most expensive here. The boat is a large, wide-beamed yawl, with a diminutive three or four horse-power engine, and there are numbers of small launches of similar fittings in the bay. The boatman and gaffer sits amidships. Another seat extends from rail to rail, with two comfortable chairs facing astern for oneself and companion. Thus equipped, rods in hand, the boat is shoved off and cuts the smooth waters of the bay. It is to be yellowtail, and the lines are run out sixty feet, the engine slows down to about the rate of slow rowing, the course set along the kelp-lined shore, about which the rocks rise in picturesque bluffs and cliffs, reaching back to melt into the mountains of the interior. It is July or August, but the air is cool, and as far as the eye can reach the sea is like glass.

The anglers are lost in the beauty of the surroundings when z-e-e, z-e-e-e goes the reel, its high staccato notes rising so loudly that an angler in a boat near by shouts his congratulations. The fish are plungers. Down into the deep blue they go; z-e-e-e, z-e-e-e-e-e! rising on the soft tremulous air, the line humming its peculiar music. Now, started by the big multiplier, the fish comes up, breaking away with feet and inches to again plunge, circling the boat with savage onward rushes. Lines cross, but rods are passed over and under. Ten, twenty minutes have passed away, and as fast as the fish comes in, it breaks away again to the melody of the singing reel. Finally, deep in the blue water a dazzling spot appears; then another, and up they come, by a marvel not fouling. Now one circles the boat; away it goes at sight of the gaff, z-e-e-e! to come in again. Five times it circles the boat, displaying its beauties to the anglers; a blaze of glory, canted upward, its silvery belly gleaming in the morning sun, its back an iridescent green, the fins, median line and tail yellow. The boatman is fingering his gaff. "Now, then!" whispers the angler. The tip of the rod goes forward, a quick movement, a blinding splash of water with the last compliments of the yellowtail, and the gaffer straightens up with the fish of fishes quivering, trembling, still fighting, to receive its quietus. "Thirty-two and a half pounds, sir," and glancing at his watch, "in twenty-two minutes."

The common fish is the yellowtail (*Seriola dorsalis*), a sociable fellow, coming within ten feet of the boat to take the bait, playing about in full view, its golden tints flashing with gleams of green and blue. It is usually caught trolling slowly; but from the wharf or from a boat it is often taken by allowing the bait to lie on the bottom. The cleverness and discrimination of the yellowtail are unequaled. Toss over a handful of sardines, and the big fish will dash at them, picking up every one except that containing the hook. In many years' fishing at this island, I have never seen a yellowtail under seven pounds, the largest weighing sixty-three; but a specimen has been taken which, headless and cleaned, weighed eighty pounds.

The yellowtails arrive in March and April, and in midsummer are at the islands in countless numbers. In August last, four rods took sixty of these fish, averaging thirty pounds, in a day. The record catch is that of Colonel C. P. Morehous, who is credited with a fifty-nine-pound fish. While yellowtail is the *pièce de résistance* of this angling feast, there is another fish in these waters—the white sea bass—which appeals to the angler. The yellowtails, which have been dashing about the boat, suddenly disappear, the color of the bottom changes to dark brown —the cause, a dense school of sardines, which are packed so closely that they seem to be a solid mass. They are being driven up the coast by the sea bass, and a change of method becomes necessary. The dead smelt is taken off and the bare hook cast into the affrighted throng. A slight jerk, and a sardine is impaled, rushing off, as lively a bait as could be imagined. Its erratic actions frighten the rest, which form a hollow down through which the blue water is seen, and into which the struggling bait sinks deeper and deeper, until it clears the school; then out of the unknown rises a mighty fish shaped like a salmon. The sardine disappears as though by magic. *Z-e-e-e, tse-e-e-e-e!* The shriek of the reel, the burning hiss of the line as it cuts the water, the flying leather from the brake tell of game worth the having. The bass cuts a mighty swath in the sardine school, and is away

on the surface—no sulker he. Fifty, one hundred, two, three hundred feet of the delicate line are jerked off to the measure of the click—music indeed, vibrant, shrill and exciting; then the brake stops the fish, and he is away. No, he is coming in, a living finny charger.

There may be multipliers quadrupled which can eat up three hundred feet of line while this magnificent fish is covering that distance at the top of his speed, but I never have seen one. On it comes, like the shadow of a cloud. The angler sees it as he reels, and knows that it has fifty feet of line towing behind; then suddenly it turns, with a magnificent swirl of its powerful tail, and is away. It is a trick that fails. The thread of line, which would part at the slightest jerk, slips beneath the brake as it comes taut, and the angler fortunately turns it, and the bass circles the boat fifty feet away, its high dorsal fin cutting the water like a scythe. Three times it goes completely around the boat, constantly increasing its pace, but always coming in. The dexterous gaffer begins to estimate the distance, and the angler is about to pass the fish to the position for gaffing, when it turns, and the reel again gives tongue. But this is the beginning of the end. For nearly thirty minutes the bass has played, and is tugging bravely, bearing off like a sturdy craft on a lee shore, its white belly lightly showing. A final turn, a beating of waters, a shower of spray, and the grand fish is held on the cruel barb, to beat the boat powerful blows, to plunge and carry the gaffer's elbow into the water in its last desperate rush. But the gaff is inexorable, and slowly the fish comes up, protesting every inch; and in the sun a thousand tints and scintillations seem to flash and play upon it. The belly is white, grading into gray; the upper portion, old gold with iridescent hues; the head a blaze of peacock blue in iridescent flashes to pink and indescribable tints ever changing in the sun. Nearly five feet in length, and tipping the scales at fifty pounds, on a sixteen-ounce rod, No. 12 line, are incidents in the verdict.

The bass (*Cynoscion nobilis*) is a cousin of the weakfish, and in these waters averages fifty pounds. Four I caught in one morning were all of this weight, or over. Like the yellowtail, the white sea bass is a very sociable fish, some of the

The Anglers and Fleet of Boats Typical of Southern California Fishing Resorts.

best catches having been made twenty feet from shore. But the season is short and uncertain, from May until July. These fishes attain a weight of one hundred pounds. The record rod catch of the Tuna Club in Avalon bay is fifty-eight pounds.

The tuna is game for the veteran, but the inexperienced angler may work up to it by practising on albicore, a gamy long-finned oceanic fish found at the Californian islands the year around. A sixty-three-pound fish towed an angler three miles before it could be brought to gaff. If larger game is desired without the extreme excitement of the tuna, the black sea bass affords it. This is the giant of the bass tribe, ranging here up to four hundred pounds. The record rod catch with 21-thread line is a four-hundred-and-twenty-five-pound fish, caught by Edward Llewellyn. The bass, like all of its kind, affects the rocks and the great beds of kelp which form halls and parterres beneath the sea, in comparatively shallow water inshore. The boat is anchored in twenty-five or thirty feet of water, and arrangements made to cast off at short notice. The equipment is a single tip rod, the line a thread of 16 or 21 strand, with long wire leader, and Van Vleck tarpon hook. The bait is four or five pounds of barracuda, or a live white fish. This is cast into the clear places in the kelp, or near it, or suspended three or four feet from the bottom, as the angler may choose; either way accomplishes the purpose and lures the big game. The strike of the tuna is a magnificent rush, sometimes a leap upward, sometimes down; that of the yellowtail a single powerful plunge, a miniature lightning stroke with electric effects; but the king of the bass is more deliberate, reminding one of the methods of the great Mexican barracuda. The line begins to move, to tremble and twitch. A few inches go over the rail, the reel sounds a note of alarm, then another, and the line runs slowly out. Five feet have gone when the angler gives the fish the butt, and the bass gives the retort courteous. I have seen a strong man jerked elbow deep—this on the handline; but with the reel, it means a long musical prelude in various keys, the bass tearing off the line by the fathom. The boatman casts off the anchor buoy, grasps his oars, and heading out to sea, surging

through the water, towing the boat, the big game is away, the sport is on.

These fishes have resorts in deeper water from an eighth to a quarter of a mile offshore, and they invariably rush to the groves of deep-lying kelp into which they can dart, soon breaking the line. The oarsman rows against the fish, the angler endeavors to stop the rush by applying the leather brake, and finally a vibrant pumping motion is felt and the bass rises gradually, then comes in, to suddenly turn and break away. The contest may be anywhere from one hour to three; the fish may tow the boat two or three miles offshore and bring it in again, or it may play within a few yards of where it was hooked. Finally the big multiplier wins and brings the fish to gaff; and be the angler a novice, there comes to him out of the depths an amazing fish, a gigantic image of the black bass, fin for fin, mahogany tinted, with silvery belly and large eyes. As it feels the gaff its ponderous tail rises, and angler and gaffer are swept with a small tidal wave. It rises, plunges, tips the boat dangerously, and must be killed before it is brought in, then almost filling the boat. Little wonder that those who fail to see such catches are affected with doubts, as the black sea bass is stupendous, and when hung up at the stand of the gaffer, with the thread-like line dangling from its mouth, and the split bamboo standing against it, it seems incomprehensible that these trifles have killed so powerful, so gigantic a fish.

These delightful waters abound in small fry that afford excellent sport. There is the sheepshead, ranging up to fifteen pounds, caught within one hundred feet of the rocks, on a twelve-ounce rod; the whitefish, calling to mind the weakfish of the East, a famous fighter, especially in a tide run when the bait can be cast down the tide. With them is the rock bass, almost identical in shape to the black bass, as gamy for a while, but without endurance. They attain a weight of ten or twelve pounds and afford fair sport. At San Nicolas Island the rock bass are very large and gamy, and there are several kinds. San Clemente is famous for its whitefish, yellowtail and sea bass. In these waters is found the barracuda, smaller than the Gulf of Mexico form, rarely exceeding twelve pounds. They are taken slowly trolling, and with an eight or ten ounce rod sometimes afford excellent fishing.

The vicinity of Monterey is a famous locality for angling. The streams abound in trout and the bay in salmon from early spring until late in the fall. The latter fish appear in a series of runs, governed by the bait supply—sardines and smelts. The tackle must in the majority of cases be a stiff rod, as a heavy sinker, weighing from a quarter to half a pound, is often used to take the bait down to the level of the salmon, which do not play on the surface like the yellowtail, but lurk beneath the big school of sardines. Fairly smooth water is found in Monterey and Santa Cruz bays, and from four to fifteen salmon have been taken in a day by a single rod, the fish weighing from ten to forty pounds.

If the fishes of Southern California disappoint the angler, it is because, possibly, of the tackle, as the average visiting angler fishes with a stiff rod. My own rods, which, of course, might not suit everyone, are the result of experience: for tuna a greenheart, or noibe wood, single joint, weighing sixteen ounces, about seven feet in length including butt. This is much longer than the average, six feet nine inches being the requirement. This rod is also for black sea bass; the line, a 21-cuttyhunk. For yellowtail an eight-foot two-jointed rod is used, about twelve ounces in weight, not too slender, but pliable, with a No. 12 line; for white sea bass (fifty pounds) a seven-foot four-inch rod, two joints, pliable and light, and the same line. This can be used for sheepshead and barracuda; but for whitefish and ten-pound rock bass an eight-and-a-half-foot light bass rod is used, reel seat above the hand. All these rods have cork or left-hand grips above the reel seat, and are of greenheart. In thus adapting the tackle to the fish, all its game qualities are put to the test, and the angler has the supreme satisfaction of knowing that he has accorded all the advantage to the dumb animal which is affording him so much sport. The salmon fisherman who has landed a fifty-pound fish may consider the seven-foot fourteen ounce rod a cruel weapon for this fish, when salmon of equal size are taken with a very long rod, but it should be remembered that there is no comparison between the strength of a yellowtail or sea bass of fifty pounds and a salmon of equal weight. It would be a question of hours to take a large yellowtail with salmon tackle, for the water is deep, and the fish takes advantage of it, and plunges into its blue depths.

The introduction by the United States Fish Commission of striped bass into the waters of San Francisco Bay has added another fine game fish to those caught in California. The fish are remarkably gamy, and are found in such numbers that a striped bass club has been formed. Occasionally the yellowtail ventures into Monterey Bay, and the big sea bass is caught there as well as far down the coast. A new fishing ground has been found at or near Tiburon Island, in the Gulf of California, where sea bass of remarkable size are found and are caught in great numbers from the beach. At Ensenada there is excellent fishing with the rod, and doubtless when Lower California is developed, other fine fishing grounds will be found. There are fine fishing waters in the northern part of the State, which will be taken up in an article soon to follow this one.

The New Sequoia Forests of California
(1878)

THE NEW SEQUOIA FORESTS OF CALIFORNIA.

THE main forest belt of the Sierra Nevada is restricted to the western flank, and extends unbrokenly from one extremity of the range to the other, waving compliantly over countless ridges and cañons at an elevation of from three to eight thousand feet above the level of the sea.

Here grow the noblest conifers in the world, averaging about two hundred feet in height, and from five to twenty feet in diameter—the majestic Douglass spruce; the libocedrus, with warm yellow-green, plumelike foliage; the two silver-firs (*Picea amabilis* and *P. grandis*), towering to a height of more than two hundred feet, with branches pinnated like ferns, and whorled around the trunk in regular collars, like the leaves of lilies; the yellow pine, forming arrowy spires of verdure; and the priestly sugar-pine, with feathery arms outspread as if addressing the forest. But the great master-existence of these unrivalled woods is *Sequoia gigantea*, or "big tree"—a monarch of monarchs.

By reference to the map on page 815 it will be seen that the sequoia belt extends from the well-known Calaveras groves on the north to the head of Deer Creek on the south—a distance of nearly two hundred miles; the northern limit being a little above the thirty-eighth parallel, the southern a little below the thirty-sixth, and the elevation above sea-level varies from about five to eight thousand feet.

From the Calaveras to the south fork of King's River the sequoia occurs only in small isolated groves and patches, so sparsely distributed along the belt that two gaps occur nearly forty miles in width, one between the Calaveras and Tuolumne groves, the other between those of the Fresno and King's River. But from here southward nearly to Deer Creek the trees are nowhere gathered together into small sequestered groups, but stretch majestically across the broad rugged basins of the Kaweah and Tule in noble forests a distance of nearly

GROUP OF SEQUOIAS, OF ALL AGES, IN THE SOUTHERN FOREST OF KAWEAH.

dred; in the Tuolumne and Merced groups there is less than one hundred; in the well-known Mariposa grove, about six hundred; and in the North King's River grove, less than half as many; but the Fresno group, the largest congregation of the north, occupies an area of three or four square miles.

The average stature attained by the Big Tree under favorable conditions is perhaps about 275 feet, with a diameter of twenty feet. Few full-grown specimens fall much short of this, while many are twenty-five feet in diameter and nearly 300 feet high. Fortunate trees, so situated as to have escaped the destructive action of fire, are occasionally found measuring thirty feet in diameter, and very rarely one that is much larger.

Yet so exquisitely harmonious are even the very mightiest of these monarchs in all their proportions and circumstances, there never is any thing overgrown or huge-looking about them, not to say monstrous; and the first exclamation on coming upon a group for the first time is usually, "See what *beautiful* trees!" Their real godlike grandeur in the mean time is invisible, but to the loving eye it will be manifested

seventy miles, the continuity of this magnificent belt being broken only by deep sheer-walled cañons.

The trees in most of the small northern groups have been counted. Those of the Calaveras number twelve or thirteen hun-

sooner or later, stealing slowly on the senses like the grandeur of Niagara, or of some lofty Yosemite dome. Even the mere arithmetical greatness is never guessed by the inexperienced as long as the tree is comprehended from a little distance in one harmonious view. When, however, we approach so near that only the lower portion of the trunk is seen, and walk round and round the wide bulging base, then we begin to wonder at their vastness, and seek a measuring rod.

Sequoias bulge considerably at the base, yet not more than is required for beauty and safety; and the only reason that this bulging is so often remarked as excessive is because so small a section of the shaft is seen at once. The real taper of the trunk, beheld as a unit, is perfectly charming in its exquisite fineness, and the appreciative eye ranges the massive columns, from the swelling muscular instep to the lofty summit dissolving in a crown of verd-

outlines so firmly drawn and so constantly subordinate to a special type. A knotty, angular, ungovernable-looking branch eight or ten feet thick may often be seen pushing out abruptly from the trunk, as if sure to throw the outline curves into confusion, but as soon as the general outline is approached it stops short, and dissolves in spreading, cushiony bosses of law-abiding sprays, just as if every tree were growing underneath some huge invisible bell-glass, against whose curves every branch is pressed and moulded, yet somehow indulging so many small departures that there is still an appearance of perfect freedom.

The foliage of the saplings is dark bluish-green in color, while the older trees fre-

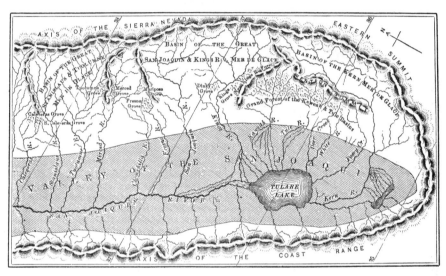

MAP OF THE SEQUOIA BELT.

ure, rejoicing in the unrivalled display of giant grandeur and giant loveliness.

About a hundred feet or more of the trunk is usually branchless, but its massive simplicity is relieved by the fluting bark furrows, and loose tufts and rosettes of slender sprays that wave lightly on the breeze and cast flecks of shade, seeming to have been pinned on here and there for the sake of beauty alone.

The young trees wear slender, simple branches all the way down to the ground, put on with strict regularity, sharply aspiring at top, horizontal about half-way down, and drooping in handsome curves at the base. By the time the sapling is five or six hundred years old, this spiry, feathery, juvenile habit merges into the firm rounded dome form of middle age, which in turn takes on the eccentric picturesqueness of old age. No other tree in the Sierra forests has foliage so densely massed, or presents

quently ripen to a warm yellow tint like the libocedrus. The bark is rich cinnamon brown, purplish in younger trees, and in shady portions of the old, while all the ground is covered with brown burs and leaves, forming color masses of extraordinary richness, not to mention the flowers and underbrush that brighten and bloom in their season.

Walk the sequoia woods at any time of year, and you will say they are the most beautiful on earth. Rare and impressive contrasts meet you every where—the colors of tree and flower, rock and sky, light and shade, strength and frailty, endurance and evanescence. Tangles of supple hazel bushes, tree pillars rigid as granite domes, roses and violets around the very feet of the giants, and rugs of the low blooming chamæbatia where the light falls free. Then in winter the trees themselves break forth in universal bloom, myriads of small four-sided

SNOW-CRUSHED SAPLINGS IN THE FRESNO GROUP.

conelets crowd the ends of the slender sprays, coloring the whole tree, and, when ripe, dusting all the air and the ground with golden pollen. The fertile cones are bright grass green, measuring about two inches in length by one and a half in thickness, and are made up of about forty firm rhomboidal scales densely packed, with from five to eight seeds at the base of each. A single cone, therefore, contains from two to three hundred seeds, about a fourth of an inch long by three-sixteenths wide, including a thin flat margin that makes them go glancing and wavering in their fall like a boy's kite. The irrepressible fruitfulness of sequoia may be illustrated by the fact that upon two specimen branches one and a half and two inches in diameter respectively I counted 480 cones clustered together like grapes. No other California conifer produces nearly so many seeds. Millions are ripened annually by a single tree, and the product of one of the small northern groves in a fruitful year would suffice to plant all the mountain ranges of the globe.

Nature takes care, however, that not one seed in a million shall germinate at all, and of those that do perhaps not one in ten thousand is suffered to live through the many vicissitudes of storm, drought, fire, and snow-crushing that beset their youth.

The Douglass squirrel, the "chickaree" of the West, is the happy harvester of most of the sequoia cones. Out of every hundred perhaps ninety-nine fall to his share, and unless cut off by his sharp ivory sickle, they shake out their seeds and remain firmly attached to the tree for many years. Watching the squirrels in their Indian-summer harvest days is one of the most delightful diversions imaginable. The woods are calm then, and the ripe colors are blazing in all their glory. The cone-laden trees poise motionless in the warm smoky air, and you may see the crimson-crested woodcock, the prince of Sierra woodpeckers, drilling the giant trees with his ivory pick, and ever and anon filling the glens with his careless cackle; the humming-bird, too, glancing among the pentstemons, or resting wing-weary on some leafless twig; and the old familiar robin of the orchards; and the great, grizzly or brown bear, so obviously fitted for these majestic solitudes—mammoth brown bears harmonizing grandly with mammoth brown trees. But the Douglass squirrel gives forth more appreciable life than all the birds, bears, and humming insects taken together. His movements are perfect jets and flashes of energy, as if surcharged with the refined fire and spice of the woods in which he feeds. He cuts off his food cones with one or two snips of his keen chisel teeth, and without waiting to see what becomes of them, cuts off another and another, keeping up a dripping, bumping shower for hours together. Then, after three or four bushels are thus harvested, he

SEQUOIA DOMES LOOMING INTO VIEW ABOVE THE FIRS AND SUGAR-PINES.

comes down to gather them, carrying them away patiently one by one in his mouth, with jaws grotesquely stretched, storing them in hollows beneath logs or under the roots of standing trees, in many different places, so that when his many granaries are full, his bread is indeed sure. Some demand has sprung up for sequoia seeds in foreign and American markets, and several thousand dollars' worth is annually collected, most of which is stolen from the squirrels.

Sequoia gigantea has hitherto been regarded as a lonely, companionless species not properly belonging to the present geological age, and therefore doomed to speedy extinction. The scattered groves are supposed generally to be the remnants of extensive ancient forests, vanquished, in the so-called struggle for life, by pines and firs, and now driven into their last fortresses of cool glens, where moisture and general climate are specially favorable. These notions are grounded on the aspects and circumstances of the few isolated northern groups, the only ones known to botanists, where there are but few young trees or saplings growing up around the failing old ones to perpetuate the race.

The most notable tree in the well-known Mariposa Grove is the Grizzly Giant, some thirty feet in diameter, growing on the top of a stony ridge. When this tree falls, it will make so extensive a basin by the up-tearing of its huge roots, and so deep and broad a ditch by the blow of its ponderous trunk, that even supposing that the trunk itself be speedily burned, traces of its existence will nevertheless remain patent for thousands of years. Because, being on a ridge, the root hollow and trunk ditch made by its fall will not be filled up by rain-washing, neither will they be obliterated by falling leaves, for leaves are constantly consumed in forest fires; and if by any chance they should not be thus consumed, the humus resulting from their decay would

OLD SUGAR-PINE.

still indicate the fallen sequoia by a long straight strip of special soil, and special growth to which it would give birth.

I obtained glorious views in the broad forest-filled basin of the Fresno: innumerable spires of the yellow pine, ranking above one another on the braided slopes; miles of

sugar-pine, with long arms outstretched in the lavish sunshine; while away toward the southwest, on the verge of the landscape, I discovered the noble dome-like crowns of sequoia swelling massively against the sky, singly or in imposing congregations.

The forest was now full of noon sunshine, and while pushing my way over huge brown trunks and through the autumn-tinted hazel and dogwood of the lower portion of the avalanche ravine, the gable of a handsome cottage appeared suddenly through the leaves, with quaint, old-fashioned chimney and trim, neatly jointed log walls, so fresh and unweathered they were still redolent of gum and balsam, like a newly felled sugar-pine. So tasteful and unique a cabin would be sure to excite attention any where, but beneath the shadows of this ancient wood it seemed the work of enchantment. Strolling forward, wondering to what my strange discovery would lead, I found an old gray-haired man, weary-eyed and unspeculative, sitting on a bark stool at the door. He looked up slowly from his book, as if wondering how his fine hermitage had been discovered. After explaining that I was only a tree-lover sauntering along the mountains to study sequoia, he bade me welcome, advising me to bring my mule down to a little carex meadow before his door, and camp beside him for a few days, promising to lead me to his pet sequoias, and indicate many things bearing on my studies. Stray bits of human company are delightfully refreshing in long mountain excursions, and I gladly complied, choosing a camp ground a little way back of the cabin, where I had a fine view down the woods southward through a long sunny colonnade. Then returning to the hermit, and drinking of the burn that trickles past his door, I sat down beside him, and bit by bit he gave me his history, which in the main is only a sad illustration of early California life during the gold period. A succession of intense experiences—now borne forward in exciting successes, now down in crushing reverses, exploring ledges and placers over many a mountain, the day of life waning the while far into the afternoon, and long shadows turning to the east, health gone and gold, the game played and lost; and now, creeping into the solitude of the woods, he awaits the coming of night.

I pushed on southward across the wide corrugated basin of the San Joaquin in search of new groves or vestiges of old ones, surveying a wild tempest-tossed sea of pines from many a ridge and dome, but

THE HERMIT OF THE FRESNO FOREST.

not a single sequoia crown appeared, nor any trace of a fallen trunk. The first grove found after leaving the Fresno is located on Dinky Creek, one of the northmost tributaries of King's River. It was discovered several years ago by a couple of hunters who were in pursuit of a wounded bear; but because of its remoteness and inaccessibility it is known only to a few mountaineers.

I was greatly interested to find a vigorous company of sequoias near the northern limit of the grove growing upon the top of a granite precipice thinly besprinkled with soil, and scarce at all changed since it came to the light from beneath the ice sheet toward the close of the glacial period—a fact of great significance in its bearings on sequoia history in the Sierra.

One of the most striking of the simpler features of the grove is a water-fall, made by a bright little stream that comes pouring through the woods from the north, and leaps a granite precipice. All the cañons of the Sierra are embroidered with water-falls, yet each possesses a character of its own, made more beautiful by each other's

CONNATE TRUNK OF A "FAITHFUL COUPLE," TWO
HUNDRED AND SEVENTY-FIVE FEET HIGH.

beauty, instead of suffering by mere vulgar arithmetical contrast. The booming cataract of Yosemite, half a mile high, is one thing; this little woodland fairy is another. Its plain spiritual beauty is most impressively brought forward by the gray rocks and the huge brown trees, several of which stand with wet feet in its spray; and then it is decked with golden-rods that wave overhead, and with ferns that lean out along its white wavering edges, the whole forming a bit of pure picture of a kind rarely seen amid the sublimities of sequoia woods.

Hence I led my mule down the cañon, forded the north fork of King's River, and climbed the dividing ridge between the north and middle forks. In making my way from here across the main King's River cañon I was compelled to make a descent of 7000 feet at a single swoop, thus passing at once from cool shadowy woods to tropic sun glare. Every pine-tree vanished long ere I reached the river—scrubby oaks with bark white as milk cast their hot shadows on the sunburned ground, and not a single

flower was left for company. Plants, climate, landscapes changing as if one had crossed an ocean to some far strange land. Here the river is broad and rapid, and when I heard it roaring I feared my short-legged mule would be carried away. But I was so fortunate as to strike a trail near an Indian rancheria that conducted to a regular ford about ten miles below the King's River Yosemite, where I crossed without the slightest difficulty, and gladly began climbing again toward the cool spicy woods. The lofty ridge forming the south wall of the great King's River cañon is planted with sugar-pine, but through rare vistas I was delighted to behold the well-known crowns of sequoia once more swelling grandly against the sky only six or seven miles distant. Pushing eagerly forward, I soon found myself in the well-known "King's River Grove," on the summit of the Kaweah and King's River divide. Then bearing off northwestward along the rim of the cañon, I discovered a grand forest about six miles long by two in width, composed almost exclusively of sequoia. *This is the northmost portion of the sequoia belt that can fairly be called a forest.* The species here covers many a hill and dale and gorge, and rocky ridge-top and boggy ravine, as the principal tree, without manifesting the slightest tendency toward extinction.

On a bed of gravelly flood soil fifteen yards square, once occupied by four large sugar-pines, I found ninety-four young sequoias—an instance of the present existence of conditions under which the sequoia is stronger than its rival in acquiring possession of the soil and sunshine.

Here I also noted eighty-six seedlings, from one to fifty feet high, upon an irregular patch of ground that had been prepared for their reception by fire. Bare virgin ground is one of the essential conditions for the growth of coniferous trees from the seed, and it is interesting to notice that fire, the great destroyer of tree life, also furnishes one of the conditions for its renewal. The fall of old trees, however, furnishes fresh soil in sufficient quantities for the maintenance of the forests. The ground is thus upturned and mellowed, and many trees are planted for every one that falls. Floods and avalanches also give rise to fresh soil beds available for the growth of forest trees in this climate, and an occasional tree may owe its existence and particular location to some pawing squirrel or bear. The most influential, however, of the natural factors concerned in the maintenance of the sequoia forests by the planting of seeds are the falling trees.

That sequoia is so obviously and remarkably grouped in twos and threes is no doubt owing to the restricted action of this factor as regards area. Thus when an old tree falls, a piece of ground forty or fifty feet in diameter will be cleared by the upturning roots, and a group of seedlings with an even start will speedily take its place. Out of this seedling thicket perhaps two or three may become trees, and then those groups called "Three Graces," "Faithful Couples," etc., will be formed. For even supposing they should stand twenty or thirty feet apart while young, by the time they are full grown they will touch and crowd and become "faithful." Also the branches on the inside of each will die for want of light, and the partial crowns be modelled into one, and the trunks, if close pressed, will appear as a forked specimen derived from one seed, leaning outward toward the top, on account of the outside of each being loaded with branches.

As soon as any mishap befalls the crown of sequoia, such as being stricken off by lightning, or broken by storms, then the branches beneath, no matter how situated, at once become excited, like a colony of bees that have lost their queen, and all seem anxious to repair the damage. Limbs that have grown outward for centuries at right angles to the trunk at once turn upward, and push eagerly on to assist in making a new crown, each speedily assuming the special outline curves of true summits. Even in the case of mere stumps burned half-way, some small ornamental sprout will seem to receive a special call to go aloft and do its best as a leader.

Less than a mile from the southern extremity of this noble forest we enter the so-called "King's River Grove," extending southward to the Kaweah divide. Here during a former visit I heard the sound of axes, indicating a group of busy men preparing a section of one of the trees they had felled for exhibition at the Centennial. It was twenty-five feet in diameter at the base, and so fine was the taper, it measured ten feet in diameter at 200 feet from the ground. The age, as counted by three different persons, is from 2125 to 2317, the fineness of the annual wood rings making accuracy in the count rather difficult.

Yet this specimen was by no means a very old-looking tree, and some are undoubtedly much older. A specimen observed by me in the New King's River Forest is probably over four thousand years old, as it measures thirty-five feet eight inches inside the bark, and is standing upon a dry hill-side where the growth has evidently been slow.

The forests of the south fork of the Kaweah extend up the range to a height of 8400 feet, which is the extreme upper limit of the entire sequoia belt, and here I was so fortunate as to settle definitely the question of the relationship of sequoia to the ancient glaciers, as to the soil they are growing upon. Hooker discovered that the

SEQUOIAS TWENTY AND TWENTY-FIVE FEET IN DIAMETER, WITH NEW CROWNS.

cedars of Lebanon were growing upon an ancient moraine. So also are the giant trees of California. Several years ago, toward the commencement of my glacial studies, I clearly determined the fact that all the upper portion of the general forest belt was not growing upon soil slowly crumbled from the rock by rains and dews and the decomposing atmosphere, but upon *moraine* soil ground from the mountain flank by the ancient glaciers, and scarce at all modified by post-glacial agents. *Pinus contorta, P. flexilis, P. aristata,* and *P. monticola* are planted as regularly in moraine rows and curves as the corn of an Illinois farmer. So also is a considerable portion of the *Picea amabilis* which forms the upper portion of the main heavy coniferous belt of the Sierra. Next in descending order comes *Picea grandis,* then *Pinus lambertiana,* and *P. ponderosa, Sequoia gigantea, Libocedrus decurrens,* and *Abies douglassii,* all growing upon moraine soil also, but so greatly modified and obscured by post-glacial weathering as to make its real origin dark or invisible to observers unskilled in glacial phenomena. Here, on the head of the south fork of the Kaweah, the sequoias are established upon moraines of the ancient Kaweah glacier that flowed down the south fork cañon, and scarce more changed than those occupied by the summit pines.

At the time of my visit this forest was on fire, and as fire, whether occurring naturally by lightning or through the agency of man, is the great master-scourge of forests, and especially of sequoia, I was glad of the opportunity presented to study the methods of its destruction.

Between the river and the west end of the forest there was a heavy growth of cherry, manzanita, and ceanothus, combined into one continuous sheet of chaparral, through which I had to pass on my way into the burning sequoia woods. But this chaparral also was on fire, and the flames were racing up the shaggy hill-side as fast at times as a horse could gallop. Now bending forward and feeding on the green leaves with a passionate roar, devouring acres at a breath, then halting and shooting far into the sky, with flapping edges fringed and hacked like a dandelion leaf.

It was interesting to notice how much faster these wild fires can run up hill than down. If the wind be not among the conditions, then the steeper the better for speed; but when driven by the wind, a certain slope is required for the attainment of the maximum velocity, which slope varies with the wind and the character of the chaparral.

Passing through the smoke and ashes which these wild-fire billows had given for beauty, I pushed up the mountain-side into the burning forest as far as consistent with safety. One is in no danger of being chased and hemmed in by sequoia fires, because they never run fast, the speeding winds flowing only across the tree-tops, leaving the deeps below calm, like the bottom of a sea. Furthermore, there is no generally distributed fire food in sequoia forests on which fires can move rapidly. Fire can only creep on the dead leaves and burs, because they are solidly packed. Besides the general leaf stratum on which running fires mostly depend for food, there are a good many dead branches that become available here and there. And when aged sequoias fall, their crowns are smashed as if made of glass, making perfect wood-piles, limb piled on limb, broken into lengths of two or three feet, and mingled with the dense leaf tassels. The trunks, also, are broken straight across as if sawed in logs, and when the forest fire comes creeping forward into those grand wood-piles, a most sublime blaze is produced, booming and roaring like a waterfall. But all flame and noise speedily disappear, leaving only the great logs two hundred feet long, and from twenty-five to ten feet thick, lying among the gray ashes like bars of red-hot iron, enveloped in one equal, rich, ruby, flameless glow. Sequoia fire is more beautiful in color than that of any other species I ever noticed. And now fancy a forest hillside strewn with those majestic trunks straight as arrows, smooth, and perfect in taper and roundness, and covered with a plush of flameless, enthusiastic fire, gorgeous in color as the bars of a sunset cloud. Get this picture clearly before your mind, and you have one of the most perfectly glorious fire spectacles to be found on the face of the earth.

Sequoia smoke is also surpassingly beautiful; not

BEAR WRITING ON SEQUOIA.

muddy with resiny lamp-black, like that of the pine, but fine brown and purple when well lighted.

Although the fallen trunks burn on the outside for days in succession, they never lose much of their bulk in this way. Strange to say, however, although perfectly unde-cayed, they burn *inside* for months, and in so methodical a manner that they are at length bored into regular tubes, as if by some huge auger. For it must be under-stood that all those far-famed hollow trunks, into which horsemen may gallop, are hol-lowed, after falling, through the agency of fire. No sequoia is made hollow by decay; and even supposing it possible that in rare instances they *should* become hollow, like oaks, while yet standing, they would in-evitably smash into small fragments when they fell.

Out from beneath the smoke clouds of this suffering forest I made my way across the river and up the opposite slopes into woods not a whit less noble. Brownie the meanwhile had been feeding luxuriously day after day in a ravine, among beds of leersia and wild wheat, gathering strength for new efforts. But way-making became more and more difficult—indeed impossible, in common phrase. But just before sun-down I reached a charming camp ground, with new sequoias to study and sleep be-neath. It was evidently a well-known and favorite resort of bears, which are always wise enough to choose homes in charming woods where they are secure, and have the luxury of cool meadow patches to wallow in, and clover to eat, and plenty of acid ants, wasps, and pine nuts in their season. The bark of many of the trees was furrowed pic-turesquely by their matchless paws, where they had stood up stretching their limbs like cats. Their tracks were fresh along the stream-side, and I half expected to see them resting beneath the brown trunks, or standing on some prostrate log snuffing and listening to learn the nature of the disturb-ance. Brownie listened and looked cau-tiously around, as if doubting whether the place were safe. All mules have the fear of bears before their eyes, and are marvel-lously acute in detecting them, either by night or day. No dog can scent a bear far-ther, and as long, therefore, as your mule rests quietly in a bear region, you need have no fears of their approach. But when bears *do* come into camp, mules tethered by a rope too strong to break are not infrequently killed in trying to run away. Guarding against this danger, I usually tie to an elas-tic sapling, so as to diminish the shock in case of a stampede, and perhaps thus pre-vent either neck or rope from breaking.

The starry night circled away in profound calm, and I lay steeped in its weird beauty, notwithstanding the growing danger of be-ing snow-bound, and feeling more than com-monly happy; for while climbing the river cañon I had made a fine geological discov-ery concerning the formation and origin of the quartz sands of the great "dead river" deposits of the northern Sierra.

Two days beyond this bear dell I enjoyed a very charming meeting with a group of deer in one of nature's most sequestered gardens—a spot never, perhaps, neared by human foot.

The garden lies high on the northern cliffs of the south fork. The Kaweah goes foaming past 2000 feet below, while the se-quoia forest rises shadowy along the ridge on the north. It is only about half an acre in size, full of golden-rods and eriogonæ and tall vase-like tufts of waving grasses with silky panicles, not crowded like a field of grain, but planted wide apart among the flowers, each tuft with plenty of space to manifest its own loveliness both in form and color and wind-waving, while the plant-less spots between are covered with dry leaves and burs, making a fine brown ground for both grasses and flowers. The whole is fenced in by a close hedge-like growth of wild cherry, mingled with Cali-fornia lilac and glossy evergreen manzanita, not drawn around in strict lines, but wav-ing in and out in a succession of bays and swelling bosses exquisitely painted with the best Indian summer light, and making a perfect paradise of color. I found a small silver-fir near by, from which I cut plushy boughs for a bed, and spent a delightful night sleeping away all cañon-climbing weariness.

Next morning shortly after sunrise, just as the light was beginning to come stream-ing through the trees, while I lay leaning on my elbow taking my bread and tea, and looking down across the cañon, tracing the dip of the granite headlands, and trying to plan a way to the river at a point likely to be fordable, suddenly I caught the big bright eyes of a deer gazing at me through the garden hedge. The expressive eyes, the slim black-tipped muzzle, and the large ears were as perfectly visible as if placed there at just the right distance to be seen, like a picture on a wall. She continued to gaze, while I gazed back with equal steadi-ness, motionless as a rock. In a few min-utes she ventured forward a step, exposing her fine arching neck and fore-legs, then snorted and withdrew.

This alone was a fine picture—the beau-tiful eyes framed in colored cherry leaves, the topmost sprays lightly atremble, and just glanced by the level sun rays, all the rest in shadow.

But more anon. Gaining confidence, and evidently piqued by curiosity, the trembling sprays indicated her return, and her head came into view; then another and another step, and she stood wholly exposed inside the garden hedge, gazed eagerly around, and again withdrew, but returned a moment afterward, this time advancing into the middle of the garden; and behind her I noticed a second pair of eyes, not fixed on me, but on her companion in front, as if eagerly questioning, "What in the world do you see?" Then more rustling in the hedge, and another head came slipping past the second, the two heads touching; while the first came within a few steps of me, walking with inimitable grace, expressed in every limb. My picture was being enriched and enlivened every minute; but even this was not all. After another timid little snort, as if testing my good intentions, all three disappeared; but I was true, and my wild beauties emerged once more, one, two, three, four, slipping through the dense hedge without snapping a twig, and all four came forward into the garden, grouping themselves most picturesquely, moving, changing, lifting their smooth polished limbs with charming grace—the perfect embodiment of poetic form and motion. I have oftentimes remarked in meeting with deer under various circumstances that curiosity was sufficiently strong to carry them dangerously near hunters; but in this instance they seemed to have satisfied curiosity, and began to feel so much at ease in my company that they all commenced feeding in the garden—eating breakfast with me, like gentle sheep around a shepherd—while I observed keenly, to learn their gestures and what plants they fed on. They are the daintiest feeders I ever saw, and no wonder the Indians esteem the contents of their stomachs a great delicacy. They seldom eat grass, but chiefly aromatic shrubs. The ceanothus and cherry seemed their favorites. They would cull a single cherry leaf with the utmost delicacy, then one of ceanothus, now and then stalking across the garden to snip off a leaf or two of mint, their sharp muzzle enabling them to cull out the daintiest leaves one at a time. It was delightful to feel how perfectly the most timid wild animals may confide in man. They no longer required that I should remain motionless, taking no alarm when I shifted from one elbow to the other, and even allowed me to rise and stand erect.

It then occurred to me that I might possibly steal up to one of them and catch it, not with any intention of killing it, for that was far indeed from my thoughts. I only wanted to run my hand along its beautiful curving limbs. But no sooner had I made a little advance on this line than, giving a searching look, they seemed to penetrate my conceit, and bounded off with loud shrill snorts, vanishing in the forest.

There is a wild instinctive love of animal-killing in every body, inherited, no doubt, from savage ancestors, and its promptings for the moment have occasionally made me as excitedly blood-thirsty as a wolf. But far higher is the pleasure of meeting one's fellow-animals in a friendly way without any of the hunter's gross concomitants of blood and groans.

I have often tried to understand how so many deer, and wild sheep, and bears, and flocks of grouse—nature's cattle and poultry—could be allowed to run at large through the mountain gardens without in any way marring their beauty. I was therefore all the more watchful of this feeding flock, and carefully examined the garden after they left, to see what flowers had suffered; but I could not detect the slightest disorder, much less destruction. It seemed rather that, like gardeners, they had been keeping it in order. At least I could not see a crushed flower, nor a single grass stem that was misbent or broken down. Nor among the daisy, gentian, bryanthus gardens of the Alps, where the wild sheep roam at will, have I ever noticed the effects of destructive feeding or trampling. Even the burly shuffling bears beautify the ground on which they walk, picturing it with their awe-inspiring tracks, and also writing poetry on the soft sequoia bark in boldly drawn Gothic hieroglyphics. But, strange to say, man, the crown, the sequoia of nature, brings confusion with all his best gifts, and, with the overabundant, misbegotten animals that he breeds, sweeps away the beauty of wildness like a fire.

Hence into the basin of the Tule the sequoia forests become still more extensive and interesting, and I began to doubt more than ever my ability to trace the belt to its southern boundary before the fall of winter snow. My mule became doubly jaded, and I had to drag him wearily from cañon to cañon, like a fur-trader making tedious portages with his canoe, and to further augment my difficulties, I got out of provisions, while I knew no source of supply nearer than the foot-hills far below the sequoia belt. I began to calculate how long I would be able, or how long it would be right, to live on manzanita berries, so as to save time that was extremely precious at this critical period of the year, by obviating the necessity of descending to the inhabited foot-hills only to return again.

One afternoon, after eating my last piece of bread, I stood on a commanding ridge overlooking the giant forests stretching interminably to the south, and deliberating whether to push firmly on, depending on what berries I might pick, until I should chance upon some mountaineer's camp, when a rifle-shot rang out crisp and joyfully over the woods. You may be sure I marked the bearings of that shot in a way not to be forgotten, and steered gladly through the woods in quest of the hunter. I had not gone far ere I struck the track of a shod horse, which I followed to a camp of Indians in charge of a flock of sheep.

The only Indian in camp when I arrived did not seem to understand me very well, but he quickly perceived that I was hungry, and besides, made out to say, in a mixture of words and gestures, that he had a companion who would soon be in who could "heap speak English."

Toward evening the sheep came streaming dustily in long files through the woods, and spread out on a meadow near the camp. Then the other Indian came in, to whom I explained my wants. He promised me some flour in the morning, showed me where to tether my mule, and when supper was ready urged me to eat heartily. Sitting around the camp fire, he inquired whether I had been successful in discovering gold in any of the gulches, seeming, like most white men, to be incapable of comprehending any other motive for such explorations; and as a talkative Indian is rarely found, I embraced the opportunity of trying to get some wild knowledge out of him concerning the birds and animals. Unfortunately, however, he made pretensions to civilization, and spoke contemptuously of *wild* Indians; and of course the peculiar instincts of wildness belonging to his race had become dim; neither did he seem to have any special knowledge of mountain life, not even of bears; and as for wild sheep, he never had seen them. He informed me, however, that the "big trees" still extended far south, how far he knew not, but that he had seen them in crossing the range from Visalia to Lone Pine. His only item of information likely to prove available was that a saw-mill was located somewhere on the south fork of the Tule, where I would find provisions.

Next morning, after receiving a few pounds of flour and a strip of dried mutton, I plunged again into the wilderness.

The entire upper portion of the Tule basin is magnificently forested with sequoia, the finest portion being on the north fork. This, indeed, is, I think, the noblest block of sequoia in the entire belt, surpassing even the giant forest of the Kaweah. Southward from here I thought I could detect a slight falling off in the density and general thrift of the forest, without, however, noticing any further indication of approach to the southern limit. It is a remarkable and significant fact that, upon the whole, the species becomes more and more fully the master tree of the forest belt the farther south, until within a few miles of its limit. Here it is the first tree one meets forming heavy forests, either in ascending or descending the range. Only a fringe of small or sparsely planted pines and firs occurs above it, and a like scanty fringe beneath. But although the area occupied by the species increases in so significant a degree toward the south, there is no corresponding increase in the size of individual trees. The height and girth of the largest of the old groves are, with a few marked exceptions, about equal to any I have seen in the new forests. General Grant, of the King's River Grove, has acquired considerable notoriety in California as "the biggest tree in the world," though in reality less interesting and not so large as many others of no name. The diameter of forty feet claimed for it is obtained by measuring close down on the ground around its wide-spreading craggy base. A fair measurement makes it about equal to the Mariposa giant (thirty feet diameter), which it also resembles in general appearance.

In pushing across the Tule basin I encountered terribly precipitous cañons. Even the small tributaries run in deep gorges, exceedingly difficult to get down into, and still more difficult to climb out of with a mule. I thought of abandoning saddle and blankets and turning him free, and thus turn myself free; for no mountaineer is truly free who is trammelled with friend or servant, or who has the care of more than two legs. Besides, it seems cruel to make any animal share one's toil without being capable of sharing its rewards. What cared Brownie for botany beyond grasses, or for landscapes beyond glacier meadows?

Large flocks of sheep had swept the South Tule Basin bare of grass, and of course Brownie had hard fare. After turning him loose one night to pick what little the place afforded, I busied myself building a fire, paying no attention to him, when, after prospecting the lean ground, and finding nothing but bushes to browse on, he returned to camp, stole close up to me, almost thrusting his nose against my face, and, in the solemn stillness of the gloaming, poured forth a most lamentable compound of bray and neigh, and with all its horrid blare pervaded by pathetic, supplicatory tones of hunger. The horror of so grim a vision of weariness and want I shall not attempt to tell. I hastily offered him half my little remnant of bread, made from the last of the flour given me by the Indians, and though unleavened and charred by baking on the coals, he devoured it greedily. Next morning I pushed directly down the mountains to the inhabited foot-hills, and turned him loose in a corral to botanize at will among abundance of alfalfa and barley; then procured a fresh animal from a friendly mountaineer, and climbed back to the sequoias to complete my work, or at least to remain in the woods until winter set in.

The ridge between the South Tule and Deer Creek is well planted with sequoia; but the trees are decidedly shorter and less irrepressible in aspect, and I began to feel confident that the southern limit of the species could not be very far distant. I was greatly interested here to find that the species had crossed over into the upper valley of the Kern, and planted colonies northward along the eastern slope of the western summit, or Greenhorn range. The western summit, like a branch axis, puts out from the main backbone of the Sierra at the head of King's River, trending southward, and inclosing the upper valley of the Kern on the west; and it is just where this lofty spur begins to break down on its approach to its southern termination that sequoia has been able to cross it.

Pushing on still southward over the divide between the north and south forks of Deer Creek, I found that the southern boundary was at length crossed, and a careful scrutiny of the woods beyond failed to discover a single sequoia, or any trace of its former existence; and now all that remained was to descend the range, and make a level way home along the plain.

It appears, then, from this general survey of the sequoia forest, that, notwithstanding the colossal dimensions of the trees, and their peculiarly interesting character, more than ninety per cent. of the whole number of individuals belonging to the species have hitherto remained unknown to science.

We are now ready for the question, *Was the species ever more extensively distributed on the Sierra in post-glacial times?*

We have been led to the conclusion that it never was, because, after careful search along the margins of the groves and forests and in the gaps between, we have not observed indications of any kind whatsoever of its previous existence beyond its present bounds; notwithstanding I feel confident that if every sequoia in the range were to die to-day, numerous monuments of their existence would remain of so imperishable a nature as to be available for the student more than ten thousand years hence.

In the first place, we might notice that no species of coniferous tree in the range keeps its individuals so well together as sequoia. A mile is, perhaps, about the greatest distance of any straggler from the main body, and all of those stragglers that have come under my observation are *young*, instead of old monumental trees, relics of a more extended growth.

Again, we might recall in this connection the well-known longevity of individual trees, and the fact that the trunks frequently endure for centuries after they fall. I have a specimen block cut from a fallen trunk which is in no way distinguishable from specimens taken from living trees, notwithstanding the old trunk fragment from which it was derived has lain on the damp ground for more than 380 years. The measure of time in the case is simply this: when the ponderous trunk to which the old vestige belonged fell, it sunk itself into the ground, thus making a long straight ditch, and in the middle of this ditch a silver-fir is growing that is now four feet in diameter, and 380 years old, as determined by cutting it half through and counting the rings, thus demonstrating that the remnant of the trunk that made the ditch has lain on the ground *more* than 380 years. For it is evident that, to find the whole time, we must add to the 380 years the time that the vanished portion of the trunk lay in its ditch before being burned out of the way, *plus* the time that passed ere the seed from which the monumental fir sprang fell into the prepared soil and took root. Now, because sequoia trunks are never wholly consumed in one forest fire, and these fires recur only at considerable intervals, and because sequoia ditches after being cleared are often left unplanted for centuries, then it becomes evident that the trunk remnant in question may probably have lain a thousand years or more; and this instance is by no means a rare one.

But admitting that upon those areas supposed to have been once covered with sequoia every tree may have fallen, and every trunk been burned or buried, leaving not a single remnant, many of the long straight ditches made by the fall of the trunks, and the deep wide bowls made by their upturning roots, would remain patent for thousands of years after the last remnant of the trunks that made them had disappeared. Much of this sequoia ditch-writing would no doubt be speedily effaced by the flood action of overflowing streams and rain-washing; but no inconsiderable portion would be enduringly engraved on ridge-tops beyond all such destructive action. And where all the conditions are favorable, sequoia ditch-writing is almost absolutely imperishable, as might easily be rigidly demonstrated had we sufficient space, and readers of sufficient patience. But in the mean time I only wish to fix attention on the fact that *these historic ditches and root bowls occur in all the present groves and forests of sequoia, but not the faintest vestige of one outside of them has yet presented itself.* We therefore conclude that the area covered by sequoia has not been diminished during the last eight or ten thousand years, and probably not at all in post-glacial times.

The climatic changes in progress in the Sierra, bearing upon the tenure of forest life, are wholly misapprehended, especially as to the *time* and *means* employed by nature in effecting them. It is constantly asserted, in a vague way, that the Sierra climate was vastly wetter than now, and that the increasing drought will of itself extinguish sequoia in a short time, leaving the ground to firs and pines supposed to be capable of growing upon drier soil. But that sequoia can and does grow on as dry soil as that occupied by either fir or pine is manifest in a thousand places along the main belt. "Why, then," it will be asked, "are sequoias always found in *greatest abundance* on well-watered places where small perennial streams abound?" Simply because a close growth of sequoia always produces those streams. The thirsty mountaineer knows well that in every sequoia grove he will find running water, but it is a very complete mistake to suppose that the water is the *cause*

SUGAR-PINES IN A SEQUOIA DITCH.

of the grove being there; for, on the contrary, the grove is the cause of the *water* being there. Drain off the water, and the grove will remain. But cut off the grove, and the streams and springs will at once disappear.

When attention is called to the method of sequoia stream-making, it will be apprehended at once.

The roots of this immense tree cover the ground, forming a thick dense sponge that absorbs and holds back the rains and melting snows, yet allowing them to ooze and flow gently. Indeed, every fallen leaf and rootlet, as well as long clasping root and prostrate trunk, is a dam, hoarding the bounty of storm clouds, and dispensing it in blessings all through the summer, instead of allowing it to go headlong in short-lived floods. Evaporation is also checked by the densely foliaged sequoia to a greater extent than by any other mountain tree. Thick masses of air that are soon saturated are entangled among the massive crowns, or drift slowly like icebergs around clustering islets, while thirsty winds are prevented from sponging and licking along the ground.

So great is the retention of water in many portions of the main belt that bogs and meadows are created; by the killing and consequent falling of the trees a single trunk falling across a stream often forms a dam 200 feet long and ten to thirty feet high, giving rise to a pond which kills the trees

within its reach; these dead trees fall in turn, thus clearing the ground; while sediments gradually accumulate, changing the pond into a bog or drier meadow for a growth of carices and sphagnum. In some instances a chain of small bogs rise above one another on a hill-side, which are gradually merged into one another, forming sloping bogs and meadows.

Since, then, it is a fact that thousands of sequoias are growing thriftily on what is termed dry soil, and even clinging like mountain pines to rifts on granite precipices, and since it has been shown that the extra moisture found in connection with the denser growths is an *effect* of their presence instead of a *cause* of their presence, then the prevailing notions as to the previous extension of the species and its near approach to extinction, based upon its supposed dependence on greater moisture, are seen to have in this connection no real significance.

The decrease of the rain-fall since the close of the glacial epoch in the Sierra is not nearly so great as is generally guessed. The highest post-glacial water-marks are well preserved on all the upper river channels, and they are not greatly higher than the spring flood-marks of the present, showing conclusively that no extraordinary decrease has taken place in the volume of post-glacial Sierra streams since they came into existence.

Winter on the
Isle of Summer
(1911)

Bay of Avalon from the hills

✦ WINTER ON THE ISLE OF SUMMER ✦

By CHARLES FRANCIS SAUNDERS

PHOTOS BY C. F. AND E. H. SAUNDERS

TO speak of winter on Santa Catalina Island is a concession to the almanac; for in and about Avalon — which to the transient visitor represents the whole island —one rarely sees the mercury under forty, and only so low as that on sunless mornings, or in the chill hours between midnight and dawn. To the hilltops inland Jack Frost does, during January and February, not infrequently come, but he is shy of descending to the beach, hedged about as it is by sheltering hills. In fact, the weather recorders have worked it out that the mean temperature of Avalon in winter averages but eleven degrees Fahrenheit below that of summer. Winter there, in short, is merely summer over again with a few cool rains thrown in. When New York is icebound and the middle West lies under five feet of snow, here in Avalon the sweet alyssum blooms wild on the vacant places; down by "Uncle John's" park and over by the golf links, the *malva rosa* sets its pretty buds and spreads

The island town of Avalon

its cheerful petals; in cottage gardens geranium, mignonette, yellow oxalis and glowing nasturtiums of many hues flower untiringly; and old residenters take pride in showing you tomato vines that live on from year to year, unfrosted and undaunted.

The busy season on Santa Catalina Island is from June to September. Then the hotels, the rooming-houses, the tents on the camp-grounds and the private cottages are overflowing with pleasure-seeking humanity, which sometimes crowds the capacity of the island's one little town to such a degree that the evening boat from San Pedro is held over night to shelter people unable to secure a roof over their heads on shore. We are not fond of crowds, so we made our first visit in winter.

A feature of the Santa Catalina climate that always surprises the winter visitor, who naturally expects an atmosphere more charged with moisture on a small island in the ocean than upon the mainland, is the noticeable absence of dampness.

The crescent bay of Avalon, sparkling in the winter sun

There is a balminess in the winter nights that makes them the loveliest in the world for outdoor sleeping, if one is not very robust yet likes the fresh, clean feel of a night at the sign of "The Beautiful Star."

Avalon offers ideal sport to the fisherman every month in the year. Many a mid-winter vacation is spent with rod and reel.

There being no crowd in winter—except during the mid-day hours when the steamer from the mainland is in with her load of tourists—the visitor intending to make a stay at this season has the pick of the island's accommodations at prices well within the limits of a slender purse. Then there are flats and cottages galore, furnished for light housekeeping, and procurable by the day or week or month, if you wish to enjoy the privacy and comforts of home while you stay. Indeed, if one wants to be

Pilgrim Club's tower on the right, overlooking the bay and town

Craft of varied sorts in the harbor at Avalon

quite independent and at the same time live in the most economical way, there is no better plan than to rent a small furnished cottage or a room or two in one of the many houses arranged for light housekeeping. The latter are usually in suites of two or three rooms, each suite with its little porch and outlook over the sea or into the cañons, which in winter are a glory of green. One of the rooms is always fitted up for a com-

bined kitchen and dining-room, with accommodations for cooking and running water at the door. If you can afford a little extravagance, you will find it pleasant to take the main meal of the day at the hotel or a restaurant, preparing only breakfast and lunch at home.

We spent half a day walking up one hilly street and down another, finding "to let" signs on all sorts of little camps and bunga-

Trail to a Marconi station on the edge of the ocean

The beach and picturesque shore line

lows, with queer names that must have taxed the inventive humor of their owners to the straining point—"Restabit," "Munnysunk," "Peek Inn," "Never Inn," and the like. Finally our eyes lighted upon a two-story cottage perched upon a hill, so steep of approach that we felt sure that none but true friends, the soundest in heart and most determined in will, would attempt to visit us there. We began climbing steps as soon as we were within hailing distance. The first two flights brought us to the level of the foundations of the house; two more flights delivered us, well winded, on the little porch at the front door.

To the southward, over the tops of the eucalyptus grove in which many of the summer camps of Avalon are embowered, rose the oak-dotted hills, green that January day as ever emerald was; to the eastward, at our feet, the roofs of the little town, with tree-tops and aspiring vines pushing up masses of verdure and flowers between the buildings, and further out the crescent bay of Avalon, sparkling in the sun and dotted with little craft of varied sorts; and as our delighted gaze wandered still farther eastward across the white-capped waters, lo, above the fogline of the mainland shore, the heavenly snow-topped peaks of the Sierra Madre and its outlying mountains from sixty to one hundred miles away— Old Baldy, Grayback, San Jacinto—a view

which in many of its aspects brings to mind the Bay of Naples. Indoors were a living-room, half of it windows as befitted so lovely an outlook, with a snug little fireplace in one corner; two bedrooms on the first floor, a little kitchen, a dining-room and a bathroom; upstairs were two more bedrooms and a roofed porch open on three sides to the air of heaven and with the same glorious view that had captivated us below. There was, too, a little, neglected, precipitous garden, plunging down to the neighboring houses far below; a swarm of flaming geraniums bloomed riotously there, and the first modest wild flowers of the year peeped out from the grass.

"It is the place we dreamed of," we confessed to each other in a stage whisper, "but we can never pay the price."

The agent eyed us anxiously. We composed our faces into a Gradgrind hardness and indifferently asked the rate. He was a shrinking kind of old man, and rubbing his hands apologetically, he faltered out:

"I'll have to charge you fifteen dollars a month. The owner won't take a cent less. You see it has seven rooms and a bath, and do you think mebbe you could pay fifteen?"

For answer we laid down a month's rent in advance and the old man departed promising to bring clean linen and the tea-kettle lid, which was lacking. Then sitting down in the pleasant winter sunshine, in the

Cottages where housekeepers may lead the simple life

midst of all the glory of verdant cañon side and blue sky and flashing sea and dreamy, distant mountains, we estimated ways and means averaging somewhat less than a dollar per day for each of us, with all the comforts of home and the most beautiful outlook on an island whose climate, summer and winter, has no superior on the Lord's whole lovely earth. To be sure, the estimate was based on our doing our own cooking. But then, as we pharisaically observed to each other, that meant the better cooking, and we could always have the things we liked the way we liked them. Besides, we had room enough to give afternoon teas to all our friends that came tripping by the boat, and keep some overnight, if they would remain.

"We'll stay three months!" we cried rapturously, and we did.

The charm of winter life at Avalon— apart from the perennial delight of the climate—is its leisureliness. There is a lull in the fishing then, the particular feature that has spread the island's fame, and what's the hurry? Of course there is golf, but no one hurries at that, and there are half-day trips to take, up and down the island coast by gasoline launch; there are the sea-gardens to visit and revisit, and no end of delightful climbs and walks back among the all too little frequented hills—

but after all, the uninterrupted chance to experience the simple joy of being alive, and gather inward strength for your next sally into the world beyond the mountains, is what endears Avalon in winter to you.

Hither as to that more famous Avalon whither King Arthur was borne to be healed of his grievous wound, comes many a business-buffeted pilgrim and is quite as effectually cured. Sitting upon the beach as the evening shadows lengthen, the departing steamer long since swallowed up in the mainland mists; listening to the scolding gulls and the barking of the seals and the music of the surf upon the shingle; watching the sun's level beams touch to gold the prosy sails of merchant ships bound in to San Pedro and bathing in mysterious amethystine tints the far-off mountains—he begins to feel the chains of care loosen their grip upon his inward man, and to realize that many things about which he had been worrying himself sick are not so important after all. The novel sense of isolation from the world's whirl and the knowledge that nothing can happen to him before the steamer comes again to-morrow, send a delicious thrill through his weary frame, and he does not wonder that there are people who have come to Avalon to spend a day or two and have remained for years—in fact, are there yet.

The Haunts of
the Black Sea-Bass
(1891)

Hauling Ashore the Black Sea-bass

THE HAUNTS OF THE BLACK SEA-BASS.

By Charles Frederick Holder.

It is said that when the purchase of the Northwest coast was contemplated by the United States Government, an old English *raconteur* and fly-fisherman remarked, "Oh, let the Yankees have it ; the salmon won't rise to a fly."

Southern California might go by default in this way, as fly-fishing, compared with that of the East, is not to be had, though the San Gabriel, Aroyo Leco, and other cañons have many pools where gleams of light and color flash, telling of the living rainbow lurking in the shadows. If southern California is deficient in black-bass streams and salmon pools, it possesses the finest marine fishing in North American waters ; not only in the size and gamy qualities of the fish, but in the variety of forms which follow each other as the seasons advance, adding new and constant zest to the sport.

The striped-bass fishing has its prototype here in the gamy yellow-tail, *seriola dorsalis*, which attains a weight of forty or fifty pounds, and is as rapid in its movements as the tarpon. An important personage is he who lands a yellow-tail on an ordinary striped-bass rod, reel, and line. Equally gamy as the yellow-tail is the sea-bass, ranging up to sixty pounds, while the barracuda, tuna, albicore, and others afford the sport esteemed by blue fishermen in the East.

From the Santa Barbara Islands to the Coronados, and beyond, is the field of the southern California Walton ; the islands of the Santa Barbara channel, Santa Catalina and San Clemente being particularly famous in the piscatorial annals and the Mecca of lovers of this sport—winter and summer. The island of Santa Catalina is the principal rallying-point, being the largest, possessing the small town of Avalon, a popular summer resort, with numerous bays and harbors protected from the in-shore

"Three hundred and forty-two and a half, sir."

wind that blows in beneath the steady trade. An ideal spot it is—a series of mountain ranges, from one thousand to twenty-six hundred feet, rising green-hued from the blue waters of the Pacific and extending twenty-two miles down the coast, and an equal distance from it. From the slopes of the Sierra Madre, forty miles away, the island appears formed of two lofty peaks, sloping gently to the sea ; but standing upon its highest summit I looked down upon range after range, cutting the island into a maze of cañons that wound in every direction to the sea. Near its northern portions two harbors extend in from opposite sides ; the island evidently at one time having been separated, the isthmus, as it is called, being but a few hundred feet across ; from this it widens out to six miles or more. The island seems in reality a gigantic mountain projecting from the ocean. The cliffs are majestic, beetling, rising sheer from the sea, broken into strange forms, and tinted with folds and splashes of color. The only beaches are at the mouths of the cañons, or perhaps where the continued falling of rocks in land-slides caused by the winds have formed a vantage-ground for waves. On the west coast the sea assails the cliffs with sullen roar, and the in-shore wind whirls up the cañons, beating the fog against the rocks and bearing it aloft, where it is dissipated by the radiating heat of the mountains. On the east the water is calmer and often like glass, affording favorable conditions for boating and fishing.

The air of this island in the sea seems redolent with romance. Three hundred years ago Cabrillo, a Spanish adventurer, cast anchor in one of its harbors and named it La Victoria, after one of his vessels. In 1602 Viscaino visited and gave it the present name of Santa Catalina. Father Ascencion, who accompanied him, describes the inhabitants as sun worshippers, one of whose temples he found near the two harbors. In these early days the island had a large and prosperous native population; every well-watered cañon had its village, and I have found evidences of them on some of the highest ranges.

One of my first visits to Santa Catalina was for the purpose of opening some of the ancient graves of these people, and while thinking the matter over with "Mexican Joe," who has lived thirty years on the island, I took out an old bass-rod that had seen service on the St. Lawrence, and began looking it over.

"What you catch with that?" asked my companion, with a curious look on his strong Indian face.

"Bass, black," I answered, nonchalantly, whirling the reel and listening to the music.

"What!" retorted Joe, laughing; then, "how much he weigh?"

"Five pounds," thinking of a certain afternoon on the river.

"Oh!" continued Joe, "I thought you mean black sea-bass."

"Well, how much does he weigh?" I asked.

"How much he weigh? You want catch with that?" said Joe, pointing to the rod with scorn. "Why, man, he weigh five hundred pounds. Yes, black sea-bass run from seventy-five to five hundred, seven hundred pounds."

I ran over in my mind the various heavy-weight tackles—the tarpon, striped-bass, salmon rods, and came to the conclusion that a flag-staff with a donkey-engine reel attachment might do; yet decided, then and there, to take a black sea-bass, if it was among the possibilities. I announced my determination interrogatively to my guide and oarsman.

"Of course you catch one if you know how. I show you where he live. It take patience, if you have it," was the reply.

I was well supplied with this necessary, and a few days later found myself gliding away in the deep shadows of the rocks, headed for one of the haunts of the deep-sea bass. The water here was so clear, objects forty feet below could be distinctly seen, glances into the depths showing an almost tropical condition of things. Bright-hued fishes, yellow and orange, darted by, while patches of wiry sea-weed gleamed with blue and iridescent tints. In the watery space fairy-like *medusæ* moved lazily about, rising and falling, while here, there, and everywhere flashed a veritable gem in red, gold, blue, green, and amber, the minute crustacean sapphirina.

When off a point which juts boldly into the sea, the keeper of the fortunes of the black sea-bass ceased rowing, cast anchor, and we swung in the current that ran along the rocky shores to the north. The tackle produced by my oarsman was not æsthetic. The line was almost as large as that employed in the halibut fisheries of the East, while the hook was perhaps twice as large as a tarpon-hook, arranged with a well-working swivel. Live bait, a white fish which we soon caught, was attached, with a sinker sufficient to carry it down. The line was then dropped over, and that patient waiting, which makes all successful fishermen philosophers, begun.

Three hundred — yes, one hundred years ago, a boat could not have dropped anchor here without being the object of hundreds of eyes, and the news would have been flashed from hill-top to cañon to the various camps ; now the only observers were the shag that flew along near the boat, its long, snake-like neck extended, startling the flying-fish into the air in fright, and a wondering pair of eyes that stared at us, telling of a sea-lion making the grand rounds ; while the leaping forms near shore were seals, bound for their rookery around the bend. The whistle of the plumed quail came softly over the crags from the neighboring cañon, and the gentle musical ripple of the waves lulled us to fancied repose.

I had been watching the interesting face of my Mexican guide, wondering at his life, when I noticed his eyes suddenly grow large ; then he lifted the line gently with thumb and forefinger. It trembled, thrilled like the string of a musical instrument touched by some player beneath the sea. Slowly it took his fingers down to the water's edge.

A bass? Yes. No snap, no sudden rush, no determined break for liberty as I had seen the black bass make. I was disappointed ; a simple drag. But the Mexican smiled and passed me the line, arranging with the other hand the coil in the bottom of the boat.

"He's a young one," he remarked. "Pay him out ten feet, then jerk an' stan' clear the line."

These instructions took but a few seconds, yet the line was now gliding through my hands like a living thing— four, eight, ten feet. Suddenly it tautened, and for a single second the tension hurled the sparkling drops high in air ; then, leaning forward, I jerked the line with all my strength. I have watched the silvery form of the tarpon as, like a gleam of light, it rushed into the air, shaking, quivering before the fall, and have handled large fish of many kinds, but I was unprepared for the deepwater tactics of this king of the bass. For a brief period there was no response, as if the fish had been stricken with surprise at this new sensation ; then a smoke, a succession of snake-like forms rising into the air—nothing but the line leaping from its coil. "Ah, he only a young one," said Joe ; "take hold."

In some way I had lost the line in this rush. Watching my opportunity, I seized it again, and by an effort that thoroughly tested the muscles, brought the fierce rush to an end. Then came heavy blows distinctly given, as from the shoulder, evidently produced as the fish threw its head back in quick succession.

"Take it in ! " said my companion, excitedly, and bending to the work I brought the line in, fighting for every inch that came ; when the Mexican shouted a warning. Whizz ! and the coils leaped again into the air. Nothing could withstand the rush—a header directly for the bottom and away.

The anchor had been hauled up by the Mexican at the first strike, and now, with line in hand, we were off, the boat churning through the water, hurling the spray over us, and bearing waves of gleaming foam ahead.

"Take in ! " cries Joe, who stands by the coil, and again, slowly fighting against the dull blows, the line comes in. Ten feet gained, and, whizz-eee ! as many more are lost. In it comes once more, hand over hand, the holder of the line bending this way and that, trying to preserve a balance and that tension which would prevent a sudden break. Now the fish darts to one side, tearing the water into foam, leaving a sheet of silvery bubbles, and swinging the boat around as on a pivot. Now it is at the surface—a fleeting vision followed by a rush that carries the very gunwale under water. This, followed by a sudden slacking of the line, sends despair to the heart : he is gone, the line floats. No, whizz ! and away again, down. All the tricks of the sturdy black bass this giant of the tribe indulges in, except the mid-air leaps which gladden the heart of the angler. Quick turns, downward rushes, powerful blows, mighty runs this gamy creature makes, fighting inch by inch, leaving an impression upon the mind of the fisherman that is not soon forgotten.

With a large rope, and by taking turns, the fish could have been mastered, but such methods were not considered sportsman-like here. It must be taken free-handed, a fight at arm's-length, and being such, the moments fly by ; it is half an hour, and we have not yet seen the outline of our game. Gradually the rushes grow less, the blows are lighter, and what is taken is all gain.

"It take your wind," said Joe, with a low laugh.

So it had, and I stood braced against the gunwale after a final dash—a burst of speed—to see a magnificent fish, black, lowering, with just a soupçon of white beneath, pass swiftly across the line of vision, whirling the boat around end for end.

"You've got him," from astern, is encouraging; yet I have my doubts; an honest opinion would have brought the confession that I was in the toils. But the flurry was the last. Several sweeps around the boat, and the black sea-bass lay alongside, covering boat and men with flying spray with strokes of its powerful tail.

"It is a small one," ejaculates my man, wiping the spray from his face. Imagine a small-mouthed black bass enlarged, filled out in every direction until it was six feet long, and plump in proportion; tint it in rich dark lines, almost black, with a lighter spot between the pectoral fins; give it a pair of eyes as large as an ox, powerful fins and tail, a massive head, ponderous, toothless jaws, and you have the black sea-bass, or Jew fish — the best fighter, the largest bony deep-sea fish in Pacific waters. Too large to be taken into the boat, it had to be towed in, and finally, after being stunned with an axe after the quieting method applied to muskallonge in the St. Lawrence, we got underway, the huge body floating uncomfortably behind, materially retarding the progress.

The entry to Avalon harbor was one of triumph, as at that time the capture of a bass was a new thing to visitors; and as the magnificent creature was hauled up on the sands by willing hands, the entire population gathered about to listen to the details of the sport. Then came the weighing. "Three hundred and forty-two and a half, sir," said a Mexican youth who had triced the fish up; "better than the average." Glory enough for one day.

During this summer, at Catalina, about twenty of these fish were caught, ranging from eighty pounds to three hundred and fifty. All were females, ready to spawn, and had come in to Pebble Beach for this purpose, depositing their eggs in August and September. This locality has always been a famous place for them, and ten thousand pounds were taken there in a single day four years ago. At that time there was a systematic fishery, the meat being dried and —tell it not in Gath!—sold as boneless cod. My oarsman informed me that the bass had been frightened off. These fishermen killed the fish on the spot, throwing the heads overboard, and so the bass left, only comparatively few having been seen since.

This is a native version. The fish undoubtedly migrate, going into deeper water during the winter, or possibly to the south.

It is often said that there is little pleasure in taking deep-sea fish; but to capture the black sea-bass, free-handed, play it fairly, and bring it to the gaff, is an experience that well compares in sport and excitement with hand-line tarpon fishing on the Gulf coast.

Temecula Canyon
(1893)

TEMECULA CANYON.

BY T. S. VAN DYKE.

BEFORE the railroad went through Temecula Canyon in San Diego county, California, many a deer spent the day there in summer. This canyon is a narrow water-way several hundred feet deep, through rolling hills in which deer are abundant. In places walls of granite line its sides, but most of the slopes are not difficult to scale, and there are few that a deer cannot bound up in a way that will puzzle many a good shot with the rifle.

Why the deer prefer this canyon in the heat of the day I never could divine, for its densest shade is not so cool as that of the breezy hills above, where there is plenty of shade under the solid green of the sumac, the heteromeles or lilac, and where dark green groves of live oak flourish along the sides and around the heads of the gulches. Many deer do spend the day in such places and the hunting is often good enough on the hills, but in hot weather the bottom of the canyon is a surer place to find them and will furnish all the amusement desired. Often a single deer will give a sportsman enough to talk over for the rest of the day, and think about during the night spent beneath the tent of starlit sky.

Along the waters of the creek in the shade of the overhanging alders, or where the wild grape festooned the sycamore, the cottonwood outspread its arms above the elder, the clematis twined about the willow, or hung out the plumous tails of its seed over clumps of gigantic nettles, the deer loved to lie in silence almost unbroken save by the rippling of the stream or the soft sigh of the unfailing sea-breeze through the leaves above.

Sometimes he lay near the foot of the hill where the red or cream-colored trumpets of the mimulus blew the long summer through from the chinks in the piles of granite boulders, and the broad evergreen head of the sumac shaded the space between them, but generally he preferred the bottom near the water. From the hillsides above or the deep shades about him rang often the call of the quail, but he cared as little for it as for the scream of the hawk in the upper air. Cattle and horses as wild almost as himself strayed along at times, but they never disturbed his rest unless the different tread of a horse showed that a man was on his back, a little difference that deer seem to learn very quickly.

To find deer in this canyon on any hot day was once an easy matter, but to see them before they see you is next to impossible ; while the numerous dead sticks, all dry and crackling under the slightest tread, make it impossible to approach without being heard. To avoid the keen nose is easy, for the sea-breeze blows always one way, but their ears and eyes have the advantage of you, and about the only chance to shoot is when they go bounding up the hill-side.

In the dense chaparral of the hills the deer often hides and allows you to pass within a few feet, well knowing that you do not see him. But in the bottom he rarely resorts to this strategy. Lying there in calm content, he still keeps constant watch with head well up and large flaring ears all attention. The first thing you see is a whirl of white and gray and big ears, accompanied by the crack of brush and the thump of hoofs upon the ground. But quite as often you see nothing, and the heavy thump of hoofs or crack of brush is the only intimation that the game is started.

It is generally best and often necessary for two to hunt together, each one on a side of the canyon. A yell from either or the report of a rifle is the signal to the other that the game is up. And then wild scrambling often follows for a position on the hillside that commands a view of the situation, with a delightful uncertainty about the course the deer will take, whether down the bottom and out of sight until too far to shoot, or up some little side ravine, leaving you pondering on the vanity of earthly hopes, or whether he will go bounding up the opposite hillside in full view in case you gain a point above the timber in the canyon.

By good skirmishing it is quite possible to reach a position on one hillside that gives a shot. And what a shot it generally is! Sometimes, with that fatal curiosity that even the wildest have, the deer stops and looks back to see what alarmed him; but more often he is in no hurry to learn until well out of danger, and then the only chance is to catch him while bounding up the hillside. Up the steepest hill he often speeds as if slopes were made for him to play with, and over big granite boulders, as if they were holes in the ground. The stiff and ragged red arms of the manzanita are to him as a shaven lawn, and through the toughest and thorniest of the wild lilac he sails as though it were a shadow. And all this with a perfect bound in which all four feet strike the ground together, sending the deer aloft like a ball, with all four legs grouped together beneath his body ready to strike the ground again with heavy thump at the descent and rise again lightly as a sunbeam from the glistening boulder beside him. How an animal of such size, yet so light of limb, can hold such a gait, clearing from ten to fifteen feet and over at a bound, on a slope that the toughest hunter often hesitates about climbing, is a mystery. Yet hold it he will, and up a thousand feet or more of the steepest hillside among rocks and brush of all kinds without ever missing a step.

Vainly the bullets hiss and splash from the smooth rocks around the flying game, or tear up the dirt just ahead of or behind it. Often you raise the rifle with its sights so exactly in line with the shining whirl as it curves in air above some boulder that you cannot resist the impulse to pull the trigger; and yet by the time the ball reaches the spot the glistening fur is not there but a whole leap ahead, and you have only the satisfaction of seeing the dry dust fly from beyond the point of space at which you aimed, while the target is rising from another bound as deceptive in its speed and curve as the last. And how nobly you determine to correct the error at the next shot, and how philosophically, in the brief instant allowed, you hold the sights of the rifle just the right distance ahead of the massive breast that is smashing so grandly through the brush!

Bang goes the rifle and *wheee-ooo* sings the ball away over the rim of the hill beyond, and a puff of dry dirt from the ground just in line and not an inch ahead of the descending curve of gray you thought to intercept, tells you made a good shot. In the little time allowed for reflection you draw what consolation you can; and well you may, for perhaps it is the last you see of your game in available shape.

Few of the tricks and pranks of the deer that, for steady amusement, make him the most attractive of all big game to the lover of the rifle, equal the ease with which he can disappear about the precise moment you think you have him. Just as you measure his jump, gauge his speed, and guess the time it takes your bullet to get to the point where he will be when it travels over that distance; just as you correct your former errors, and with the eye of faith see the next curve descending into the path of the ball, the gray vanishes from sight.

Where did it go? But a second ago it was in plain sight, rising in a graceful curve, and none of the brush or rocks around the place seem over a foot high. Yet the end of that curve is the end of all there is to shoot at on that hillside, and where that end is gone you know not. Perhaps it ended in a little ravine that, from the distance at which you are, seems but a wrinkle in the earth. And perhaps it tired of ricochet motion and simply dropped its head and walked off in brush that from where you are seems not a foot high. Perhaps you hit it, and often you flatter yourself you did, and lose an hour thrashing about in the hot sun on the steep, brushy hillside, only to find the tracks leading away with feet well placed and the outline of each hoof in the dry dirt, all in the proper form of a deer walking in perfect health. Then suddenly, perhaps when the trail reaches some little ravine, it breaks into spots four or five yards apart where the ground is ploughed up by four sharp hoofs descending almost together.

Bitter disappointment that, some would think ; but there is more amusement in missing game under some circumstances than in killing it under others. But the hunt is by no means over, for it was no uncommon thing a few years ago to find a dozen or more deer in this canyon in a mile or so of its length. And you may start another much nearer than you imagine, for they often care little or nothing for such noise as your rifle has just made, and if they did care the conformation of the hills would make it very puzzling for them to locate the cause of the disturbance. Hence you may at once keep both eyes and ears open as you again start down the canyon.

Perhaps you go not three hundred yards before you hear the report of your companion's rifle from the other side of the bottom, and away you dash for the hill on your side. Funny work this, running away from the game to get a shot at it, but it is your only chance. Your friend will dash for the hillside, up which the game has gone, but you never could cross even this narrow bottom in time to see anything to shoot at, and your only hope is a shot across the canyon. You reach a place where, over the trees, you see a massive buck, with glistening horns proudly erect, bounding gaily up the slope with easy pace as if in no haste. And before you can raise your rifle he stops and turns half around, and with that fatal curiosity that will often betray the wildest of game, looks back to see what the noise is about.

What a trifling difference there often is between a good shot and none at all ! Had he stopped first, he would certainly have seen you, for a deer's eyes are marvelously quick to detect a motion. But as you were at rest when he turned around, you have the advantage, because a deer's eyes are as slow to detect an object at rest as they are quick to notice it when in motion. Never does the deer show better than on a steep hillside in the bright sunlight, and never does he strike an attitude so picturesque as when roused from his bed he runs a bit, and then, concluding that he has been scared at nothing, turns around to see what it was. Little trace of alarm is there in the majesty of repose with which he stands with great ears expanded and turned full forward with the sun glittering on all the polished tines of his horns, his thick neck erect, and his whole dark, gray coat sleek with fatness down to the trim legs that are so springy when occasion requires. Not at you are his big gray ears aimed, and the black nose is turned down the side of the canyon toward the point from which he came. He is watching your comrade and does not see you, and never was there a better chance for a good broadside shot, though to tell the truth the distance is rather great and you must do some fine shooting.

As a little good fortune often changes the whole character of a hunt, a little ill fortune quite as often changes it the other way. As you raise the rifle upon the glossy coat it springs aloft with a bound that carries it out of sight behind a sumac bush, just as you hear the crack of your comrade's rifle on the other side of the timber. The deer had the same advantage over him that you just had over it, that of being at rest while the other was in motion. Your friend was seen the instant he appeared above the brow of the hill, and the snapshot with which he had to content himself was too hasty to be accurate.

Out comes the deer from behind the bush, clearing a boulder as lightly as a sunbeam skips over the morning hills, and down he goes into a mass of brush that seems heavy enough to hide him forever. But up again he comes in a curve of glistening fur, making one of the prettiest of targets for you to shoot at, provided you knew it was coming, and knew the spot into which it was coming. Then you might get a bullet under way in time to catch the fur when it arrived at the top of the curve. But as it is it makes a mark so tempting that it often misleads the best of shots.

Before you can resist the impulse you fire directly at it. The result could be predicted from the laws of motion. Your bullet throws up the dirt from the hillside, apparently in exact line with the center of the place the gray occupied a second before and just as it vanishes in the brush on the side.

Your comrade is evidently too far down the hill to see the game, and its capture devolves upon you. At such a distance and at a target with such irregular motion, speed of fire is your main reliance, and yet it must be used with great discretion. The game is moving forward and up and down at the same time, and its distance is so great that just so surely as you shoot directly at the animal just so surely will it be out of that place by the time the ball arrives. Your best hope is to fire at the place where it will strike the ground from the next spring, and fire about the time it fairly rises in that spring. If you wait till it makes the top of the curve you may be too late.

But before you have time to reason, and before the swiftest motion of the lever of your repeating rifle can reload it, an arch of gray rises again above the brush. You mark the place where it went down, and throwing the sights of the rifle well ahead of it, wait for the next bound. Not an instant do you have to delay, for up it comes again a surging line with big ears and glittering antlers pointed skyward on the high held head. Five feet or more ahead of it and below the top of the brush you aim the rifle and, with a feeling of grand confidence, pull the trigger.

There is a whirl of something in the brush, you plainly hear it crack ; and out from its lower edge comes your buck as if equipped with the wings of light. But no more with high, sweeping bound and haughty head proudly aloft. With head low and outstretched, and hugging the ground like a racer on the home stretch, he comes in full gallop directly toward you. Bang ! goes your rifle again, aimed full at his head, but the bullet tears up the dirt a yard behind, and on he comes. Bang ! goes another shot and the lead from that too he leaves behind, and splashing from a rock it goes hissing away up the hill. Right toward your companion he goes and from behind a bush his rifle rings along the hills, but the deer pays no attention to it, and goes right toward him as if he would impale him on those outstretched glittering tines. A good shot your friend is, but such a target has fooled many a better one, and his next bullet whizzes above the buck's back about an inch, while another from your rifle ploughs the earth again behind him, and still on he comes as if bound to run over both of you. You were surprised before to see the speed he could make up hill, but it is nothing to the pace directly down the hill. And the strange part of it is that the deer is practically dead and running with a single breath. Before you can fire again, and without your detecting a slip in his step or the slightest sign of faltering, he goes headlong forward through a large sumac bush, and on the other side of it turns a somersault almost at your friend's feet.

Salt Water Fisheries
of the Pacific Coast
(1892)

SALT WATER FISHERIES OF THE PACIFIC COAST.

In a paper on salt water fisheries, the immense salmon fisheries should not be included, partly because the bulk of the catch is made in the fresh water of the numerous rivers of the Coast, and partly because the industry has grown to such enormous proportions as to demand separate consideration. The fisheries north of Puget Sound might better be treated with the Alaskan fisheries. Thus the subject is narrowed to a consideration of the San Francisco fisheries and southward, with the exception of Puget Sound and Shoalwater Bay in Washington.

Oregon possesses no salt water fisheries, but does an enormous business in the Columbia River region and its tributaries. On the Sound, attempts have been made by New England capitalists to establish a fresh and salt halibut fishery but without success, on account of lack of cheap facilities for preservation and transportation. As a rule, the fisheries are carried on only sufficiently to supply the coast cities with fresh fish.

Halibut, flounders, and salmon, constitute the greater part of the catch in this region. At Shoalwater Bay quite an industry in oysters is growing up.

San Francisco is the only great fishing center of the Pacific Coast, and may be taken as a type of them all.

If a San Franciscan wishes to take a short trip to foreign parts, there is no more economical route than an early visit to Fisherman's Wharf, on the water front, under the shelter of Telegraph Hill, crowned with the ruins of a battlemented beer castle. There, before the sun appears above the Oakland hills, all is bustle and business, especially on Friday morning, from midnight until after dawn. A chatter of husky, guttural voices speaking a foreign tongue is heard, for English has no place on Fisherman's Wharf. The curious visitor can easily fancy himself transported on Sinbad's wonderful carpet to some Italian fishing port.

The dock consists of two L-shaped wharves, the overlapping wings of which inclose a protected basin 400 feet long by 350 feet wide, where the feluccas are moored side by side; those on the right are painted white with blue gunwales, and blue or pink decks; the boats on the left are mostly white with green trimmings. On the approaches to the dock there are numerous wagons, receiving boxes of fish of great variety.

The feluccas are boarded by the customers, the fare, or catch, looked over, and the bargains made. Of these purchasers many are Chinamen, with their baskets on the wharf; many are fish dealers bargaining for a particular part of the fare.

Standing on the wharf and looking over the dock, you will notice the numerous boxes of fish stacked up against the fisherman's market, or piled up inside that large shed-like structure. There may be a hundred boxes of fish, or more, the result of the steam fishing-tugs' trawl-seine or paranzella catch.

While you are looking over these boxes, your attention is attracted by the rattling of the anchor rope on the gunwale of a felucca, as a new arrival casts anchor in the basin near you, makes all snug on board, and prepares to clean up the nets and pick out the numerous king-fish from the two gill-nets piled on the aft deck. Just beyond the end of the wharf another boat is swiftly approaching under full sail, lateen and jib, borne by the fresh ocean breeze as gracefully and lightly as a sea gull.

The boat does not shorten sail. You conclude that she is going to pass. Suddenly the foggy-voiced command of the Italian skipper is heard; two men scramble over the deck, the jib collapses in an instant, the large lateen sail folds itself like the wings of a sea-bird, and the skipper with a dexterous turn of the helm steers around the outer side of the closed rectangle, through an opening forty feet wide, bringing the bow of his boat around to face the direction whence he came ; one more turn and the boat is rowed with long oars to its moorings beside her thirty or forty mates. The " Morning Star" has arrived. This name on her bow is the only bit of English in sight or hearing.

The sun has got well up now, and the crowd of purchasers on the wharf has scattered ; even the huckster with his hand-baskets, or the more pretentious owner of a bay-horse-frame tied with bale rope to the broken shafts of a rickety old cart, has bought the remnant of half-spoiled tom-cod and crawled away.

Turning to examine the large shed of somewhat pretentious external appearance, one is disappointed in the barn-like, dirty, white-washed interior. All around the structure are sale counters with marble tops, but no fish are in sight save two or three boxes of boiled cray-fish in the middle of the room, and a patch of fish about a yard square at the entrance, for sale by a sleepy old man, lazily leaning his folded arms on the counter while puffing a broken pipe.

All about the counters are piled high with dry nets. Up among the rafters like pigeon lofts are many more lockers filled with nets, boxes, and various articles of the trade.

Without, sitting or standing about some large boxes, is a group of five or six Italians and Greeks, earnestly conversing in their own tongues. Now and then one becomes more emphatic, and with gesticulation lays down the law to

his interested listeners in a voice that seems to have embodied an echo of the roar of the surf. Some are wearing high rubber boots folded down to the knee, some wear blue, some wear red, sashes, in all stages of decomposition, separating woolen shirts of no particular color at all from anything that might pass for trousers.

A slouch felt hat, sufficiently faded to suit an artist, or a still more faded Tam o' Shanter, covers a swarthy, weather-beaten countenance, behind a heavy, black, piratical moustache.

Many of the boats present quite a busy appearance. The crew of the " Morning Star " are washing their net, one man switching it about in the water, and another coiling it in the stern, and picking out any small fish not already washed from its meshes.

On other boats they are washing down the decks, and scrubbing them with long round swabs like stiff sink-brushes. One man has just taken out of the hold a queer utensil, apparently a cross between a round cast-iron slop-hopper and a plumber's furnace. He swings it about in the water, and then fills the upper part, above the grating, with charcoal, and sets it on deck, in the wind. After starting the fire, it is put down in the hold next to the mast, and breakfast is prepared.

On the deck of another felucca four men are eating from a white china bowl filled with a sort of stew mixed with lumps of water-bread. A half-consumed semi-circular loaf of water-bread is resting on an oar one side of the boat. The men are grouped about this dish on the after hatch ; two of them have forks, and two case knives. Each man dips in at will, and fishes out a morsel between his thumb and knife or fork, which he holds in his fist. There are two bottles of claret beside them, with peculiar whistle-shaped mouth pieces, which they frequently raise above their heads, and put into the side of their mouths. One young man raises the bottle on high, and drinks half its contents without a breath, releasing his hold only after the violent protest of his partners, uttered in an angry, guttural tone.

About the wharf are stretched nets, which the fishermen are busy repairing. Among them very few words are spoken; each man attends strictly to his business.

On the raised rail about the wharf many nets are drying; the small smelt gill-net, the flounder-net, and the salmon-net, varying in the size of their meshes, may be found here. Stretched out on the wharf is a trawling-seine, which is operated by two fishing boats, dragging this large bag-net between them.

Out on the end of the wharf is a shed with five or six large cauldrons for tanning the nets and the sails.

Moored near this shed is a boat that presents an odd appearance. From a distance it looks as if it had eight crab nets arranged equally on two sides, with the lines coiled on top. On more careful investigation they are seen to be the coils of the trawl line fishermen, who drop their lines among the rocks off the rocky headlands north of Golden Gate, or about the Farallone Islands. A circular flat basket is used to hold the coil, into the rim of which the 150 or 180 hooks are pressed, making a complete circle of steel hooks, which are 3½ feet apart on the line when it is stretched. When the chosen grounds are reached, a stone weighing about five pounds is fastened to one end, and a red or blue buoy, resembling a painted milk can, made fast to the other, and the 100 fathoms of line allowed to drift, after it has been baited with sardines, for rock-cod and codfish. From thirty to forty baskets of trawl lines are carried by each boat when trawling.

A great variety of apparatus is carried by each boat, on account of the frequent changes in the fishing caused by the appearance and departure of certain species. It is common for a boat to be fitted with seines, hand and trawl lines, salmon gill-nets, herring, or smelt, and flounder nets. These are stored on shore, for only those which are required for immediate use are taken on board.

The larger boats generally fish for the salmon, shad, smelt, herring, flounder, rock-cod, and sturgeon, in their respective seasons. All the boats carry eight or ten hand lines, to occupy the idle hours and help out the daily catch, of which the hand line may sometimes constitute two thirds.

The size of the craft and the fishery it pursues governs the number of the crew, which varies from two to six men. At present, according to George H. Koppitz, Deputy Fish Commissioner, there are about 175 fishing boats in the bay, exclusive of 42 Chinese junks, although all of them are not fishing all the year around. Speaking in this regard, the same authority says: " Of these about 120 use net and seine, and are subject to pay an annual license. About 30 use nets for the purpose of catching crabs, and the remainder (25) are boats that use trawl lines and fish beyond the Heads, and are not subject to pay a license."

In January, February, and March, also in September, this number is increased by a number of boats that come down in the bay to fish on account of the scarcity of salmon in the rivers, which is growing greater every year.

The crab fishermen have separate wharves at Harbor View, near the government Presidio, carrying on an independent trade along their favorite fisheries between Black Point and the Golden Gate. The boats used in this industry are the smallest used in fishing, and carry about twelve nets apiece. Their nets are made of two concentric iron hoops, one about twice the size of the other, so woven together that when drawn up they form a basket. When resting on the bottom with a piece of bait, meat or offal from neighboring packing houses, they are flat, and are quite accessible to the greedy crab. These nets are lowered along near the shore and attached to log floats. They are also set outside the Golden Gate, where the best crabs are captured. So abundant are these common crabs, *Cancer magister*, and so simple the apparatus required for their capture, that many a penniless old drunkard or tramp may be seen on a pleasant day sunning himself on a pile on the northern shore of the city, while he waits for crabs to crawl into his nets. After boiling his morning's catch in a rusty can on the sea shore, over a fire of drift-wood, the whisky-soaked old human driftwood peddles his wares around the neighborhood for ten cents or two beers apiece.

The regular crab fishermen use submerged cages run on ways like an elevator, in which they preserve their catch alive until marketed; retailing at the rate of three for twenty-five cents. In 1887, according to the Fish Commissioners' Report, by actual count, the sale in the San Francisco market alone amounted to 300,000, averaging one pound each, and netting $15,000.

Only the ordinary fisheries have thus far been spoken of.

The most important development of the industry is the introduction of steam fisheries over the sandy bottom of the banks which stretch from Point Reyes to the Golden Gate, the most extensive fishing ground on the Pacific Coast so far developed.

Outside the kelp, in other parts of the coast, the paranzella, a mode of fishing similar to the trawl-net fishing might be used, but the markets are too small and undeveloped to be profitable. There are no definite off-shore fisheries south of the Straits of Juan de Fuca, says Professor Jordan, in his report to the Fish Commissioners in 1887. Off those straits, eight miles north of Cape Flattery, there is an extensive halibut bank, but the market is undeveloped, and recent investigations made by the Albatross have shown these to be less valuable than reported.

The proximity of a large market led Peter Koster & Co., an association of five Spanish, Greek, and Italian dealers, to introduce the paranzella from the Mediterranean waters. So far as I have heard, this method is unknown elsewhere in the United States. Its introduction greatly increased the supply of fish in the San Francisco market, and consequently the price was greatly lowered. Before it was in use tom-cod sold wholesale at from 25 to 40 cents, and never reached a lower price than 8 cents per pound in the summer. In 1876 fishermen with seines sometimes made as high as twenty-five dollars per night for each seine. Three steamers are now engaged in this fishery. Until recently two small steam tugs operated a paranzella between them, but the latest innovation is the introduction by an opposition company of a system of booms projecting from the stern of the boat twenty-five feet on each side, from the extremities of which powerful hawsers 400 feet long extend to the wings of the large bag-net sunk in forty fathoms of water. These ropes are weighted with one-hundred-pound sinkers of lead, ten, twelve, or even twenty on each side. The bottom of the strongly made net is heavily loaded with lead, and the top floated by large pieces of cork.

The net has a conical bag in the middle about eighteen feet deep, forty feet long, and five feet wide at the mouth, from which extend wings about one hundred and fifty feet long, though some have wings of only forty feet. The size of the meshes decreases from the extremities to the center of the bag, which has a half-inch mesh.

With this apparatus the tug moves along slowly over the sandy bottom where flounders abound, scooping in a great variety of sea life. When the operators think they have a full net, they bring in the booms, take a turn on the drum of the donkey-engine, and bring in the net with care. When the net is alongside, the bag is carefully hoisted on davits to the surface. Immense

There are cod fish of different kinds, shad, sturgeon, sharks, silver skate, star fish, sting-ray, jelly fish, crabs, devil fish, and sometimes an electric ray, which seems to be a kind of marine drop-a-

Photo by C. A. Adams

FISHERMAN'S WHARF. SAN FRANCISCO.

scoops are used to transfer the marketable fish to a large fish box in the stern of the vessel. Only sufficient fish are scooped up to supply the immediate demands of the market at profitable prices. The two wings of the net are then released, the apex of the bag secured, and the net dragged along inside out. Tons of fish are thus thrown into the water, including great numbers of tiny flounders and other small fish, crushed or asphyxiated by the jam in the bag of the net.

A great variety of sea life is brought to the surface, flounders being the principal part of the catch.

nickel - in - the -slot-and-test-your-nerves apparatus, without the nickel.

All the tugs belong to one company now, but a smaller paranzella is operated by sail boats. One of the larger boats brings in about seventy boxes a day with ordinary luck.

The variety of marketable fish is very great. The flounders and soles are abundant throughout the year. In general the name flounder is applied to most of the flat fish brought in except the best of the flounders, which is called a sole. This confusion in names indicates how impossible it is to give an accurate account of the fish product without the scientific names. Mr. John Kessing, an American who has been in the business many years, told me that, owing to the lack of general intelligence among fish dealers, there was no accuracy in naming the fish, a hap-hazard nomenclature having sprung up.

Striped bass were introduced from Eastern waters in 1885, and now constitute the choicest of California's market fish. Shad is caught in San Pablo Bay and outside the Heads. A supply also comes from the northern part of Monterey Bay. It is captured in gill-nets from

Photo by G. W. Reed

FELUCCA, OUTWARD BOUND.

Smelt are plentiful, codfish of all kinds, including rock-cod, black and red, which latter is more marketable in spite of its learned soubriquet, *Sebastichthys ruber.* Perches of different kinds abound, which Professor David S. Jordan thinks a misnomer applied to surf-fish. The "sea-bass," or "white sea bass," like many of the neighbors of Fisherman's Wharf goes under an *alias, Cynoscion nobilis.* The white sturgeon is abundant, being sold in restaurants under the title of sea bass; and a particular delicate cut is christened "tenderloin of sole." It is also known as "bass" and "white salmon."

April to December, but a few are found throughout the year, a thing unknown in the East, whence the fish was introduced by the United States Fish Commission. Barracuda, herring, sardines, and anchovies, are abundant in season. The sardine is almost exactly the same as the sardine of Europe, and might be made a great canning industry if developed. The German carp and fresh water cat-fish are thriving imported species.

The Chinese consume skates, shark's fins, dogfish, squid, abalones, clams, and shrimps, the last two being also in general demand.

The supply of oysters is limited to the local production of two companies, who have established beds in San Francisco Bay, near Milbrae, where transplanted Eastern oysters are raised for the local market and shipment to the interior towns.

The marketing of fish in San Francisco, though the most highly developed on the Coast, is still in a primitive condition. The fishermen are not organized as formerly, and much needless expense is incurred by their rivalry.

Very recently steps have been taken by the Caucasian fishermen to organize politically, for the purpose of securing laws which will be sufficient to stop the wholesale destruction of young fish by the Chinese and the paranzella, when operated close in shore. It is said that in Italy this method is prohibited within five miles of shore.

The fishing grounds are far from the city, out around the Farallones or northward to Bolinas Bay, Drake's Bay, and Tomales Bay, and southward about forty miles along the coast. In cases of calm and in hot weather the fish is often spoiled before the fare is landed, for the fishermen stay out sometimes two and three days. A system of steam transports might be employed to advantage, if the foreigners who monopolize the trade could be persuaded to suppress their mutual distrust and jealousy, and combine to organize the industry. There are about fifteen wholesale dealers, twenty-five retail dealers, and many hucksters. The methods of doing business are crude, only a few of the larger companies keeping any records.

The business is carried on almost exclusively by foreigners from southern Europe, the Greeks, Italians, Spanish, Portuguese, and Slavs, many of whom are naturalized. Rarely is an American to be found among them, and few Germans, French, or Scandinavians.

IN RICHARDSON'S BAY.

THE CRAB FISHER'S RETURN.

On account of the dense ignorance of this class, who live for the day, and their suspicious nature, it is difficult to extract much accurate information from them. As a class they are industrious, and law-abiding citizens as far as the fisheries are concerned. Some of the large dealers are intelligent men, but they cannot compensate for the general ignorance.

From one or two of these large dealers I was surprised to learn the extent of territory receiving fresh iced fish from the San Francisco market. A supply is sent all over California, and choice varieties, striped bass, pompano, or shad, when out of season north, are shipped to Portland, Seattle, and Tacoma One dealer alone sends yearly ten tons of fresh fish to Butte City, Montana, and one ton to Laramie, Wyoming.

Another dealer ships to Tombstone and Tucson in boxes with pounded ice, which are placed in the ordinary closed freight car, and re-iced at Los Angeles and Yuma. Recently, fresh fish have been sent to the City of Mexico, at a rate amounting to about five tons a year for a single dealer.

Recent statistics of the U. S. Fish Commissioners' report are surprising, placing San Francisco the leading whaling station of America. This is but in small part a Pacific Coast fishery, but it is largely operated with San Francisco capital. The value of the products landed from the San Francisco fleet in 1889 was $540,927, as against $346,255 for the New Bedford fleet rendezvousing in San Francisco. This was an extremely poor year, but it serves to illustrate the relative standing of the two whaling centers.

San Francisco is the only port on the Pacific Coast of the United States to prosecute the cod fishery, which has declined materially of late years on account of lack of demand, the keen competition of Eastern producers in Western markets, and the attraction of capital to the more profitable salmon canning industry of the north. The two companies engaged in this trade have curing and outfitting stations in Marin County, one at California City, and one on Richardson's Bay.

These fisheries, prosecuted in Alaskan waters mostly, are not properly within the scope of this article.

The exact amount of the fresh fish products sold in San Francisco by peddlers, marketmen, and wholesale dealers who ship to interior ports, can not be determined, for no records are kept. Mr. W. A. Wilcox and Mr. A. B. Alexander, of the Fish Commission, after a "careful estimate, however, based upon the experience of the most observant and conservative dealers, and upon the records of transportation agencies," give the following figures : —

In 1889, the fish product of all kinds amounted to 4863 tons, of the retail value of $696,300 ; the mollusks, crustaceans, etc., were consumed to the value of $741,228, making a total of $1,437,528 for the year. To obtain an adequate idea of the amount of fish caught, one third should be added for loss of weight in cleaning, and then the great amount of fish destroyed and returned to the waters should be taken into consideration. The paranzella fishery necessarily crushes to death or asphyxiates great quantities of small flounders and other fish in their big nets, beside destroying many skates, halibut, and other unmarketable fish. This is the case when the immense drag-net is operated close in shore, as it is at Drake's Bay.

The value of apparatus and capital invested in the market fishery is $1,989,030, consisting of vessels, boats, apparatus of capture, (such as gill-nets, trammel-nets, seines, bag-nets, pots, hand-lines, and trawl-lines,) shore property and cash capital.

With this amount of capital invested,

Photo by Lowden

IN SUISUN BAY.

BREAKFAST FOR THE GULLS.

it is natural that the Caucasian fishermen should look with apprehension upon the illegal and destructive fisheries of the Chinese, who have established camps about the Bay and along the coast as far as San Diego.

There are at present, according to Deputy Koppitz, 42 junks of differing sizes from the two to the five-man junk, employing about 205 men to fish, and about 75 more to pack and dry.

Not only the Chinese but some among the other fishermen are fishing carelessly with very small-meshed bag-nets, and destroying large quantities of small fish. Mr. Alfred V. La Motte is authority for the statement that he has seen a seine hauled up on Richardson's Bay, with sufficient small fish to cover an area 12 feet square, 18 inches deep. Through this pile the fisherman waded, kicking the fish about, and picking out one of sufficient size here and there. When returned to the water they were almost all dead, and fell a prey to the gulls.

The sea-lion is another great enemy of the development of the salmon supply. Thousands of these animals frequent the coast about the Cliff House of San Francisco and the Farallone Islands, where they are practically safe from molestation. Both the fishermen and the Fish Commissioners' deputies agree that a wise law would be to set a bounty on their scalps. When salmon are scarce they enter the Bay, and pursue their prey far up the great rivers. They are so intelligent that they follow a fisherman's boat, and wait to rob his gill-net, when set. Two of them will sometimes devour or bite pieces out of a dozen or more ensnared salmon out of a catch of fourteen. A favorite meal is to bite the heads off from their victims, and leave the body to float free from the net. If one or two can produce such destruction, it can only be imagined what amount of marketable fish is consumed by the thousands on our fishing grounds.

However great this may be, it cannot reach the magnitude of the injury done our fisheries by the wholesale capture of shrimps and little fish carried on by the Chinese. The shrimps are taken legally in enormous quantities, even in spawning time, and dried for export to China ; but with them, whenever they think they are not watched, large quan- tities of small fish are taken illegally,

Fish camps of a similar nature at Pes- cadero, Monterey, Santa Barbara, and San Diego, are mostly engaged in dry- ing abalones and squid for the Chinese export trade.

The camps about San Francisco are given up to shrimp drying, which as- sumes considerable proportions in spite of the growing scarcity of their prey.

A Chinese fish camp is unlike other

Photo by E. L. Wood

A CHINESE FISH CAMP.

which should be returned to the water immediately, under penalty of indict- ment for misdemeanor. Seven or eight camps are established at various points on the Bay, such as Belmont, San Bruno, Point Richmond, and San Pedro, the lat- ter being the most important, where at one time in 1880 there were 1500 men at work.

At present in this camp, there are 8 junks of 5 men each, 5 boats of 4 men each, beside 10 or 12 smaller ones ; in all there are about 100 men, some of whom are engaged in preparing and packing the product.

camps, from the fact that it is easily found in the dark by the sense of smell. The fishermen do not mind it, for their olfactory nerves are paralyzed by over work. The camp is always located on the edge of the water, near the fishing grounds, often protected from an invad- ing tax collector at low tide by a wide stretch of mud. A confused jumble of rickety shanties are crowding to get a foothold on the shore, and the smaller ones have been elbowed off into the mud. Strewn about are old Chinese baskets, ducks, filthy boxes, pieces of dirty mat- ting, piles of garbage and decaying fish,

Photo by Lowden

A CHINESE JUNK.

old sacks, and rotten sails; here and there a mangy, half-fed dog, or a black cat stretched in the sun, on the sill of a smoke-blackened hovel. A charitable squash vine has taken root among some old rusty cans, and tries its best to cover some of the abominations of the camp. A short distance from the camp a number of small junks are pulled up on the shore, not far from the queer oblong shrimp boiler. On a slope close by are several barren patches of considera-

ble extent, an acre or so, where the cooked shrimps, and perhaps some small fish, are drying, if illegal work has been going on, which is frequent.

The boy who has been reading Captain Kidd would be much frightened to meet a Chinese junk of the large size, manned by five men. The craft is extremely dirty, unpainted, and weather-stained. Approaching nearer, the countenances of the men are anything but reassuring. An old pirate squatting on the after deck, with a piece of red flannel tied around his head, and a very dirty shirt, glowers at the intruder; another man has no shirt at all, but wears the regular Chinese straw hat, shaped like an inverted basket.

The junk sails up to the line of bag-nets so anchored in a current as to catch most of the small fish that come in or go out with the tide. The bag-net, or strap is a huge cone-shaped bag, forty-two feet long and twenty-four feet wide at the mouth, which is held open by stakes driven into the water at low tide. The apex of the bag is four feet wide, which, when set, is tied up with a puckering string. This end of the bag is taken up when the net is hauled, the string loosened, and the contents dropped into the boat; the meshes of this net are decreased in size toward the apex, where they measure only half an inch. Such a net, set for shrimps, should not be more than two feet high, but when not watched they are set three or four feet high to catch all the small fish possible.

These nets are set according to the currents in the tide, forming a complete blockade. It matters not to these aliens whether the shrimps caught are filled with spawn or not; they are here to catch all they can, regardless of the future. "All is fish that comes to their nets." As there is no law protecting shrimps, the Fish Commissioners are powerless to stop this evil. As it is, they are so exerting themselves to prevent the illegal capture of small fish that, at the present writing, the shrimp fisheries have stopped, and none are to be had in the markets. The fact that shrimp fishing has stopped when illegal fishing is stopped would seem to indicate that the profit in the business comes from the illegal taking of young fish.

The law is peculiar on this point. While there is no law to prevent the taking of young fish, it is a misdemeanor to neglect returning them to the water

immediately, alive. When a Chinaman gets anything of value in his possession, it is almost impossible for him to let it go. Hence the constant struggle to maintain the law.

The wholesale catching of shrimps (which ceases only when the rains stop the drying) has so depleted the supply that whereas, in 1880, fifteen hundred men were engaged in this camp at Point San Pedro, at present only one hundred are employed. This depletion is bitterly lamented by the Caucasian fishermen, who claim that it is ruining the Bay fishing by destroying the food supply of the larger fish.

At the turn of the tide the nets are brought close to the boat by an awkward windlass rigged amidships, and the contents of the bag emptied; the nets are then reset to suit the change of tide. With a favorable catch of two tons of shrimp, the junk is headed for the drying ground. The shrimp are loaded into large Chinese baskets, suspended on a pole in the usual manner, and carried to the boiler. A portion of the catch, however, is preserved for the local market.

The vat is ten or twelve feet long and three or four feet wide, with wooden sides; the bottom and ends of boiler iron. On one end is a rude mass of brick and mud, from which an old stove pipe protrudes. The water which is prepared with sea-salt is already simmering. Into this the shrimps are dumped, and covered over with a wooden cover, to be cooked with a gentle heat for twenty minutes. From the boiler they are spread out to dry on the bare ground, after it has been wet down, dried, and swept. From time to time the shrimps are turned with a curious wooden rake. By this time they have become shriveled, hard, and tough, and about the color of the yolk of an egg. A corrugated wooden roller is then run over them, pushed by two men, after which they are swept up and put through a primitive fanning machine, to separate the meat from the shell. With the shrimp are sometimes quantities of small flounders, soles, kingfish, and smelt. The gravel mixed with the fish is removed, and the fish sorted by means of graduated seives, after which they are sacked and ready for shipment to China. In 1888, the export was 769,660 pounds of meat, worth $76,966, and 3,842,200 pounds of shells, valued at $38,482.

The only other fishery the Chinese pursue to any extent is that of the sturgeon, from which they make caviar, and extract the white spinal cord, which they consider a delicacy. As with the other fishery, their methods are cruel and wasteful. The sturgeon trawl has been introduced from China, though it is illegal. Of this Mr. Alexander says :—

Each trawl has an average of eighty barbless hooks, which are as sharp as needles. They are fastened to the gagings in clusters of eight and ten, and when in the water are swung about by the action of the tide like the tentacles of an octopus reaching out for prey. A fish which approaches within a length of itself is pretty sure of being hooked by one or more of these treacherous devices. When a fish of any considerable size gets fastened to a hook it is sure in its struggle for freedom to become entangled with other hooks, and finally, in its flouncing about, will become completely incased in a network of gagings and hooks, like a shark which has rolled itself up in a net. . . . The trawl is always set off bottom, and from three to five fathoms below the surface, according to the depth of the water, and the way in which the fish caught are thought or known to be moving.

The lines are anchored and buoyed in the same manner as cod lines.

The Chinese fishermen are fertile in resource. Mr. A. V. La Motte has observed a novel mode of entrapping sturgeon in great quantities. At low tide a long, single-wire, barbed-wire fence is constructed for several hundred yards. The wire is 6 or 8 inches above the mud flats where they are built. At high tide the sturgeon pass safely over the obstruction, to feed on the crustaceans near shore. As the tide slackens they recede, with their heads shoreward, until their tails strike on the barbed-wire fence. They endeavor to go shoreward, but the receding tide backs them down against the fence, which they cannot pass over or under. The fisherman then passes along on the outside of the fence with his scow, and clubs his victims to death, pulls in those he wants with his gaff, and leaves the others to float away on the next tide.

Great pains are taken by these Oriental fishermen. At the Chinese camp at Pescadero a strange method of frightening fish into the gill-nets, set near the rocks close to shore, was seen. A small scow is sculled around them, while a man stands in the bow, and throws a pole into the water in such a manner that it will return to his hands, and another man squats on the bottom of the boat, and drums on the middle seat with two sticks.

At all the principal fisheries, such as San Diego, San Pedro, Port Harford, Monterey, and the Channel Islands, the Chinese pursue their trade of gathering abalones and squid for export to China, selling the shells of the abalones to Americans, for ornamental shell work. At San Diego there are fifty-two men engaged in gathering abalones.

Monterey is the principal squid and octopus fishery, of which the export value was $13,620 in 1888.

At that time there were 934 Chinese employed in the fisheries of California, exporting abalone shells and meat to the value of $78,576, and shrimps and prawns worth $141,688.

As the development of the fishing industry in the great center is quite incomplete, the same is even more true of the lesser salt water fishing centers, such as Puget Sound, Monterey Bay, Port Harford, Santa Barbara, San Pedro, and San Diego.

Monterey Bay is well known for the abundance and variety of its fish, and is especially noted as the dividing line of navigation of many species found in the north and south. Salmon are rare south of this line, and species found in great abundance further south, such as the barracuda, bonito, mackerel, horse mackerel, sea-bass, and pompano, are seldom found in great numbers north of Monterey Bay.

The methods of fishing in the south are the same as those north, with the exception of trolling for barracuda and bonito, which is unknown north of Monterey Bay.

A troll line consists of a line about sixty feet long, with a drail of bone or iron three or four inches long, with a barbless hook fastened to it, that the hook may be extracted easily. When trolling, the vessel moves along under easy sail, with six or eight lines out. No bait is used, for the fish bite readily at the drails. To prevent fouling of lines, they are sometimes attached to short booms rigged on each side of the boat.

Both north and south of San Francisco, as a rule, only sufficient salt water fish are caught to supply the local market. In the south, the hot weather and frequent calms often deprive the fisherman of the fruit of his labor, for he has no facilities, such as ice or welled boats, for preserving his catch until marketed. Around the rocky islands off the coast there is an abundance of yellow-tail, barracuda, and mackerel, in season, which are dried and exported to Honolulu and Hong Kong. The mackerel is too poor to satisfy domestic consumers. Crayfish grounds are numerous along the coast of the mainland and off the islands, whence comes a supply to the San Francisco market, where the local catch is not abundant.

The man that delights to pore over statistics finds a feast in the Report of the U. S. Commissioner of Fish and Fisheries for 1891, on the Fisheries of the Pacific Coast of the United States, from which reliable source the following figures are taken.

In 1888, there were 3,988 Caucasian fishermen employed on boats and vessels, exclusive of those engaged in Arctic whaling and fresh water fisheries, with a working capital of $2,348,200, producing a yearly product of $1,144,547 of fish, and $769,299 worth of mollusks, crustaceans, etc., at retail valuation.

Of this capital, San Francisco furnishes $1,989,030, occupying 2,512 fishermen, including 807 Chinese. San Francisco thus furnishes two thirds of the capital and more than half of the men engaged in the salt water fisheries of the Pacific Coast.

Philip L. Weaver, Jr.

The Raisin Industry
in California
(1892)

THE RAISIN INDUSTRY IN CALIFORNIA.

THE history of California's development since the advent of the Americans displays a succession of transformation scenes more rapid and surprising than ever before exhibited on the stage of the world. In this drama of destiny the curtain rose on a scene of peaceful beauty. The Mission churches in their pleasant locations by the seaside, the neighboring princely estates with their haciendas, the vast unpeopled plains of the interior, the endless stretch of mountains in the background, formed a setting to which the padres and their Indian proselytes, the dons and their native retainers, the vaqueros and their countless herds gave a completing touch of pastoral simplicity and loveliness.

The motive of the piece suddenly changed. A scene of turbulence and excitement followed. The solemn religious chant was drowned in the roar of traffic; commercial cities encroached upon and crowded the Missions aside; the estates and haciendas were overrun and disappeared; the plains were alive with processions of adventurers; the solitary mountains became the theater of furious energy and tumultuous life.

But another change came; not so suddenly as the first, but swiftly in comparison with the time in which industrial revolutions are usually brought about. In disappointment some turned from the mines to the barren plains, to see if the apparently sterile expanses would respond to the processes of husbandry. The arid wastes were seeded, more in doubt than faith; but, lo! a miracle. The glad soil rewarded its tillers with the repressed fertility of centuries, yielding such abundance of harvest as had never been seen. Illimitable fields of golden grain formed the central feature of California's new scenic display.

In a little while, and before the observer was fully conscious of it, yet another change had come. Sweeping inland, like a silent mist from the ocean, enveloping hillside, cañon, and plain alike, came vineyards, orchards, orange groves, and similar marvels, until we waked to discover that the wastes and grainfields were disappearing, and the landscape was like a garden of the Lord or a dream of Hesperides. The change from the pastoral to the mining, from the mining to the agricultural, was scarcely more rapid and complete than that which has given to our State its present horticultural complexion. The passing show is being enacted in a scene whose chief features are interminable vistas of fruit trees and vines.

What is the setting of the next act in the drama of California's destiny to be? In view of the surprises of the past forty-four years it would be rash to make a positive prediction. Some surpassing resource or adaptability yet undiscovered may turn her fortune unexpectedly awry and project it on a new line of development. This has occurred thrice in her brief history already. The discovery of extensive deposits of petroleum, natural gas, coal, iron, and other minerals, may give her fate a different cast, and make her a rival of Pennsylvania; or demonstration of the special adaptability of her soil and climate to the culture of ramie, hemp, flax, rice, tobacco, the sugar beet, the tea plant, and other products as yet but imperfectly experimented with, may cause an equally radical revolution in the character of her industries. But it is not at all probable. The field of possibilities has been pretty thoroughly explored, and it is likely that California has found and is pursuing the right course to her high destiny. Nature has favored her beyond all other spots on earth with horticultural and viticultural advantages, and it would be a derogation she is not likely to be guilty of to abandon her proud superiority in these respects to engage in lowlier and more common pursuits. The likelihood is that development will continue upon the present lines, but with ever-increasing variety and range. Already the fig, the olive, the lemon, the perfume field are coming forward to take a place of prominence with the peach, the prune, the orange, and the vineyard. Other rare species will in turn push to the front, until the nations shall look to California for the choicest growth of every variety of semi-tropical products.

Among the transformations that have characterized the development of California during the few decades of her real history, no single feature is more interesting or important than the growth of the raisin industry. Within twenty years it has vaulted from an experimental stage to the position of one of the foremost interests of the State. And though just at present it appears to have exceeded the temporary need and passed the limits of financial success, it will be found that it is no more stationary now than at any former period of its history. Constantly extending markets will give renewed impetus to it, and it is destined to expand to dimensions only to be gauged by universal and ever-increasing demand.

Raisins are merely the proper varieties of grapes properly dried. It is popularly supposed that sugar is used in curing them, but such is not the case. The only sugar in raisins is that produced from the juice of the grape in the process of drying. All raisin grapes are of the green variety. The rich purple or chocolate color is imparted to them by the sun while they are being cured. The same grapes dried in the shade, whether by the air or by artificial means, have a sickly greenish hue. Difference

of soils, of degrees of ripeness, of the proportions of water in the grapes, all affect the color of the raisins, but only within a certain range of lighter or deeper shades. The uniformly rich tones which characterize all shades alike are due entirely to the action of the sun.

Experiments in raisin making in California probably date back to the time of the first vineyards. Nature herself, if no one else, must unavoidably have been forced to try her hand at it. Grapes left upon the vines until they become overripe undergo the processes of curing, though not so rapidly, the same as if picked and spread in the sun. In our hot interior valleys a very considerable part of the crop not infrequently becomes thus prematurely dried. But those early experiments, if such there were, could have resulted, as did much later ones, in nothing but dried grapes,— as the cured product of the wine and table varieties is called,— for the true raisin grape does not appear to have been experimented with for many years. So-called raisins, made from Feher Zagos grapes, attracted some attention, but they must necessarily have been of a very inferior quality. The Malaga grape was also tried, and is largely made use of yet in some sections. Its name led many to suppose it the genuine raisin grape. But in that respect, as in every other, it is a fraud. Among the grape family it is what the carp is among fish,—a magnificent deception, dry and tasteless as sawdust. Both as a table grape and a raisin it is an imposition. It is grown extensively because it is hardy and bears prolifically. The size and beauty of its bunches, whether green or dried, ensnare the inexperienced and render it one of the most marketable products of the vineyard; but the sooner it is excluded from the raisin field the better it will be for that industry.

The genuine raisin grape is the Muscat. Of all grapes it alone has the qualities that give to raisins their peculiar taste and pungency. There are many varieties to which the name is applied, but only two of them are used in raisin making—the Muscat of Alexandria and the Muscatel Gordo Blanco. At one time there was much contention over their relative merits, but of late years it seems to have died out. It may with safety be suffered to remain buried, as for all practical purposes there is no choice between them, a slight difference in the shape of the berries and in the looseness of the bunches being the only distinctions, and even these are not always plainly marked.

The Sultana, a small seedless grape, with a fruity flavor which renders it very desirable for cooking purposes, is cultivated quite extensively also, and Corinth and Zante currants are grown in the State on a small scale, but so far their culture has not proved successful.

Colonel Agaston Haraszthy imported the Muscat of Alexandria, from Malaga, in 1852; and while visiting that place in 1861, he secured cuttings of the Muscatel Gordo Blanco and the Sultana. To him, therefore, belongs the credit of having first introduced raisin vines into this State. Another importation of the Muscat of Alexandria was made by A. Delmas in 1855, and G. G. Briggs subsequently brought cuttings of the same variety directly from Spain. In 1876 W. S. Chapman imported the supposed choicest varieties, but they proved to be in no way superior to those already growing here. Other importations may have been made; but it is a matter of no material consequence, as no improvement has ever been made on the stock originally imported by Colonel Haraszthy.

But, though the true raisin vine was thus early introduced, no one appears to have utilized it for many years. It will never be known who produced the first raisins in California. Doctor J. Strentzel made an exhibit of raisins at the State Fair in 1863; but it is alike uncertain if they were genuine Muscat raisins, or if they were the first produced in the State. The first distinctively raisin vineyards — or, at least, the first to prove successful and attract attention to the industry — were those of G. G. Briggs at Davisville, in Solano County, and R. B. Blowers at Woodland, in Yolo County, planted in 1863. The former was of the Muscat of Alexandria variety, imported directly from Spain; the latter of the Muscatel Gordo Blanco, secured from Colonel Haraszthy. Both these vineyards produced raisins as early as 1867, but the product made no figure in the market until 1873, when 6,000 boxes were marketed, which may be considered to have inaugurated the raisin trade of the State.

From the time it was generally known that the proper varieties of grapes had been secured, and that merchantable raisins could be produced in California, the industry spread rapidly, and for twenty years it has kept on increasing at an astonishing ratio. As nearly as can be ascertained the production has been as follows:

Years.	Boxes.	Pounds.
1873	6,000	120,000
1874	9,000	180,000
1875	11,000	220,000
1876	19,000	380,000
1877	32,000	640,000
1878	48,000	960,000
1879	65,000	1,300,000
1880	75,000	1,500,000
1881	90,000	1,800,000
1882	115,000	2,300,000
1883	125,000	2,500,000
1884	175,000	3,500,000
1885	475,000	9,500,000
1886	703,000	14,060,000
1887	800,000	16,000,000
1888	1,250,000	25,500,000
1889	1,633,990	32,678,000
1890	2,341,463	46,829,260
1891 (estimated)	2,600,000	52,000,000

The Muscat is the most delicate of all varieties of the vine, and to insure good crops from it and their proper curing peculiar conditions of soil and climate are required. Hence, many localities where ordinary grapes can be successfully grown are not suitable for the raisin industry. A rich, heavy soil is a prerequisite to a thrifty growth of the vine and its full bearing, and a warm, dry climate is indispensable to the early ripening of the fruit and its conversion into raisins. The soil of the coast counties is well enough adapted to the growing of the vine, but the fog and dews cause mildew, and render drying in the sun impracticable. These considerations have driven the business to the interior valleys whither the moisture of the ocean does not penetrate. Apart from this there is no reason why it may not be successfully prosecuted anywhere from Shasta to San Diego.

All inland localities, however, are not equally favorable to the industry. Suitable soils can be found throughout the whole length of the State, but to the northward later spring frosts endanger the crops, and earlier autumn rains render drying difficult; while to the extreme south a like hazard in curing is experienced in consequence of the grapes not ripening until several weeks later. The most favorable conditions in every respect appear thus far to be afforded by the San Joaquin Valley. These are an abundance of the richest soils, thorough systems of irrigation, absence of dews and fogs, a uniform high temperature, which gives unusual flavor and perfection to the grape, and a protracted warm and dry season that enables the curing processes to be carried on in the sun with scarcely a liability to interruption. These advantages have led to a continuous expansion of the industry in that region, until one half the raisin crop of the State is now produced in Fresno County alone. Tulare, Kern, Merced, Stanislaus, and San Joaquin counties, with equal facilities for irrigation, should prove equally successful in the same line of effort. The crop of 1891 has not all been moved yet, but the following figures, giving the actual shipments of the crop of 1890, will show the relative importance of the various localities at that time:

	Boxes.
Fresno	1,050,000
San Bernardino	629,913
Yolo	300,000
San Diego	175,000
Los Angeles	40,000
Sutter	17,000
Shasta	6,000
Solano	14,000
Yuba	17,550
Santa Clara	40,000
Sonoma	15,000
Merced	17,000
Ventura	10,000
Colusa, Tehama, etc.	10,000
Total	2,341,463

The proper planting of a raisin vineyard involves a great amount of care and labor. As on any but thoroughly sub-irrigated land the vines will require irrigation, it is a precedent condition that they must be planted on level ground; and it is better under all circumstances that the ground be leveled or graded, otherwise in excessively rainy seasons the water will stand in the depressions and interfere with the prosecution of work at the proper time. It is seldom, even on the apparently smooth plains, that land is to be found sufficiently level in its natural state. To bring it to the right condition the elevations have to be scraped off and the depressions filled in. The labor required to accomplish this varies according to the original roughness of the land and the degree of levelness to which it is brought. Land cannot ordinarily be leveled perfectly at an expense averaging less than fifty dollars an acre, but grading enough to prevent pools of water accumulating can generally be done at a comparatively small cost.

When the land has been satisfactorily leveled or graded, it is plowed and harrowed until the ground is in as soft and smooth condition as it is possible to get it. It is then laid off into fields or checks, their size and shape being regulated commonly by the necessary ditches and avenues.

At this stage several questions present themselves for consideration which,

is likely to never be definitively settled, but expediency determines it in favor of the former on large vineyards. In order to do the necessary work within the proper time, pruning has to be begun about the first of December, and as good, if not better, results are obtained by this practice.

And here again, at the very first stage of the year's work, another perplexity is encountered in the matter of close or liberal pruning. Like the other ques-

fresh growth will be developed from dormant buds concealed in the rough bark of the head ; if too many, only a sufficient number of canes will grow strongly, the others being arrested at different stages of development. It is a singular feature of Muscat vines in California that suckers bear fruit the same as canes springing from the previous year's growth ; hence, the shoots forced from dormant buds compensate for illiberal pruning.

Photo by Nutting.

GOOD RAISIN LAND.

tions in dispute, it admits of no authoritative settlement. So long as the pruning is confined anywhere within reasonable bounds — say within a range of from six to fifteen spurs of two buds each for full-grown vines — there will not be a very perceptible difference in the result. Vines have a wonderful power of regulating themselves, and find within their own resources a compensation for improper treatment. If too few spurs have been left, a vigorous

As fast as the pruning is finished and the brush disposed of,— which is usually done by burning it in the vineyard, — plowing is begun, generally about the first of January. A back-furrow is turned in the center of the space between the rows, and the earth thrown away from the vines until nothing is left but a narrow ridge. This is broken with a shovel in some cases, but in most instances the vineyard is cross-plowed, leaving only a little square at each vine

Photo by Nutting.

A SIX MONTHS OLD VINEYARD.

to be spaded or hoed. The soil is allowed to receive the rains and the action of the atmosphere in the loose condition in which the plowing has left it until late in March, when the work of cultivating commences. The cultivators are run lengthwise and crosswise, until the ground becomes pulverized and smooth and no weeds are to be seen. The oftener the operation is repeated the better, but two or three cultivations are the usual number, the last in May, after which time the vines attain a size that renders further cultivating impracticable. The weeds that spring up later are cut out with hoes.

Meanwhile other necessary operations have to be attended to. The first of these, in point of time, is sulphuring the vines. The greatest danger to the raisin crop comes from mildew. Its presence is indicated by a filmy network, like a spider web, upon the bud clusters, and a whitish incrustation on the leaves. The first effect is the dreaded coulure, or dropping of the fruit. The berries on bunches thus affected fall off at the time of blossoming, leaving the stem entirely bare, or at best with only a few straggling grapes clinging to it ; hence, a bad attack of mildew may result in an almost total loss of the first crop. The later effects are the drying up and falling of the badly mildewed leaves, a sickly appearance of the foliage generally, and a failure of the new growth of wood to mature properly. Repeated attacks of mildew will dwarf vines, and eventually destroy them. The cause of the evil and the conditions that favor it are not definitely known, its appearance and action being too capricious for the formulation of any certain theory respecting it. It comes or stays away at its own pleasure, regardless of any fixed meteorological conditions ; it will select for its ravages a strip as clearly defined as a roadway, attack irregular patches at random, or spread over an entire vineyard, — all in a way wholly unaccountable. It commonly, however, most severely attacks young vines, and those on poor soil and elevated places ; and it is more prevalent in cold and cloudy seasons, especially if there be strong north winds. A moist atmosphere is also favorable to its development ; while, singularly enough, a copious rain destroys

RAISIN DRYING.

cipally employed for packing. Some of these houses afford work for more than five hundred hands. Women and girls come to the towns from all directions during the packing season, parties of them not infrequently renting houses or living gypsy-like in tents.

There are few brighter or more animated scenes than a raisin packing-house in full operation. The women pack the layers, or choice goods. Considerable skill is required to do this well and rapidly, and as they are paid by the form, the amount that each one earns depends upon her taste and dexterity. Earnings range from $1.25 to $3 per day. A form is a metal or wooden frame, the size of an ordinary raisin box, in which five pounds of cluster raisins, surrounded by plain paper, are arranged compactly and tastefully.

The raisins are then pressed and slid into the packing boxes. These are made in three sizes, — quarter, half and whole boxes, holding respectively five, ten, and twenty pounds, but the last is always understood when speaking of a box of raisins. The top layer is surrounded with ornamental paper in addition to the plain white. The packer's label is placed over this, the printed cover nailed on, the edges nicely trimmed, and the box is ready for the market.

Less care is required with loose raisins. It is in handling them that the greatest improvement has been made upon the Spanish methods of packing. A combined stemmer and grader has been perfected, by which large quantities are handled with very little labor. The raisins are fed from a hopper into the space between a woven-wire cylinder revolving

SOME RAISIN PICKERS

within a larger cylinder of the same material, where they are broken from their stems; they then fall into a fanning-mill, by which the stems and dirt are blown away; after which they pass through a series of screens that grade them into as many different sizes as are desired. The better grades of loose raisins are packed in boxes, with paper and labels, giving them an appearance nearly as attractive as that of layers; but the inferior qualities are now generally shipped in sacks.

lishments, costing from $5,000 to $10,000, to comparatively inexpensive devices, in which the drying is effected simply by heat and ventilation. It would be better for the industry if no attempt were made to cure the second crop. Inferior raisins only can be made from it, as the grapes never contain sufficient sugar. To facilitate the curing of second-crop grapes they are sometimes dipped in lye and made into what are known as Valencia raisins. The lye cracks the skins, and in consequence of the resulting

THE STEMMER.

The treatment of the second crop, which usually ripens early in October, or about the time the first crop is out of the way, is the same in every respect, except that the trays frequently have to be stacked to protect the raisins from rain, which is almost sure to come before they are cured. The drying of this crop in the open air is extremely hazardous at all times, and wholly impracticable in bad seasons. Principally with a view to saving it, many raisin growers have built driers, varying from large steam estab-

evaporation the grapes will dry twice as quickly as undipped ones. The product, however, has not met with favor from dealers; hence the method is not extensively practiced.

The Sultana raisin, which was comparatively neglected for a time, is steadily growing in favor. There will be an immense demand for it when its excellence for cooking purposes is generally known. To insure good bearing, canes three or four feet long have to be trained from the ground every year and tied to

RAISIN PACKING.

stakes, which is a laborious and expensive task; but the vine is a heavy bearer, little liable to be affected by mildew, and its fruit is easily dried and stemmed, so that upon the whole the Sultana crop is equally profitable with the Muscat, and a much surer one.

The cost of labor will always prevent California from competing with Spain in some of the niceties of the raisin business. It would not pay us to trim and nurse the grapes upon the vines in order to secure perfect bunches and large berries, nor to handle the clusters by the stems only throughout all the manipulations in order to preserve their bloom. Neither could we afford to do the fancy facing bestowed upon the choicer Spanish packs. These things could be done here as well as in Spain, but with the present rates of labor it would be at a cost far in excess of the price obtainable for the goods. But with the exception of such fancy work, comparison with our great rival will all be in favor of California. Our grapes are more meaty, and have a richer flavor; our raisins are better cured, and will keep twice as long without deteriorating; our grading is fairer and our packing honester, on the average. These are points of superiority that will gradually obtain recognition everywhere, and eventually gain us the markets of the world.

Just now it is devoutly to be wished that a greater portion of that future trade was already secured. Within a year or two production has increased more rapidly than the market could be extended, or than it has been, at least. The consequence was extremely low prices the past season. This state of affairs, however, is not likely to continue. It is probable that the low price itself will assist materially in enlarging the market, as at home it will bring our raisins to the notice of many who have not hitherto used them, and will allow of their being extensively exported with a certainty of profit. But with only the ordinary increase in consumption, the demand will soon exceed the supply again. The history of all industries is marked by periods of depression. It was not to be expected that raisin growing would prove an exception to the rule.

It has encountered a check just at present which was plainly to be foreseen. But with proper attention to finding new markets, with caution in not swelling the production too rapidly, with constant improvement in growing, curing, and packing, the raisin industry of California will continue to flourish and expand until the world has reached its ultimate limit of prosperity.

Joseph T. Goodman.

Staging in the Mendocino Redwoods (1892)

THE

OVERLAND MONTHLY.

VOL. XX. (SECOND SERIES.) — AUGUST, 1892. — No. 116.

STAGING IN THE MENDOCINO REDWOODS. I.

F all the stage routes open to the traveler in California, probably none offer such wild diversity of the picturesque as the various lines intersecting Mendocino. These have their focal point at Ukiah, which is a beautiful wooded town situated on the Russian River at the terminus of the San Francisco and North Pacific Railroad.

Before noon on week days one sees from the windows of the hotel some half dozen cumbrous, weather-stained coaches, all entering the main thoroughfare from various side streets, and not one more than a few minutes behind the rest. With a fine dash and clatter, and important cracks of the whip, each driver pulls up his steaming four-in-hand before the express and post offices opposite, hands out the regulation iron box and leather mail bags, amid a score of hearty questions and answers, and then, with a word to the champing leaders, the short turn to the hotel is faultlessly executed, and the cramped passengers eagerly alight for dinner.

No other personage in a mountain town has the prestige of the stage driver. Every one greets him with liking and respect, and his trifling foibles are passed over with admirable indulgence. If he takes a glass too much when off duty, or spins a yarn to the utmost limit of credibility, by tacit consent the matter is not emphasized by his patrons. In most instances, they have known him since their childhood, when imagination made a hero of the stalwart, free-hearted young man who handled broncos as if they were rabbits, and who never failed to give a "lift" to dusty little legs measuring the long lane to the country school.

In fact, one cannot journey far with a professional driver, before becoming convinced that he merits all the grateful recognition so unostentatiously bestowed upon him. For years he has been equal to a tele-

Bacon & Company, Printers.

TRAINING HOP VINES.

Indeed, the memory of the stage driver has infinite capacity. Seldom a station, camp, or shanty, but has its daily message or package for him to deliver to some one on the route. These commissions are rarely forgotten, though meanwhile the most exacting passenger is not conscious of the least neglect of his personal comfort or entertainment.

To ordinary thinking the word "comfort" is hardly to be used in connection with stage riding, even on a picked road. Nevertheless, this is scarcely a fair conclusion. The popular conception of this unfashionable mode of travel includes the dismembering, muscle-wrenching vehicle of primitive periods; whereas, the stage of today is quite another affair, — yielding of spring, delightfully rocking in motion, capacious, cushioned and curtained in a style wholly luxurious by comparison. Then, if the right time of the year be selected for north country riding, one is totally free from that most serious drawback to California travel, the dust. By the middle of May, there is spring time riot on the mountains, the wood-embossed valleys were never so tenderly gay and green, and the frequent streams are like running quicksilver.

phone between the remote settlements on his line. To him is due the latest news from the logging camps in the redwoods, and the particulars of the last accident at the mill, all told with graphic homeliness of phrase. From the same source the masters learn how sheep shearing progresses on the high, breezy slopes, the day their fattest beeves may be expected at market, and how the droves of sharp-snouted hogs thrive on the acorn crop. To others interested he imparts the condition of the young fruit trees at Prairie Camp, the number of ties split in a day by the new crew, how the tan-bark hunters are back for the summer, and the exact symptoms of "Mis' Hodges' bilious spell" at Comptche.

Without a day's delay, I spoke for a through seat to the coast beside Jack Crow, the driver, and the same afternoon we made start for the redwoods. My first sense was of disappointment that neither route took in that daintiest of mountain mirrors, Leonard Lake. However, there was little room for regret of any sort, for all the valley lay warm and lovable under the far upreaching of mountains snow-silvered on the outer rim of a cloud-buffeted horizon.

Under this inimitable reflex of sun and shadow we careered up the broad lanes, past poppy-hedged wheat fields, and wide bottom levels of shooting hop-vines. There were plodding Indians at work, training the tendrils up the leafless poles.

YOUNG JIM CROW.

Photo by O. Carpenter

A SHEPHERD'S ARCADY.

"Those poles must be all o' ten feet high," the driver remarked, pointing toward them with his whip. "You'd hardly believe it, but a young smarty from the State University came here a year or two ago an' bought up a lot of old telegraph poles to start his hop patch. He said science taught him that the higher you made the vines climb, the better would be the crop. I hain't heard of his getting anyone fool enough to plant his poles for him yet, an' guess likely he's cut his wisdom teeth since an' give up the notion."

The hop plantations along Russian River are the most romantically situated of any in the State. Everywhere, the white oaks stand singly or in groups about the fields, or spread protecting arms over the home eaves of the farmer. In the orchards, clusters of baby fruit were already visible, sheltered by new leaves so flushed they were all but flowers.

Crossing the river on the long bridge several miles out from Ukiah, we turned hillward up a charming pass, through thickets of blossoming chemisal and wild white lilac. Here that loveliest of forest trees, the madroño, rivals the oak in girth, the graceful, twisted branches shining like lustrous cinnamon satin through the parting folds of its worn winter jacket. At this season it is gradually replacing the old leaves by fluted bunches of new, resembling nothing so much as velvety blooms of a lively shade of crimson.

Aside from its undisputed right of beauty, the madroño has a commercial value hardly estimated by even its most ardent admirers. The wood is of exquisite color, grain, and hardness, and susceptible of a beautiful polish eminently desirable for indoor ornamentation. The Indians hereabout are not ignorant of its virtues. One of their number, who has become shrewd from years of asso-

the country, sheep men had their choice of government lands for pasture, and their wool brought them forty cents a pound. They had no taxes to pay and no improvements to make. Now there is more or less fencing required in order to control a range, and the price of wool has gone down to half its former figure, owing to the immense importation from other countries. Add to these disadvantages the appropriation of the best lands by settlers, and it is easy to see the general interests of the country have advanced at the expense of the sheep owners. Notwithstanding these drawbacks, however, the wool produced in Humboldt and Mendocino has the reputation of being the finest in the State.

There is something indescribably harmonious in all pioneer life, with its obedience to rude necessity and its primitive makeshifts. The means employed are always so aptly fitted to the end, and savor so directly of human needs and affections. A shepherd's cabin on a wind-swept height gave us a bit of artistic effect. This building was made of short sections of unbarked logs piled up like cordwood, a rough stone chimney in the rear, and the knotty boughs of a handsome oak thrown carelessly across the unpainted roof. There was nothing short of art in the unpremeditated picturesqueness of this simple dwelling.

On reaching the summit we gave a farewell glance at the glorious chain of peaks separating Ukiah Valley from Clear Lake, with old Sanhedrim rearing a frosty line above the others. Below us, on either hand, we saw through a sudden mist of rain the great, green bowls of the valleys. A moment, and

Photo by O. Carpenter

GREENWOOD TRESTLE, ELK CREEK.

Photo by O. Carpenter

LOADING LUMBER AT POINT ARENA.

the sun broke out afresh, dashing a torrent of gold across the dripping wildwood. The air steamed up in fragrance, —a delicious mingling of flower-breaths with the balsam of rosiny bud and leaf, and the faint smell of rankly growing ferns.

Under the fluttering groves of oak and maple saplings, the thimbleberries clambered riotously, their snowy, silklike flowers resting flat on the soft, serrated leaves. The buckeyes thrust up their curving plumes beside straight young firs, looking blither than their wont in a fresh drapery of pea green needles.

These Coast Range oaks present a fantastic venerableness, with their Alpine beards of grizzly moss trailing a yard or more from underneath their huge, gnarly limbs. Many of them carry more moss than leaves, all the branches being thickly wrapped in the coarse gray fiber. An entire landscape of these veiled oaks is a weird picture, especially when beheld through the muffling fog so common to this region. When winds are up, the gray, weblike tresses are loosened and fall to the ground, much to the delectation of sheep and deer, which munch them greedily.

Descending the grade, we passed piles of tan-bark newly peeled from the trunks of numberless chestnut oaks. A week or two later when the roads have dried, this bark is teamed to Cloverdale or Greenwood for shipment.

The tracks of the tan-bark hunter can be traced through all these Mendocino forests, by the reckless felling of the choicest trees which are afterwards left as useless waste. This variety of the oak makes excellent fuel, if worked up before the fiber becomes spongy. The bark is stripped during the three months of summer when it is easily separated from the body of the tree. Fortunately it is a rapid grower, or with the present unrestricted destruction the species would soon become extinct.

Our first night out was spent in Anderson Valley, a narrow strip following the Navarro River seventeen miles on its seaward way. On the north and south are unbroken ranges of high mountains. The cradled valley between has many opulent orchards and fields. Now and again one sees through luxuriant foliage the funnel-shaped top of a hop kiln, or the similar roof of a fruit-evaporator. Several of the hop-plantations are skirted by redwoods, and these groves make ideal camps for the pickers gathered here in the fall. When the day's work is done, it is said, the young folks dance in some stately sylvan hall, while close at hand, in one of Nature's grandest cathedrals, their elders hold prayer and praise meetings.

The seclusion enjoyed by these Anderson farmers has its disadvantages. They must haul their produce thirty miles, over rough mountain roads, to reach the nearest market. The majority of them have lived here for years, patiently awaiting the day when the ax shall sound in their magnificent forest, and the smoke of mills ascend from the streams. The most feasible outlet for the valley is through the redwood wilderness on the Navarro. In fact, the logging railway from the mouth of this river is steadily heading that way. Twenty or thirty miles more of track, and the road will be open to navigable waters.

The oldest settlers of Anderson Valley are the owners of large bands of sheep. Owing to the nearness of the mountains, their ranges extend almost to the doors of their houses. These sheep masters have adopted certain pe-

culiar methods in the care of their flocks which afford them a deal of recreation. Like other keepers of sheep in the mountains, they have to contend with the serious depredations of wild cats, lions, coyotes, and even grizzlies. Instead of following the usual custom of hiring shepherds, they have trained horses and hounds, and frequently go a-hunting in fine style, killing off the enemy with skilled certainty, and leaving their gentle charges wholly unguarded by day and night.

Of course, this practice incurs considerable expense, probably fully as much as, or more than to hire regular herders, but then, as one of the hunters dryly observed,—

" Think of the fun of it ! "

Before sunrise we were again under way, striking straight for the barricade of western summits climbed by rank on rank of redwoods. These early rides in a spring dawn have a charm all their own. The world is at its best and freshest, and nothing could be more exquisite than the soft outpouring of cool, scented air. Then the loveliest colors ever granted to human eyes are those of morning clouds after rain ! The light showers of the night had passed, and the crests of the peaks wore the glory of the risen sun.

We crossed a mountain stream called Indian Creek, where there were cosy nests of homes with luxuriant gardens and orchards. Along its flashing current our road made a winding passage through the rich brown of tree trunks and outcropping rocks mottled with moss, with borders of white trilliums, ferns, and lilied flags. The gray squirrel flashed electrically from limb to limb, prospecting for future forage ; a bevy of quail made delightful noises in the underbrush ; and blue jays darted and scolded in and out the redwoods which towered in unscathed majesty back of a roadside church.

Never do I behold these matchless

trees without an instinctive outstretching of my arms in greeting! We had now entered their peculiar domain, for the redwood is exclusive, always keeping near the sea, and not being found outside the Coast Range and the Sierra Nevadas. A mountain covered with these kingly trees is inconceivably sublime; and no words can depict the solemn impressiveness of a deep gorge filled with the gigantic upright shafts. There is something, too, almost super-

THE REGULAR PASSENGER.

natural in their profound silence. Birds and all manner of small furry creatures shun the perpetual twilight found here. Only monster slugs make viscous trails over the mottled leaf needles underfoot in the vast soundless aisles.

These Coast Range redwoods, *Sequoia sempervirens*, are only second in size to their renowned brothers of the Sierra. The finest specimens are in Mendocino and Humboldt, and are all the way from ten to twenty-four feet in diameter, with clean, columnar trunks running up to a height of three hundred and even four hundred feet.

Of all the trees in the rich forests of California, not one has the industrial value of her coast redwood. Its popularity is steadily on the increase, in spite of the expense and the ingenious means required to render it marketable. There are today all of 900,000 acres of redwoods still in Mendocino, though the timber next the ocean is cut off to the average depth of eight miles.

Here and there we passed the camps where Portuguese or Russian Finns were at work splitting the beaded boles. The mountains resounded with the echoing blows of their axes. The hands of these burly woodsmen were mahogany stained from the juices of the wood. A man gets twelve to fifteen cents for making a tie, according to its size, and boards himself. The ties are hauled to Greenwood, six or eight horses being used for a load, which usually consists of two wagons coupled together, each piled with seventy-five or a hundred of these split timbers.

Before the redwoods crowded us there were dashes of color everywhere — the scarlet of columbine and larkspur, the pale indigo of lilacs and hardy iris, roses innumerable, and the hair-fringed bells of lemon-hued calochortus. The eye reveled in the unspeakable beauty of this flowering wildness.

Now the gloomy underworld of the sequoias showed no brighter shades than the faded pink of oxalis, and the green and purple foliage of endless huckleberry bushes.

"Here's my regular passenger!" and the driver slowed down his mud-spattered horses.

For the moment we did not see the drift of his remark. Then two tiny figures took shape in the shadows, standing motionless beside a hydra-headed stump. The girl wore a prim hat and carried a tin pail and a book. Though it was barely seven o'clock, she was evidently on her way to school. She and the boy looked ghostly in the obscure light, and neither smiled nor responded to the driver's kindly salutation.

When we stopped, the sister spoke a few words in Russian to the bareheaded boy, and then hastily climbed into the vacant back seat. There was something so unchildlike in her pinched, solemn little visage, that one could not help fancying that the burden of the dumb, sunless forest oppressed her young life. Indeed, the chill of the place was so invincible that the cheer of an occasional patch of sunlight can hardly be imagined.

An hour or so later we came to a diminutive school-house where the "regular passenger" got down, and soberly joined a half dozen other children,—the total number of her schoolmates. Close by was a low-roofed, untidy building, where we stopped ten minutes to change horses. The long morning's ride had so sharpened my appetite that I begged a morsel of food of the pretty school-ma'am who boarded here. She led me back to the fire in a rude kitchen, and hospitably served bread, butter, and dried peaches, on my lap. Nothing ever tasted so good. When the familiar "all aboard" brought me hurriedly to the front steps, it was with the last thick slice in my hand.

At Soda Creek we paused for a drink of the cold, effervescent water. A young girl came running out of a modest dwelling, and asked the driver to take a bonnet she had just trimmed to a lady in Greenwood. After much good-natured raillery, she pinned the paper parcel on his back to insure it from getting jammed, and the amiable fellow carried it thus to the end of the journey.

As we approached Greenwood the

THE SCHOOL MA'AM'S TREAT.

grandeur of the forest disappeared, for we had reached the "chopped out" district. The presence of innumerable blackened stumps, and the tall, charred spires of pines and the Douglas spruce, contrasted vividly with the fresh green of new growths clustering about the parent roots. In some localities once covered with redwoods the ceanothus, locally termed the "blue blossom," has literally possessed the soil. For miles we drove through a continuous cloud of these delicate honey-sweet blooms.

The cañons nearest the coast are curtained from crown to base with a wonderful profusion of wild berry vines. These western slopes furnish the most prodigal berry patches in the world. In June and July many families from the interior cross the redwoods to camp and pick blackberries and raspberries. They bring with them wagon loads of coal oil cans, in which to pack the fruit after they have preserved it on the grounds.

A gap in the hills revealed the blue plain of the ocean, not a white-cap in sight, and scarcely a wrinkle on its burnished surface. Farther still a dim sail was discernible, and just off a rocky point a vessel in the cove was taking on lumber. In the bottom of a willow-trimmed gorge, Greenwood Creek poured its crystal fountains. Just before it reaches the sea its waters are confined by a dam, in which was an enormous jam of logs. Before the rains the river-beds far up their source are rolled full of logs, to be brought down to the mill in high water. In this manner all these coast streams are made of incalculable service to the lumberman. When the river supply is disposed of, steam is called into requisition, and the logging train is now an indispensable adjunct of California lumbering. The Greenwood railway extends six miles back to the timber, a branch line crossing Elk Creek on a splendid iron truss bridge.

The mill at Greenwood is a new plant, and shows an immense expenditure of capital. It is equipped with the latest improvements in machinery, and when both sides are in operation turns out daily ninety-thousand feet of lumber.

Below in the boom a man was leaping from log to log, steering three or four at a time on to the carriage, which is drawn up the logway to the platform by wire cables run by steam power. A donkey engine was hard at work lifting the "sinkers." These heavy butts of redwood can only be kept to the surface by making them secure to lighter logs. The most valuable lumber in redwood comes from the "sinkers," as the grain is finer and harder next the roots of the tree, and takes a smoother finish.

A village is sure to grow up around a large mill, with the saloons usually outnumbering the dwelling houses. The array of empty bottles stacked alongside a Greenwood street is appallingly suggestive. The company's store is a comprehensive affair, including all manner of necessaries which are purchased by the employees. By this means a fair percentage of the wages paid out finds its way back to the original pocket. This is not at all a bad arrangement, but when the same source provides the whisky and beer, the contemplative mind is troubled with doubts.

The coast shore of Mendocino is extremely rugged, the sandstone cliffs having an elevation of one hundred to five hundred feet, with jagged caverns, arches, and detached rocks burrowed out by the waves. For a hundred miles the road is along this sea-wall, and here one experiences the very poetry of staging. No heat or dust even in summer,— only a great salt freshness blowing in from the shining highway of the ships; and on the other hand, the eternal mountains. We counted two steamers and four schooners in sight, besides the spreading canvas of a vessel far away to the north.

Shortly after noon we made an abrupt curve round the Greenwood bluffs above pale green floating beds of kelp. The dense forests traversed in the morning were visible only between wide openings in round, grassy foothills. We saw a puffing engine dragging a long train of loaded flat cars around the poppy-tipped cliffs. A few days before twenty of these cars, piled with logs, went over the embankment into the surf.

Following us south were fields with grazing cattle, and emerald stretches of uncut hay. The larger portion of this Point Arena country is given up to dairying, and delicious and wholesome is the butter made from these blossoming pastures. All the downs and meadows are sown to flowers. There were acres of purple violets, asters of blue and gold, daisies, cream cups, nemophilæ, pale-edged poppies, clover-blooms and dandelions, all heading so evenly they made a smooth mosaic of incomparable hue and pattern.

Then there were knolls and sweeping hollows, where one sees the effectiveness of grass, pure and simple. And such grass as it is, sweet and juicy, and full of the virtues of dairy products! It is delightful to watch the Jerseys eat it. They wrap their tongues about the succulent bunches with a sound that is truly appetizing.

This feed is kept green three fourths of the year by constant cool winds and fogs; afterwards, corn fodder is fed to the cows, and great mangel-wurzel beets and Belgian carrots, pulled from the plowed fields next the comfortable homes.

The butter from this section finds its principal market in San Francisco, though hundreds of pounds are also disposed of at the lumber settlements. The business is mainly in the hands of Americans, the most of the dairies being owned by old residents who came here in the fifties. Many of them make use of all the new appliances of machinery for separating the cream and working the butter, and the utmost care is taken as to cleanliness and the proper packing of the rolls.

There are thousands of acres of available agricultural and pasture lands around Point Arena, though much of this is still unoccupied, unless one excepts the desultory sojourning of half a hundred Diggers. The lumber interests of the place are now confined to the making and shipping of posts, staves, shakes, and railroad ties, which are brought down a seven-mile flume, and loaded on vessels by means of wire cables. As many as thirty-five hundred ties are thus transferred in a single day. The same ingenious method is employed in the shipment of cordwood, hides, tanbark, and potatoes, the other leading products of the country.

One comes upon the town quite unexpectedly. A turn in the road, and you are bowling down the incline of the main street, the pleasant dwellings tilted back against windy hills putting up their shoulders to the sea.

The drives hereabout are delightful, that to the light-house being usually the first proposed to visitors. This handsome building stands on the northwest extremity of a flower-enameled promontory jutting three miles beyond the mainland. From the dizzy tower one has a memorable view of the ocean, with its curving margin of white, broken cliffs, the numerous islets off shore, and fronting this fair sea picture the green dairy farms rolling back to a dark ridge of mountains.

Some of the nearest rocks are clambered over by writhing sea-lions. These animals are semi-annually killed off for their oil, and are a profitable investment to the man that owns the rocks.

The road to the Indian rancheria is a particularly romantic one, and a more picturesque site for a primitive village could not have been chosen. On a grassy swell just out from the woods hiding the beautiful Garcia River are built the rude huts of the natives, with their cir-

RANCHERIA AT POINT ARENA.

cular sweat house in the midst. A few squatty figures were packing homeward heavy burdens in baskets strapped to their backs.

This remnant of a decaying tribe lives by hunting and fishing, and doing odd jobs about the farms and dairies. In the fall of each year they join the hop pickers on the Russian River, and are considered better hands than either the whites or the Chinese. In spite of poverty and excess of vermin and filth, these Diggers are as care-free and happy as children.

Through this fine landscape the Garcia makes a joyous descent to the ocean, its translucent current bearing many a lusty trout and salmon. While going through the redwoods these western streams take on a solemn chant, in keeping with the reverent forest. But as soon as they emerge into oak and laurel openings, or when cascading past the curving summits of berry hills, their glad exuberance knows no bounds. It is only when they broaden to meet the sea that the shouting, swirling waters drop into a measured flow, and advance with serene majesty.

Fording the Garcia, our north-bound stage was driven up the gravelly lanes at a rollicking pace, sometimes plunging down grades quite frightful to contem-

plate. Of these the Mal Paso is the largest and steepest, and its legendary history the most exciting. The pioneer settlers came into the country through this almost impassable gulch.

"It was off that split," said the driver, "that my grandmother lost her life. She was overturned, an' her neck broken. The rest of the wagons was took to pieces an' let down by ropes. My folks was the first to begin stock raising here. That was before they commenced taking out lumber. The Morse family came in by sea on a chartered schooner. They landed in the sand at Fish Rock, an' Gran'ma Morse an' the three children had to foot it ten miles across a rough country before they reached camp. The old lady is still living at Point Arena, an' is hale an' hearty."

For some distance on ahead a white church showed starkly on the treeless brink of the high gray cliffs. On coming nearer we found it was not so isolated as it had first appeared. There were, in fact, several dozen dilapidated, tenantless buildings scattered over the same bench, their windows broken and roofs fallen in. Stacked about were rotting shakes and ties, and the remains of chutes and tramways, with all the other belongings of a once flourishing lumber port.

The church, standing with its back to the sea, was the only modern feature of the place, unless one excepts a neatly fenced graveyard alongside, with its freshly painted crosses and headboards. Nothing more forlorn and desolate than this deserted village can be pictured. The driver volunteered the following scraps of its history :—

"Th's is Cuffey's Cove. There was once millions of feet of lumber shipped from off them rocks, an' such loads of potatoes ! You must have heard of the Cuffey Cove potatoes, for in them days they had a big name all over the State. The first man that come here was Nigger Nat, an' after that the men called the place ' Cuffey' as a sort of joke. That was nigh on to forty years ago. Oh, yes, Nat 's living still, an' pretty near as young as ever ! Likely 'nough you 'll run across him fishing up on Big River. He 's mostly there this time o' year."

Ten miles beyond Cuffey's Cove, and Navarro is reached. At the mouth of the river two vessels were being loaded with lumber directly from the wharf. This is done by means of two chutes, each sixty feet long and on opposite sides of the wharf, so both vessels can take on loads at the same time. By this double arrangement two hundred thousand feet of lumber is transferred from flat-cars to the schooners in a day.

The main town of Navarro is huddled on a sand flat which is nearly on a level with the tide. After some days of country fare our accommodations at the superintendent's home seemed the acme of luxury. Indeed, it was an occasion when one is tempted to believe that soft living has its spiritual advantage, so inexpressibly restful was the Sabbath spent here.

All the previous night it rained ; not in persuasive showers, but a sheeted downpour that set the river to boiling, and sent all hands up stream at sunrise. Such a heavy freshet so late in the season had not been known in twenty-five years.

And how the logs came tumbling and crunching down the turbid flood, here and there thrusting up a defiant butt

with the water streaming off like a mane ! The men worked like beavers, some in boats, others along shore, and those more venturesome on the heaving logs. With their long pike poles they steered the renegade logs into course, and broke up jams in the sharp bends of the stream. It was desperate work at times, with a spice of real danger, but withal wildly exhilarating.

After nightfall the men straggled to camp, exhausted, wet to their waists,

CHASING LOGGING TRAIN.

but exultant ; they had brought down to the boom more than four thousand logs.

There are from seventy to a hundred families at Navarro, including those on the "Navarro Ridge." For the most part their houses are small box-shaped buildings, with streets between scarcely wider than footpaths. In the diminutive square stand the church and a new hall. The expense of keeping up the former is defrayed in part by the company, and the remainder is subscribed by the men. The services are well attended, not a few of the congregation walking two and even four miles from the wood camps.

The public hall at Navarro is the latest pride of the neighborhood. It was built for the purpose of encouraging more innocent amusements among them than gambling and drinking. The drapery of the stage represents a faded view of Naples, and struck me as oddly familiar. It was in fact a portion of the drop curtain of the old California theater in San Francisco.

Navarro is one of the most active lumber districts on the Coast. When its great sawmill is in full blast, the pay roll of the company numbers eight hundred men. The majority of these are Russians, Finns, Swedes, Danes, and Norwegians, their overseers being Americans. These foreigners have a monopoly of the lumber business in California, and as a class are steady workers. They are robust, powerfully muscled fellows, who stand a tremendous amount of hardship and bad whisky. There is but little variety in their life, their hours being long and the work largely of the treadmill sort.

Common hands in the mills and logging camps are paid thirty dollars a month, the married men, who board with their families, receiving the additional sum of ten dollars. The company has a flourishing store and eating-houses, which the employees are expected to patronize. The cooks are usually Chinamen, who also fill the places of water carriers. They have not the physical strength to make good wood hands, nor the mechanical skill to serve in the mills.

Unlike the generality of lumber towns, Navarro refuses to sell intoxicating liquor to the men. They get it in some way, of course, but necessarily in limited quantities. On a first occasion of drunkenness, a man is reprimanded by the superintendent. On a repetition of the offense the delinquent gets a peremptory dis-

charge. This strict discipline is not without a salutary effect. Navarro can boast of a better class of inhabitants than is customarily found in a lumber settlement.

Altogether, there are more than a thousand laborers in and around Navarro, who get their livelihood out of the various branches of the lumber trade. From two hundred to three hundred of these are engaged in taking out split timber, the bulk of which consists of railroad ties. The rest of these men come under the head of mill hands, wood hands, and railroad hands.

There are thirty-five miles of unbroken wilderness running back from the Navarro landing, with an average width of two to fifteen miles. This noble forest is already penetrated by twelve miles of railroad built by the company.

"We shall be in time to get the noon train," the superintendent hurriedly remarked, with a glance at his watch.

As we hastened across the street we heard the spiteful shriek of a locomotive, and caught a glimpse of a long tail of empty flat-cars whisking around an angle of the glen.

The superintendent was not without resources.

"Jim," he shouted, "take us aboard your engine, and chase the logging train!"

A moment more, and we were perched on a queer little dummy which included boiler, tender, and a seat for passengers, all on four wheels. With an avenging whistle we darted forward, past the smoking mill and wide boom choked with logs; on, where the narrow track glinted like a silver-edged ribbon in the wet grass, and the laurels clasped boughs overhead.

Through a whirlwind of cinders there were fleeting visions of gaping woodsmen, girls in red calicoes, and a bewildering chaos of mountains, rivers, and trees. Every second we quickened speed till the landscape rushed by in dizzy circles, and the wind tore at our breath and clothes. It was magnificent riding!

On we flew, over bridges, rocking, bumping, and zigzagging around curves and chasms, all the while keeping our seat with difficulty. A minute later we sighted the rear car of the logging train, and the black plume of smoke from the engine. Our locomotive sent up deafening whistles, while the superintendent frantically waved his handkerchief, and I took a firmer hold of the iron railing.

After what seemed a hopeless amount of signaling, we saw the train slow down; at last we had been seen or heard.

" What time did we make ?" we asked when breathlessly alighting.

The engineer gave a satisfied grin,— " All of forty miles an hour."

Boarding the train we proceeded more leisurely up the cañon, the entire way being full of interest. A deserted logging camp on our left made a melancholy picture. The shanties and ox stalls were empty, and the skid roads and landings almost obliterated by vegetation. Sections of old chutes clung dejectedly to the mountain side, and the whole place was eloquent of disuse and decay. We were now in the midst of a worked-out tract, the face of the country appearing as though a hurricane had passed over it. The mountains, scorched by fire, retained but a thinned-out array of spindling pines, their ragged branches blown stiffly one way. Everywhere in the heaped-up debris of bark and branch were the black, massive stumps of redwoods. Some of these giants had vainly perished, for their prostrate columns were split the full length in falling.

Later in the day while walking up the new track, we came to one of these splintered trunks.

" There's four thousand feet o' lumber gone to waste," —and the rheumatic old time-keeper at my side gazed at it gloomily.

" There ain't no 'scuse for it neither, but 'nfernal ca'lessness," he went on emphatically. " It 's jes' this way. A chopper ought 'er know where a tree 's to fall, and make a lay out. It don't

THE LOGGING CAMP.

Photo by O. Carpenter

Photo by Meta Hanen

NEW GROWTH ON THE RIVER.

take half an eye to see that it 'ud smash if that holler wa'n't filled in with brush an' stumps. A redwood is diff'rent from most other trees; it carries its bigness good. A tree like that 'ud turn out nine or ten sixteen-foot logs. How ole be they? Well, Noah's flood was little less 'n six thousand years ago, an' it's the sup'sition them redwoods hez ben growin' ever since. 'Cordin' to that, it'll take the same time for the likes o' this to be stan'in here again."

The logic of the old foreman was unanswerable, and we gravely returned his salute as he hobbled off to inspect the gang at work in a side cañon.

Ninetta Eames.

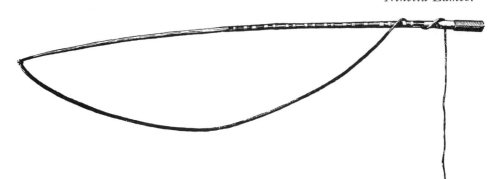

STAGING IN THE MENDOCINO REDWOODS. II.

HERE can be no more picturesque scenes conceived than those daily recurring in a logging camp. First, there is the cutting down of the tree, which is always an absorbing matter to the looker-on. This is oftenest done in winter when the ground is soft, for the redwood is a brittle tree, and liable to split if it strikes hard. If the tree selected is marred in any way at the butt, the scaffold is built of sufficient height to bring the incision above the deformity. Usually two men work together at opposite ends of the platform, the one chopping right handed, the other left handed. When well through the bark, a ten-foot falling-saw is used to complete the job. This saw is much narrower than the regular cross-cut saw afterwards used to divide the trunk into sections. It takes a day and a half to fell an ordinary-sized redwood.

The value of a chopper is in his knowing just where a tree will fall. To the untrained eye it appears perfectly straight, and its "lay out," therefore, easily determined. But the expert chopper sees differently, and makes his plans accord with the slight deviation from the vertical of that towering stem.

Before the sawyers begin on the prostrate trees a fire is kindled, to burn off the obstructing brush. During the conflagration the "swampers" are vigilantly at work, going about with buckets of water to prevent the destruction of valuable timber other than the redwood. There is no danger of the flames injuring the latter, owing to the great thickness of its bark.

Photo by Meta Hanen.

BROUGHT TO THE "DUMP."

440

A few hours and the fire has completed the devastation of what Nature was hundreds of years in building. The sawyers now fall to with a will, their sooty faces and hands making them look like colliers. Were it not for the previous burning, no work could be more delightfully clean than theirs, barring the stain of the fragrant juice, and the infinitesimal particles arising from the madder-hued wood, with flecks of leaf and bark.

The trunks are cut in lengths suitable for the market, the average being from ten to sixteen feet. When the barkers have performed their part, the under side of one end of the stripped log is sniped, causing it to bear a rude resemblance to the runner of a sled. This work is performed by the "snipers," or team crew, which consists of six men, including the bull-teamster and the chain-tender.

The logs are often on a side hill above the skid road, where the ponderous oxen travel up and down. When the question is asked as to how steep this road can be safely made, the answer is invariably the same,—

"Just as steep as the cattle can climb."

It is the part of the "jackscrewers" to roll the logs within reach of the team crew. In fact, without the simple instrument known as the "jackscrew," the handling of redwood would be impossible. Even in exercising the utmost caution, there is always danger to the jackscrewers from the unexpected rolling of a log.

Good judgment must be used in making up the load for the oxen, and the chain-tender's position is one of exceptional responsibility. The heaviest butt is carefully chosen to go on ahead, and all are joined by chains with dog-hooks driven well down on the under side of the logs. The chain-tender takes the precaution to wear cork heels on his boots to prevent him from slipping. If he be not a novice, he will bravely ride the front log, keeping a sharp eye to the water-carrier, whose duty is hardly less important than his own. It is the business of the water-carrier to go between the head log and the rear oxen, and wet the skids in the road so the logs will slip easier. A cup of water missing its aim will often cause the logs to jump the track. The skids are set five feet apart, and the Chinaman is supposed to throw a cup of water upon each one. He carries two buckets swinging from the ends of a pole, and it is surprising to see how long his supply of water holds out.

The six to eight yoke of bulls tugging at the long line of bumping logs is one of the most animated scenes in a lumber camp. These brutes are of enormous size, stolidly obedient to the "Whoa haws" and "Gees" of the teamsters, and surprisingly quick to get out of the way of a flying log. In a hard pull the faithful creatures fairly get down upon their knees to make it.

When the logs are brought to the landing or "dump," the oxen are turned back up the skid road, and the jackscrewers roll the boles on the flat-cars, or into the stream, whichever is the most convenient way to get them to the mills.

Another common method of bringing the logs to the river is sending them in a box flume. This is an exciting spectacle. Each naked bole comes smoking down at a terrific speed, and makes a noble splash when it strikes the water.

The cars used for transporting lumber are strongly constructed flats, nearly square in shape, and each set upon four wheels. They are so arranged that by close coupling, a combination car can be made. When a load of logs is brought to the sawmill, they are slid up inclined timbers, by hooking around them wire cables which are worked by machinery.

Owing to the colossal proportions of the redwood, the machinery used in our Coast milling differs widely from that employed in the sawmills of other coun-

THE LOG CHUTE.

tries. All first-class mills here have double band saws, the circular saw being no longer in favor. One of the advantages of this exchange is the saving of the sawdust, which is utilized as fuel for the engines. There is endless fascination in watching the glistening steel slice up a mammoth seventeen-foot log as a knife would cut through cheese; nevertheless the friction is greater than it appears, for the saw must be changed for another every three hours.

The heap of refuse lumber thrown off rate piles, distributed along four side tracks. Each pile has a neat sign-board on which is labeled the dimensions and quality of the lumber. The ground between is planked over, and the whole yard comes under electric light.

Since the year 1811, when a Russian colony commenced logging operations at Fort Ross, California's lumber interest has steadily increased. Today the output from this industry has reached a marvelous figure in the commercial catalogue of the State.

Photo by O. Carpenter

THE BAND SAW.

by the slab elevator at the waste dump is kept burning continually. The mill and the wharf are lit by electricity, so in case of pressure vessels are loaded by night as well as by day. A model sawmill includes under its roof a carpenter shop, a machine shop, a blacksmith shop, and an attic where the saws are kept and repaired.

The piling ground is arranged with strict regard to system and convenience. It has a capacity of ten millions feet of lumber, made into eight hundred separate

Another morning of crisp, white sunshine, and our stage was lumbering up the Navarro Ridge, en route for Big River.

There are two daily stages running up and down the Mendocino coast,—one the regular mail line, and the other the "Portuguese Opposition." The respective drivers keep up a petty feud, which furnishes no little amusement to passengers. On the morning in question the Portuguese stage pulled out a few minutes in advance of us. Our driver, a

Photo by Carpenter.

MENDOCINO CITY.

bilious young man with a morbid view of things in general, and the whole Portuguese race in particular, interpreted this spurt of energy on the part of his rival as a fresh instance of insolence.

THE "OPPOSITION."

"Talk about the Chinese," he grumbled, "why, they're a wholesale blessing to a country compared to these good-for-nothing for'ners. There hain't no work in Mendocino City but's run by a pack o' Portuguese. Say, can't you help them plugs o' yourn along faster?"

The last in a loud voice, for his horses' noses were scraping the canvas cover of the "Opposition," and it was impossible to pass abreast on the narrow road.

A swarthy, pudgy-cheeked man thrust his head back at us with an exasperating grin. Our driver choked down an oath or two, and then yelled again:—

"Why don't you git out o' the road? I can't hold my team from running over you!"

Then to the passengers,—

"That idiot's hull four ain't equal to one o' my horses."

When we approached the staid little

NAT.

hamlet of Biggerville, there was a new grievance. Was the "Opposition" going to get either of those persons waiting to be taken aboard?

"G' long, Prince! *Duke!*"

Thus urged by their lordly titles and the snap of the lash about their ears, our horses bounded forward, and both stages reached the hotel together. The passengers turned out to be a couple of Chinese "swampers" on their way to Fort Bragg. They unhesitatingly climbed into the Portuguese stage, already occupied by two of their countrymen; our driver meanwhile remarking, with a disgusted sniff, that he was n't "hankering for no such load." With this parting fling he made the customary disappearance into the bar-room, from which he emerged shortly, wiping his mouth on the back of his hand.

A glance at the other stage showed the driver's seat still vacant, and we heard the clinking of glasses through the half open door of a near saloon. The opportunity was not to be lost. A moment later we were making a gallant exit from the sleepy town, the horses tossing their manes and widening their nostrils to take in the cool salt breeze, while the sharp blows of their hoofs sent up showers of flinty sparks. A half hour of this brisk trotting, and the "Opposition" was hopelessly distanced.

At Whitesboro we found the village nearly deserted, its lumber exports being now limited to the shipping of ties and cordwood.

Seven miles south of Mendocino City we crossed the Albion River, a pretty stream, averaging a width of a hundred yards for a mile or two up its abrupt, wooded banks. The immediate coast line is bare of trees, its sharply indented wall bordered for miles by outlying rocks. In the shoal ground off the south point of the little harbor, is Pinnacle Rock, standing in range of the smokestack of the saw mill. In the throat of the inner cove Mooring Rock is seen, girdled by a rusty mooring chain. Vessels of ninety tons burden, and drawing six and a half feet of water, are loaded off the mill wharf, while lighters are used for transferring freight to large schooners lying at Mooring Rock. The forests accessible to Albion Cove are almost exhausted, and the quaint old mill stands in a wasteful disorder of logs and lumber.

We passed stock ranches next the bluffs, with dwarf pines straggled about. The low hills on the east were blotched with burnt stumps, indicating the one time existence of vast numbers of trees. There was no longer a lavish outspread of flowers, though many painted blooms still nodded to us behind the moss-grown rails of the fences. The handsomest of these, and for that matter altogether the most beautiful flower we had yet seen, was the *Rhododendron Californicum*, which is said not to grow farther south than Mendocino. The people hereabout call them "wild oleanders." The flaring, roseate blossoms form compact clusters on the branchlets of a large evergreen shrub, whose peculiar habitat is the well drained peat of these bench lands.

The country grew more hilly as we journeyed north, and was frequently cut through by gorges dark with pine and redwood, or cañons whose streams dance to the sea under the lightsome foliage of

ROWING UP BIG RIVER.

Photo by Meta Hanen.

THE BOOM ON BIG RIVER.

alders, or spicy nutmeg trees and lithe-limbed spruce. In many localities the soil is rich and friable, presenting to the eye a varied landscape of billowy pasture lands alternating with squares of plowed patches and fields of waving oats.

The dwellings of these coast farmers hint of homely ways and wholesome contentment. They are mostly broad and simple in structure, and painted white, with a virtuous regularity of window and door, and a welcoming look about the clean-swept porches fronting old-fashioned posy beds. At times we drove by some old steep-roofed barn, and the odor of milch cows was mingled with the briny scent of dulse and kelp. The cattle lingered to chew their cud in the shade of the lean-to, and a stray hog lazily scratched itself on the convenient edge of a loosened board. From the hay loft there sounded the wild jollification of hens over new-laid eggs, and a sheeny chanticleer in the yard crowed lustily in

conjugal sympathy. The orchards we saw were set on the inland slope of hills which served as windbreaks, or thrifty gums made a hedge on the side next the ocean.

A mile below Little River Harbor is Stillwell Point, a bold cliff two hundred feet high. Soon after passing this conspicuous landmark we sighted the pretty town of Little River. When our horses came to a slow climb, we took advantage of the lull to question the driver, and learned that the lumber industry here is reduced to the shipping of ties. The sawmill was silent, the swampy boom gorged with whitening logs, and the yards stacked with discolored lumber and the debris of past milling. A number of coasting schooners have been built here, and brought out at high water. The timber used in their construction is the California fir, which grows in that vicinity. This wood is marketed under the name of Oregon pine, but is a tougher and stronger wood than the regular pine found north of the boundary of California.

From the tableland lying between Little River and Mendocino Bay one has the first glimpse of Mendocino City, the oldest and most picturesque of all the coast towns. It occupies the rolling bench on the north side of the ragged curve of the bay. Viewed from a distance on shore or at sea the city seems to have an imposing array of cupolas, which are in reality water tanks, with windmills of every known pattern. There is in fact an individuality about the water works of this town not found in any other place of its size. Every family or group of families has its separate well and windmill, thus obviating the necessity of a general source of water supply. One sees windmills painted in red, white, or blue, or dark shades of maroon and yellow, and still others so ancient and wind-tortured that their distinctive color can only be guessed.

When the wind blows, and there is rarely a day herd it does not, these divers windmills set up a medley of discordant creaks and groans, each pitched in a different key, and whether heard singly or collectively, all equally nerve-rending It is presumable one could get used to the constant slapping, straining, and screeching, for nowhere are there people more serene, healthy, and home-loving, than in this breezy town of Mendocino. Many of them are pioneers of this section, and have lived here since the early fifties. They must have had no end of brave, warm purpose, judging from the work they have done, and the superiority of the families they have reared in the midst of inconceivable hardships, and the wild exigencies of a remote timber district.

Not a few of the children of these oak-hearted pioneers have built elegant homes beside the primitive dwellings of their parents. The first house made of sawed lumber still stands in the heart

of the town, and is yet occupied by the original owner. The first settler on the present site of Mendocino City was one William Kaston, a voyager up the coast in 1850, who was forced by stress of weather to seek shelter in the bay. It was not known why he concluded to take up his abode on a bleak, isolated headland, or whether he had companions other than the Indians who hunted and fished along the beautiful river.

A year or two after the arrival of Kaston, a richly laden vessel from China was driven on the beach at the mouth of the Noyo, and parties came up from Bodega to gather salvage from the wreck. These men took back glowing accounts of the wonderful forests on Big River, and their contiguity to a good port — a desideratum of special moment at a time when the price of lumber was greatly out of proportion to the wages paid for hire.

The first to avail himself of this immense timber wealth was Harry Meiggs, who in 1852 brought in the brig Ontario a crew of men, and the machinery necessary to erect a sawmill on the point flanking the north side of the harbor. The oxen used to draw the logs to this mill were sent overland from Bodega. A village sprung up, which was called in those days "Meiggsville" or Big River Landing. Many of the families lived in tents or Indian wick-i-ups, and other poor makeshifts against the inclemency of the weather, the petty depredations of the Indians, and the nightly prowlings of wild beasts.

Coasting steamers call regularly at Mendocino City. The passengers are taken off in boats, and the freight is discharged in lighters and afterwards hoisted by a swinging derrick to a platform on the brink of the cliff. On the northwest face of the head there are two chutes down which lumber is transferred to small schooners, the deeper vessels being loaded from lighters.

The lumber interests of Big River are

at a standstill. No smoke issues from the enormous brick chimney of the saw-mill. Unless a moneyed company buys the mill and builds railroads to the uncut forests higher up the stream, this charming seaside town must share the decline of her sister villages. Her horticultural resources are not sufficient in themselves to support the present population, and a return to prosperity must depend upon the further development of her timber industry. There is plenty of good land here, but the almost indestructibility of the redwood stumps and roots renders its clearing a difficult undertaking.

A day spent in rowing up and down Big River is an enviable pastime, especially in latter May, when not even the feather of a cloud mars the lovely blue of the sky, and water and woods are aglow in a downpour of sun-gold. Across the long bridge, where the terminal forest dips lightly into the white sand of the bar, one comes upon the summer camp of " Nigger Nat," who is still a famous hand at the oar. Indeed, Nat looks surprisingly young for a man who must be upwards of sixty-five or seventy, for history has it he came to the coast in '52, and was then in the prime of early manhood.

" Yes, ma'am, yer right. I was the first white man that come to Cuffey's Cove, an' Portugee Frank was the next un."

So said the old pioneer, as he smoked in the shade of a pepper-wood, just up from the river. It was evident the word "white" was not intended to be facetious, for the bright eyes that met mine had no twinkle in their depths, and the mobile lips wore a respectful smile. He probably used the term in contradistinction to Indian, but the humor of it was irresistible. One could see he was pleased with the prospect of a customer, for he rose with alacrity, calling to Julie, his wife, to help him shove off the boat.

Julie and the dog Bob are Nat's inseparable companions, and both do their full share toward earning the livelihood. She is a good-looking, middle-aged squaw, who amiably cooks the meals, mends nets, fishes, and sets traps, and deftly removes the skins of lions, wild cats, and otter, which Bob and his master bring back from the hunt.

I give Bob precedence, because in reality he is the more successful hunter of the two, rarely failing to chase down a deer so it takes to the water, when, with Nat and Julie actively on hand in the boat, and Bob warily on guard in the brush, the fate of the terrified animal is assured.

Nat related his prowess, while our boat was midway in the stream, Bob decorously squatting by my side, with his one eye intent on the lunch basket, and his remaining ear — he had lost the other in a paw-to-paw combat with a wildcat — pricked attentively. Upon hearing his name, he commenced pounding the seat with his stub tail.

On either hand the river made sweeping curves through uprising banks, clothed with young piney growths that press to the verge, to mirror their graceful greenery in the noontide current. Surely, no stream was ever more beautifully margined than this " Bool-dam " of the Indian ! The name signifies "big holes," and was suggested by the curious blow holes seen in the rocks near its mouth. The American interpretation, however, is " Big River," owing to its being the largest of the coast streams in Mendocino.

We were passing a verdant level, and Nat pointed out a tumble-down shanty and corral : —

" That's ' Ha'nted Flat,' " said he, pushing his hat off his forehead to wipe the dripping perspiration. " I don't go much on ha'nted things myself, but there's cert'nly somthin' curi's 'bout that place. Long ago a man killed his pardner there, an' since then, folks say, cattle put there breaks through the corral an' runs off. Guess it's prob'ble the musquiters won't let 'em stan', fur they 's dreadful pesky here o' nights. One man tol' me he foun' his oxen ready yoked at sunrise, an' durin' the night he heard scary noises. Likely 'nough 't was the 'Singin' Fish.' You hain't heard o' the 'Singin' Fish?' 'Well, that 's sing'lar! Some folks calls 't the 'Drum Fish.' 'T ain't exactly singin' it does, but a sort o' rumble, soundin' mournful down the river till yer hair stan's up. It begins 'bout sunset, and lasts fur two 'r three months every summer. It 's a leetle too early fur it yet,— say 'bout the first o' June. Folks come way up from the city to hear it, an' they 's all puzzled to know what does the singin'; but mostly thinks

His vessel was a ship's boat, schooner rigged, and owned by himself.

After two or three years of ferrying, Nat's blood took fire at the rumors of splendid hunting in the Mendocino ranges; so he sold his boat, and forthwith started for the redwoods. Not many weeks later "Nigger Nat," as he was called, was accounted the best shot on the coast; and, in consequence, was of great service to lumbermen, who made regular contracts with him to furnish their supplies of meat.

"Me an' Greenwood hunted together," Nat went on, while resting on his oars. "There was more elk here than there 's cattle now. The trouble with elk meat, it 's tallowy,— like mutton fat, only more

"BOB."

it 's a fish. I 've made up my mind it 's the bullhead, but that ain't sayin' how it makes the music alongside the logs."

Here Bob gave an expressive yawn, and whined uneasily, while fixing his round, watery eye on a particular copse alongshore.

"He rec'lects that spot; don't ye, Bob? Jest under them salmon berries is where he fetched a deer up once."

Nat proved a most interesting companion. His strength and energy seemed hardly impaired by age, and his memory was unfailing. Before he came to Cuffey's Cove he ran the first ferry-boat between Sausalito and San Francisco, and charged sixteen dollars for single fare.

so. The men was always willin' to pay more fur ven'son, an' more fur black an' brown bear than fur grizzly. If we 'd had such guns as they hev nowdays we would n't 'a' left any game in the country. Sometimes, when we 's campin', we got so hungry fur salt I 'd go fifteen miles to the beach to get a sack o' kelp. By the time I got back, there was plenty o' salt shook out in the bottom o' the sack. We used to slice up the cold livers o' deer and elk an' call it bread, an' sometimes the folks at the mills wa' n't no better off. I 've went clean to Anderson Valley to git meal. It was so coarse we had to mix it with a spoon. It wa' n't long 'fore there was plenty o' potatoes, an' such big ones I once actu'lly took a pile of 'em fur firewood."

While we lunched, and I listened to Nat's modest recitals, Bob was kept quiet by giving him cake and sandwiches. We were now four miles up the river, where there were eight thousand logs wedged in a boom. They had been here a year or more, but were in no danger of rotting in a much longer period, as redwood is quite as impervious to water as it is to fire. A sportsman was swinging his legs off one of these immense logs while fishing for trout.

Big River drains a wide scope of forested country, and in past years millions of feet of logs have been floated on its bosom to the mill. In high tide the water is brackish for eight miles up from its mouth. In the fall salmon come in from the ocean, Nat declaring he had once hauled in fifteen thousand within the space of ten minutes.

"They last till June," he said, "an' then comes herrin', yaller perch, an' flounders, an' there's always plenty bullheads, though a lot of 'em is killed by the fresh water comin' down. Ye see that log, like an' island with grass on top? When an otter's fishin' he lies on one them logs out o' sight in the grass, an' there's jest where I set my trap an' ketch 'em every time."

Nat's one vanity appeared to be the narrow strip of otter fur ornamenting the neck of his woolen shirt.

We found an easy landing, and making fast our boat went ashore. All about us were tropical ferns a dozen feet in height, growing in the dense shade of pepper-wood and pine. Several rods farther along a well-worn trail the shadows were fancifully played upon by circles of sunlight filtered through the scant drapery of white-limbed alders. In this sequestered grove is a narrow lake known as Bishop's Pond. Above its peaceful bosom the withe-like branches of the alders meet and braid themselves into a leafy arch, which is darkly reflected upon the surface. There were white pondlilies, *Nymphœa odorata*, in the lake, the first I had seen in California.

When rowing homeward, the horizontal rays of the sinking sun lay goldenly upon the river, touching the young trees to a tenderer green, and lighting even the black masts of the few patriarch redwoods that had escaped the ax. The massive logs lodged out in the current were mimic green gardens, and every visible head of a "sinker" was whiskered and plumed with seeded grass. On a marshy spot a crook-necked crane waded, and along the sand flats near the mill, flocks of gulls wrangled over the bodies of bullhead fish washed ashore. Nat made powerful strokes against the incoming tide, and landed us among these gluttonous fowls when it was yet early twilight.

The day after the river excursion I took the delightful ten-mile ride up the coast to Fort Bragg. Every bight of the sea on the way had its stream and sawmill, though only the Caspar mill was running, Fort Bragg being the Aaron's rod that had swallowed all the others. This lively lumber town was full of excitement over the prospective launching of a "cigar" raft, which lay in its cradle upon ways six hundred feet long. The raft itself measured three hundred and sixty-five feet in length, with a diameter of twenty-one feet. It was equipped with rudder and steering gear, and had a pilot house perched on top, from which a flag floated. The raft contained more than 1,200,000 feet of piling, saw logs, and ties, all bound together in the shape of a cigar by means of wire ropes placed twelve feet apart, with a core or center chain of solid stud link cable, by which it was to be towed.

For the three months previous the building of this raft, the first of the kind ever attempted on the Pacific Coast, was the one absorbing topic of interest to lumber companies. Should the venture prove successful, they would dupli-

THE MASTER WORKMAN.

cate their mills in the large seaport cities, where all the refuse lumber could be sold for fuel. The carrying out of this plan would not appreciably diminish the work done at the present mills, as only the smaller logs can be made into rafts, thus utilizing trees which are either burnt or left standing.

Unfortunately, the Fort Bragg raft was not launched in deep enough water, and the bow struck the sand when the stern still rested upon a hundred feet of ways. It took days of perplexing labor to get her fairly afloat, by which time the strain had so loosened her bands that she parted at sea, and thousands of dollars worth of logs were lost. The experiment, though a failure in this instance, has at least demonstrated that this manner of raft can be built and launched at certain lumber ports along the Pacific, if the ways are made to run far enough back, and have sufficient elevation to secure the right momentum to the sliding raft.

In 1857 Fort Bragg was a military post, erected for the protection of the " Noyo Indian Reservation," but ten years later was abandoned. Several of the barrack buildings yet stand on the

open plateau occupied by the present town. The place has a noisy, commercial air, its great mill and eating-house and the extensive lumber yards surrounding them being the first objects that meet the eye of the visitor. The total shipment of lumber from this point during the last year was 3,500,000 feet, besides immense quantities of pickets, shingles, and ties. A railroad runs up Pudding Creek seven miles to the Glen Blair mill, which has the reputation of sending out the best selected lumber in the State.

A tunnel of 1,123 feet is nearly completed between Pudding Creek and the Noyo River, by which thousands of acres of virgin timber will be made accessible to Fort Bragg.

The trip back to Ukiah was taken by way of Mendocino City, and thence the road climbs to the Mendocino Barrens, through redwood and pine, with here and there a rhododendron, like a huge bouquet stuck in the somber background of their foliage. Upon gaining the ashen soil of the highland, the forest thins to a few meager trees, raising distorted limbs above the thorny clumps of chemisal. The Barrens indeed would be unspeakably monotonous if it were not for the rhododendron, which here holds queenly sway, transforming the arid stretch into a wonderful profusion of blooms, which look for all the world like vast gardens of roses.

Shortly after entering an unbroken wilderness of stately timber, a man stepped quickly out of the shade and signed to the driver to take him aboard. The Wells, Fargo messenger who was the sole occupant of the interior of the stage made an instinctive clutch at his gun, and glanced askance at the stranger who composedly took the seat by his side. In the conversation that followed, we learned that the new comer was a wood cutter on his way to an upper logging camp.

There was something about this young woodsman, who could hardly have been much past twenty, that aroused interest. It might have been a touch of daring in the keen, dark eyes, or a hint of concealment in the handsome mouth. His manner and speech were respectful and intelligent, and his voice betrayed a curious mingling of suavity and insistence. Though he conversed with modesty and apparent candor, one felt that he was withholding more than he imparted.

"I commenced as a water slinger, when I was a boy," he replied in answer to a question from the messenger, "and have been in logging camps ever since. The work ain't so bad, if the men were treated right. They have to work twelve hours out of the twenty-four, and have only a half hour for dinner. Their pay comes every three months, and then in drafts on San Francisco banks which takes time and money to cash. Now this ain't fair treatment, for we men pay back at least three fourths of our wages into the company's stores, so they ain t losing nothing on us. We sent them respectful petitions to correct these things, but they don't pay no attention, and what we've got to do is to unite

and compel them to give us our rights. It took me three months to get the first thirty names on our list, and now we have 1,400 names, all of Mendocino woodsmen. I don't work in a place only just long enough to let the men understand what we want 'em to do. The Russians held out the longest, but they're now coming in fast. The Humboldt companies all give their men what we're asking for. We only want our rights, and we don't mean to do anything that ain't peaceable to get 'em," with a contradictory flash of his dark eyes.

There was a rude eloquence in this recital of grievances, and I had reason to know the facts of the case had not been exaggerated. In further discussion, the young man had the fairness to admit that there was something to be said on the side of the companies.

"They ain't any of 'em much more 'n making expenses, but all the same they ought to be fair with us," he added stubbornly.

With the present limited market, there is no doubt California's lumber trade is greatly overstocked. This depression would not continue if cheaper methods of transportation were brought about, whereby redwood and other valuable timber in the State could be shipped to the East and elsewhere.

When the woodsman was about to leave us, it was not in human nature to refrain from asking his name.

"I'm a Master Workman, madam," with a smile and bow of no mean grace, and the somber wood shut in his upright figure.

Look as intently as we might, we could detect no sign of house or camp, only the crowding of gigantic, corrugated pillars, and a stillness that was awesome even at midday. In Tom Bell Gulch the grandeur of the redwoods exceeded anything we had yet seen. The entire length of this supremely picturesque cañon we rode through lofty branchless columns, keeping their ranks closed in, and supporting a plumy roof more than two hundred feet above us.

Upon emerging into the "logged-out" claim along the Albion, the driver deposited a sack of flour on a stump, saying, considerately,—

"I reckon that's out o' reach o' the varmints, if Jerry don't come for it to night."

We now had glimpses of the river— fleeting pools of silver banked by tangles of man-root and poison oak, or masses of blue lilacs, like fallen clouds in the ravine. At the small settlements of Prairie Camp and Comptche there are bearing orchards, with now and again a burly stump to break up the rows. When well over Madroño Hill we stopped to rest the horses upon a ridge so blade-like that the driver declared,—

" If a bucket o' water was poured on top, it would run both ways."

On the one hand, at the bottom of a terrifying precipice, the Albion twinkled faintly through the treetops; while to the left, at an equal depth below, we could hear the impetuous tumbling on the rocks of the north fork of Big River. From our high altitude we saw over a world of mountains; vast, hazy heights grandly steepled by black, motionless forests.

At the foot of the grade we changed horses at Low Gap, and were soon beyond the redwood belt and into the oaks and laurels. On the warm slopes deer were feeding, or sheep that were quite as timid. Rounding the Devil's Elbow we dashed down the smooth red road, taking into our pulses the wild, soft beauty of the landscape, and the perfume of whole mountain-sides of flowers. The rest of the way we followed the pretty windings of Orr Creek, leading us past fragrant haycocks, and the green fields and orchards of suburban Ukiah.

For the next day or two I rested at the springs, a few miles out of town, en-joying the invigorating baths, and making heroic attempts to drink the warm mineral water which every one assures you is delightful. I saw one pale little invalid quaff four dipperfuls, with hardly a pause between. For my part, I preferred a cool fountain farther up the glen, which has all the effervescent quality of the warm springs without their nauseating temperature. The Ukiah people do most of their bathing at this favorite resort, and others come from much greater distances. Aside from the properties of the water, the scenery of the cañon is of that reposeful nature so eminently soothing to tired nerves and brains.

One perfect summer day I returned to Ukiah, in time to get the stage which takes the tourist within a mile or two of Montgomery Wood,— a wonderful grove of redwoods, which is the chief scenic attraction of a romantic resort, where there are hot mineral springs The ride to these springs covers sixteen miles of good mountain road, which in flower time is the loveliest bit of traveling in all California. From the dizzy elevation of the last grade, one looks down upon the roofs of the buildings hundreds of feet below in the gorge. The newest and most picturesque of these several houses spans the stream, its foundations resting upon either bank. The view from the dormer windows in the upper story takes in the redwoods towering to the topmost peaks of the cañon ; while along the creek there are pepperwood, alders and maple, and that fair handmaiden of the sequoias — the dogwood, with its placid, moon-shaped blossoms.

Some rods back of the hot mineral baths are the Chemisal Falls, which

make four successive plunges over perpendicular rocks. At the foot of each a basin is hollowed in the stone, and worn smooth by the action of the water. These circular wells are all of twelve feet deep.

Montgomery Wood is two miles beyond the springs. We walked up this magnificent cañon, the light meanwhile becoming fainter as the trees increased in size and number. The moist mats of

soil to give nourishment to delicate ferns and vines. These air gardens are extremely pretty, and are the one touch of ornamentation found on the dignified sequoia.

In Montgomery Wood proper the trees have a uniform immensity seen nowhere else in Mendocino. The largest measures twenty-three feet and three inches in diameter, and the short, bristling limbs do not begin for nearly one

"UNCLE JIM" MILLER.

leaf needles rendered our feet noiseless, as though sandal shod. Here and there a century-old log thrust up its fire-scorched roots like a monster black claw. Rich mosses and purple lichens made a gay winding sheet for these prone giants. Where there were oozing springs, some of the redwoods had fungus excrescences high up the trunks. On these protuberances leaves had lodged, and created in time sufficient

hundred feet up the bole. Others of its brothers are almost equal to it in girth, the difference not being perceptible to the eye. This congregation of giants is closely grouped about a wide depression in the glen, and margined by blocks of granite, piled up with a noble regard for picturesque proportion and contrast. The majesty and hush of the place are sublime. Nature dwells here alone, and before her august face man's jaunty self-

Photo by Carpenter.

CHEMISAL FALLS.

sufficiency falls off like a garment, leaving the soul convicted of nakedness. Here the Master Architect had been at work rearing these mighty columns, and fashioning a sun-proof ceiling for this "House of the Lord," in whose dim aisles the human voice is an impertinence and laughter a sacrilege.

On the rim of the Woods is a dilapidated shanty, built some years ago by an ambitious would-be mill man, who

"Uncle Jim's" tall figure is seen sauntering along the streets, his plaid coat buttoned smoothly across his capacious chest, and the smoke of an excellent cigar curling above the brim of his gray felt. There are those in the State who remember him as a remarkably handsome young man in gay sombrero, and Mexican trousers trimmed with silver buttons; or in winter garb of felt hat, with a gold serpent for its band, and

Photo by Carpenter.

COMING OUT OF THE REDWOODS.

thought he had discovered a flaw in the title of the present claimant to this superb forest.

Of all the stage drivers who make Ukiah their headquarters, no other is so widely known throughout Northern California as Jim Miller. Every day, for a couple of hours after the arrival of his "Tourists' Stage,—one is tempted to use the word "chariot" instead, so ostentatiously grand is this equipage,—

a princely overcoat of black bear skin, lined with satin. With all these striking appeals to feminine favor, one marvels that so gallant a driver should have remained a bachelor.

Though well up in years, and weighing over two hundred pounds, Jim Miller is still a fine looking man, possessed of a good deal of personal magnetism, and a voice so pleasant and persuasive that it is a luxury to listen to his road yarns.

MONTGOMERY WOOD.

Like every other visitor to Ukiah I had heard of his prodigious watch, and, while enjoying a glorious ride to Blue Lakes, took occasion to ask about it. "Uncle Jim" tossed away the stub of his cigar, and, looking quietly pleased by my cordial interest, related the following : —

"It was twenty-five years ago, and I was new on the road, or I would n't have did such a foolhardy thing. When I seen four highwaymen pointing guns and ordering me to hand over the box, I was that mad I did n't stop to think, but just gave the horses the silk, and they went out like a shot. The bullets came bang, bang! through the top of the coach, and the passengers screamed and swore ; but I yelped at my six mustangs till they lit out faster 'n ever, and those fellers behind me had to give up the chase. There was a big lot o' money in the box, and the Wells, Fargo men was so glad to have it saved they asked me what I'd like best, and I told 'em

I'd always wanted a big watch. What did they do but take four pounds of bullion, an' put half of it in a chain an' the rest in a watch. I wore the chain round my neck for years, an' then had it cut off, like you see it now," showing me the thick silver fob, attached to a watch so absurdly large it made one's wrist ache to hold it.

The trip to Blue Lakes took less than four hours' riding, over the smoothest road we had yet traversed. From the summit we beheld the lakelets, nestled in the heart of mountains rounding up from their brimming basins. In the fading day their color-beauty was a revelation. On through the wildwood skirting the steep banks, past summer resorts and camps, we came to a sequestered group of rustic cottages built on the smaller lake. Here I slept and dreamed to the mystic leaf music of the laurels, and the soft lapping of wavelets under my window.

Ninetta Eames.

An American Tin Mine
(1892)

Photo by Schumacher
HOISTING WORKS AND REDUCTION BUILDING FROM CAJALCO LEDGE.

AN AMERICAN TIN MINE.

AT the present writing, the end of the year 1891, it can be said that the Temescal tin mine, in the hills of that name that seem to form a detached fragment of the Sierra Madre Range, and only eight miles easterly from the Santa Fè station at South Riverside, California, has produced the first and only American tin ever sent to the market.

Curiosity has led me to collect some facts about other excitements in this country over the alleged finding of tin ore, long before the first discoveries here, nearly a quarter of a century ago, the only fruit of which was the sending of a sample of tin metal to the Philadelphia Exposition in 1876, which

sample is now in the National Museum in Washington, where, by the way, nearly, if not all, of the samples of metal tin ever produced in this country up to the last year, have found their final resting place. The "Broad Arrow" mines, in Alabama, were thoroughly tried years ago, and as recently as 1883 it was claimed they were being worked and that new lodes were being discovered. It is now learned, however, that no ore was ever found that yielded over one and one half per cent, and the work was abandoned years ago. In fact it never counted in tin production, and yet it appears to have been once considered a probable success. Another supposed extensive ore region was the James River Gap of the Blue Ridge, Virginia. This also failed to show results, after much prospecting. In North Carolina and Maine shafts have been sunk along thin tin veins, but no considerable ore body has ever been struck. One of the most noteworthy speculations in this line was occasioned by the discovery of tin in the White Mountains, the exact spot being Jackson, New Hampshire, something over fifty years ago. It was a veritable craze and for months divided the attention of the people of the region with the great " Hard Cider " Campaign of 1840.

This also seems to be the natural connection in which to refer to the Black Hills, Dakota, which, it is now definitely understood and agreed, is the only probable source of tin supply, other than the one I am about to describe. These mines are generally designated as well defined tin bearing lodes, which Professor Blake reports will yield good returns, the grieson rock showing from two to six per cent ore. English capital is reported to have been brought to bear upon this field also, and thorough examinations are now being made over a very wide region. Large bodies of ore have been taken out and it is stated that concentrating plants and smelting furnaces are soon to be set going.

The experts and others at the Temescal mines are watching the Dakota experiments with sharp and constant interest, but decline to venture any opinion as to the outcome, as they cannot, at this distance, get at sufficient facts. The peculiar interest now attaching to the tin industry has let a flood of light on the whole subject, and I observe that our Mexican neighbors have resumed operations upon one old mine, and that a carload of the metal has just been received in Pittsburg, from Durango; but nothing definite can be obtained as to the promise of the mine at this writing.

Tin is an absolutely unique production, being wholly from one type of ore, cassiterite. Mr. G. P. Merrill, in a recent contribution to *Stone*, gives the following scientific summing up of its characteristics:

To fully appreciate this peculiarity of the metal, we have but to recall the fact that gold occurs and is mined as native, in at least three sulphurets, and as a telluride; silver as native, in two sulphurets, two sulphantimonides, an arsenide, telluride, and chloride; copper as native, in the form of three sulphides, a sulphantimonide, sulpharsenide, oxide, carbonate, and silicate; lead as a sulphide, sulphate, and carbonate; iron in the form of three oxides, and as carbonate; and zinc as oxide, silicate, carbonate, and sulphide. Indeed, aside from cassiterite there is known but one natural compound in which tin plays a prominent part — this is the sulphide of tin, *stannite*, which however is rare even as a mineral.

Tin is pre-eminently an old metal, that is, found *in situ* only in the older rocks. Its occurrence in more recent deposits, or alluvial formations, is due to the decomposition of these older rocks and the accumulation of the tin as gravel.

According to Whitney the ore deposits of this metal occur in four principal forms. These are (first) in flat sheets or beds lying between the laminæ of the schists and granites and parallel with one another. Each such deposit is usually quite limited. Such are called floors by the Cornish miners. The second form is the so-called stock work, in which the ore is concentrated in innumerable small veins ramifying through the rock. The third form of occurrence is in true fissure veins, and the fourth in alluvial deposits, which yield the so-called stream tin. This last form is wholly secondary and the ore may have been derived from any one or all of the others mentioned.

There is still a fifth form closely allied to the stock work deposits, but which is of sufficient importance to merit especial attention. In these deposits the cassiterite is found impregnating for varying distances the wall rock adjacent to the true veins, as at the East Huel Lovell mines in Cornwall, or again disseminated throughout the rock apparently quite independently of or but remotely connected with veins, as at some of the Saxon mines, or as is illustrated in a more striking manner in the so-called carbonas of the St. Ives Consuls, also in Cornwall. Such are known as impregnations.

While upon the technical part of the subject it may be observed that the Temescal mines have secured a suitable share of attention from the industrial journals of the country, and although no attempts have been made to give assays or any other technical reporting, they have been, by common consent, accorded a consequence never before known towards a like property in the country.

"The San Jacinto Estate, Limited," is the title of the new ownership of the Temescal mines, which for over twenty years after their discovery were tied up in litigation.   Colonel E. N. Robinson, through whose efforts most of the developments and improvements have been made, effected a sale of the property to this new English company a year ago last August.   By a provision of the transfer it is guaranteed to the former American owners that they may be re-instated in interest again in agreed proportion of ownership by making good certain advances for purchase and development; but the English stockholders are to retain control in any event. It is not undertaken here to state details of the deal, nor is it deemed pertinent to the purpose of this paper.   It is a vast property of over 45,000 acres, a considerable portion of which is productive and easily tilled land and has, besides, a valuable water right and showings of gold in one place that will some day be followed up, or rather down.   Sir John Stokes, of London, Vice-President of the Suez Canal Company, is Chairman of the Company; Mr. Hugh Stephen, General Representative; Mr. E. C. West, Engineer, and Captain Stephen Harris, for forty years a Cornwall mine manager, Superintendent of the Mining Department.

These latter gentlemen have recently

Photo by Schumacher.

OFFICE BUILDING AND TIN LEDGE, CAJALCO.

been sent out from England and are under instructions to concentrate all their efforts upon the development of the ore-bearing lode already opened, the "Cajalco," in which is being led a third level, and preparations made for the most thorough test of the extent and quality of the ore. There are thirty or more lodes, with substantially the same tracings and croppings as this one, and their long black lines stretch across the crests of the low lying sandy hills that form the mining camp, as one has seen weather-beaten fences show their black outlines above wasting snow banks. These lodes are only a few rods apart and can be marked from one out-cropping to another for half a mile even by the unpracticed eye.

Some twenty buildings, neatly kept and planted about with young trees and flowers, make up the camp; and a pretty sight it is, on a December morning, set off against the distant snow mountains whereon winter has placed her sentinel outposts whose helmets glisten like burnished silver in the quivering sun-lit atmosphere. All work upon the property is stopped, except the tin mining and the occasional "feeling" of the other lodes, as opportunity offers, it being, as I have said, the policy of the new company to develop this one source and in the meantime to realize as much as possible for the product, the average British stockholder having become somewhat weary, it is said, in contemplating the nebulous nature of many of his recent American investments. The company is so simplifying that the very restaurant has been let to outside parties, who board the hundred and more men for twenty-five cents a meal, the company only supplying bunk room.

The disadvantages and obstacles, as the casual observer can see, are various and serious. The fuel used is the lowest grade of soft coal and is hauled eighteen miles from Elsinore, the last three miles being over the rude trail

that traverses the very pinnacles of the hills, no serious attempt having been yet made to construct easy grades. The coal costs, laid down, $5.25 per ton. Everything else, also, is necessarily taken over this rude mountain roadway. By and by, no doubt, a short branch railway to the Santa Fè station at South Riverside, about seven miles away, will be built. These later considerations, however, have little to do with what I am led to believe the people are acutely anxious to know,— namely, the probable product and promise of the first real attempt to make AMERICAN tin.

When President Harrison was in Southern California last spring and stepped out upon the platform station at South Riverside, he was greeted with the vision of a pile of tin fifteen feet high, bearing the legend "First American Tin, April 23, 1891"; and standing alongside of it he made one of the happiest addresses of a series notable for tact and grace. But it was not till a short time ago that constant and systematic work began, when one could see with his own eyes, as he can now do daily, the hoisting and crushing of ore, the working concentrating machines, the smelting, and the hauling away for shipment into the market, the pig tin of commerce. There has been exasperating and gross if not fraudulent exaggeration about the product and the management of these mines. On the one hand it was, last fall, broadly published that many tons a day were being sent out to supply tin-plate factories, and we should soon be producing all our tin; while on the other, it was asserted that no tin was really turned out and the only work being done was by imported, cheap labor that was supplanting our own. Add to the mischief of this political coloring the nimble fancy of the local press, and it is no wonder the sincere seeker after truth has had a hard time of it.

The writer, on a recent visit to the mines, was allowed to see the confidential reports of the directors of the Company, also of the experts, and given the fullest use of all official information. The amount of ore being daily handled, now that things are working well, is something over thirty tons, and the tin metal product about three fourths of a ton. Captain Harris assured the Company, during his visit and yield of ore. With the third level he expects to get better ore, the present yield being about four per cent.

The reader will remember that only one lode of the thirty is being worked, and this under plain restrictions in the way of machinery, fuel supply, etc. The expected early increase of percentage in the ore yield will also increase the production. The gross value of a ton of 2240 lbs. of pig tin, at the high-

Photo by Schumacher.

THE HOISTING MACHINERY.

to England last summer, that he expected soon to be able to make the mine pay expenses; and he says he is now doing it. The product for December was twenty-five tons marketed (a little being left over from November), the actual amount smelted was slightly more than twenty tons. He estimates the output of this one lode for 1892 at 250 tons, at the present rate of work est price yet paid, 23 cents, is $515. The Superintendent's conservative estimate, however, is $450 a ton; and this year, then, working the ore near the surface and taking into account only this one lode, will, at the lowest estimate, bring to the Company, in round numbers, $112,000. Were it not for the high price of labor and the present rude conditions of manufacturing and marketing the product, there would be a handsome profit in working ore that yields even four cent, that being more than double the yield of the Cornwall mines. The prices for labor are as follows, per day :—

Engineer, Carpenter, etc	$5.00
Engineman	3.25
Able miners	2.75
Common surface laborers	2.25

The miners that work by contract make about $3. The lowest price paid any man is $2.25. and this leaves him, after paying his day's board, $1.50 a day clear. As to imported labor, there are a few Cornish miners, but they have been years in this country; and even if they were to come from England to-morrow, they would demand and receive the local market price of labor, which, in California, has always ruled high. Of course, this is not only the philosophy of the labor question, but it is the necessity of every situation.

I have thus set down the exact facts as to the present product, the worth of it, the price of labor, and a conservative estimate of this coming year's operations. In addition to this I give Captain Harris's answer to my question, " Do you feel that this enterprise has passed the experimental stage ? "

" Everything about mining," said he, "is constant experiment. Sometimes a vein of ore will cut off in the most unexpected way and calculations based on former experience seem to go for nothing. The most common result is that mines get worked out as to paying ore, and are abandoned. Out of a hundred Cornwall mines that I have known, only fifteen are now productive. But as to this mine, I expect to find the ore much better as we go down, and if it proves to be so, it will be the richest mine I have ever known. The average yield now is more than twice as much as those of Cornwall. Of course, if this were not so, we could not touch it,

with the many disadvantages, and particularly the greater cost of labor. I propose to develop this one lode for all it is worth, producing meantime twenty tons or more of tin a month. If it continues to improve, as it promises, and as we have a right to expect, then we have about thirty more just as rich and extensive, and it will be a big and valuable property. I expect this to be the case, and yet, I tell you, there is always speculation in digging for what is out of sight."

Interpreting these words by the help of the man's manner, the language of confidential reports whose terms I do not feel at liberty to quote, and by the fact that after many months of examination and experting, the Company has already put three quarters of a million dollars into the enterprise, it is evident they expect it will finally turn out a great paying property. But it will necessarily be a long time before the amount of tin produced will have any considerable effect upon the world's yearly supply, which is, in round numbers, at present, 56,000 tons, according to the best attainable returns. Of this, England — which is erroneously supposed to control the tin product and the markets — produces only 9000 tons; the Malay Peninsula and islands, 28,000 tons; Australia, 6,500 tons, and all the rest of the world the balance of 12,500 tons.

I wish it were possible to make estimates and predictions as to the future of the Temescal Mines more specific and satisfactory, but I have contented myself with presenting all of the obtainable facts and the best opinions of men, who, it would seem, are entitled to be believed. My own opinion is that the work now being done, and which is bringing in returns that cover the cost of these twenty or more tons a month, will be doubled before another year, and thereafter increased precisely as fast as the new lodes can be advantageously worked; for there are many things to

THE CONCENTRATOR.

be attended to all the while, like providing a better and cheaper fuel supply, improving the roads, and generally lessening cost and waste.

But there is even now an assured American tin mine. There is no doubt about it. It is very easy to work, the ore cropping out so near the surface of these little low-lying hills over and among which one may ride anywhere in a buggy. It is near a great railway, and in the midst of a rich, cultivated country. I cannot learn that any other deposit of tin ore of equal richness and amount, has ever been found that could be so easily developed and handled; and I am very positive that the men who have staked reputation and capital upon this venture feel that they have made no mistake.

I count it a great gain and assurance of success that English capital has been enlisted here. It has always freely followed significant beckonings. It is instinct almost, with the British bent for mines and mining. This investment means an indorsement of the claims made on behalf of the property and the placing of it where its merits may justify. To put things at their best here, it was desirable, it was necessary, it was inevitable, it should come to this. To enlist this capital was to bring to the enterprise pluck, thrift, and the experience and traditions of a race that has always led in this line of industrial productions. It is one of the many combinations that are surely establishing the balance and symmetry of things in this sunny Southern land and helping to make the measure of its material interests match the marvel of its skies

Enoch Knight.

Cross-Country Riding in Southern California (1897)

CROSS-COUNTRY RIDING
IN SOUTHERN CALIFORNIA.

By Henry G. Tinsley.

RABBIT-CHASING is a form of equestrian sport, generally participated in by the young men and women of Southern California. In the winter months, when the army of tourists and health seekers from the Eastern States lives temporarily in the land of fruits and flowers, large parties eagerly follow it. It is to the sport-loving Californian what fox-hunting is to the hard riders of the older East and Southeast. Many people who have followed hounds in England and the United States enthusiastically assert that no field sport surpasses in variety of scenery, vigor of riding and excitement a genuine rabbit-chase.

The season of rabbit-chasing begins in Southern California in October and ends some time in early March, when the ranchmen plant their broad areas to grain and set up notices of no trespass. The country in the hunt season is the most beautiful in the world. The warm summer is past, the rains have fallen, the face of Nature has been washed, the brooks from the mountain cañons are once more gurgling with water, and all vegetation has had a thrill of new life under the freshening showers. The orange and lemon groves with their deep olive foliage cleansed, glisten in the clear sun as if varnished.

As far as the eye can reach across the valleys there are waving masses of color; broad sweeps of the rich yellow of wild poppies, areas of flowering cactus, clumps of golden-rod and eschscholtzia, and enormous beds, acres wide, of marguerites, wild heliotrope, lupines and geranium. Hedges of green cypress, of a score of varieties of roses and of laurestine extend up and down the roadways in every direction as lines of demarcation between the holdings.

Hundreds of cottages, the homes of ranchmen and fruit-growers, literally embowered amid tangled masses of the rarest climbing roses, and all manner of fragrant, blossoming vines, dot the landscape, and appear at a distance like stupendous bouquets of roses. To the north and east the Sierras rear themselves thousands of feet high,' their rugged sides and snow-capped peaks adding to the picturesqueness of the scene. Away to the west are the tossing blue waves of the Pacific. To the south are the foothills, now green as emerald, with fields of alfalfa and alfileria. The air comes as soft as a caress from the ocean, and the heavens are for days at a time an azure peculiar to a California sky.

One of the numerous rabbit-chasing clubs in Los Angeles or Santa Barbara counties has fixed upon a day for a hunt. The secretary sends out invitations to a score of ladies and gentlemen to join in the pleasure of following the hounds.

The trysting-place is a well-known mesa, a mile or so from town, and the hour is probably seven A.M. The morning is clear and cool.

As the moment for the start approaches, the saddles are cinched tighter, the last whiffs of pipe or cigarette are hastily taken, and the dogs are called up. There is a moment of silence as each person gathers reins in hand, and, with foot in stirrup, awaits the signal for the start. The master of hounds blows a sharp musical toot on a silver horn. In a second the dogs are off like rockets, while the riders, amid a jangling of heavy Mexican spurs and bridle chains, start down the mesa, following the master of hounds at a rapid rate.

Under the direction of the master of hounds and his assistants the party spreads out, covering, perhaps, a quarter of a mile. The horses settle down to steady pace. The hounds keep several hundred feet ahead, now and then stopping and looking wistfully around, then moving on again. The riders move across a field of barley stubble, and through a grove of live oaks, and then the hounds lead the way across an upland of olive trees. A turn is made to the left, and the party rides quickly over a mile or so of broad adobe country road lined by giant palm trees, close beside one of the historic and lonely Franciscan missions of the last century. Beyond is a seeming boundless area of alfalfa and barley fields, now barren since the summer harvest.

A small muddy-gray animal has darted from the brush under the front horses. For a second the apparition is startling to those of the party, who are having their first ride after the hounds. The creature has an inquisitive head, a pair of enormous black-tipped ears, erect and rakish. For a fraction of a moment the rabbit stands, and then by leaps of ten and twelve feet each, it shoots forward in full view of all. The hounds follow in pursuit like mad, the horses plunge forward, and every one is fired with zest and excitement. The field is now away fast and furious.

All the dogs gradually close in upon the jack-rabbit, and the irresistible cry, " hi, hi, hi ! " goes up and down the line of riders. The rabbit, an experienced old fellow, begins the run as if he had been seeking just such sport. He leaps four or five feet in the air to clear a

bowlder or to skim a piece of chaparral. One almost believes he could hop over a whole country if really hard pressed. For a few hundred yards he goes in a straight line, never diverging for any obstruction. The dogs are exerting every muscle, and glide along through the short vegetation like animated arrows. Such sinuosity, such grace were never better seen in animals. The pace is a hard one for novices, but other riders are taking everything. Narrow arroyas are jumped, fences are leaped with ease, and irrigation ditches are crossed at a bound. At the end of two miles several riders have fallen by the wayside, and are considering the old saw of discretion and the better part of valor. But most of the hunters are still going, and are well up with the hounds.

The rabbit has stopped several times as if in actual ridicule of his pursuers, and now turning dashes at the horses, whose riders pull them on their haunches and take the new direction. Down into a hollow, or through an old river bed, now across a vineyard they go. The rabbit slips under a horse's feet, and a hound snaps at him while the horse rears and snorts. For a moment the jack is confused, and then is off again outdoing the dogs in dodging, and at last saving himself from death by reaching a high mesa of scrub oaks and manzanita, after wearing out half-a-dozen horses and several hounds, and, as one old New England fox-hunter and cross-country rider says, providing more excitement than could be mustered in a dozen paper-chases.

The panting dogs, with tongues extending, seek the nearest irrigating ditch which is fed by the icy mountain streams. The riders halt their horses for a brief rest in the shade of umbrella trees about a ranch house. Nearly every one dismounts. By this time the ladies and gentlemen have lost much of their freshness and extreme neatness so noticeable an hour ago when the hunt started. White riding trousers are sadly soiled by rude contact with the hedges and the foliage of orchards ; several ladies' riding habits are spotted with mud and discolored with the stains of wild flowers. One or two riders have suspicious earth stains across their shoulders, that cause general merriment.

The master of hounds sounds his horn

again, and the field is away. This time the riders turn to the southeast, where there are smooth broad rural roads and fewer hedges. The route leads toward Santa Anita, the rural beauty spot and the "show" ranch of Los Angeles county. A veritable garden of Hesperides stretches away in every direction— a checker-board of vineyards, a lily farm with acres of snowy bloom, olive and prune orchards, orange groves, grain plots and mammoth patches of eschscholtzias, daisies, bluebells and violets.

In fifteen minutes another rabbit is started up in a heavy growth of wild heliotrope by a hound away off the left of the riders. The rabbit bounds ahead by several hundred feet, and is breaking away for adjacent cover, opening and shutting automatically like a jack-knife. Surely nothing on four feet ever traveled faster. The old fellow is not to have his own way long, for a dog that has many rabbits' ears and scalps to his credit, does not waste his wind in the early part of the run, but wisely notices the direction the rabbit is taking and then starts upon a course which will head off the swift jack.

"Watch out ! watch out !" shouts the master as the rabbit turns again, quick as a flash, and comes like a streak of gray right in front of the horses. The dogs are terribly excited, and as they dash under the very horses' feet in close pursuit of the rabbit, two gentlemen are unhorsed. There is no time for more than a passing glance at the fellows scrambling to their feet, for the field is a hundred yards away. The horses have become thoroughly warmed up. They leap ditches and fences and tear through brush with as much spirit as the hounds. A lean, sagacious dog that has served a long apprenticeship has closed in upon his victim, and now by an adroit movement, that only a shrewd hound knows, the rabbit is intercepted just as it is about to plunge through a bunch of laurestine or seek refuge in a waving sea of wild mustard.

The rabbit is caught — a vigorous shake by the dog and its life is ended. In a few seconds more the hunters gather at the scene of the capture. The gentleman who first seizes the dead rabbit, cuts off its long ears and presents them to the lady who has kept up with the hounds and is first "in at the death."

After another rest for dogs and horses, and a few minutes of conversation, the field is off on another chase. Thus the runs are made in succession until the noon hour comes and the ears which are fastened to the girdles of the ladies number seven pairs. The master of the hounds has led the party seventeen miles from the starting-place. He has planned to finish the last run of the morning near the mouth of a cañon, where there is cooling shade beneath sycamore trees, among which a little stream of water twists and swirls on its way down into the valley. This has been previously fixed upon as the place for luncheon, and some older people and invited guests have come there in carriages to watch the chase through fieldglasses, and to have luncheon with the riders.

The hampers of food are opened, and their contents arranged upon the tables beside the brook, where the shade is most inviting and the grass is heaviest. There are bunches of freshly picked carnations, roses and verbenas, garlands of wistaria and ivy geranium to decorate the tables, and a score or more of little bouquets for the ladies and gentlemen. All the riders bring to the luncheon appetites thoroughly sharpened by the exhilaration of the past few hours. Sitting there in the coolness of the sycamore grove two jolly hours are passed.

The chief pleasure of following a pack of greyhounds across country lies mainly in the variety. The dogs are models of grace, beauty and intelligence, and the rider, despite the speed, finds more actual enjoyment than in hunting with fox hounds.

The greyhound, notwithstanding some writers, is most intelligent and affectionate, and in a short run often makes remarkable exhibitions of shrewdness and rare judgment of topographical conditions. The more finely bred greyhounds have rarely a good sense of smell ; they depend upon their marvelously accurate eyes, and when once the game is in sight their extraordinary speed should enable them to capture it. One dog, a beauty of her type, has tactics of her own. When she has lost sight of her game in brush or tall grass, she occasionally leaps high above the cover, and while suspended a second she looks quickly about and sees the waving of the grass caused by the fleeing form.

By repeating this maneuver, she is enabled to locate the rabbit until it is again forced to the open.

After luncheon and a restful smoke the sport begins anew. There are but half a dozen more runs. The riders are now even more excited and reckless. The horses catch the spirit of the thing as good horses will. The hounds dart this way and that, while the riders, wild with enthusiasm urge the pack with ringing calls. It is the last spurt. The rabbit, after a gallant effort, is seized from behind by a blue dog, and tossed, dead or dying, into the air.

The master of the hounds blows a signal that the last run of the afternoon is finished, and the last trophy ears are had. The field slowly rides back to town. The sun is dipping in the dimpling blue of the Pacific and the rough and rugged sides of mountains are bronzed with the rays of sunshine. Even the most tired among the riders enjoys the panorama of royal scenery which graces the homeward route.